RICHARD ALDINGTON
AND LAWRENCE OF ARABIA

RICHARD ALDINGTON and LAWRENCE of ARABIA

A Cautionary Tale

Fred D. Crawford

Southern Illinois University Press

Carbondale and Edwardsville

Library of Congress Cataloging-in-Publication Data

Crawford, Fred D.
Richard Aldington and Lawrence of Arabia : a cautionary tale /
Fred D. Crawford.
p.   cm.
Includes bibliographical references (p.   ) and index.
1. Aldington, Richard, 1892–1962. Lawrence of Arabia.
2. Lawrence, T. E. (Thomas Edward), 1888–1935.   3. British—Middle
East—History—20th century.   4. Aldington, Richard, 1892–1962—
Censorship.   5. Publishers and publishing—Great Britain.
6. Freedom of the press—Great Britain.   I. Title.
DS568.4.L45A633   1998
940.4'15—dc21
ISBN 0-8093-2166-1 (cloth : alk. paper)
97-25418
CIP

Frontispiece: Richard Aldington, from a passport photograph probably taken in 1962,
the year of his death. Courtesy of Catherine Guillaume-Aldington
and Alister Kershaw.

For Rodelle and Stanley Weintraub

CONTENTS

Contents

PREFACE

THIS BOOK EXAMINES the history of Richard Aldington's *Lawrence of Arabia: A Biographical Enquiry* (1955) from 1949, when Aldington selected T. E. Lawrence as a biographical subject, to the present, when controversy about the enigmatic TEL continues along the lines that Aldington defined. The behind-the-scenes activities to suppress and denigrate Aldington's book, coordinated by B. H. Liddell Hart, show how private interests can influence what the public is allowed to read.

This is "a cautionary tale" about the precarious position of an author who presumes to challenge the established view of a national hero, the extensive legal means available to those who can afford them to force a publisher to alter or suppress a manuscript, and the ability of an influential coterie to damage the reputation of a book even before people have had a chance to read it. The nearly successful attempts to suppress Aldington's book reveal how little freedom of the press can mean when a book displeases or discomfits influential people with positions—or myths—to maintain. Many eminent historians, biographers, and literary scholars attacked Aldington's book as untruthful even while they admitted among themselves that some of his allegations were valid, thus betraying their professed commitment to value truth over personal concerns. Claiming to add to our knowledge, they worked to conceal information from those outside their privileged circle.

Aldington was not, as his critics charged, prosecuting or persecuting TEL and his admirers but simply telling the truth as he saw it. Even those who reject Aldington's views should acknowledge that he had the right to present his findings before the tribunal of the reading public. His treatment at the hands of the establishment, in a country whose subjects pride themselves on freedom of expression, was hypocritical at best and reprehensible at worst.

The consequences of the campaign against Aldington have been enduring. Appreciating his contribution to our knowledge of TEL still inspires contempt from TEL's admirers, while regarding TEL's achievements as in any way remarkable elicits a similar response from Aldington's supporters. My sympathies are with Aldington in his struggle to print what he discovered, but I also feel that TEL's accomplishments deserve genuine respect. Later exaggerations, by TEL as well as by others, do not diminish the reality behind them. His importance to history and letters is unassailable.

I did not believe this in 1983 when I decided to write Aldington's biography. I had first read Aldington in 1972 at the suggestion of Stanley Weintraub, who recommended the 1929 novel *Death of a Hero*. Recently out of uniform myself, I enjoyed Aldington's ex-soldier diatribe against civilians. Aldington's satiric power did not diminish when he changed subject or genre. I included an Aldington chapter in a book about the influence of *The Waste Land* on modern novels and discussed his Imagist war verse in a later book about British World War I poets. When I learned that no Aldington biography existed, I promptly nominated myself to write his life.

That aspiration was short-lived. Alister Kershaw, with whom I had corresponded since 1977, informed me that Charles Doyle had been at work on Aldington's life since 1976 (his authoritative biography appeared in 1989), so instead of attempting a full-scale biography, I decided to investigate the Aldington/TEL controversy. Phillip Knightley's 1973 article "Aldington's Enquiry Concerning T. E. Lawrence" had made the startling claim that an influential group of TEL's partisans, including Winston Churchill, had tried to suppress Aldington's book. I felt that this deserved more attention.

When I began my research, I knew little about TEL beyond *Seven Pillars of Wisdom* (1935), the 1962 *Lawrence of Arabia* film, and Aldington's book, which I accepted without question. As I read more by and about TEL, my opinion of him altered markedly. Embellishments of the TEL legend aside, he did adapt to the customs of the Arabs, speak their language, win their respect, endure hardship with them, and coordinate their plans with Allenby's, at great personal cost. His physical endurance and courage during the Arab Revolt are beyond dispute. This did not diminish my admiration for Aldington's biography. His exposure of the exaggerations of the TEL legend was little short of miraculous, given the limited material at his disposal, and his refusal to tolerate cant led to important discoveries about TEL.

Perhaps the main reason for my becoming more appreciative of TEL was the subsequent scholarship that has grown from Aldington's pioneering study. Post-Aldington scholars have had access to material unavailable to Aldington, chiefly the records of the British government that became available in 1968. Many, following Aldington, have criticized aspects of TEL's actions and character during the Arab Revolt and after, questioned his military value to Allenby, and identified him as the source of much of the

Preface

legend that he publicly repudiated. Even TEL's critics, however, recognize that he was essential to the ultimate success of Allenby's campaign by keeping the Arabs friendly. In the more candid atmosphere that Aldington made possible, John E. Mack's psychological biography, *A Prince of Our Disorder* (1976), even while admitting that TEL was not always veracious, could validate his greatness and address both the sources and consequences of his psychological confusion. It has become possible to put Aldington's revelations about TEL into a context that makes him a more sympathetic figure.

The wealth of unpublished material in the Aldington collection at Southern Illinois University offered a great deal of support for my early assumptions about the Aldington/TEL controversy. However, when I spent the summer of 1988 at the Liddell Hart Centre for Military Archives, King's College London, and thus had access to the correspondence of those whom Liddell Hart had led in their collective opposition to Aldington's book, I had a few surprises. One was that many who knew TEL, contrary to Aldington's skeptical view of their motives, defended him despite his idiosyncrasies because they genuinely admired him. They spoke from their personal knowledge of TEL, and the sincerity of their regard for him was unmistakable. Another surprise was the uncomfortable position of Aldington's publisher, Collins, who had to contend with opposing interests. While Aldington had reason to regret his association with Collins, he did not fully appreciate the constraints under which Collins, and any other publisher, must function. Surviving private correspondence reveals what Aldington and his opposition were doing while Collins was trying to find middle ground between the two. In attempting to come to terms with the behind-the-scenes history of Aldington's book, I have had access to material unavailable to Aldington or his publisher or his opposition, including facts that would have surprised them all.

The Morris Library at Southern Illinois University holds some seven thousand letters by and to Aldington, most of which relate directly to his TEL book. The Liddell Hart Centre for Military Archives, King's College London, has the file copies of Liddell Hart's voluminous correspondence, including the letters he received. These archives, supplemented by others listed in my acknowledgments and notes, provided most of the new information about the Aldington/TEL controversy from 1949 to the present.

Aldington's daily letters to Alister Kershaw and correspondence with his publishers and others verify his later claims that he began his research with no predisposition against TEL and that his contempt for TEL grew from what his research revealed. How Aldington decided to write about

TEL and how his research led him to his conclusions are the subjects of chapters 1 and 2.

Aldington erroneously believed that someone at Collins's firm was in league with TEL's partisans to suppress his book. He attributed to this apocryphal saboteur many of the revisions that Collins and his lawyers demanded, condemning their "editorial" changes as blatant censorship. At the same time, the demands imposed by Collins were far removed from normal publishing practice. Chapter 3 examines the uneasy relationship between Aldington and Collins as they worked at cross-purposes.

TEL's partisans began their efforts to suppress Aldington's book in January 1954, a year before its publication, knowing only that Aldington was hostile to TEL. Their tactics ranged from threats of legal action to political pressure, including letters from Prime Minister Winston Churchill and even a petition to Queen Elizabeth II. The mobilization of opposition to Aldington's book and the attempts of eminent TEL partisans to suppress it are the concern of chapter 4.

Collins, who had agreed to publish Aldington's book before reading it, found himself in a dilemma. He felt an obligation to honor a commitment to his author, but he also knew the consequences for his firm of an injunction for libel or infringement of copyright, and he did not want to incur the lasting resentment of powerful and influential people who insisted that he withdraw the book. How Collins proceeded with publication is the subject of chapter 5.

When Aldington's book appeared on 31 January 1955, it was the target of a campaign of vicious, abusive, and even mendacious reviews. Many of TEL's Machiavellian partisans decided that defending TEL justified any means. Chapter 6 focuses on the campaign to discredit Aldington's book, from its appearance in England in 1955 until Aldington's death in 1962.

After the publication of Aldington's book, the climate for TEL studies changed markedly. Aldington's investigation made it possible for later scholars to study aspects of TEL that had been hitherto the guarded preserve of a group relishing its exclusive, and often flawed, knowledge. The guardians of TEL's reputation, alerted by Aldington's inferences from published material, made it more difficult to gain access to unpublished sources and exercised greater caution when granting permission to quote material protected by copyright. They also tried to suppress or mitigate the influence of books unfavorable to TEL. Attempts to limit Aldington's influence and to control later publications about TEL are the subject of chapter 7.

For four decades, TEL's partisans have tried to dismiss Aldington's re-

Preface

search, but his findings have stood up well despite the efforts of a dedicated opposition with much more evidence at its disposal than was available to Aldington. Chapter 8 addresses the long-term significance of Aldington's allegations about TEL and the failure of subsequent attempts to dispose of Aldington's contentions.

Chapter 9 addresses the significance and implications of the controversy as they impinge on the nature of publishing and on the control of information by hidden censorship. The history of Aldington's book includes virtually every means by which a determined and energetic opposition can impose on an author. Such methods remain legally available today.

Note on the Text

Quotations retain variant spellings of names (Feisal, Faisal, Feysal) and places (Deraa, Der'a, Dera) as well as idiosyncratic usage. I have silently corrected obvious typographical errors from unpublished correspondence and typescripts.

ACKNOWLEDGMENTS

THIS BOOK WOULD not have been possible without extensive support and encouragement from many people during the past decade. I owe a great debt to those who read the entire manuscript and who offered invaluable suggestions and criticism: Catherine Aldington, Charles "Mike" Doyle, Norman T. Gates, Alister Kershaw, Lady Kathleen Liddell Hart, Michel W. Pharand, Patrick Quinn, Stanley Weintraub, David J. Wilkinson, and Caroline Zilboorg.

The following individuals (or, as noted, their heirs or literary executors) kindly gave me permission to quote from letters and interviews: Richard Aldington (by permission of Catherine Aldington), Staige D. Blackford, Lord Mark Bonham-Carter, Malcolm Brown, Winston Churchill (by permission of Curtis Brown Ltd, London on behalf of the Estate of Sir Winston S. Churchill. Copyright Winston S. Churchill), W. A. R. Collins (by permission of W. J. Collins), Robert Graves (by permission of The Robert Graves Copyright Trust), Sir Alec Guinness, Alister Kershaw, A. W. Lawrence and T. E. Lawrence (by permission of The Trustees of the Seven Pillars of Wisdom Trust), B. H. Liddell Hart (by permission of Lady Kathleen Liddell Hart), Dr. John E. Mack, Suleiman Mousa, A. L. Rowse, Lowell Thomas (by permission of Lowell Thomas, Jr.), Stanley Weintraub, and Henry Williamson (by permission of Anne Williamson, Manager, Henry Williamson Literary Estate).

Many others with firsthand knowledge of the Aldington/TEL controversy, either from direct involvement with Aldington's TEL book or from their experiences with post-Aldington publications, have generously provided information and insights through interviews and correspondence. These include Alan Bird, L. J. Browning, Anita Engle, M. V. Carey, Lawrence James, Phillip Knightley, Adrian Liddell Hart, Lady Kathleen Liddell Hart, Rob Lyle, Christopher Matheson, Jeffrey Meyers, Philip M. O'Brien, Alison Palmer, Henry Regnery, Stephen E. Tabachnick, and F.-J. Temple. Jeremy Wilson also provided useful information in a forum in the pages of *T. E. Notes*, edited by Denis W. McDonnell.

Richard E. Winslow III located and sent copies of many unlisted articles from journals and newspapers. Ruth M. Helwig and Mary Halfmann successfully ordered reams of material through interlibrary loan, even when I had only fragmentary or erroneous citations gleaned from passing references in unpublished correspondence. Central Michigan University provided a summer research grant that enabled me to visit several manuscript repositories in 1988.

I am particularly grateful to the following organizations for the use of material in their archives and for the unfailing assistance and cheerful cooperation of the named individuals: Alderman Library, University of Virginia (Michael Plunkett and Robin D. Wear); BBC Written Archives Centre, Caversham Park, Reading (Jeff Walden); British Library (J. Conway and J. M. Smethurst); Harry Ransom Humanities Research Center, University of Texas at Austin (Winston Atkins, John Kirkpatrick, Thomas F. Staley, and Christopher M. Stutz); Henry Williamson Literary Estate (Anne Williamson); Hoover Institution on War, Revolution, and Peace, Stanford, California (Charles G. Palm and Dale Reed); Imperial War Museum (T. C. Charman, Nigel Steel, and Martin Taylor); Liddell Hart Centre for Military Archives, King's College London (Jane Branfield; Derek G. Law, Director of Information Services and Systems; Nicholas Malton; Patricia C. Methven, College Archivist; Kate O'Brien, Military Archivist; Michael Page; Jane Platt; Marie Stewart; and Marie Walsh); Lowell Thomas Communications Center Archives, Marist College, Poughkeepsie, New York (Emily Burdis, Claire Keith, and Laura Kline); British Ministry of Defence (I. D. Goode and S. J. Spear); Morris Library, Southern Illinois University at Carbondale (Shelley Cox, David V. Koch, Peggy Roche, and Sheila Ryan); National Library of Australia (Graeme Powell); Royal United Services Institute for Defence Studies (Jonny Mendelsson); and University of Reading Library (Michael Bott and J. A. Edwards).

Others who have helped in a variety of ways include Ronnie Apter, Dean Baldwin, Adrian Barlow, Miriam J. Benkovitz, John A. Bertolini, William Brevda, Gordon R. Button, Cass Canfield, Jr., Gerald Carter, Ian Chapman, Ralph Colp, Jr., Capt. Hugh Corbett, Anne Crawford (no relation), Carlo D'Este, Deborah L. DeYoung, Lori and Richard Dietrich, Lori and Phil Dillman, Robert C. Doyle, Beate Engel-Doyle, Frances and Tom Evans, Hans F. Fetting, Hugh Ford, C. J. Fox, Nancy and Peter Fries, Brian Fullagar, Henry L. Fulton, John T. Gage, Helen Greathead, Stanley B. and Thelma C. Greenfield, Robert Grudin, Barbara Guest, Pat and Russell Gula, Gary Hewitt, Joel Hodson, James F. Howell, Leon H. Hugo, Cliff Irwin, Ronald L. Johnstone, Lionel Kelly, Jelka Kershaw, Sylvain Kershaw, Frank Kersnowski, Valerie Kettley, Peter T. Koper, Ray Kytle, Robert Langenfeld, Dan H. Laurence, Dick Leech, Harold Leffingwell, J. N. Lockman, Christopher

Acknowledgments

Logue, Jay Luvaas, Ian S. MacNiven, Wendy Madge, G. H. Martin, Robert Martin, Denis W. McDonnell, Mary E. McDonnell, James H. McGrath, Edwards Metcalf, Peter Metcalfe, Susan and William Miles, Francis J. Molson, Clara Lee Moodie, Thomas J. Moore, John A. Morris, L. Robert Morris, Frederick and Ruth Newberry, Harold Orlans, Carole A. Pasch, William H. Peck, Sigrid P. Perry, Margot Peters, John R. Pfeiffer, John M. Pickering, Anne and Jeremy Powell, Diane and Rick Quarton, Catherine Quinn, Steve Rantz, Lawrence Raskin, John Redman, Alfred S. Regnery, Susan Reighard, Janet A. Reisman, Susannah Ringel, Jean Rose, Alfred W. Satterthwaite, Maarten Schild, Susan Schreibman, Susan Seitner, Arthur Sherbo, Roger Smith, Michael E. Stamm, Carol A. Swan, Sanford G. Thatcher, Ann Warnford-Davis, Kingsley Weatherhead, Daniel B. Weber, Rodelle Weintraub, James L. W. West III, Thomas M. Whitehead, George Wickes, David J. and Tina Wilkinson, Patricia C. Willis, Philip Winsor, Chet Wolford, Roma Woodnutt, and H. M. Young.

I am also very grateful to Carol Burns, James D. Simmons, and John K. Wilson of Southern Illinois University Press for their invaluable help and guidance. I particularly appreciate the diligence and zeal that Cindy Milstein has applied to the process of copyediting my manuscript.

No one can embark on such an enterprise without the support and even indulgence of one's family. I am particularly grateful for the sympathetic tolerance of Charles and Sharon Crawford, J. Edward Crawford, Darcy and Derek Christianson, Albert and Margaret Krajnik, and, most of all, MaryAnn.

RICHARD ALDINGTON
AND LAWRENCE OF ARABIA

1

THE UNLIKELY BIOGRAPHER

I wish I could get back to novels; but somehow in the war I got on to this line of biogs and can't now get off them. Unluckily a biog needs the same concentration of nervous energy as a novel and about five times as much work plus the damned bore of accuracy or trying for accuracy.

—Richard Aldington to Eric Warman, 27 July 1950

And the principle that you are not to say anything impolite about the work or character of a writer who has been dead 20 years destroys both honest criticism and honest biography. Why must we be so damned mealy-mouthed?

—Richard Aldington to Alan Bird, 15 August 1952

He was a strange man, Aldington—genuinely an écorché vif. His sensitivity was unbelievably intense and he reacted with a degree of violence which seemed incomprehensible on occasion. I never knew—I don't think anyone did—what had so scarred him.

The odd thing, however, is that he was much more relaxed and urbane and cheerful in private life than he ever was when he wrote.

—Alister Kershaw to Fred D. Crawford, 18 March 1983

In *Lawrence of Arabia: A Biographical Enquiry* (1955), Richard Aldington presented a scathing indictment of TEL. According to Aldington, "the national hero turned out at least half a fraud."[1] Aldington became convinced that TEL was a vainglorious liar, a self-advertising poseur, and a charlatan. Aldington concluded that TEL's military exploits were strategically worthless, that the Arab Revolt that TEL himself had called "a sideshow of a sideshow" had little significance to the Great War or even to General Allenby's successes in Palestine, and that TEL had exaggerated his exploits. When he learned that TEL was illegitimate, he concluded that TEL's shame and humiliation had led him to compensate by inflating his accomplishments. Aldington also inferred, from what he admitted was only tenuous evidence, that TEL was homosexual.

Aldington regarded TEL's reputation as a popular mythology fostered by Lowell Thomas's 1919 film-lectures and 1924 biography, extended by the hero-worshiping biographies by Robert Graves and B. H. Liddell Hart and by the gushing memoirs that appeared after TEL's death in 1935. After he learned that TEL had helped Thomas with his film-show and had assisted Graves and Liddell Hart with their biographies, even writing many passages for each work, Aldington became certain that the Lawrence legend was essentially TEL's own fabrication: "The legend of Lawrence has been built up by nearly all those writers who have taken Lawrence as their subject, whether for a full-scale biography or for a three-page reminiscence. The edifice shows a fairly solid front to the uncritical reader but once it has been examined it is shown to be an inverted pyramid at the base of which stands Lawrence himself on whom the legend rests" (RA, *Lawrence of Arabia,* 13). For Aldington, TEL was a sham hero whose propaganda value the British establishment exploited to justify the ruinous cost of the Great War.

In retrospect, it seems odd that the first serious challenge to the TEL legend came not from a military historian but from a biographer better known as a poet, translator, critic, editor, and novelist. Few writers succeed in more than one genre, but Aldington achieved mastery in several. In addition to his early Imagist poetry, he wrote some of the most vital love lyrics and truthful war poetry of the century. He was also a superb translator of Greek, Renaissance Latin, French, and Italian, and his renditions of Voltaire's *Candide* (1927) and Boccaccio's *Decameron* (1930) remain standard texts. His insights as a critic are impressive, and he edited more than a dozen works by D. H. Lawrence, including the *Selected Letters* introduced by Aldous Huxley in 1950. His mordant fiction attracted wide readership. *Death of a Hero* (1929), a best-seller and one of the finest of the World War I novels, earned him an international reputation. He wrote seven more novels that did not deal directly with the war. Among them, *The Colonel's Daughter* (1931) focused on the plight of single women who could not find husbands after the carnage of World War I, *All Men Are Enemies* (1933) depicted a quest for love in the postwar world, *Women Must Work* (1934) called attention to the struggles of women trying to make their way independently, and *Seven Against Reeves* (1938) took a comic view of the vexations of a retired businessman based on A. S. Frere (whose original surname was Frere-Reeves).

Aldington had also written successful biographies of Voltaire, the Duke of Wellington, D. H. Lawrence, and others. When he began *Voltaire* (1925), he was already an acknowledged expert on Voltaire's work. *The Duke, Being an Account of the Life and Achievements of Arthur Wellesley, 1st Duke of Wellington* (1943) derived from his interest in Wellington's character and won the prestigious James Tait Black Memorial Prize in 1947. *The Strange Life of Charles Waterton, 1782–1865* (1949) developed from his fascination with an eccentric squire about whom he had published a long essay in 1934. His unrivaled knowledge of D. H. Lawrence's work, his friendship with him, and his access to privileged information (including unpublished correspondence) helped him to make *Portrait of a Genius, But . . .* (1950) the first reliable D. H. Lawrence biography.

When Aldington decided to undertake a biography of TEL, however, he had no prior interest in the man or his writing. He had not read TEL's autobiographical *Seven Pillars of Wisdom* (1935) or the earlier shorter version, *Revolt in the Desert* (1927), much less TEL's more obscure *Crusader Castles* (1936), *Secret Despatches from Arabia* (1939), and *Men in Print* (1940). He was unaware of three significant 1938 publications: David Garnett's edition of *The Letters of T. E. Lawrence, T. E. Lawrence to His Biographer Robert Graves*, and *T. E. Lawrence to His Biographer Liddell Hart*. He had not read Thomas's *With Lawrence in Arabia* (1924), Graves's *Lawrence and the Arabs* (1927), or Liddell Hart's *"T. E. Lawrence": In Arabia and After* (1934), nor had he seen *T. E. Lawrence by His Friends* (1937), edited by A. W. Lawrence.

Aldington had never met TEL despite some tangential connections. During TEL's lifetime, Ezra Pound, Wyndham Lewis, A. S. Frere, and others knew both Aldington and TEL. Howard Coster photographed both, and Pound included the two in his *Cantos* (Aldington in Canto 16 and TEL in Canto 74). Dagobert von Mikusch translated Aldington's *Death of a Hero* and TEL's *Revolt in the Desert* and *Seven Pillars of Wisdom* into German. Bruce Rogers printed, and Paul Nash illustrated, their volumes. TEL and Aldington helped and encouraged novelists Frederic Manning and James Hanley. They both wrote reams of letters, yet their marginal associations did not occasion any correspondence between them, even during their mutual involvement, known to both, with the translation of Pierre Custot's *Sturly*. Aldington mentioned in his autobiography that he had successfully translated *Sturly* after TEL had abandoned the attempt, and TEL wrote a blurb for the dust jacket when Jonathan Cape published Aldington's translation in 1924.

Neither Aldington nor TEL was an ideal reader of the other. In 1950, *Nine* published a letter to Ezra Pound dated 20 August 1920 in which TEL suggested that, as poets, "surely R. Aldington and W. B. Yeats are no good?"[2] (If Aldington knew about this before his TEL book appeared, he did not mention it in his letters, and criticism by someone incapable of finding poetic merit in Yeats would not have bothered him.) In a letter to K. W. Marshall dated 9 March 1931, TEL took a dim view of Aldington's introduction to James Hanley's 1930 novel *The German Prisoner*: "But why, in God's name, an introduction by Richard Aldington? Honestly, that's low. Hanley writes a damn sight better than R. A. and doesn't pule in print. Why not an intro. by Sir A. Quiller Couch? Why not let it rip without any chaperon?"[3] (Aldington knew nothing about this comment, which did not appear in print until 1993.)

Aldington's choice of TEL as a biographical subject was the result of a well-meant suggestion by Alister Kershaw, a twenty-six-year-old Australian poet who had admired Aldington since reading *Death of a Hero* in 1937. Kershaw had come to London in 1947 to hazard a literary career and to meet three writers whose work had influenced him profoundly: Roy Campbell, Henry Williamson, and Aldington. Kershaw was penniless, having depleted his meager resources to pay for steerage passage from Melbourne, but Campbell, who was a Talks Producer with the BBC, gave him enough assignments to let him scrape by. Lacking Aldington's address, Kershaw wrote to him in care of his publisher Heinemann and received a quick response that Aldington was now living in Paris but would be happy to receive Kershaw should he ever find himself in the Boulevard Montparnasse. Another assignment from Campbell provided the funds, and in June, Kershaw went to Paris.

After reading *Death of a Hero* and the later novels, Kershaw expected to meet "a scowling and splenetic malcontent, a sullen Timon," but in person, Aldington was not the curmudgeon suggested by "passages of lacerating bitterness and disillusionment."[4] Aldington and his wife, Netta, overcame Kershaw's shyness by insisting that the young man join them for breakfast every morning and spend his days in Paris with them. He returned to London feeling that his meeting with Aldington had made his journey from Australia worthwhile. When the Aldingtons moved to the Villa Aucassin in Le Lavandou, in the South of France, they invited Kershaw for an extended visit.

For many years, Aldington had been very busy with literary work. When he, Netta, and their daughter, Catherine, had reached the United States on 17 February 1939, they had intended to remain. (Aldington's original title for his 1941 autobiography was "Farewell to Europe.") For a few years, his books appeared in the United States but not in England, where wartime paper shortages severely curtailed publishing. He worked constantly on screenwriting and literary assignments, and by early 1946, he was on the verge of nervous collapse. After a short visit to Netta's mother in Jamaica, the Aldingtons decided to return to France. As Aldington wrote to Lawrence Powell on 28 July 1946, "After much discussion and a good deal of mental distress, we have come to a compromise. Netta cannot endure America, and I find it a bit raucous myself; she would like England, but I say to hell with it, damn England; Catherine wants to stay in Jamaica. So we have decided to risk rationing and revolution and return to France, if we can circumvent the immigration officials (upon whom be hell and brimstone) of U.S., England, and France!"[5]

In 1947, Heinemann and other English publishers began issuing books by Aldington that had appeared only in the United States. Consequently, while he was planning his D. H. Lawrence biography, he found himself corresponding with an overwhelming number of publishers, agents, and sundry "pestilential bastards." He dreaded the daily arrival of the mail, and when Kershaw offered to answer letters for him (including the "personal" ones that, for Aldington, were "the worst of the lot"), Aldington was easily persuaded. By May 1948, Kershaw had become indispensable as Aldington's unpaid secretary, confidant, and companion. Aldington, who took holidays only to recover from overwork, had again exhausted himself by October. The strain of writing the introductions for fourteen works by D. H. Lawrence that Heinemann and Penguin issued while he was working on the D. H. Lawrence biography had been too much. He had even considered dropping the biography, but he persevered. He completed the first draft by 20 May 1949 and sent the final typescript to American and English publishers in July. When Aldington finished *Portrait of a Genius, But* . . . , he was depressed, fully expecting "the British Intelligentsia" to discredit him. He was weak after a lengthy bout with bronchitis, exhausted by his labors, and worried about his finances.

One drain on his resources was Brigit Patmore, with whom he had lived and traveled from 1928 until 1936. She called herself Mrs. Aldington, was sensitive about being obviously older than her "husband," and was outraged when Aldington began a passionate affair with her daughter-in-law, Netta McCulloch Patmore. By mid–February 1937, Aldington and Netta were living together at the Pensione Balesti in Florence. When Netta became pregnant, the two sought divorces from their respective spouses so that their child could be born in wedlock. H.D., whom Aldington had married on 18 October 1913 and from whom he had separated in 1919, was extremely cooperative and generous, even paying the lawyers' fees, but extricating Netta from her marriage to Michael Patmore was more difficult. Aldington had voluntarily signed an agreement to pay Brigit £250 per year, a substantial portion of his estimated annual income of £1,000, but this was not enough to satisfy the Patmores, who brought suit. On 23 November 1937, the London *Evening Standard* reported the results under the headline "Richard Aldington to Pay £1,500 Divorce Damages." In addition, his earlier commitment to provide Brigit with an annuity continued. In 1949, Aldington learned that his brother Tony, who handled Aldington's business dealings, had neglected to pay the Patmores, requiring him to send a substantial lump sum. He decided that writing another biography would resolve his financial pinch.

While finishing the D. H. Lawrence biography, Aldington had considered writing the life of Balzac or of Maupassant, both of whose works he knew well, but Kershaw offered

> a much brighter suggestion—the other Lawrence, T. E. Lawrence, Lawrence of Arabia. Richard knew practically nothing about him. I knew it all, the lot. To begin with, I explained to Richard, there was the brilliant strategist who—single-handed, if you please—had overthrown the Ottoman Empire; then there was the archaeologist, the greatest archaeologist ever ("My dear boy, aren't you forgetting Schliemann and Leakey [actually an anthropologist] and . . . ?") [ellipsis in original]; why, the astonishing fellow, I went on, had created the Arab nation ("*What* Arab nation?"), he was a visionary, a mystic, a scholar, a hero. Poor booby, I knew the lot; and, knee-deep in good intentions, I finished by talking Richard into writing the great man's biography.[6]

Despite his amusement at Kershaw's enthusiasm, which had derived in part from conversations with TEL's friend Henry Williamson, Aldington realized that a biography of TEL could have great commercial appeal. Two decades earlier, Aldington had been very successful with a novel about a soldier in the trenches. Why not now write about a hero of the desert war who still fascinated the British public? TEL seemed the ideal subject for a biography that would be easy to write and would do well in the marketplace.

Aldington did not realize that a hostile biography was inevitable when he measured his subject against the standards and circumstances of his own life.[7] Chief among these was his grim experience in the trenches. He wrote to D. H. Lawrence during the war, "There are two kinds of men, those who have been to the front and those who haven't."[8] During the April 1917 battle for Vimy Ridge, he was under bombardment in the Loos area, and after he received his commission in November 1917, he was part of the advance on the Somme front that breached the Hindenburg Line. Early in 1917, as he wrote to Count Geoffrey Potocki on 12 March 1959, he "was on the receiving end of a great German experiment in gas shelling"[9] that condemned him to bronchitis attacks and other respiratory ailments for the rest of his life. Aldington wrote to Kershaw on 5 July 1951, while drafting his chapters on the Arab Revolt, "I hope to finish the war in 10 days, and then the worst will be over. These potty little skirmishes and sabotage raids which [Liddell] Hart and Lawrence call battles are somewhat belly-aching to one who did the Somme, Vimy, Loos etc."[10] Aldington regarded as sheer effrontery TEL's comment at the end of *Seven Pillars* that "When Damascus fell, the Eastern war—probably the whole war—drew to an end."[11] Aldington found this "typical of Lawrence's blatant propaganda . . . " (RA, *Lawrence of Arabia*, 247).

For Aldington, the Arab Revolt occurred on a minor front, TEL's role was political rather than military, the railroad that was the target of many raids was "puny," the Arab victories were usually won by others or were insignificant, and the real object of TEL's activities was not to help Allenby or the British war effort but to "biff the French out of all hope of Syria" (165, 266). Aldington's contrasts between the comparative safety of TEL's hit-and-run exploits and the horrors of the western front were both frequent and sarcastic. The lavish sums that TEL distributed among the Bedouin seemed disproportionate: The gold "was packed in thirty bags each weighing 22 pounds and containing 1,000 sovereigns, about the equivalent (in paper money) of a year's pay for 1,000 British cannon-fodder tommies" (219). For Aldington, TEL's carelessness or indifference was detrimental to the British war effort, beginning with TEL's stint in the Map Department: "Lawrence's conception of his duties was strictly personal, for when told to provide a map of Sinai he put together and delivered the 68 manuscript sheets—'some of it was accurate and the rest I invented,' which obviously would save troops many casualties" (124).

Even worse, Aldington saw TEL as a security risk:

> On the 18th March [1915], Lawrence wrote Hogarth an uncensored private letter excited in expression and highly indiscreet in contents, since over a month before the landing at Gallipoli (25th April), it contains the words: "the Australians and New Zealanders, and some Indians are going to the Dardanelles, with the French, and Ian Hamilton's army." No wonder the Turks were ready on Gallipoli when such indiscretions occurred! Evidently Lawrence was now in possession of highly important secrets, and clearly a most untrustworthy person to have them, for the letter is filled with confidential military information. (134–35)

Hints that TEL manipulated the truth in official reports, altered the wording of telegrams as they passed between Feisal and Hussein, and compromised security convinced Aldington that during the war, TEL was not serving the British but his own personal and political ends: "They call Lawrence a Crusader—but on whose side? Not on ours" (144). For Aldington and others in the trenches, the staff had been incompetent enough without adding flippant chicanery to ineptitude.

Aldington also resented TEL's claim that he was a self-made man. When his father went bankrupt, Aldington had to leave the University of London. TEL graduated from Oxford. Although Aldington's parents insisted that he find a safe and respectable clerk's job, he deliberately chose the riskier course of a writing career. TEL found a secure position as an archaeologist through the influence of D. G. Hogarth and other Oxford connections. Aldington's war service began with the indignities of basic training for the "other ranks" and involved prolonged discomfort and danger when he took part in pushing the Germans back to Mons during the final months of his second tour of duty. TEL received a staff commission in an office without even having to submit to a physical examination and spent most of his service in camel riding, conversation, and commuting. After the war, Aldington wrote criticism and book reviews to make ends meet. TEL received an All Souls' fellowship to write his war book. Aldington doggedly completed assignments. TEL abandoned projects when his enthusiasm waned. TEL's claim to be a man of letters particularly annoyed Aldington, who had labored since 1912 to convey his viewpoint to the public through poetry, criticism, fiction, and biography. TEL seemed to prefer being "known as the writer of a mysterious, unprocurable masterpiece rather than to have it read" (328) and failed to dedicate himself single-mindedly to writing. In such contrasts, Aldington saw the vanity and hypocrisy that he had satirized for years.

There was another sharp contrast in how they recorded their war experiences. On 2 January 1918, Aldington had written to Amy Lowell of his war poems, "They are not popular—I mean they are bitter, anguish-stricken, realistic, not like [Rupert] Brooke or [Alfred] Noyes or anybody like that. They are stern truth, and I have hesitated about publishing them." [12] Aldington did not find "stern truth" in *Seven Pillars* and asked, "If a book, above all a war book, is not completely sincere and as exact as the author can achieve, what is the use of it? Was Lawrence writing a true account of the desert warfare, or merely producing a pretext for pretty printing; so that it didn't matter what he said if the page lay-out was satisfactory to his Oxford aestheticism?" (RA, *Lawrence of Arabia,* 321). For Aldington, TEL could not "claim the merit of a serious recorder of an intensely-felt experience which he longed passionately to convey to others, for them to share and to take warning, not for self-glorification and the plugging of some political 'cause' " (328). That TEL might devote his literary skills to such base purposes as self-advertisement and political ends, instead of to serve truth, struck Aldington as TEL's greatest perversion.

From his early years, Aldington had an intense passion for truth. Of Aldington's three siblings, only Margery Lyon-Gilbert, six years younger than he, was close enough to have a sense of his childhood. In an interview with David J. Wilkinson, she described her brother's characteristic attitude: "In retrospect I can see that every time he saw hypocrisy, falseness, snobbery, class distinction, and that sort of thing, he put his head down and he went straight at it, and said what *he* thought . . . the truth [ellipsis in original]. 'Let us face the truth.' That was always his attitude, I think, towards life and everything." [13] He demanded that truth be the basis of national policy, as he wrote to Alan Bird on 11 February 1953: "[. . .] I believe this Lawrence book is much more than a mere biography—it is the showing up and repudiation of a whole phase of our national life with Winston [Churchill] at the head. True, *he* is a hero, but . . . [ellipsis in original]. Our life as a nation must *not* be based on lies and liars, on slick 'policies.' We must have the truth." [14]

Aldington also despised TEL's anti-life philosophy. In a letter to Ker-

The Unlikely Biographer

shaw dated 13 November 1953, more than a year after the TEL manuscript
had gone to the publisher, Aldington enumerated

> facts and passages telling *against* L. which I either never put in or cut out
> or reduced to the merest reference unintelligible except to a reader of
> TEL. Thus I did not quote his "silly accidents of cruelty, perversions,
> lusts"; his "we wrote our lesson with gun or whip in the sullen flesh of
> the sufferer"; his "Arab skin was an affectation only"; "dung flowed like
> green soup"; the shooting of Hamed (I hope and think he invented this
> atrocity); the belching green-slavering camels; the goat-buggering shep-
> herds; the Sharif who "encouraged nits"; the "chopping" of the Circas-
> sian's feet; the torturing [of] a prisoner; the horrid feast with Abd el Kader
> (descendant of one of the greatest Arab aristocrats and heroes) "spitting
> and belching and picking his teeth"; the German doctor who had made
> the Arabs "swallow their lice"; the setting up [of] a kindergarten for the
> Staff; children crawling "wormlike out of their mothers' wombs, embod-
> ied proofs of consummated lust"; the hideous story of Jem[a]l Pasha
> throwing the old man into an engine furnace and waiting for his skull
> to explode; the prisoners with "the bruises of their urging blue across the
> ivory backs"; the description of the pregnant woman on the bayonet to
> which I merely referred; the "hot pissy aura" of British soldiers; the hos-
> pital in Damascus; and finally that description of the woman's lavatory
> on the troop-ship [in *The Mint*].

For Aldington, "Lawrence was one of Mr. [T. S.] Eliot's hollow men,
and both make a virtue of the same unwholesome incapacity for living—
that genius for accepting the world which was so greatly the gift of D. H.
Lawrence and, in a quite different but equally authentic way, is the gift of
Roy Campbell" (RA, *Lawrence of Arabia,* 376). Aldington had expressed his
own philosophy in the title of his 1941 autobiography, *Life for Life's Sake.*
Throughout his career, he had encountered censorship and hostility for
celebrating passion and the life-loving individual who defies conventional
respectability or patriotic cant, as well as for defending others, such as D. H.
Lawrence, who did the same. Aldington complained that TEL "was too
often excited only by what was violent or horrible or disgusting" (73), and
he found TEL's work replete with callous descriptions, sadistic details, and
a contempt for women that he found repugnant in view of his own passionate susceptibility to women. He regarded *The Mint* as "almost insane
in its attack on female sex" (333).

While TEL's homoerotic impulses reinforced Aldington's view that
TEL was an enemy of life, this was less important to Aldington than TEL's

perceived mendacity. Aldington wrote to Lawrence Durrell on 20 August 1960,

> No, Larry, my main point against the bogus Prince of Mecca is not that he was so obviously an impudent sod, but that he was an impudent mythomaniac whose lies about himself and his alleged deeds were put into a film-lecture by a slick yank advertiser [Lowell Thomas] and taken up enthusiastically by H[is] M[ajesty's] G[overnment] in 1919 because it distracted attention from the fearful slaughter on the Western front, the failure of the invincible British Armada, and similar uncomfortable truths. Only a propagandist could doubt his pederasty. What I want to see is the removal of his bust from St Paul's where it insults the tombs of Nelson and Wellington.[15]

When Aldington became convinced that the British establishment exploited the TEL legend as propaganda, his rancor became even more intense. He already had several grievances against the British government. When he was beginning to build his literary reputation, it had forced him into the trenches, putting him in mortal peril and ending, as he then thought, his hopes for a literary career. It taxed him ruinously, demanding 42.5 percent of the income of writers living abroad on the grounds that literary income was "unearned." It restricted his ability to travel. It also enforced the censorship of his own work and that of D. H. Lawrence, whom he had helped by distributing copies of the banned *Lady Chatterley's Lover*. For Aldington, the political establishment was clearly the enemy of his freedom.

That he emerged as TEL's debunker surprised even Aldington. When he wrote to Henry Williamson on 31 January 1953, nearly a year after he had sent the manuscript to his publisher and two years before the book appeared in England, he deprecated his achievement: "I have no illusions about the value of my share in the TEL book. It is not I but the story and his immense renommé. I just happened to be the first person who took the trouble to collect, sift and verify all the available evidence and to put it down with no particular bias."[16] This might explain why Aldington had found many contradictions, lacunae, and fabrications in the accepted view of TEL, but not why he had reacted against TEL and his legend so vehemently.

Such a reaction had long been part of Aldington's character. He entered into friendships, literary associations, and love relationships wholeheartedly, with extremely high expectations. When others seemed to let him down or accord him less than his due, Aldington responded with intense outrage. Whenever he decided that his confidence in another had been misplaced, his rejection was both total and final. No friendship with Aldington could survive his discovery of a deliberate lie. Had he learned that Henry Williamson had misled him about the purpose of his last meeting with TEL, Aldington would have cut Williamson dead. When Aldington became convinced that TEL was a vainglorious liar who had fabricated his own legend at the expense of the real heroes of the Great War, he could view TEL only with loathing and express his antipathy only in the most forceful terms.

On 18 December 1952, months after he had finished his manuscript, he wrote to Williamson that "It is the only documented life of TEL, and damn near killed me in the writing, but it is worth while because it is the TRUTH as near as can be found. I am glad now I did not know him, so can write in complete calm and non-partisanship. It is not a life to be written by enemies or friends. And fascinating."[17] He had not set out to debunk TEL, but convinced that he had inadvertently exposed a national fraud, he was determined to tell the world the truth.

2

FROM "BIOGRAPHY" TO "BIOGRAPHICAL ENQUIRY"

The TEL is the hardest book I have ever attempted, and I despair of success. Practically everything he professed at one time he denied at another; he gives contradictory accounts of the same event or motive; his friends contradict him and each other. I sometimes feel it would be easier to prove that he was the invention of a powerful clique than to discover what really happened. . . . The disentangling is heart-breaking. Which doesn't mean that the whole adventure wasn't an achievement for an Oxford archaeologist with no military training but The Church Lads' Brigade and the O.T.C.

—Richard Aldington to Henry Williamson, 4 January 1951

By the way, did you know TEL prophesied me? Sir Arnold Wilson, he says in effect, wrote like a bull in a china shop, but one day there will arrive a more subtle devil who will sap under me, and bring me down. Of course he knew he was a fraud.

—Richard Aldington to Alister Kershaw, 5 August 1952

My book is, as the title states, a biographical enquiry and not a biography, and, like John Locke, I have considered it "ambition enough to be employed as an under-labourer clearing the ground a little and removing some of the rubbish that lies in the way of knowledge."

—Richard Aldington, *Lawrence of Arabia*

ALDINGTON'S APPROACH TO biography was to gather all the available facts and then let the evidence determine his conclusions. One of his pointed criticisms of TEL's honors thesis, published as *Crusader Castles* in 1936, was that TEL "had wisely formed his theory first and then set out to look for the evidence"[1] instead of letting his findings shape his conclusions. Between November 1949, when Aldington decided to write TEL's biography, and April 1952, when he submitted his manuscript, he consulted published material by and about TEL, derived further information from unpublished manuscripts and correspondence, and let his discoveries form his evolving view of TEL. Aldington did not realize that his biography would be hostile to TEL until more than a year after beginning his research.

In Le Lavandou, Aldington did not have ready access to major archives, so he relied on a small but devoted team to supply books, copy manuscripts at the British Museum and other repositories, and make inquiries on his behalf. Kershaw, who had moved back to London in 1949, was singularly well-placed to negotiate with publishers. Henry Williamson, who had visited the Aldingtons in April 1949 while on honeymoon with his second wife, Christine, lent letters from TEL and copies of books, including his own *Genius of Friendship* (1941). W. Denison Deasey, to whom Kershaw had introduced Aldington in 1948, copied material at the British Museum, including revealing manuscript correspondence between TEL and Charlotte Shaw, wife of the playwright. William Dibben, an English civil servant with an uncanny knack for locating obscure books, found many vital out-of-print items. Alan Bird, a graduate student at Wadham College, Oxford, investigated TEL's early years in Oxford and at the university, unearthing essential documents. F.-J. Temple solicited information from French officials and records. A. S. Frere of Heinemann, L. J. Browning of Evans Brothers, and Charles Duell of Duell, Sloan & Pearce made inquiries on Aldington's behalf. The help of these nine men made Aldington's TEL research possible, but coordinating everything by mail was often frustrating. Deasey frequently traveled on business, Bird accepted a lectureship in Cairo and then another in Madrid, and Dibben inexplicably stopped corresponding for some weeks (it turned out that he had been ill).

When Kershaw had originally proposed that Aldington write TEL's life, Aldington responded that Kershaw should do it. Kershaw soon abandoned the project, and Aldington wrote on 13 November that he had reconsidered and would attempt a full-length biography of TEL. Kershaw acted quickly.

From "Biography" to "Biographical Enquiry"

On 18 November, he wrote that he had discussed arrangements with Browning for Evans Brothers to publish the book in England and that Browning agreed to advance Dibben money for purchasing TEL books. Kershaw had written to his mother in Australia to send his own TEL collection, including limited editions of *Secret Despatches* and *Men in Print*. He identified *T. E. Lawrence by His Friends* (1937), Vyvyan Richards's *Portrait of T. E. Lawrence* (1936), and David Garnett's edition of *The Letters of T. E. Lawrence* (1938) as sources for information about TEL's early years. He offered to seek firsthand information from TEL's surviving younger brother, Professor A. W. Lawrence (AWL).

Kershaw also outlined how Aldington might gain access to *The Mint*, TEL's account of his early R.A.F. experiences:

> I have this morning received a letter from B[rowning], wherefrom I quote: "I have had a word with Raymond Savage [TEL's literary agent, associated with Evans Brothers] regarding THE MINT and he is quite prepared to allow you to read it in this office. For many reasons he feels it would be dangerous to allow the MS to leave this office." Now this refers only to my own personal desire to read this work but it seems to imply that we must—I must—persuade B. to have a copy made—it's about 60,000 words—to be sent to you and eventually returned. I doubt you could keep the copy—I don't know—because much of it is inflammable, seditious, and libellous stuff. . . . [2]

During the protracted negotiations to gain access to *The Mint*, Aldington became convinced that AWL and the other Seven Pillars of Wisdom Trustees, who controlled TEL's copyrights on behalf of a charitable trust, would try to restrict what he could write about TEL. On 16 January 1950, Kershaw wrote to reassure him:

> There was never any need for you to go "cap in hand" to either T.E.'s brother or Savage. Briefly the position is this. All T.E.'s copyrights are controlled by his brother, A.W., who is (a) not keen on seeing further writings on T.E. appear, and (b) anxious to ensure, if they do, that they are not hostile to T.E. Savage's idea was that you should write to him—S.—not asking any sort of permission but merely saying that you were thinking of writing on T.E. and chattily outlining your approach. He would then show this to A.W.—whom he knows—with the comment that it seemed a good idea and urging A.W. to allow you to quote. Whatever line you suggested in your preliminary letter need have no relevance to what you eventually write. Browning and I feel that we could draft this letter for you out of our knowledge (derived from Savage) as to what A.W. would respond to.

From "Biography" to "Biographical Enquiry"

Savage's precarious position with Evans Brothers soon made negotiations more delicate, as Kershaw wrote on 23 February:

> As I have told you, all T.E.'s copyrights are controlled by his brother, A.W.,
> and permission to quote can best—perhaps only—be obtained from him
> through Raymond Savage. But Savage's contract with Evans will not be
> renewed and he must be informed of this soon—indeed, would have been
> so informed already but for my explaining the set-up to Browning. On
> learning that he is going, S—who is at present wildly enthusiastic—
> may lose some of his exuberance and even become definitely obstruc-
> tive. WHETHER YOU FINALLY DECIDE TO DO THE BOOK OR
> NOT WE MUST GET A.W. LAWRENCE'S O.K. *NOW* and this can
> only be done by your writing a note to Browning which he can show
> to Savage who will show it to A.W. THIS WILL COMMIT YOU
> TO NOTHING EITHER IN WHAT LINE YOU TAKE OR
> WHETHER YOU DO THE BOOK at all.

On 13 March, Aldington sent Kershaw a letter from Savage that suggested
limits on what Aldington might write: "I enclose a letter from Savage
which I have not answered. Now, the only line for me as a biographer is
truth-telling, and I cannot bind myself to write a panegyric of the defunct
such as will please his weeping family with their black-edged hankies in
one hand and TEL's estate in the other. I am being put in a false position."[3]
On 16 March, Kershaw tried to allay Aldington's fears: "I REPEAT: IT IS
ABSOLUTELY UNDERSTOOD THAT A.W.L. WILL BE SHOWN
THE TYPESCRIPT AS A COURTESY BUT WILL HAVE NO
POWER OF VETO."

Aldington, who had already encountered censorship of *Death of a Hero*,
The Colonel's Daughter, and *All Men Are Enemies*, as well as efforts to suppress
publication in England of his satire of T. S. Eliot in *Stepping Heavenward*
(1931), was extremely sensitive to the merest hint of limits on his freedom
of expression. He reacted forcefully and defensively to comments that even
faintly suggested an attempt to direct his thinking, as he did in his 30 March
letter to Kershaw: "What, are you too 'critic-bitten'? What have I said now?
Why do you jump on a chance phrase to torment me? Surely you know
that I shall weigh all the evidence carefully, and that if it is as you say I shall
so state. You know ever so much more about Tel [*sic*] than I do, but I don't
commit myself beforehand. Let me find out what I think." Aldington's
defensiveness went beyond his impatience with the frustrating correspondence and the delays in obtaining a copy of *The Mint*. While he had been

reading about TEL, financial and domestic problems had distracted him from his research.

In January 1950, after learning that his brother, Tony, had again failed to pay the Patmores, who were clamoring for their money, Aldington found out that Tony had also not paid taxes on £1,700 in royalties from Aldington's Wellington biography. As these assaults on his limited resources grew more pressing, he had another shock. Netta, who had departed on 2 January to visit her mother in Jamaica, decided to remain in London rather than return to Le Lavandou, requiring Aldington to supervise his daughter's education and upbringing by himself as well as cope with her emotional reaction to her mother's desertion. Although there were other reasons, Aldington blamed Netta's departure on his financial woes. On 24 February 1950, he wrote to Kershaw that "Netta is quite right—my career as an earning writer is finished, owing partly to my own imprudence, partly to political events, partly to the malice of enemies."

Frequent lapses of confidence nearly convinced Aldington to drop the TEL book. On 27 January, he wrote to Kershaw that "To undertake a book like the TEL is out of the question," and by 6 February he complained that "It would be ludicrous to write that letter about TEL. I can scarcely write this. How could I undertake a book, and such a book? I begin to think I shall not write another. I pulled the old long bow once too often, and it came to pieces in me 'ands. I can't, I can't, I can't." He also worried about the reception of his D. H. Lawrence biography, submitted to Frere in June 1949 for publication by Heinemann in April 1950. This biography had been unexpectedly difficult. Aldington had complained to Lawrence Powell on 10 March 1949 that "This Life of Lawrence is the hardest book I've ever undertaken. He chops and changes and contradicts himself so often, and the people who wrote about him make so many mistakes in facts and dates that it all drives me nuts."[4] Frere, not expecting *Portrait of a Genius, But . . .* to sell, had shown little interest in the TEL book, which is one reason that Aldington intended Evans Brothers to publish it in England. The combination of overwork, financial pressures, and lack of confidence in his D. H. Lawrence biography had exhausted Aldington. He ended his letter to Kershaw of 30 March 1950, "PLEASE remember I have fringed a complete nervous breakdown, and am not as tough as I ought to be."

Despite the stridency of Aldington's complaints, his position improved when *Portrait of a Genius* had respectable sales and when both Evans Brothers and Duell, Sloan & Pearce paid advances against the future earnings of the TEL book. On 2 April 1950, Aldington wrote to Kershaw that he needed "six months for collecting material, six months for first writing, and six more for checking and revision." This schedule did not account for the time that Aldington had to spend seeking elusive answers, pursuing unexpected leads, and documenting "everything" to anticipate opposition to his book. Still, when he completed his 456-page manuscript on 21 April 1952, he was only six months behind his proposed schedule. Early in May 1950, Aldington confided to Kershaw that he had not begun reading the TEL books that he had collected. On 8 May he asked Kershaw for "(a) any unpublished letters, (b) any new stuff on TEL's early life to 20, (c) about his parents and family." He wrote to Savage on 19 June to thank him for arranging access to *The Mint* and for lending his personal copy of *Crusader Castles*. He also asked Savage to thank AWL for him since he did not have AWL's address, declaring that "I willingly accept Mr Lawrence's conditions which are most fair and reasonable." The only stipulations were to prevent others from gaining access to *The Mint* and to let AWL read the TEL manuscript prior to publication.[5]

After Savage had sent the address, Aldington wrote directly to AWL on 30 June to thank him for access to *The Mint* and to ask, "If you have leisure will you tell me (1) if I might have further information of your ancestry on both sides, how long the family lived in Ireland, any unpublished information about T.E.'s boyhood; (2) if there exists any collection of newspaper cuttings about his career." In a postscript dated 1 July, Aldington added that *The Mint* had arrived safely.[6] Aldington did not then realize that questions about TEL's Irish "ancestry" would be particularly disturbing to AWL. TEL's father had abandoned his wife and four daughters in Ireland to elope with their governess, who ultimately bore him five sons. Since he and TEL's mother had never married, TEL and his brothers were illegitimate. AWL had come to terms with this years earlier, but he wanted to protect his mother, who was still living.

On 1 July, Aldington informed Savage that he had received the books that Savage had sent and that he had written to AWL.

> I think I now have most of what I need among the T.E.L. material. "The Wilderness of Zin"—which he did, as you know, in collaboration with Woolley—still eludes me; but it was a Penguin and Alister has asked Allen Lane to lend the file copy. And there's Henry Williamson's "Genius of Friendship" still to come: H.W. is lending me his own copy. So many of the books are out of print and quite unobtainable. Some of them will inevitably prove useless when they do turn up; but I don't want not to have read anything on T.E. which is available.

He asked Savage to suggest how he might learn more about TEL's family and early years.[7]

Aldington had also written to David Garnett, with whom he had corresponded about D. H. Lawrence, and the response of 27 June was encouraging. Garnett had recently completed "a biography of T.E. in his own words," to be called *The Essential T.E. Lawrence,* and promised to send proofs when they were available. He also offered some advice:

> 1) You should see, make friends with, & study Lawrence's mother who is still alive.
> 2) You should see, make friends with, & study Lawrence's brother Professor A. W. Lawrence 51 Madingly Road Cambridge.
> 3) You speak of Lawrence as "a poor devil whose misfortunes . . . " [ellipsis in original]. This implies that you think he was a *victim*. No doubt you can put up a case for such a view, but I think Bernard Shaw was nearer the mark. He regarded him as a triumphantly happy man who always got what he wanted. The real question is why he wanted it. I suppose you will study T.E.L. by his friends. There is a lot in that.[8]

After preliminary correspondence with Savage, AWL, and Garnett, Aldington began studying the books that he had at hand. On 7 July, he informed Kershaw that he was "Working hard on T.E. I am converted to him by The Mint, with the smug feeling that while he was a great guerilla general I was a better private soldier." He had read enough to recognize that AWL had limited what appeared in print about TEL, but he did not find this particularly disturbing at this point. He wrote to Kershaw on 9 July that

> I've finished T.E. by his friends, and am now going through the Letters, where Crusaders supplements and at times duplicates Garnett and yet the texts are not complete. Letters to mother rather dull (oh what a good boy am I) but those to Scroggs [C.F.C. Beeson] lively and clever—he even mentions with approval the Arles WIMMEN!!!! How come the pudic A.W. didn't suppress that? T.E. wild with enthusiasm on reaching and bathing in the Mediterranean, at Aigues Mortes. . . . I hope the letters get more interesting—so cultured and boring after DH [Lawrence].

On 27 July, Aldington informed Kershaw that his researches were assuming an unexpected dimension: "The more I think of it, the more I get to feel that in spite of practically insuperable difficulties there IS a real book to be made here—an attempt at the impartiality I gave DH. Trouble is that TE is the treasured possession of a clique and much essential information is withheld. I propose to say so. The cuts in the letters are sometimes done to make them less voluminous, but also as Garnett hints he was often not allowed to print." He had told Kershaw on 10 July that "Garnett seems to have omitted an awful lot from the letters for reasons of prudence." Garnett had carefully indicated how much he had omitted from each letter— twenty-five lines here, forty-six lines there—throughout the edition. After wading through more published material, Aldington summarized his progress for Kershaw on 8 November: "I have finished taking notes from TE's letters, but find to my annoyance that some of [H. S.] Ede's were omitted by Garnett. Also that TE's letters to Bruce Rogers don't seem to be all here. The amount of unpublished letters and omissions from Garnett's ed[ition] is very considerable."

Aldington continued to worry that, in return for access to *The Mint*, AWL would impose restrictions on what he could write about TEL. He wrote to Kershaw on 8 November, "I have sent Browning the letter you had from Savage about The Mint—a letter which still fills me with distrust of AWL and the whole boiling. Browning has not answered, probably investigating. I am convinced this Mint bogey has been invented as a means of killing my book if I am not properly respectful to the Great Man. That is Browning's affair, but I still think the material I have, though too voluminous, omits too much for any authoritative work." Aldington had decided that publications about TEL concealed as much as they revealed. Of memoirs of TEL's boyhood, Aldington later commented that "the solemnity of his hagiographers (one might call them the Lawrence Bureau) [was] so unsuspecting that the instances they cite often strike an outsider as either ludicrous or highly improbable or both." Of such sources as *T. E. Lawrence by His Friends*, a collection of reminiscences by eighty people, he noted that "none of it is contemporary while the accounts were mainly written in an atmosphere of posthumous hero-worship heightened by the sense of loss at his recent death."[9] Even so, Aldington found several important clues in that collection. One was Lowell Thomas's statement that, despite later denials, TEL had helped Thomas with the film-show and book that made TEL world-famous. Another was that M. R. "Bob" Lawrence, TEL's elder brother, was born around December 1885/January 1886, which later helped Aldington document one of his more sensational discoveries.

Aldington wrote to Alan Bird on 12 November for background information on Oxford University. He did not identify TEL as his subject, but he had TEL in mind when he asked Bird on 24 November about Oxford traditions of misogyny and posing. By 12 December, he had reached chapter 83 of TEL's *Seven Pillars of Wisdom* (about 70 percent of the way through the book) and had taken some thirty pages of notes. He complained to Kershaw on 22 December that he had not yet put "5000 words of the first draft of T.E. on paper. I know it sounds foolish to say so, but the real biographical material is so scanty though the stuff to be gone through is wearisome and voluminous. T.E. does at times reveal himself, but mostly he is hiding behind his words. I think he is harder to know than any character in history." By the end of 1950, Aldington had learned that the published record of TEL's life was incomplete, but the same held true for any public figure with living relatives and influential friends. He had discovered that TEL's estate tried to protect TEL's reputation, but that was hardly unusual. He had noticed several inconsistencies in accounts of TEL's adventures but nothing that would threaten TEL's stature as either hero or chronicler of the Arab Revolt. He sensed that TEL's admirers were hiding something, but he had no idea what that might be or even whether it was significant.

Aldington wrote defiantly to Kershaw on 29 December, "I don't give a stuff for AWL and TE's friends and I intend to write the truth as I see it, send the script to John [Browning] and Duell, and let them fight it out. If they cut a word, I shall insist on saying so in a preface. They can cut what they like, but I shall insist on saying there have been cuts." He wrote to Williamson on 4 January 1951, "There *is* some mystery about his family, a skeleton somewhere. I am trying to discover it. But the book will probably be mutilated if it ever appears, as his brother and Trustees are very arrogant in claiming [the right] to direct one."[10] There was little justification for these outbursts since he had discovered practically nothing worth censoring. This changed early in 1951, however, when he found evidence convincing him that TEL was a liar, discovered that the published record of his accomplishments rested largely on his own unsupported testimony, and learned about TEL's illegitimacy. By May 1951, Aldington had shifted from biography to "biographical enquiry," relying on "outside" sources to verify or refute accounts by TEL and his admirers, reevaluating books by and about TEL in the light of unexpected discoveries, and documenting "everything."

The first major breakthrough, early in January 1951, was evidence that seriously impeached TEL's veracity. Aldington had seen claims in TEL's correspondence (and would encounter similar claims in *T. E. Lawrence to His Biographer Liddell Hart*) that TEL had been offered the post of High Commissioner of Egypt in 1922 (when Allenby threatened to vacate the position) and in 1925 (when Allenby actually did resign). Browning had arranged for Colin Mann, then Public Relations Officer of the Conservative Party, to write to Leo S. Amery (member of the Privy Council in 1922 and a colonial secretary and cabinet minister in 1925), Lord David Lloyd (son of Lord George Lloyd, who succeeded Allenby in 1925), and Sir Ronald Storrs (civil governor of Jerusalem and Judea from 1920 until 1926, when he became governor of Cyprus), asking whether TEL ever received such an offer.

Aldington reported to Kershaw on 5 January, "Letter from John Browning. Amery, present Lord Lloyd and Storrs all scoff at the idea of TE being 'offered Egypt' or 'Home defence.' I have copied passages from Letters and Friends and asked J.B. to send them to Storrs 'in case he is sufficiently interested in the memory of his friend to comment on them.' " Describing the situation to Williamson, Aldington wrote on 22 January, "Some of TE's upstage friends don't know as much about him as they pretend. Suspecting this I rigged up a fairly primitive booby-trap through a third party. Incontinent Amery, Storrs and the present Lord Lloyd fell flop into it. I have now sent Storrs the proof that [TEL] was talking bunk with a mild question, Would he care to comment? So far, no answer. 'Say something, Bill!' "[11]

The "booby-trap" was having Mann ask them whether anyone had offered "Egypt" or "Home Defence" to TEL without mentioning that TEL had boasted of such offers. After Storrs declared it "grotesquely improbable" that anyone had offered TEL either post, Aldington had Browning send Storrs excerpts from TEL's 1926 letter to Charlotte Shaw and his 1934 letter to Lord George Lloyd stating that Churchill had offered TEL "Egypt." Browning also sent Churchill's recollection from *T. E. Lawrence by His Friends* that he had said to TEL, "The greatest employments are open to you if you care to pursue your new career in the Colonial service."[12] Since neither "Egypt" nor "Home Defence" came under the Colonial Office, neither had been Churchill's to give. Storrs sent Browning's letter and enclosures to Churchill on 20 March, and Churchill responded on 12 April, thanking Storrs for telling him about Aldington's forthcoming biography of TEL. Instead of commenting directly on the enclosures, Churchill merely wrote, "I do not recollect any details of posts that may have been offered to Lawrence although I certainly hoped that he would take a commanding part in Middle East Defence."[13]

Churchill already knew about Aldington's research from a 14 February letter from Lord John Hope announcing that Heinemann was planning to publish a biography of TEL by Aldington and that A. S. Frere, chairman of Heinemann, had asked Lord Hope to put three questions to Churchill. First,

From "Biography" to "Biographical Enquiry"

"Was this post [High Commissioner of Egypt] ever *officially* offered to Colonel Lawrence? Or, did Mr. Churchill ever mention it as a possibility, unofficially, in private conversation?" Second, was TEL ever "asked to re-organise Home Defence[?] In connection with this Mr. Churchill is quoted as saying he had hoped to see Lawrence 'take a commanding part in facing the dangers which now threaten the country.' " Third, would Churchill "consent to quotation of his answers in a forthcoming biography of T. E. Lawrence[?]"[14] Churchill responded on 21 February, "In reply to the questions you ask, I do not recollect any of these details; and I think the first is certainly unfounded. With regard to the quotation, I certainly hoped Colonel Lawrence would play such a part; but all this was before the [1939–45] war broke out."[15] Churchill omitted permission to quote.

Aldington had found several statements by TEL that cast doubt on his truthfulness, but they were usually trifling, such as turning kilometers into miles or dollars into pounds to make a bicycle tour or a literary earning more impressive, and other exaggerations were easy to dismiss as playful leg-pulling. Lying about the High Commissioner of Egypt offer was different. For TEL to inflate a purely personal exploit was harmless, but to lie about affairs of state, knowing that his statements would become part of the historical record, was a serious matter.

Aldington had not mentioned his TEL research to Williamson until 3 November 1950, more than a year after he had begun. According to Aldington's sources, TEL had disavowed the title "Prince of Mecca," had refused a CB and DSO, and had disposed of a Legion of Honour and Croix de Guerre by tossing them into the river, returning them to the French, or tying them around the neck of Hogarth's dog, depending on who was telling the story. The title and honors, however, appeared in TEL's *Who's Who* entries. Aldington particularly wanted to know whether TEL had compiled his own *Who's Who* entries or whether someone working for *Who's Who* had prepared them without TEL. On 22 January 1951, Aldington asked Williamson to act as his intermediary with *Who's Who* since "Now directly I approach somebody they know it is a biographer and are cagey or busy."[16]

Williamson accordingly wrote to A. & C. Black, publisher of *Who's Who*, on 28 January: "I wonder if you would be so good as to help me in a matter concerning a friend of mine, the late 'T. E. Lawrence' of Arabia. Looking in your *Who's Who* of 1920, at the Lawrence entry, I wonder if Lawrence himself wrote this? I know that generally the entries are contributed by the subjects themselves—as in the case of my own entry—but could it have occurred that the 1920 T. E. Lawrence entry was supplied by someone other than himself? I would be so grateful if you would be so good as to tell me."[17] A. & C. Black responded on 31 January: "In reply to your letter received today we have to say that T. E. Lawrence apparently did not himself complete our form for the first entry to appear under his name, in Who's Who 1920. He did however himself amplify the entry for the 1921 edition and frequently modified it in subsequent years either on our annual proof or by personal calls at our office here."[18] Aldington now had evidence that TEL had edited the *Who's Who* entries that claimed his ostensibly repudiated honors.

A second major breakthrough was evidence that TEL had helped to create his own legend. This came from Lowell Thomas, whose 1919 film-show and 1924 *With Lawrence in Arabia* had propelled TEL from obscurity to worldwide renown. Aldington had seen Thomas's statement in *T. E. Lawrence by His Friends* that TEL had helped with the film-show and book. On 20 July 1950, Aldington wrote to Charles Duell of Duell, Sloan & Pearce, then under contract to publish Aldington's TEL book in the United States,

> If you are able to talk with the excellent Lowell Thomas, will you ask him the nearest possible or exact date of (1) his first lecture on TEL in USA, and (2) ditto in GB [Great Britain] [?] (3) Does he still have and could he lend us a copy of the script of his original lecture? (4) Was he responsible for the whole film and talk, or did TEL make suggestions? (5) What was his reason for turning the attention of the USA away from the vast, murderous and decisive battles on the Russian and Franco-British fronts in France and Salonika, the Italian, to a side-show like the Arab revolt? (6) May it be hinted that the hitherto unknown author of the famous proverb about backing into the limelight was no other than Shaik Abdül'owel ibn Thomas?[19]

On 16 October 1950, Thomas sent Duell a lengthy response to "one or two of Mr. Aldington's questions." He described the history of the world-famous film-show "With Allenby in Palestine and Lawrence in Arabia," including the circumstances under which Thomas brought his show to London in 1919 and then took it on a tour of English-speaking countries, where he presented his show some three thousand times.[20]

Aldington wrote directly to Thomas on 19 October requesting permission to publish the facts from his letter, repeating the question about the film-show script, and asking specifically "to what extent did Lawrence co-operate with you?" and whether Thomas had seen any of TEL's "own notes or any part of The Seven Pillars of Wisdom?"[21] Thomas's response of 8 December revealed more than he may have intended. Answering one of Aldington's questions, Thomas stated,

> Yes, Lawrence helped me in every way that I asked—but only to that extent. He never made any suggestions unless I asked for them. He was cooperative about pictures, but no more so than all the other important figures I have dealt with down through the years. His attitude was one of rather normal indifference, combined with amusement. He had none of the irritating false modesty that you sometimes find among people who are lens hounds but don't want you to know it. If I asked him for something he seemed to take it for granted that I had a sound reason and let it go at that. It isn't easy to explain just what I mean. But, Lawrence's attitude was what you might call: decidedly British, and that is meant as a hundred percent compliment.

This supported Aldington's conviction that TEL's reiterated aversion to publicity was merely a pose. Thomas generously added, "It is quite all right to use anything I give you in your book. But, when you have your manuscript in final form I would appreciate it greatly if you would send me a carbon copy. If I am one tenth as important to the narrative as you suggest then I am anxious to help you get everything as near right as possible." Thomas ended his letter by asking, "By the way, how did you happen to get interested in Lawrence, and what is it that you are attempting to do?"[22]

Aldington replied on 27 December, "I thought Charlie Duell had told you that I am under contract to him and a London publisher [Evans Brothers] to write a life of TEL." He then addressed some of Thomas's responses:

> You say L. did not show you any of his notes or any part of Seven Pillars. But passages in your book (e.g. 1st par[agraph] on page 79) are almost verbatim the same as the text of L's Despatches and/or Seven Pillars, which were published long after "With Lawrence in Arabia." I assume that they came to you from the four articles published in The World's Work, July-Oct 1921? Don't think I'm making a mountain out of a molehill or in any way doubting your word and TEL's. But so much has been made of these paragraphs with the implication that TE while pretending not to was actually letting you quote from his papers that I want to be able to contradict the story.[23]

Aldington wrote to Kershaw on 2 January 1951, "Charlie [Duell] got a very interesting long statement out of Lowell Thomas. It appears that T.E. knew all about the lecture, co-operated freely all through, jeered at scruples

T. E. Lawrence poses before a draped backdrop in Lowell Thomas's London flat in 1919. Thomas wanted more material for his film-show "With Allenby in Palestine and Lawrence in Arabia" and later included a cropped version of this photograph in *With Lawrence in Arabia* (1924). The uncropped print supports Aldington's claim that Lawrence helped to create his own legend. Courtesy of Lowell Thomas, Jr., and the Lowell Thomas Communications Center Archives, Marist College.

about fact, was often present at performances, and was enchanted by the publicity! (Why not? He hadn't realised its dangers then.) It was a film not slides, but the reels have perished in storage—what a loss." (Thomas never realized that the Imperial War Museum had carefully preserved its August 1918 copy of his original rough footage.) On 9 January, Duell conveyed Aldington's thanks to Thomas "for the material you gave me to pass on to him," quoting a paragraph from Aldington "which I think will please and amuse you":

> If you and L.T. can't see I'm on his side you're a coupla pie-faced mutts. Of course I must differ with L.T. over some of his facts and over his opinions and estimates, but I mean to justify his good faith and to prove his decisive influence in TEL's life. L.T. probably doesn't know how the British highbrow fans of TEL have high-hatted him. I am the only writer on TEL who know[s] what a good speaker L.T. is, having heard him not only on the radio often in [the] US, but throughout a most enjoyable evening at the Dutch Treat Club.[24]

Aldington wrote to Thomas again, nearly a year later, on 2 August 1951:

> It's me again, damn me.
> (1) Can you give me the exact or approximate date when you and Mr Chase arrived at Akaba in the tramp steamer? (What a journey that was!)
> (2) How long were you with Lawrence in Arabia—exactly or approximately?
> (3) Where did you personally go besides Akaba? I ask because T.E.L. in his note on your visit is vague. He mentions, as you do, that he was up country when you arrived, but does not say exactly how long you were there. Surely, with the prejudices of the Bedouin it would have been most dangerous to take you far inland? Or were you able to wangle it?
> I know this is a bore. Please excuse on the genuine grounds of anxiety to get facts as near right as possible.[25]

Thomas, however, did not respond. Aldington commented to Williamson on 14 September 1953, "After I had got some interesting letters from [Thomas], I wrote him point blank: Were you with Lawrence on any of the expeditions you describe? He didn't answer! Of course he wasn't."[26]

Learning that TEL was the major source of Thomas's narrative had made Aldington wonder how much Graves and Liddell Hart's books owed to TEL, but he did not see copies of *T. E. Lawrence to His Biographer Robert Graves* or *T. E. Lawrence to His Biographer Liddell Hart* until April 1951. Aldington learned that despite the published statement in Graves's *Lawrence and the Arabs* that "my completed manuscript could not be submitted to [TEL] before publication," TEL "read and passed every word" of Graves's biography.[27] As Aldington wrote to Kershaw on 14 April, TEL "seems to have amused himself by telling Graves incompatible yarns at enormous length on innumerable occasions!" On 18 April, he added that Graves's correspondence with TEL was "very interesting" and "makes TEL to me much more attractive. When he socks RG [Robert Graves] for his damned Laura Riding [*sic*] highbrowism, I cheer." (The outspoken American intellectual and poet Laura Riding had been Graves's mistress.)

Aldington had read Liddell Hart's authoritative biography months earlier. He wrote to Kershaw on 29 December 1950,

> Since you are in Paris will you go to Librarie Champion (Quai Malaquais) and try to get me any books on the French view of the Arab Revolt. According to Liddell Hart, Colonel Brémond has published his account, but the shit (Hart) gives no bibliography. Garnett has no mention of Brémond even in his Index. I have never read such sloppy biographies. There is NO attempt at critical accuracy. And no proper bibliogs. The book recommended so highly by AWL, Victoria Ocampo's 338171 T.E. (may I call you 338?) is sentimental bilge of a highly inaccurate nature.

Letters from TEL to Liddell Hart reinforced Aldington's conviction that Liddell Hart's methods were shoddy, as he wrote to Kershaw on 21 April 1951:

> Back here by 11, and settled down to the last slug at Hart's notes on TEL's talk plus unpub[lished] letters and many answers to LH's (mostly idiotic) questions. LH is a really tip-top Brit military historian. His idea of "checking" on the Arab doings was not to consult Turkish records and the reports of Joyce and other independent members but merely to ask TEL—whose propensity for leg pulling did not fade with age. He eventually told LH he had been "asked to take Hankey's place"—only Home Secretary!—provided the Cabinet side were divorced from the C.I.D. [Committee of Imperial Defence].

Aldington learned that TEL had contributed extensively to Liddell Hart's biography, even writing portions of it. Realizing that TEL had heavily influenced the books by Thomas, Graves, and Liddell Hart, he concluded that the "written record" was no more reliable than TEL.

Ironically enough, Aldington greeted the first inklings of another breakthrough with considerable skepticism. For reasons that are obvious in retrospect, AWL had provided no information about TEL's family background or ancestry in response to Aldington's queries. When Kershaw reported rumors from Williamson of TEL's illegitimacy, Aldington was inclined to dismiss them, as he wrote to Kershaw on 29 December 1950:

> I laughed at your account of the TE birth scandal, having spent the morning being very ironical about the "reticence." But I think I can placate A.W. by putting in a sentence: "This should dispose finally of all foolish stories about etc." I still doubt the story, because (a) the [birth] certificate is proof of legitimacy in law, ([b]) the difficulty of getting away with a false return is enormous, since it is the duty of the Registrar to check and see that the declaring parties of a legitimate birth are legally married. You can't fake a marriage certificate. In any case that certificate itself is proof of the marriage, but will you get in touch again with John [Browning] and ask him to get the Marriage Certificate of Thomas Lawrence and Sarah Maden? M. R. Lawrence was born in Dec 85 or Jan 86. Therefore the marriage occurred (supposing all strictly legit, as I believe) in 1885 or a little before. Can't have been much earlier or the old cow wouldn't still be alive. I think the bastardy story a can-ard, as Caax says. ["Caax" is Ezra Pound, whom Aldington had satirized as Archibald Cox in "Nobody's Baby," published in *Soft Answers* in 1932.] There's some other nigger on [*sic*] the woodpile. Sarey was perchance a Gamp or something ungenteel. If she was so bloody releegious would she dam 5 bastards? Let's find her marriage certif.

Williamson had erroneously connected TEL with the Nugent family, based on what his close friend Dick de la Mare and the publisher Geoffrey Faber had told him shortly after TEL's death. He sent Aldington a photograph of TEL's purported cousin, Sir Terence Nugent, so that Aldington could see the resemblance for himself. Aldington responded on 22 January 1951 that although there was some family skeleton, "the story you got is bull-dust, distorted on the way. Extensive researches are now under way, and something may or may not be discovered. . . . Meanwhile, do let me beg you not to put that Nugent rumour into writing again or even to tell it to anyone. . . . The Nugent story is a criminal libel (or slander) on Mrs. L. and on the two surviving L. boys. So perpend!"[28]

Within a week, as he reported to Kershaw on 28 January, Aldington had learned that "The real name of TE's father was Thomas Robert Chapman. His mother was S. Maden, b. 1863, daughter of John Maden and Jane Haworth—therefore not 'a Gordon' as TE claimed. No birth certificate of Robert Lawrence, TE's elder brother, is extant under the name Lawrence. Therefore change occurred between Dec 1885 and Aug 1888 [the birthdates of M. Robert Lawrence and TEL]. Search for Chapman now on. Needless to say this is *not* a gentleman's—county gentleman's—name. Obviously something squalid somewhere."

Aldington had misidentified TEL's mother, and Chapman really *was* the name of an Irish baronet, but learning that TEL's father's real name was Chapman put him on the right track. He had found this information in Sir Ronald Storrs's entry on TEL in the *Dictionary of National Biography, 1931–1940*:

> His father, Thomas Robert Chapman (who had assumed the name of Lawrence), the younger son of an Anglo-Irish landowning family, had followed up a sound classical schooling with an agricultural course and some years of continental travel and mountaineering; he lived on private means permitting of comfort though not luxury; became keenly interested in church architecture and in photography; and was an enthusiastic yachtsman, shot, and (from the early days of the safety bicycle) cyclist. His mother, Sarah Maden, the daughter of a Sunderland engineer, was brought up in the Highlands and afterwards in Skye. Both parents were devout, evangelical members of the Church of England.[29]

Aldington had considerable difficulty following up this lead. He wrote to Kershaw on 12 February that "Extensive searches of Chapman find only blanks in the national archives. This is probably a Storrs-Lawrence blind." Perhaps wishing to flaunt his insider's knowledge, however, Storrs had used Chapman's real name despite Sarah Lawrence's request for reticence. She had written to Storrs on 29 August 1946 that "if he would say nothing about Lawrence's antecedents other than that his father was Irish and his mother Scottish he would 'make an old woman of 85 most grateful.' "[30] Aldington and his publisher later searched extensively for documentary proof of TEL's illegitimacy in case they had to defend themselves in a libel suit. They did not realize that Léon Boussard had published the information in 1941 in *Le Secret du Colonel Lawrence*, reissued in 1946. Boussard's book buried TEL's illegitimacy in a subordinate clause: "Cet écolier précoce, fils d'un baronet irlandais nommé Chapman qui vit maritalement avec l'ancienne gouvernante de sa femme devenue folle et qui, elle, porte le nom de Lawrence, ce gamin . . . " (This precocious student, the son of an Irish baronet named Chapman who lived maritally with the former governess of his wife, who had become mad, who [the governess] bore the name of Lawrence, this youngster . . .).[31] The baronet had not decamped with the governess because his wife was insane, but Boussard had Chapman's real name, rank, and nationality. Kershaw, as he wrote to Aldington on 9 February 1951, had ordered Boussard's book ("listed in Stefan's [Stéphane's] bibliography"), but he could not find a copy, and Aldington made no use of Boussard in his TEL research.

That TEL was the illegitimate son of Sir Thomas Robert Tighe Chapman, seventh and last baronet, resolved much of the TEL mystery for Aldington and provided a rational basis for his earlier claim that he would have to mutilate his book to see it in print. He wrote to Kershaw on 21 March that

> We shall never get it published intact, Alister. AWL will never consent to such an exposé as inevitably comes from an impartial recording of the facts. All I can do is write the book and leave Browning and Duell to fight for publication. I've done my part. The rest is up to them. It is a pity that AWL is such a fool and snob, for the true story is infinitely pathetic and a man who sounds like a senseless bragging zany can be shown as one wrecked from boyhood by the knowledge of his bastardy, the frightful tyranny of his mother, his resulting self-consciousness, his yearning for distinction which led him to lie and to brag, and then to recoil from himself in disgust. And then from the moment he became notorious there was always the danger that someone would find out about his parents! I don't think he cared *morally*, but *personally* he resented it bitterly. Remember he didn't even attend his father's funeral!

Another source of concern for Aldington was his growing conviction that TEL was homosexual. He had informed Bird on 7 February that his biographical subject was TEL. On 23 February, he added that TEL's sexual orientation was perplexing because "Whatever his *practice*, of which one can naturally know nothing except by his own confession which doesn't exist, his *sympathy* was entirely with homos and against heteros." He went further when he wrote to Deasey on 28 February that "It was a favorite trick of TEL to ingratiate himself with old famous men like Hardy and Shaw by flattering their ancient spouses, which he could do with complete immunity as he was obviously a homo."[32] Imputation of TEL's homosexuality, as he wrote to Bird on 23 February, put Aldington "under the threat of censorship from Prof A. W. Lawrence and the literary Trustees, who write menacing and truculent letters the moment this topic is hinted at!"[33] He informed Kershaw on 21 March, "I have thought it only right and honourable to inform both publishers of the gist of my discoveries, in case of their feeling that the whole thing must in consequence be called off." Both Browning and Duell encouraged Aldington to continue. Still, as he wrote to Kershaw on 28 March, "the difficulty will be to get it past AWL. I know things about his brother he doesn't know. You will have to be prepared for some shocks. One reason I go so slowly is that every sentence is documented. AWL can object because it spills the beans, but not because it isn't true."

Aldington wrote to Williamson on 26 March that he had decided to abandon a traditional approach because

> what makes it all so impossible and disheartening is the knowledge that Prof L. sits there in his conceit ready to use the Copyright Acts to suppress any truth which might affect him. And there is Garnett with all sorts of withheld material in his possession waiting to produce it in triumph to prove me mistaken. The only way out is to abandon the straight biography, and to call the book a biographical enquiry—and set out the pros and cons as conscientiously and impersonally as possible. I must say in a brief foreword that all I can do is to set before the reader the evidence I can find—what has been wilfully withheld must be the concern of my more fortunate successors. Or words to that effect. But I wish I had never undertaken it, there's so much which leaves a rather nasty taste. The whole thing makes me nervous and unhappy.[34]

In his letter to Williamson, he was not entirely candid about why fierce opposition to his book was inevitable.

Trying to make sense of his discoveries, Aldington had written to Kershaw on 20 March, "I have found in [A. P.] Wavell that Lawrence and the Arabs did not 'liberate' Damazcus [sic]. The 3rd A.L.H. [Australian Light Horse] Bgde. were in and through the city in pursuit hours before! I'm rather sorry about this myself." To Deasey, Aldington wrote on the same day that he was still trying to document TEL's illegitimacy and that "I think among TEL's numerous lies is that he and his ruffians got into Damascus 'ahead of the Australians.' "[35] (This was not news to the Australian Deasey. In 1927, David Roseler had published the fact in his TEL book.[36] In London, in 1919, Thomas's film-show had proclaimed that the Arabs entered Damascus first, but when Thomas toured Australia in 1920, he corrected his film-show in favor of the Australian Light Horse.) By the end of March, Deasey had provided copies from the British Museum of TEL's letters to Charlotte Shaw that supported Aldington's view of the causes of TEL's erratic behavior. Aldington, who had now reached most of his negative conclusions, began reevaluating his sources in the context of his discoveries.

He soon had to interrupt his work. In December 1950, Aldington had received notice that he had to vacate Villa Aucassin by the end of April 1951 since the owners wanted to resume occupancy. While working on his research and first draft, Aldington had been seeking another place to live. He ultimately chose Montpellier, chiefly because there was a fine lycée there for his daughter. On 21 April, he wrote to Kershaw that he planned to carry with him "41 TEL and related books in [the] car, having taken notes from some dozens of others, and still far from complete," intending to work steadily on the project. More than a month passed, however, between departing with Catha from Le Lavandou on 25 April and settling into rooms at the pension Villa les Rosiers in Montpellier. They spent the interim in a hotel, and since Catha could not begin school until 28 May, Aldington devoted most of his time to her needs. He wrote to Kershaw on 21 May, "I must think up some way of getting to work on TEL, but of course in a town without friends Catha is rather lost." Many of the books that Aldington needed to resume his writing had remained in storage at Le Lavandou.

His attitude toward his sources had changed dramatically. Earlier, as he had written to Kershaw on 27 February, he had expected to depend on primary sources: "I MUST have all FIRST HAND evidence about TEL or take the rap from Graves, Garnett, et al. Second-hand stuff like Malraux is of no real importance. It is the first-hand evidence that matters. Ditto Caldwell. The Graves-Hart stuff from TE was apparently published by Faber (perhaps sheets of B. Rogers?) and is real biographical material; so too, the Mrs Shaw letters and all the Lionel Curtis stuff." After concluding that the only eyewitness to key events was unreliable, however, Aldington no longer trusted primary sources. He wrote to Kershaw on 26 May that

> The whole enterprise is a difficult and dangerous one, for much of the evidence is "cooked," and much of essential importance is either still hidden or will be refused publication. The Foreign Office refuses to show their papers which are probably the only documents which can show whether TEL lied about his exploits or told the truth. A most interesting character who, if his damned silly relatives and friends would only be frank, might be justified from the suspicions the present state of evidence arouses. I can do no more than sketch a biographical enquiry, and leave the real book to a successor unhamp[er]ed [by] Professor Lawrence.

Aldington's new approach required more objective sources than the TEL-based standard works, but such material was difficult to find. He wrote to Kershaw on 24 July, "Though I have used 7 Pills occasionally I have avoided repeating Graves's mere paraphrase of L's narrative and above all Hart's incredibly pretentious 'military history,' using as authorities the Secret Despatches, the Official War History, Wavell, Barrow, Brémond, Bray, Young, and any outside authority who is not merely parroting TEL. A difficult almost maddening job for which I shall get no thanks from anyone. But I suggest it will be the first account to put truth before propaganda and drama." There were moments of discouragement—he wrote to Kershaw on 21 August that "There are so many difficulties I feel I shall never get this job done"—but by this time, the major problem was to put his hands on the books that he needed, such as Hubert Young's *Independent Arab* and Major N. N. E. Bray's *Paladin of Arabia*, a biography of Gerard Leachman. Aldington joked to Kershaw on 5 November about his frustrations: "Did you gather from my recent [letter] that I got TWO Hubert Youngs and NO Bray? As they come from contemporary England I was not surprised at a blunder; what surprised me was that they didn't emit TWO BRAYS and no Young."

Aldington found several accounts by those outside TEL's circle that he used to test the TEL legend. A. P. Wavell's *Palestine Campaigns* (1928) and *Allenby—A Study in Greatness* (1940) suggested that TEL and the Arabs contributed very little to Allenby's campaign and that Allenby, despite his public praise, privately suspected that TEL was something of a charlatan. In *The Fire of Life* (1942), General Sir George de S. Barrow quoted Allenby on TEL: "Besides, we know Lawrence. He thinks himself a hell of a soldier, and loves posturing in the limelight."[37] Aldington later reported Barrow's response when TEL had ostensibly stated that "the murders, robberies and tortures of Deraa were the Arabs' idea of war": " 'It's not our idea of war,' said Barrow, 'and if you can't remove them, I will' (which Barrow immediately contrived to do with little difficulty)."[38] In Sir Andrew Macphail's *Three Persons* (1929), Aldington had found confirmation for TEL's "unconscious cruelty and savagery" in TEL's indifference, after a train wreck, to the pleas of Turkish passengers begging for protection from vengeful Bedouins.[39]

TEL had described his elaborate search for a leader of the Arab Revolt in *Seven Pillars of Wisdom*. Aldington, however, found a statement in Brémond's *Le Hedjaz dans la Guerre Mondiale* (1931) that he described to Bird on 30 June: "First thing which struck my evil eye was a remark of Général Brémond (himself apparently a genuine Arabisant) that Abdulla spoke only Arabic and Turkish, but Feisal EXCELLENT ENGLISH!!! Now we begin to see why Abdulla was no good and Feisal the chosen one."[40] Lieutenant-Colonel J. I. Eadie offered additional evidence in the *Times Literary Supplement* (22 June 1951) that TEL's command of Arabic was limited. W. E. Johns's eyewitness account of "How Lawrence Joined the R.A.F." in the *Sunday Times* (8 April 1951) provided a version markedly different from that in *The Mint*. These and other sources outside the "Lawrence Bureau" (a pun on the Arab Bureau), Aldington's umbrella term for those with a vested interest in TEL's reputation, further convinced him that the legend had no objective basis. Aldington had greater difficulty and less success obtaining official documents, as he indicated to Kershaw on 1 June: "Did I tell you that the Foreign Office sent Browning a high-hat snoot refusing to allow access to the F.O. [Foreign Office] report on the Arab Revolt made over 30 years ago—on the grounds that it is 'confidential'! And USA, France and England are already publishing ALL documents connected with the war of 1939–45." (His comment about access to 1939–45 records is demonstrably inaccurate). He did manage to examine published documents, however, such as those in *Military Operations, Egypt and Palestine* (1927–28), and his attempts at cross-verification were frequently revealing. For instance, former Prime Minister David Lloyd George's *Truth About the Peace Treaties* (1939) contradicted TEL in such particulars as which sessions Feisal had attended.

In *Papers Relative to the Foreign Relations of the United States*, Aldington discovered an important clue that had eluded Garnett, among others. On 18 May 1919, while flying to Cairo on a Handley-Page military aircraft, TEL had survived a crash in Rome that killed his pilot and copilot. Garnett quotes another pilot's report that "it had been given out" that TEL "was returning to Cairo merely to collect his kit," but the report that Garnett quotes adds that "it was fairly obvious that this was not the real reason. Anyway, not the whole story."[41] Aldington found his answer in the minutes of a 20 March 1919 meeting of the Commissioners Plenipotentiary of the United States: "(5) Memorandum No. 168 was read in which [U.S. Army] General [Marlborough] Churchill submitted a proposal that Captain William Yale accept an invitation tendered to him by Colonel Lawrence to accompany the British forces on an expedition which they are planning for the month of May against the tribes of the Nejd." After four previous attempts had failed, Abdulla led a force against Ibn Saud's Wahabis, who wiped out Abdulla's army in a night attack on 25–26 May 1919. Abdulla and his staff barely escaped with their lives. Aldington concluded that TEL had planned to join Abdulla for this ill-starred campaign and that, "But for the plane-crash, Lawrence might have perished and would certainly have lost his military reputation in the disaster which overtook Abdulla's forces at a place called Turaba, before they ever reached Khurma."[42]

Aldington also drew from accounts of other nations involved in the Arab Revolt. He rejected the claims by TEL (as well as Thomas, Graves, and Liddell Hart) that the Turks had offered a reward of £5,000 or £50,000 (depending on the source) for TEL's apprehension when he learned that neither General Liman von Sanders nor Jemal Pasha had mentioned TEL at all in their memoirs of the Turkish campaign. After some delay, Dibben provided a copy of George Antonius's *Arab Awakening* (1938), and Aldington wrote to Kershaw on 8 January 1952 that "it is a very statement of the whole show from the point of view of the Arab nationalists and contains very many documents I have hunted for in vain." According to Antonius, the Imperial General Staff had suggested the plan to take Akaba in 1916, months before TEL saw the Hejaz, and then Auda had proposed and executed the operation, with TEL merely accompanying the expedition. Aldington decided reluctantly, as he informed Kershaw on 29 December, that he had to reread *Seven Pillars of Wisdom* "before tackling the campaigns of the Man Who Won the War with Allenby's mob doing a little guerilla stuff on his left flank." Most of what he subsequently encountered, as he wrote Kershaw, merely reinforced his conclusions—that "L. was little known even to the Arabs until the cinema, newspapers, etc. made him famous" (5 February 1952), that TEL's account of the Battle of Tafileh strained credulity (12 February 1952), and so on—and Aldington focused his energies on preparing a polished final draft.

After Aldington had gained a firmer sense of his approach, the writing went fairly quickly. On 30 August 1951, he summarized his position to Kershaw:

> I don't think there will be any trouble about anyone save AW Lawrence [*sic*] and the Trustees, though they might if nasty persuade Cape and Garnett for example to refuse [permissions to quote] too. You must remember that since we got that go-ahead from Savage I have found out the whole secret of TE's birth, almost overwhelming proofs of his homosexuality, his written admission that he did not stick it out at Deraa but yielded to stop the flogging, and a whole set of unpublished letters at the B[ritish] M[useum] which prove his bastardy and the fact that "one of the three or four reasons" for his joining the RAF was to get away from his mother. Also I am forced time and time again to bring together conflicting testimony which leaves no option but to admit that he was lying.

You must remember that he had an Irishman's imagination and an Irishman's love of telling a good tale about himself; also, he loved mystifying people, and admits that he "kidded" so perpetually that he didn't himself know where truth ended and fiction began.

All this I have faithfully recorded, with references for every statement. In re-writing I shall strive hard for a coolly impersonal tone; but you will see that these facts (and they cannot be denied) may infuriate AWL into refusing permission.

Throughout his research, Aldington had informed Kershaw of his discoveries as they had developed, but Kershaw did not see the manuscript until it was complete.

Aldington's sarcastic summations in literally hundreds of letters had aroused Kershaw's apprehension that the book's tone toward TEL would be transparently hostile. Aldington's letter to Kershaw dated 10 February 1951 is representative in this regard:

Did you know that Wavell says Allenby always thought T.E. a charlatan? Also Storrs is a bugger of the Hugh Walpole kind. Of course T.E. was a sod. And a fearful liar. I think he invented that battle despatch for which he got the D.S.O., and then got frightened and pretended it was "a bitter parody." Parody my arse. I believe the malaria caught at Aigues Mortes in 1908 destroyed him, and he developed just the same awful depression and bull-shitting that Roy [Campbell] has. Of course his war experiences developed it frightfully. It is a terrible and pathetic story, however you look at it. But believe me I think he is just about as reliable as Roy. I am told it is a known thing in malaria patients, but am looking for proper medical confirmation. . . . The fearful depression resulting from the action of the trypanosomes on the blood corpuscles seems to cause the curious re-action of bull-shitting. TE was never "offered Egypt" or "Home Defence," any more than Roy. And the more I read 7 Pills the more I wonder. He may have believed it. I have a written declaration from Lowell Thomas that TE not only knew of but helped prepare that lecture, and scoffed at T[homas]'s scruples about fact! He also posed for the photos. Then, having got the publicity, loftily refers to "a Mr L.T."!!!! If only I could get some peace and quiet, I think I could do a perfectly fair book and really get as near the truth as is now possible. He vos a bugger, but he vos not a bloody bugger.

(The last sentence parodies Giuseppe "Pino" Orioli's considered assessment of Lytton Strachey.)

Usually Kershaw refrained from commenting on matters of tone, but he had written on 8 July 1951, "I shiver when you mention T.E. Do not hoe into him too hard, I conjure you—not because he should be treated as sentimentally sacrosanct at all but because surely the value of your biography will be the objectivity (and surely he *was* a remarkable man?)." After finishing the first draft of the book and starting the final version, Aldington wrote to Kershaw on 19 September 1951 that "I have at last managed to hit the right tone. I hope so. I want it to be cool, impersonal, without bias, but interesting." Kershaw, despite Aldington's optimism, still had his doubts, as he revealed in his letter of 22 September:

> I don't want to fret you by my comments on the biography: only I put it to you that the whole essence of the project is strict objectivity. You hate the fellow—fine; but if you can[,] conceal the fact—he's been anti-ed as well as pro-ed already: it is impartiality that has never come up before.
>
> And it is surely important to remember that liar or not, phoney or not, there must have been *something* rare about him that so impressed so many people.

Aldington's response, on 29 September, was to declare that "I think I have at last found the way to tell what I think [is] the truth about TEL (all documented) and still keep him sympathetic."

To Williamson, Aldington wrote on 6 February 1952, "I fear that this laborious method [of conscientious documentation] will as you say 'take the life out' of [the TEL book]. Never mind, this will be the first book on T.E.L. which has seriously tried to discover the facts—without which no biography is possible."[43] He reported to Kershaw on 29 March 1952 that when Deasey had visited Aldington at Villa les Rosiers, "Looking over my collections of 'evidence' here—the worst of which I haven't used—he now hints that I'm pulling my punches at the Colonel! Il ne manquait que ça."

Throughout his research, Aldington had emphasized his desire to be fair to TEL despite the pressures he was under and the difficulty of seeking the truth from fragmentary evidence. He had informed Kershaw on 27 February 1951, "I have had to slow down and almost stop work on TEL. The strain with all the other worries is too great, and it makes me unfair to him through irritation." The methodology of the "biographical enquiry" as Aldington applied it, however, obscured his efforts to be impartial. So much of the written record derived from TEL that it was impossible to separate an attack on the published sources from an assault on the man. In addition, Aldington's virtual exclusion of testimony favorable to TEL, except to refute it, suggested extreme bias in his selection of sources. He felt that documenting "everything" would prove his objectivity, but since many of the contradictions and inaccuracies in statements by and about TEL were trivial, his exhaustive notes made him seem nit-picking and vindictive. After his extensive efforts, however, Aldington had absolute confidence in the manuscript and could not understand why it provoked intense hostility.

Aldington finished his text on 7 April 1952, completed the bibliography and notes by 20 April, and sent the manuscript to Kershaw the following day. When Kershaw finally saw Aldington's manuscript, he found the "biographical enquiry" convincing beyond refutation. Although there were sardonic barbs throughout the text, he regarded Aldington's handling of TEL as generally balanced and his case against TEL and the "Lawrence Bureau" proven. Aldington felt that he had done his work. The rest would be up to his publishers.

3

DANGEROUS LIAISONS

Collins is likely to have bought a best-seller, a series of expensive law suits, and infinite trouble.

—Richard Aldington to Alister Kershaw, 15 April 1952

I have been re-reading the law of libel, and it seems to me that almost any slightly critical statement will be "defamatory" in English law, and as the law presumes that "publication" implies that the writer intended malice and that it has damaged the plaintiff . . . ! [ellipsis in original] I don't think people realise how the law of libel and law of "obscenity" have been carefully warped during the last 150 years to act as a hidden censorship of books.

—Richard Aldington to Alan Bird, 22 November 1952

But is it not strange that English law makes it so easy for TEL and his friends to circulate their lies, and so hard for me to expose them?

—Richard Aldington to Alan Bird, 23 October 1953

THE LONDON PUBLISHER on whom Aldington depended was not L. J. Browning of Evans Brothers, as originally arranged, but William Collins. This had resulted from the efforts of John Holroyd-Reece of Albatross, publisher of English-language editions for distribution on the Continent. Actuated solely by his desire to help Aldington, he had persuaded Collins to offer an impressive advance of £4,500 and to agree to a contract with a trust, enabling Aldington to avoid the 42.5 percent tax that the British government imposed on royalties of authors living abroad. For Collins, a popular biography of TEL by a well-known author justified this unusual arrangement. Aldington had accepted an advance of £1,750 from Evans Brothers, but after Kershaw explained how the arrangement with Collins would resolve Aldington's desperate financial situation, Browning generously released Aldington from his Evans Brothers contract, and Aldington later returned the advance. Holroyd-Reece, acting as liaison, prepared a two-page handwritten summary of the agreement with Collins in a memorandum dated 15 October 1951. The next day, Collins, who was on holiday in Paris, signed the document, and Holroyd-Reece took it across town to Kershaw, who signed it on Aldington's behalf. This memorandum was the only formal written agreement that Collins would publish the TEL book.[1]

Aldington had long expected fierce opposition from the "Lawrence Bureau." He had written to Kershaw on 6 March 1952, a month before sending his manuscript, that "not only Savage, but AWL and the Lawrence Trust will fight like devils to get this book suppressed or hopelessly mangled. . . . I don't know that it's safe to agree to 'make any cuts that are needed' [as Collins had proposed] for AWL & Co will want to cut it to pieces. But I must be specifically guarded against libel and the getting quote permissions bogey."[2] A few days after he had finished his text, on 7 April, he again wrote to Kershaw on the subject: "I trust you and [Holroyd-Reece] are prepared for a really dirty battle with the Lawrence Bureau, for they'll invoke libel and infringement of copyright for all they're worth. What I fear is that Collins will rat, and turn round on me." In his first major battle with censorship, more than a year before the "Lawrence Bureau" learned that his book was hostile to TEL, his adversary was his publisher. Aldington and Collins had never met. Both would have ample cause to regret their association.

Although Aldington had mailed his manuscript to Kershaw in April,

Dangerous Liaisons

Collins did not see it for three months. Holroyd-Reece had arranged to have the typing done in his London office, and to ensure that the contents remained absolutely confidential, he had his secretary type the entire 456-page manuscript after business hours, which took three full months, and even then it was riddled with errors. Collins, despite frequent requests, did not receive the typescript until late July. He soon realized that he had committed his firm to a publisher's nightmare. The author himself had admitted that the book was libelous and had refused to indemnify the publisher. The book was certain to outrage the "Lawrence Bureau" since, in addition to revealing TEL's illegitimacy and accusing him of fabricating his exploits, it maligned virtually everyone who had published books and articles favorable to TEL. Those who were unable or unwilling to sue for libel would pounce on a chance to bring action for copyright infringement if Aldington quoted too many words from published books about TEL or quoted unpublished sources without permission. The Seven Pillars of Wisdom Trustees (then consisting of AWL, his wife, his daughter, and his architect friend M. A. Sisson) held all rights over TEL's writing, published and unpublished, and were not likely to grant permission to quote, nor were the authors of standard books about TEL. The power and influence of TEL's partisans, many of whom Aldington's book attacked directly, would generate heated opposition from high levels. An assault on a national hero would tarnish the image of the firm. Collins felt a pressing need for legal counsel and for a materially revised manuscript.

As a publisher, Collins was in an awkward position. On the one hand, there was a good deal of profit in books that make provocative revelations about public figures, and he had already committed his firm by paying an advance of £4,500. On the other hand, the laws of libel and copyright, intended to protect individuals from unwarranted and malicious assaults on their characters and to prevent the theft of literary property, could impose ruinous penalties on a publisher that was insufficiently cautious. The real force of legal actions for libel and copyright infringement lay not in their actual use, but in their threat. As a result, the most stringent censors of manuscripts were usually publishers who went beyond the requirements of the law by deleting marginally actionable or offensive statements to protect themselves against injunction. Aldington had no sympathy for such concerns. If libel laws offered legitimate protection against calumny, they also dissuaded writers and publishers from exposing unpleasant facts. If copyright restrictions were safeguards against literary theft, they also gave leverage to those trying to suppress the truth. Aldington sincerely believed everything that he had written about TEL and his partisans, and he expected his publisher to support him without reservation. He regarded "editorial" emendations or changes that the firm's lawyers advised as attempts to censor him.

Since neither Aldington nor Kershaw knew Collins, all three depended on Holroyd-Reece, who was an odd liaison—a publisher serving as an author's intermediary in another publisher's office. Holroyd-Reece failed miserably in this role. As Kershaw later remarked, Holroyd-Reece "was constitutionally incapable of expressing clearly what he had in mind." Kershaw recalls Holroyd-Reece as "an excellent fellow and genuinely anxious to help Richard; but he adored navigating among appalling difficulties to such a degree that when no such difficulties existed he deployed all his considerable intelligence in creating them."[3] To prevent Aldington's lathering himself into a state of frenzy, Holroyd-Reece often withheld bad news, and to avoid alienating Collins, he frequently neglected to tell the publisher some of Aldington's more important concerns and requirements. The result was that Collins and Aldington continually worked against each other while believing that they were in accord. Holroyd-Reece's travels between his offices in London, Paris, and Florence constantly caused further delays.

Aldington, simultaneously concerned about censorship, publication date, serial and foreign rights, and a formal contract between Collins and the Aldington trust, caused additional problems. The slightest delay would upset him and impel him to act, usually against his best interest. Although he repeatedly promised to leave details to Kershaw and Holroyd-Reece, he frequently intervened. With one inopportune letter, he would undermine arrangements that had taken Kershaw and Holroyd-Reece considerable time, trouble, and tact to conclude with Collins. There was no center of control, and no one really knew what was going on.

Collins wrote to Kershaw on 12 August that he had "read with great interest" Aldington's manuscript, that "there are quite a number of points to be taken up," and that his head editor, F. T. Smith, would submit a full report. He referred to "a certain amount of repetition especially in points building up the case against Lawrence" that Collins felt would "alienate a number of reviewers."[4] Kershaw did not feel that he could forward this to Aldington, who soon began to wonder why he had heard nothing from his publisher. When Aldington finally received Smith's lengthy report early in September, its editorial presumption outraged him. Smith wanted a virtual rewrite of the manuscript on grounds that Aldington, in his letter to Kershaw of 7 September, described as "stupid, short-sighted and even ignorant": "Collins want[s] to exploit the bastardy scandal 'with all details' and 'how and where the parents lived together'! What price AWL and libel if that was done? I still think that the lawyers may say even my modest and carefully toned-down exposé is libellous. But this 'Editor' is too stupid to see that the very quiet, careful toneless exposition is intended to show a judge and jury that I'm not trying to exploit a scandal." Aldington sent a separate letter dated "Sunday" [7 September], indicating in detail how Kershaw should respond to Smith's report: "I do not wish in any way to exploit this domestic scandal for the sake of sales. I have pried into the private life of a family—the least I can do is to record my discoveries as quietly and briefly as possible. I consider exploitation of this situation (the woman and two sons being still alive) as caddish. (Use that word.)"

Smith's impertinence in telling Aldington how to write a book rankled. Aldington sent Kershaw a thirteen-page single-spaced refutation of Smith, dated 8 September 1952 and addressed to Collins. Smith had suggested that Aldington change his title to either "The Lawrence Legend" or "T. E. Lawrence: The Legend and the Man." Aldington considered the first confusing since people might think this was another Aldington book about D. H. Lawrence, and he found the second title "cheap." Smith had also wanted to incorporate a prefatory chapter to explain that TEL's claims to have been offered the post of High Commissioner of Egypt had led Aldington to question TEL's veracity, removing the "Egypt" episode from its proper place in the narrative structure and thus destroying Aldington's "slow but unswerving building up of the evidence from the beginning." Smith also had wanted Aldington to provide a thumbnail biography every time a new figure appeared, which Aldington resented as interference with his style.

In his letter to Collins, Aldington complained that Smith "is not fully aware of the complexities of the subject, makes objections which he fails to substantiate, and seems very eager to make 'scores' off the writer. On the other hand, some of his generalisations are vague and others manifestly self-contradictory. In some cases of detail, criticisms are based on misquotations from my text; and in others the passage queried has been carelessly read and misunderstood." Aldington felt compelled to remind Collins that, despite Smith's claim, Aldington had presented "no case against Lawrence," but "I record the facts." He demolished Smith's objections to "factual" statements and identified the sources for his own statements. In response to Smith's repeated complaints about criticisms of Liddell Hart, Aldington wrote Collins, "I don't understand your flutter about Liddell Hart. Are you afraid of him?" At one point, Smith had surmised that Lowell Thomas was "probably still alive," to which Aldington retorted, "I'll tell the world. I have very recent letters from him, and he's on the US radio every week." Aldington concluded that Smith "puts up a good bluff, but he knows very little about the subject on which he tries to pose as an authority."[5]

The editor's report had convinced Aldington that Smith was an enemy within the firm, trying to suppress Aldington's findings on behalf of the "Lawrence Bureau." He also concluded, as he wrote to Kershaw on 7 September, "Clearly, there is war between this editor and [Holroyd-Reece]." As Collins's 12 August letter to Kershaw revealed, however, Collins had read the typescript and formed his opinions before Smith wrote his "attack." Far from influencing Collins's views, Smith was dutifully evaluating the manuscript in terms of his employer's expectations and requirements. Part of the problem was that Aldington and Smith were strangers. An editor who knew Aldington would have approached him more tactfully, and Aldington might have responded less defensively.

Mark Bonham-Carter, a member of Collins's firm at the time, remembered Smith as "a sort of journeyman publisher in Collins who had been there all his life, who was expected to do what he was told, . . . who did the donkey work at Collins and kept out of the limelight, and was kept out of the limelight." He recalled Collins as "a man who was rather sensitive to what he thought was his reputation." Collins was worried about the

> cult of Lawrence which was composed of quite powerful members of the establishment, and which consisted of two groups of people: one, intellectuals, who thought he was a man of action; and the other, men of action, who thought he was an intellectual. Thus you had on one side Liddell Hart, [Sir Lewis] Namier, E. M. Forster, all passionately devoted to Lawrence in one way or another. On the other side you had Lady Astor, Mr. Churchill (though he wasn't involved in this sort of thing), Lord Trenchard (who had been head of the Air Force), and various other people like that who valued him as a great literary and intellectual figure, and therefore the affront to his reputation which it was believed that Aldington's book did, and the pain which it was assumed that it was then to inflict on his old mother, who was still alive, produced a great head of steam. . . . [T]he last thing [Collins] wanted was for people like that to think ill of him.[6]

Aldington's reaction did not surprise Kershaw, for Holroyd-Reece had dictated a letter to Kershaw on 29 August to prepare him for Smith's report. After saying that his own job was to make "all the people in the organisation feel desperately enthusiastic and convinced that they've got something that they can make big sales with" and that their ineptitude in expressing their views was deplorable but beside the point, Holroyd-Reece emphasized that "the notes and suggestions of Collins deserve proper consideration because what we need for Richard is big sales. There will be some minor points in their notes which express certain unimportant fears, namely a slight tenderness towards Mr. Liddle-Heart [*sic*] and Robert Graves," but Holroyd-Reece did not feel that Collins took this seriously because Collins, who had published Liddell Hart's edition of *The Rommel Papers*, would naturally want to avoid friction with one of his firm's authors.[7]

On 8 September, Kershaw wrote directly to Collins that he and Aldington were preparing a "detailed answer" to the editor's report. Then he presented Aldington's general response to Smith's points. Aldington agreed to alter the title but preferred "Lawrence of Arabia / The Legend and the Facts" to Smith's suggestions, and he reluctantly agreed to write a prefatory chapter despite feeling that it would "harm the proportions of the book." He was "in the highest degree unwilling to alter the presentation of Lawrence's family background," however, since TEL's mother was still living and thus sensationalizing would merely invite action for libel and violate standards of good taste. He was "exceedingly unwilling" to abridge the Arab Revolt section, and he did not want to "burden the book [with] descriptions of monotonous days in barracks and the minor uninteresting happenings of Lawrence's last years."

This letter crossed one from Collins to Kershaw, also dated 8 September. Collins wrote, "As I told you John Holroyd-Reece saw all the material we sent you and he seemed very much in agreement with all that we said. I do want to make it clear, too, that I feel very much the same as our head editor. I quite realise that it will take some time for Aldington to reply and don't want to hurry things in any way." On 9 September, Kershaw wrote to Holroyd-Reece that "Richard, as I knew would be the case, has got into all his states. He has made some concessions, may make others, but is already talking of 'enemies,' conspiracies, usw [*und so weiter* (and so on)]." He referred to Aldington's "detailed (and I must say, very convincing) reply to the Editor's report; I hope to tone this down and send it to Collins: you shall have a copy." Collins did not reply to Kershaw until 24 September, and then merely to say that he had nothing to say until he could see a corrected typescript. He did, however, remark on the title: "We much prefer T. E. LAWRENCE: THE LEGEND AND THE MAN to THE LEGEND AND THE FACTS. I can't quite understand why Aldington should think the first title cheap. I have tried it out on one or two people here whose opinion I really value and they are unanimous. Perhaps LAWRENCE OF ARABIA is better than T. E. LAWRENCE." Apparently the "one or two" who predictably echoed the opinion of their employer did not include Smith, who had written to Kershaw on 10 September, "Thank you for the new suggestion regarding title, which I like better than THE LEGEND AND THE MAN. I am most grateful."[8] Collins indicated that the lawyers were not ready to submit their report, and there matters rested.

While awaiting word from the lawyers, Aldington wrote to Alan Bird on 8 October regarding the need to have "experts" validate his manuscript. "Kershaw and I agree that both a military and a scholarly adviser are needed. For the soldier we have decided to ask N. N. E. Bray (Indian Army) who was not one of the Lawrence Bureau." Bray did read the manuscript as military expert for Collins, and Bird acted as scholarly adviser for Aldington. With the editor's report in mind, Aldington specified to Bird on 4 February 1953, "I much want to hear if you think I have been unfair to TE anywhere and if you think any of the little jokes misplaced."[9] To Aldington's acute discomfort, he learned that Collins's legal counsel would be Joynson-Hicks and Company (like its founder, commonly called "Jix"). In *Portrait of a Genius, But . . .* , Aldington had criticized the Right Honourable Sir William Joynson-Hicks, who was Home Secretary during the seizing of some of D. H. Lawrence's manuscripts and the banning of *Lady Chatterley's Lover*. Aldington was apprehensive that this would predispose the lawyers against him.

After comparing the typescript with Smith's report and Aldington's response, Jix prepared a preliminary report dated 14 October 1952, stating that "In our opinion, this manuscript contains a very large number of passages which are, prima facie, defamatory of a considerable number of people." Jix focused on "two major problems" that required Aldington's immediate attention: TEL's family history and the copyright status of TEL's letters to Charlotte Shaw. This hardly surprised Aldington, who had been telling Holroyd-Reece to warn Collins about these very issues for some fifteen months. Legal vulnerability in detailing TEL's family history lay not in exposing TEL's illegitimacy (one cannot libel the dead), but in revealing that TEL's mother had never married his father and had borne five illegitimate children. Thus, TEL's mother and two surviving brothers could sue for libel, and that required ironclad legal proof that the libelous statements were true. The unpublished letters from TEL to Charlotte Shaw were in the British Museum, and therefore available to the public, but the Seven Pillars Trust held copyright. Publishing a word from these letters without permission would be grounds for a charge of copyright infringement.

Jix felt that Aldington lacked sufficient evidence to defend in a libel suit: "some difficulty will be experienced in basing a defense of justification solely on the authority of a letter written by T. E. Lawrence—3 volumes of manuscript are devoted to proving him to have been an unequivocal liar from the cradle to the grave." Jix had "seen no evidence whatever that the union between Lawrence's Father and Mother was not legal, either in the eyes of the Church or the State." Aldington needed unequivocal proof that the T. R. Chapman who had deserted his family in Ireland and the T. R. Lawrence who subsequently became the father of TEL were the same person. Jix, however, had found the birth certificate of Sarah Junner, born on 31 August 1861 in Sunderland, "the Father being described as a Shipwright Journeyman," which conformed to the details that Storrs had given in his *Dictionary of National Biography* article on TEL.[10]

Kershaw forwarded extracts of this report to Aldington, who responded on 23 October that he saw little difficulty resolving the problem imposed by TEL's illegitimacy. He declared that he could expand his explanation of the Chapman and Junner backgrounds—"I made it too laconic"—and then provided his own suggestions for acquiring further proof that T. R. Chapman and T. R. Lawrence were the same. These included sending an emissary to Burke or Debrett to ask "how he learned that Sir TRC was dead on the 9th April 1919," acquiring Lady Chapman's death certificate, searching for Sarah Junner's marriage certificate, locating the birth certificate of M. R. Lawrence ("as that was their first attempt at false declarations something might be learned"), studying wills and income tax records for evidence that Chapman money had come to T. R. Lawrence, and photographing "the *original declarations* of birth of the Chapman children and of the Lawrence children" to compare the signatures of T. R. Chapman and T. R. Lawrence. As for the TEL/Charlotte Shaw letters, he would simply paraphrase, documenting his statements of fact with references to the manuscript correspondence at the British Museum.

Despite Jix's promise to provide a more fully detailed report "within the course of the next day or two," Aldington did not see it until 11 November. Aldington felt that Jix's objections went beyond the requirements of the law. He wrote to Kershaw on 20 November,

Having looked over the Jix-Collins script with their notes and remarks, I must tell you that I don't see much chance of the book seeing the light with a publisher so ignorant and hostile, and a lawyer so ignorant and stupid. Some of their comments are incredible. One splendid one is a sapient note to the List of Sources, running: "Are these annotations to be published with the book? They greatly increase the chances of libel"! I ask you—a set of references designed to prove that what I say is based on such and such are described as "annotations" and libellous! Some distance into the book I find the plaintive note: "What is 'T.E.L. by his Friends'?" Again, I quote Graves's well-known statement that L's Ma said "We'd no use for girls in our house" which raises the comment—"Is this true? What is the authority?" The sentence is marked "13," and that gives "Lawrence and the Arabs by R. Graves, pp. 12, 13." What is the good of my giving references if neither publisher nor lawyer looks at them, and follows any fanciful inference of his own from a hasty reading? I observe in these "legal" notes that Graves is always "attacked" and Thomas always "ridiculed."

He wrote to Bird in more restrained terms on 13 November that

I am brooding over an immense epistle from Joynson Hicks who says I have libelled (1) Ma Lawrence, as to five counts; (2) Professor Lawrence and his [living] brother; (3) Liddell Hart; (4) Lowell Thomas 14 times; (5) Graves 18 times; (6) Sir John Rhys; (7) D. G. Hogarth! I have pointed out plaintively that Rhys and Hogarth died long ago. You will be glad to learn that Jix by inference advance[s] the principle that to convict a man of a misstatement in a biography is libel. I wish I'd known that earlier.[11]

Particularly exasperating to Aldington, as he indicated to Kershaw on 1 December, was that "Jix [is] airily saying paragraphs are libellous when they are actually a toning down of what Hart, Graves and Thomas themselves confess!!!!"

Aldington had written to Collins on 6 November to reiterate his objections to Smith's report, indicate what he had done to resolve the problem of the TEL/Charlotte Shaw letters, and suggest ways to relieve Jix's concern about libel.

I have re-written all the passages derived from the Shaw-Shaw letters in the [British] Museum; I have cut the repetitions and pasted blank paper over the spaces; and I have corrected (I hope) all the typing errors and have made a number of smaller improvements. All that now remains is to add the full legal proof (if obtainable) of the Lawrence-Chapman identity. Taking advantage of your kind offer I asked Kershaw to suggest means of finding this. Do you not think that Joynson Hicks might help by suggesting lines of enquiry?

Collins's response on 5 December emphasized that Holroyd-Reece "saw Mr. Smith's criticisms, said they were very helpful and that he would write you very fully." Collins also defended Jix as "a very excellent firm" that "only want[s] to be helpful" and stressed that searching for further proof of TEL's illegitimacy, which "would normally be the biographer's responsibility," required "much time, not to say expense." He repeated the lawyers' insistence that Aldington "bring his use and treatment of the Shaw letters within the limits defined in the Philip v. Pennell Judgment which we quoted." Collins felt that "If these two main issues can be resolved definitely, we can face with comparative equanimity any other changes that may be necessary."

Aldington's reaction was exactly the opposite of what Collins had hoped. On 11 December, Aldington wrote to Kershaw that

> I have been looking over the documents and letters in this Collins case, and there can be no doubt there is double crossing somewhere. . . .
> ⟨ . . . What infuriates me is that Collins does nothing and Jix apparently gives no advice of where to look for evidence. What the hell is the damn fool solicitor there for? Apparently to scribble idiotic remarks on a text he is too dumb to understand and to give such utterly wrong advice as the suggestion to leave out all Lists of Sources!!! That would be really smart. Collins complains of "the time and expense" of his researches when, as you well know half an hour to an hour and a few shillings will procure any Will at S[omerset] [H]ouse especially when you have the exact day of demise. He remarks plaintively that he hasn't a "library of Lawrence literature"—then what right has he to question my text which is founded on such a library?

The problem was not so much double-crossing as a breakdown in communications, chiefly the result of Holroyd-Reece's failure to pass unpleasant news in either direction. Holroyd-Reece had been spending most of his time trying to extricate himself from financial and legal problems involving Albatross. While Aldington and Kershaw thought that he was actively protecting Aldington's interests, he had been out of touch with Collins for some months. He failed to follow through on arrangements to establish the Aldington trust and held back various messages from Aldington to the firm and from the firm to Aldington, even as he promised to pass them on. Finally, on 13 December, he sent a long handwritten explanation to Kershaw confessing that he had been doing virtually nothing at Collins's firm, describing the pressures he had been under, and declaring that he would do better if given another chance. He asked Kershaw to have Aldington send a wire to his London office formally authorizing him to continue acting on Aldington's behalf.

Even before he learned of Holroyd-Reece's plight and consequent "defection," Aldington had blamed Holroyd-Reece for the abominable state of his liaison with Collins. He had written to Kershaw on 5 November that "At the bottom of all this is the Bird [Holroyd-Reece]. No doubt he means well, but he hasn't the influence with Collins he pretends (he is merely a book scout) and he has shown himself incapable of carrying out his promises. It is due largely to his footling dawdling that we are now nearly *seven months* after the sending in of the script and nothing done." When Kershaw informed him that Holroyd-Reece had indeed impeded progress by inaction, Aldington responded on 16 December that "This tangled web with Collins is very largely his fault."

Since Aldington still needed someone to represent him with Collins, he wrote to Holroyd-Reece on 18 December that he had sent the required telegram. He also had instructions:

> I write this to insist that *you* insist to Collins on definite action being taken to clear up these points of libel and copyright, points on which I warned you long ago, and with which Collins now reproaches me as if I had sprung them on him. . . .
>   (1) Clear up this Chapman-Lawrence business one way or [the] other;
>   (2) Find out from the lawyer if my paraphrasing of the Shaw-Shaw letters meets requirements. If not, why?
>   (3) Clear up this nonsense about libels on Liddell Harts and Graves[es] and Lowell Thomases and the rest of the fools and frauds.

He ended by declaring, "If it is held that the Chapman-Lawrence evidence is insufficient, you'll just have to cut it. I'll publish it in America and we'll get out the complete version in the Albatross."[12]

Aldington's telegram to Holroyd-Reece—"OF COURSE MOST HAPPY TO LEAVE ALL ARRANGEMENTS CONCERNING LAWRENCE BOOK TO YOU"—was timely. On 18 December, there was a meeting at the offices of Joynson-Hicks to resolve problems of libel and copyright. Alan Rees-Reynolds and his assistant, Mr. Allison, represented Jix, Smith sat in for Collins, and Holroyd-Reece acted for Aldington. Holroyd-Reece sent Kershaw and Aldington a memorandum dated 23

December summarizing the meeting. While Aldington had convinced Jix "that Thomas Chapman assumed the name of Lawrence and is the father of T. E. Lawrence born out of wedlock," the lawyers felt "that the documents submitted did not furnish legal evidence that (a) Sir Thomas R. Chapman and T.E.L.'s father are identical, (b) T.E.L.'s mother was not married lawfully to T.E.L.'s father."

The lawyers defined the evidence that they regarded necessary to protect the publisher and author from injunction. Their preferred proof was a conclusive comparison of the signatures of T. R. Chapman and T. R. Lawrence. Failing that, the lawyers wanted a letter from one of Sir Thomas's daughters reporting that he had absconded with TEL's mother. They even suggested soliciting such a letter from Sarah Lawrence herself. Failing that, they wanted a statement from the executor of T. R. Lawrence's will identifying T. R. Lawrence as Chapman or evidence of bequests from any wills indicating that T. R. Lawrence was a Chapman heir. They also said that it would be helpful to have statements from Sir Ronald Storrs and others who could provide convincing testimony in the witness-box. Finally, since the TEL/Charlotte Shaw letters were accessible at the British Museum, the lawyers recommended including a statement at the beginning of the list of sources identifying the letters as unpublished but open to public scrutiny.

Aldington received this on 27 December and mailed a detailed response to the lawyers' suggestions the next day, including his own notions of where to find T. R. Chapman and T. R. Lawrence signatures. He emphatically rejected the idea of approaching Chapman's daughters since "they have spent their lives as a sacrifice to hushing up a scandal, and I would not for anything try to involve them." The notion of extracting a confession from Sarah Lawrence struck him as "impossible," and he felt that approaching the executor of T. R. Lawrence's will would be futile because the lawyer "would be silent in the interests of his former client" and would notify AWL. He liked the idea of tracing bequests from Chapman wills to T. R. Lawrence very much since he had repeatedly suggested this himself, and he produced a list of five wills most likely to provide useful evidence. He indicated that eliciting information from Storrs would be risky since "Storrs is a fanatical pro-Lawrence, and would rush off to Prof Lawrence at once, and raise hell" and since he would "be a wholly hostile witness in any case." Aldington preferred to put his trust in documentary evidence rather than in living witnesses who were likely to use any means available to prevent his telling what he knew.

In a slightly altered version of his report, "REPLIES TO QUERIES

BY J. H-R," Aldington cautioned, "Leave [Storrs] to talk, but give no promise of secrecy. They would have told me under seal of secrecy if I had not evaded."[13] As far as the status of the TEL/Charlotte Shaw letters was concerned, Aldington approved the lawyers' suggested statement but still wanted to know whether his paraphrases were acceptable to Jix.[14] Perhaps to compensate for his earlier dereliction, Holroyd-Reece spent the Christmas holiday in London, as he wrote to Kershaw on 5 January 1953, checking Smith's queries and Jix's elaborate but frequently erroneous notations on the revised manuscript.

Even as Holroyd-Reece's resumption of his role seemed to improve liaison, conflict with Collins arose over the marketing of the book in the United States. Aldington, early in 1952, had begun to stress the importance of American publication as a way to forestall attempts to suppress his manuscript under English libel law. He wrote to Kershaw on 20 March, "Keep in mind that from our present point of view, Collins ranks only fourth—the order of priority is: 1. US serial; 2. a different US publisher; 3. Brit serial." After Aldington had secured his release from Duell, Sloan & Pearce, he explained his strategy to Kershaw more fully on 20 June: "If we can get intact or nearly intact publication in US and rest of world, it is worth making a deal with the [TEL] Trustees to expurgate the British edition. They will know—or learn—that they are helpless against Uncle Sam, and agree. You will have to try to keep enough of the scandal stuff to get Collins home. But England doesn't matter compared with US and rest of world."

The 15 October 1951 memorandum of agreement with Collins had stipulated that U.S. rights remained under Aldington's control, but Holroyd-Reece had exacted Aldington's promise to let Collins try to place the manuscript in New York. Aldington later rescinded this, preferring to market the U.S. rights himself, but Collins had promoted the manuscript during his October 1952 trip to New York. In his letter of 6 November 1952, Aldington called this "unnecessary." When Collins responded on 5 December, he said in his postscript,

> I was puzzled by your reference to America. Holroyd-Reece told me quite definitely that I was to handle the book for you in America, and as a result I approached Cass Canfield [of Harper's] and other leading American publishers about it, and got them very interested. I can assure you it is not as easy as all that now to get big advances and get a book well placed in America. Publishing conditions and the position of individual firms [have] changed very much in the last few years. Is there some misunderstanding about this between you and Holroyd-Reece? I asked him par-

ticularly about this in writing to make quite sure and he was absolutely definite.

Canfield wrote to Collins on 12 December that Aldington had submitted a typescript and then had suddenly withdrawn it. Canfield felt that the book was "interesting" but "overlong and somewhat vitriolic," requiring extensive changes, and that Harper's could not pay a substantial advance for a book that was more suited to the English market. He emphasized that "this letter is confidential, inasmuch as Aldington is not aware of our reaction to his material."[15] Collins, possibly because Canfield agreed so closely with his own assessment of the manuscript, passed the "confidential" letter to Holroyd-Reece, demanding that he convince Aldington to stop showing the book.

Collins's conflicting interest as Aldington's British publisher made him an unsuitable agent for Aldington in New York. Aldington wanted simultaneous publication in the United States, which required potential publishers to see the manuscript as soon as possible. Collins, particularly after investing £4,500, was in no hurry to see a competing edition and promoted the manuscript without showing it. Aldington, wanting his manuscript to appear intact, sent it out in its pre-Smith and pre-Jix form. Collins did not want another edition to include anything beyond what his own firm would publish. Kershaw tried to convince Aldington to leave the U.S. rights to him and Holroyd-Reece, but Aldington was adamant. He did not want to risk his only chance of publishing the book intact by entrusting it to the very people who, in his view, were conspiring to suppress it. Kershaw, however, visited Aldington and, as Kershaw wrote to Holroyd-Reece from Montpellier on 25 January 1953, persuaded Aldington to leave the U.S. marketing to Holroyd-Reece and Collins.

Holroyd-Reece and Smith continued to work on the manuscript through January. Kershaw received a letter from Collins dated 22 January 1953 stating that "J.H.R. absolutely agreed on going through the manuscript that it would have been fatal to put it out as it stood, and felt that the comments on Liddell Hart and others were made in such a way that they would have given rise to a lot of criticism, and would have badly damaged the chances of the book's success." On 31 January, Holroyd-Reece sent Kershaw a thick sheaf of papers enumerating the specific alterations by Jix, Smith, and himself. Kershaw went through these notes, altered the manuscript at some points, refused to change it at others, and referred the more specialized queries to Aldington.

The documents as a whole focused on three major concerns—repetition of negative comments that had an unpleasant cumulative effect, phrases that were too close to the original wording of the TEL/Charlotte Shaw letters, and sneers such as "solemn mountebanks" that invited litigation. Aside from the issue of TEL's illegitimacy, the notes reflected trivial concerns. Allison of Jix prepared one report identifying twenty-six instances that, in his view, libeled Thomas, Graves, and Liddell Hart by implying that they "were not the authors of their own books but merely puppets, hirelings or propagandists writing on Lawrence's behalf." Allison added, in a tortuous and idiosyncratically punctuated sentence, that "It is defamatory to suggest that an author as such lacks integrity and passages such as: 'L. allowed G[raves] to say'; (this does not quite square with 'L. passed every word of G.'s book'); 'Told Hart'; 'Lawrence-sponsored books'; taken cumulatively suggest this." Rees-Reynolds raised the point that "Half the cynicism at Oxford's expense is perhaps unwarranted."[16]

Holroyd-Reece decided to try to circumvent the lawyers with a scheme that would remove Collins's fears of injunction or suit. His plan was to have the London *Daily Mail* serialize the book simultaneously with Collins's publication. The *Daily Mail* would not only provide additional money for Aldington but also assume liability for any resultant litigation. He had approached Lord Rothermere through Basil Burton, Rothermere's cousin, hoping that Rothermere's *Daily Mail* would welcome both the scoop and any publicity that would result from a court action. On 24 January, Holroyd-Reece wrote a confidential memorandum to Kershaw in which he argued that "Collins is quite prepared to run what he considers to be a reasonable risk of litigation though of course you cannot expect a reputable firm of publishers to admit that they will run this risk" for the sake of sales-producing publicity. Holroyd-Reece felt that if the *Daily Mail* would accept legal responsibility for libel, then all that would remain for the lawyers to settle would be the questions of copyright.

The book's legal status might have remained unresolved forever had it not been for Bird. As Aldington had pointed out to Kershaw on 12 December 1952,

> Since all this bobbery started with Smith's idiot memorandum, the *only* piece of new evidence supplied has come from Alan Bird, who got a letter from the Home Office (Registrar of Baronetage) stating that Sir TRChapman died 8th April, 1919 (same day as TRL), that his widow was still living in 1924, and that the Home Office [was] not notified of Chapper's death until 1924. No slightest mention of this piece of evidence

from Jix and Collins, but bland remarks such as "we must also remember to find out if possible if Lady Chapman outlived her husband"!!!!!!!

Bird's greatest contribution, however, was to locate the birth certificate of TEL's elder brother, registered not as M. R. Lawrence but as Montagu Robert Chapman, son of Thomas Chapman and Sarah Chapman, *née* Laurence.

On 4 February 1953, Aldington wrote to Bird,

> . . . I think this discovery of Montagu Robert Junner's birth certificate important. We had searched everywhere and failed to find it because we looked under *Lawrence*! The identification of the two Montagu Roberts— Chapman and Lawrence—is not so difficult. First we have the fact that in the will of Caroline Chapman (d. 1911) a sum of about [£]20,000 was bequeathed to Thomas Robert Chapman and one of the trustees was Charles Athill Stanuell, who was also an executor and trustee under the Will of Thomas Robert Lawrence. Second, the Will of Thomas Robert Lawrence gives the name of his eldest son as Montagu Robert—surely impossible as a coincidence, especially since in TEL by his Friends M. Robert Lawrence says he was born 2 yrs and 8 months before TEL. 2.8 before Aug 1888 brings us to *December 1885*! *Another* coincidence, m' lud and gentlemen of the jury? I think you've found it. . . . Note also that we have in this certificate a third family name for Sarah—in this case Lawrence or Laurence (spelling immaterial) which is also suggestive.[17]

As Kershaw wrote to Holroyd-Reece on 5 February, Bird's discovery offered other possibilities: "Before raising the various points which I noted from my conversations with Richard Aldington, I want to ask you whether the fact of our now possessing the signatures of T. R. Lawrence (on his Will) and T. R. Chapman (on M. R. Lawrence's birth certificate) does not enable a comparison to be made between the signatures which will provide the lawyers with final evidence?" On Thursday, 21 February, Holroyd-Reece informed Kershaw that on the following Monday, the lawyers would decree whether the birth certificate of M. R. Chapman/Lawrence would be enough to prove in court that TEL and his brothers were illegitimate.

Rees-Reynolds wrote an "aide-memoire" on 25 February that announced the lawyers' provisional approval to proceed with the book. There were references to documents that had so far eluded searches and a few loose ends, but counsel's opinion was that "once the handwriting expert's certificate has been obtained [showing that T. R. Chapman's signature on

M. R. Chapman's birth certificate was the same handwriting as T. R. Lawrence's signature on his will], we will be able to go ahead without waiting on these other documents."[18] While there remained the need for formal permission to quote from published sources, the lawyers had finally declared that the manuscript was not vulnerable to charges of libel.

Aldington felt that M. R. Chapman's birth certificate removed all cause or excuse for further delay. On 6 February, two days after he had received the evidence from Bird, he wrote to Kershaw,

> When you see Collins do please urge that he start setting [galley proofs] at once. Tell him that any of this additional bastardy legal evidence can easily be written into proofs if they are galleys, and should not take up more than a par[agraph] or two. I assume he will want to reproduce these photostats [of the T. R. Chapman and T. R. Lawrence signatures].
>
> As touching alterations to the text, make the concession that any *verbal* quips at Harts and Graveses and Thomases will be removed if he *and* [Holroyd-Reece] (not Smith) agree, but point out that the structure of the book (which is based on all those carefully collected quotes) cannot be altered without great labour, great expense of time and great risk of confusion and error.

Holroyd-Reece, however, wrote to Kershaw on 11 February to reiterate his opinion that many of Smith's and Collins's objections to the book's tone were valid. He felt that Aldington did not understand "how strong and powerful the case is which he has established. It is not only unanswerable. It is stronger than that. It is so overwhelming that there are bound to be many critics and innumerable readers who would feel that Richard is weakening his case by repetition and over-statement." For Holroyd-Reece, the "repetition and over-statement" were not in the structure of the book, but in "parentheses which can be read as sneers" and quotations of the same people "sometimes in support of Richard's evidence and sometimes as unreliable." A few months earlier, on 12 November 1952, Aldington had offended Kershaw by asking, after Kershaw had "committed" Aldington to synchronizing American publication with that of Collins, "Who are you working for, me or Collins?" He would have reacted even more vehemently against Holroyd-Reece's support of the publisher's objections to his manuscript. Aldington asked Kershaw on 19 February 1953 whether Collins "makes it a condition that his phoney journalistic friends shall not be exposed." Some of Jix's vetoes fell into this category, such as the objection to Aldington's description of Liddell Hart as a "penny-a-Maginot-liner."

Kershaw met Collins in Paris and reported to Aldington on 4 March 1953:

> Collins is gone & I am well pleased with the present position: he is fully aware of the utter urgency of both British & American serialisation & of a US contract; he is determined to publish in this Autumn; he has initiated all (few) remaining moves over the legal aspect; he is well-disposed; he is confident of success. All that remains is for me to complete the minor textual changes required by the lawyers—no change will be made (and Collins made no contrary suggestion) for any other reason.[19]

Weeks passed, however, without much evidence of activity.

After visiting Aldington in Montpellier, Kershaw wrote to Holroyd-Reece on 8 May that Aldington was "in a very disturbed state":

> After all this time setting-up has still not begun. I telephoned Collins last week and he told me that they were waiting (a) on certain permissions, (b) on the handwriting expert's certificate. But this just doesn't make sense. WHY must setting-up wait on these? Surely the obvious course is to have the book set up so that, once the permissions etc. are obtained work can go ahead on publication. Remember that R. wants two months for proof-reading: if this delay continues, how can the book be published in Autumn? Meantime, R. frets lest someone else get in first with another TEL biography, at the fact that he has published nothing for three years, at the fact that this potential money-maker is just lying idle. If Collins intends to publish at all, let him begin to set up AT ONCE and send R. the proofs. I assure [you] that any further delay will be disastrous.

To Aldington's delight, Kershaw reported that Collins had secured from Knopf a "firm offer" for U.S. publication that would include an advance of $15,000. On 16 June, Aldington responded to Kershaw, "It is therefore the most admirable and grateful news to me when you say Collins has taken over the serial and foreign publication negotiations." Six weeks later, however, as Aldington wrote to Kershaw on 31 July, the situation was far from ideal:

> I list what we have *not* got:
> (1) The two-years-discussed contract with Collins.
> (2) Any additional advance from Collins.
> (3) A contract with Knopf.
> (4) Any advance from Knopf.
> (5) Any contract for a serial or advance thereon.
> (6) Any contracts for foreign rights or any advances thereon.

(7) Any definite date of publication.

(8) Any public announcement of the book.

Fortunately for what remained of Aldington's peace of mind, Holroyd-Reece wrote to Kershaw on 6 August that Collins had started setting the book and was willing to lend an additional $10,000 (approximately £4,200) against the $15,000 that Knopf would advance if Blanche Knopf confirmed the contract.

When Aldington finally received galleys in September 1953, he was exasperated to find that the title was set as "T. E. Lawrence: The Legend and the Man" despite his earlier emphatic disapproval. He wrote to Kershaw on 4 September,

> Yesterday I received galleys 42–99A, and am still suffering from stomach ulcers and cramp in consequence. The alterations are so numerous and so unfortunate that I don't recognise my own book. One of the prettiest games has been to paraphrase a citation and thereby turn an accurate quote into an inaccurate one. If the paraphrasings are all for libel or copyright, heaven help us. I am restoring a few of the more idiotic cuts, and hope they may stick. You must tell Collins I am doing this. Of course I must have page proofs so that I can cut all quotation marks from paraphrases. What a mess.

He aired other complaints in his letter to Bird of the same date:

> Among omissions which seem to me the limit is of those four lines of Winston [Churchill]'s describing L's beauty at the Peace Conference. True, the lines made W.S.C. look an ass, but he published them himself, and how the quote can be libellous or a breach of copyright I fail to see. Again, Wavell's lines about Erzerum from the Enc[yclopedia] Brit[annica] have been clumsily paraphrased (but so poorly that they become a mere plagiarism) and as the quotation marks are left, an accurate quotation becomes an inaccurate one! . . . One more thing—they have altered or cut out *all* the references to L's collaboration with Hart and Graves! Why? Because Jix, knowing nothing of the evidence, told them to look in the H and G books, and to cut the references unless those books acknowledge collaboration! As if they would![20]

On 11 September, Aldington wrote to Kershaw that Ronald Politzer, Collins's publicity man, had visited Aldington in Montpellier. Politzer mentioned that despite encouraging correspondence from Collins and from Holroyd-Reece, there had never been "any firm bargain" with either Knopf or the *Daily Mail*. Also, AWL had announced plans to publish some "800 pages of TEL's letters to his mother," and "The suggestion was that we should 'wait' until Collins can get hold of and read a set of these proofs, and then send them to me so that I can re-write the book." Aldington saw this as yet another pretext by his "enemy" Smith to delay the book.

Events soon confirmed Politzer's gloomy prognosis. On 22 September, Aldington wrote to Kershaw that the *Daily Mail* had refused to serialize. Worse, there were problems with Knopf:

> The Knopf situation is very sticky. With great tact Collins took the book to one of Lowell Thomas's closest friends, who is also closely linked with C.B.S. [which carried Thomas's radio news program]. Collins was not present at the Knopf meeting, and Smith and Politzer let themselves be bull-dozed. I think they should have withdrawn, but they have now sent proofs to Knopf's attorney—which means of course that he will advise Thomas. I have copied out Sir Andrew Macphail's scathing exposure (parts of it) of Thomas, to send to Politzer with the idea that it might show the Knopfs that any legal action by Thomas is practically out of the question—Macphail said most of it in 1929 and L.T. did nothing.

Aldington had complained to Henry Williamson on 14 September 1953, "Why shouldn't the truth be told, even if [Thomas] is a radio commentator at 1500 bucks a week and a buddy of Blanche Knopf? To hell with them. There are plenty of other publishers, and I *won't* be censored in an under-hand way."[21]

Collins had changed the publication date from autumn 1953 to 1 February 1954, which hardly improved Aldington's mood. On 18 October, Aldington complained to Kershaw that "There is no mention whatever of the contracts! Collins gave as his excuse for not having signed up with Knopf that 'the special arrangements' I 'had required' [for the Aldington trust] had delayed the contracts so that a contract with K[nopf] could not be signed. From this I infer that Collins now claims that either he or the 'Trust' must sign the American agreement." When the contract with Knopf fell through, Aldington was incensed, attributing the reversal to Collins, who had repeatedly declared, in writing, that the sale was "firm."

Aldington suspected Collins of duplicity. He wrote to Kershaw on 27 October,

> We are dealing with cunning business men, and one of them is an enemy. I incline to think that they never intended or do intend to make an

American agreement until *after* their own publication. They will therefore be able to sell some thousands of copies of their edition to USA, and then turn round and say: "We're very sorry but the book was so difficult to place in USA that we've only now found a publisher and unfortunately he won't pay very much." It is a common trick. . . . In any case, it is now *too late* for American simultaneous publication—the only thing for which they'll pay. And the loss is entirely due to Collins.

Collins wrote to Aldington on 3 November to summarize the Knopf debacle as he saw it: "Knopf were quite adamant that they would not publish the book unless Lowell Thomas was allowed to read it first, and I think you definitely did not want this to happen." He added that he had shown the manuscript to Putnam's and Rinehart in the United States in October, but neither would advance more than $5,000. Eugene Reynal of Harcourt Brace, who would have been willing to pay an advance of $15,000, had objected to "the extreme bias in the book itself" and felt that Aldington's "obvious prejudice is extremely disconcerting and will undoubtedly have a very adverse effect upon sales." Collins declared that he had similar responses from his Canadian manager, some of his "best salesmen," and his brother.

To Aldington's intense annoyance, Collins sided with those who objected to the book's tone: "I felt this when I first read the book, but owing to the many legal problems we had to go into and which took up so much time, the importance of some of these points was naturally over-shadowed by the necessity of surmounting the many legal obstacles." Worse still, he wanted further revision. He enclosed a list of some twenty-five passages that he planned to delete from the proofs, claiming that he had "every hope that with these alterations I can still get a very good offer from America." Then he referred to his talk with the lawyers about restoring passages that Aldington felt should not have been deleted in the first place: "In some cases they agree, but in others they feel it would be very unwise, and I am sure you will agree, so we are going ahead with the page proofs on this basis." [22] The passages Collins wanted to eliminate were unimportant for the most part, such as the description of TEL as "the national hero of the Great War he never saw" and the reference to "People influential in the small but unpleasant literary world." Aldington described this letter to Kershaw on 8 November as "disagreeable and impertinent," but in his response to Collins, he agreed to all the changes on the list except for the first two, both of which paraphrased TEL's statements to Charlotte Shaw. Both survived, one identifying TEL's view that his parents "would have been well-advised not to produce children" and the other recording TEL's dismissal of Oman as "a charlatan, an imbecile and a smatterer."[23]

Aldington wrote exuberantly to Kershaw on 14 November that he had seen copy for an advertisement of the TEL book that Collins intended to place in the *Times Literary Supplement*. This, for him, was concrete evidence that Collins actually intended to publish. By 17 November, however, he had noticed that the announcement mentioned publication scheduled for "Spring," and he feared that Collins had decided to delay the book beyond February 1954. Although his anxious queries elicited no information about page proofs, publication date, serialization, or American rights, Collins did not hesitate to send him unsolicited and unwelcome news—that Collins wanted more minor alterations, that Somerset House had refused permission to reproduce T. R. Lawrence's signature from his will, and that, as Aldington complained to Bird on 18 December, "everything at all derogatory to Churchill *must* be cut! I wish on the strength of your glimpse into all this you would do a nice little essay on Free Speech in Our Time."[24]

Politzer had written that when he tried to verify the answers that Williamson had received from *Who's Who* in January 1951, the editor repudiated A. & C. Black's earlier statement. Aldington responded to Politzer on 18 December that *Who's Who* was merely evading and then expressed some of his concerns about the status of his manuscript:

> I know you will forgive me if I point out that your very kind letter passes over matters which are of much more interest to me than these minute points. You say nothing to explain why I have not received the page proofs which were promised by Collins. You say nothing about keeping to Feb 1st as publication day. The information in your letter does not justify a delay of nearly a month in replying to me. I have two books accepted by publishers in England and America, waiting on your publication; and a third in hand. I am a professional author, and the entirely unwarranted delays in your office are a serious injury to my reputation and to me financially.
>
> As I have not heard from Collins in reply to my last two letters to him, I hope you will bring this letter immediately to his attention.[25]

Politzer did show the letter to Collins, who finally responded to Aldington's earlier queries. Collins's letter, as Aldington wrote to Kershaw on 30 December, left him "trembling with rage and resentment, to such an extent that my hand shakes too much to be able to sign the letter I wrote in reply over an hour ago." Aldington had learned that Collins planned to

postpone publication until May/June 1954. "The date end May[,] beginning of June is cleverly chosen. It will be easy to find a new pretext to
postpone until autumn, and so on. What can be done I know not. I feel a
personal call from you to Collins with these letters before you is the only
way, and you must INSIST on early publication. Never mind America, tell
him, we'll risk that."

As 1953 drew to its close, Aldington still had no contract with Collins,
no arrangement for U.S. publication, no provision to shelter his earnings
in a trust, no guarantee of publication, and no reason to believe that matters would improve. During the twenty months since he had submitted his
manuscript, the combined inroads of Collins's editorial staff and legal counsel had altered his work so extensively that he no longer regarded it as his
own, and he was powerless to restore what he really wanted to say. He did
not realize that his problems were only beginning.

4

THE "LAWRENCE BUREAU" MOBILIZES

It is ominous that the "Newsweek" article (para. 3) suggests that the Lawrence legend was "produced by Englishmen for export." Anti-British publicists will fasten on to the statement that Allenby sent Lowell Thomas "to get the Lawrence story and tell it to the world"—and treat it as evidence that Machiavellian British policy was manufacturing a myth, for American consumption, to promote the interests of British imperialism. That could be very damaging if Aldington's allegations are not effectively exploded.

> —B. H. Liddell Hart, "Notes on the Article in 15 Feb. issue
> of Newsweek (U.S.) 'Lawrence: Lies or Legends' "

We have seen Storrs, Liddell Hart, Kennington and others recently, and are trying to solve this terribly difficult problem.

> —W. A. R. Collins to S. F. Newcombe, 20 March 1954

I think you know Aldington has put the Lawrence book in his "Who's Who" list as "The book Winston Churchill and others tried to suppress." A. W. told me. Cape told him. *Months* ago.

> —Eric Kennington to B. II. Liddell Hart, 24 July 1954

WHEN COLLINS AGREED to publish the TEL book in England, Aldington was strident in his demand that Collins keep the manuscript and project confidential from members of the "Lawrence Bureau," and particularly from Liddell Hart. Aldington's preoccupation with the "Lawrence Bureau" dated from his original decision to write about TEL. When he informed Kershaw on 13 November 1949 that he had decided to write the biography, Aldington mentioned that he had written L. J. Browning at his home rather than at the Evans Brothers offices partly "to stave off the rush of indignant 'friends' of TEL anxious to save him from the disgrace of me."[1] Kershaw often found Aldington's state of mind "alarming," particularly when Aldington believed that there was a "conspiracy" against him and his work.[2] There was no literal "conspiracy" since TEL's partisans were not secretive about their efforts, nor were their actions illegal, but for Aldington, the consequences were the same. Although he often seemed paranoid, he actually underestimated the later efforts of the "Lawrence Bureau" to suppress his findings and discredit his book.

On Tuesday, 19 January 1954, Tony Burt announced the nature of Aldington's TEL book in the "Londoner's Diary" column of the London *Evening Standard*: "The reputation and integrity of Lawrence of Arabia are about to come under the most devastating attack ever launched upon them. A book is due for publication in May or June which the publishers claim will 'erase Lawrence from the pages of history, except as the creator of a myth that was too readily believed by a credulous world.' " Burt named Aldington as the author and stated that his publishers had spent eighteen months "checking the basis of every allegation, and getting their lawyers to pass the manuscript." Burt was well informed. He reported that "three experts"—Leo Amery, Sir Ronald Storrs, and Lord David Lloyd—denied any offers of the post of High Commissioner of Egypt to TEL and that, as Aldington phrased it, "a 'much greater man' " (Churchill) called the claim "Wholly unfounded." Burt added that Aldington "dismissed" *Seven Pillars of Wisdom* as "a work of quasi-fiction" and that Aldington had never met TEL.[3]

Liddell Hart quickly set up a center of intelligence and operations for the anti-Aldington forces. His TEL files were extensive, and his routine already included frequent correspondence with many "Lawrence Bureau" members. After breakfast, "he spent the next several hours dictating replies to inquiries, letters to old friends, etc. After lunch he would return to his desk to write, while his secretary typed his letters and copies of notes, memoranda, and other documents from his files. There were a great many people on his 'distribution list,' so copies of a letter to one friend might well be sent—each with a covering note—to a dozen others."[4] Within days of learning about Aldington's book, Liddell Hart had written to Lord Winterton, Leo Amery, Lord Lloyd, Sir Ronald Storrs, Winston Churchill, Lord Hankey, Lionel Curtis, Lord Trenchard, Colonel W. F. Stirling, Colonel S. F. Newcombe, Lord Vansittart, and many others who had known TEL. Most would have agreed with Stirling's 25 January response to Liddell Hart: "I feel you are the one man who can wipe the floor with him [Aldington]— and I hope you will do it."[5]

After a close study of the *Evening Standard* column, Liddell Hart wrote to Collins, who had published Liddell Hart's edition of *The Rommel Papers* in 1953. On 22 January, only three days after the *Evening Standard* announcement, Ronald Politzer, answering for his employer, made a startling concession: "if you could put us on to any evidence in writing or in print that such a suggestion [the "Egypt" offer] was ever made to Lawrence, or even seriously considered by the Cabinet, we would hold up the book." Collins himself confirmed this a week later. Aldington had no idea that according to his own publisher, the existence of his book would depend on the "Egypt" question. He had resented having to move part of his "Egypt" argument to an introduction, and he had his own doubts, not about whether anyone had officially offered TEL the position, but whether TEL had deliberately lied about it. Aldington had written to Kershaw on 10 February 1951 that "the more I read 7 Pills the more I wonder. He may have believed it."[6] The issue, however, became not what TEL might have believed but whether the claim itself was true, making "Egypt" the basis for determining whether TEL was mendacious. Ultimately, this was a great stroke of luck for Aldington.

The "Egypt" question put Liddell Hart at a disadvantage. Since Burt's column quoted TEL as linking Churchill with the "Egypt" offer, Liddell Hart inferred that it must have occurred in 1922. However, the post was under the Foreign Office, then headed by Lord Curzon, no admirer of TEL, and no official offer could have come from Churchill. On 9 February 1955, shortly after Aldington's book appeared, Lord Vansittart wrote to Liddell Hart, "By the way, you may take it that no offer of the High Commissionership in Egypt was ever made to Lawrence in 1922. The appointment lay with Curzon, and I was his private secretary for nearly four years. I should certainly have heard of the suggestion if it had been made. Curzon would certainly not have entertained it. That particularly difficult post was not at all in Lawrence's line."

After learning that he could stop Aldington's book by disproving this one allegation, Liddell Hart fired off virtually identical letters to Amery, Lloyd, and Storrs on 23 January 1954, quoting the relevant paragraph from the *Evening Standard* and then asking, "Is this a correct version of what you told Aldington? If it is correct, I would appreciate your grounds for saying that there was 'no truth whatever' in Lawrence's story." Convincing Amery, Lloyd, and Storrs to withdraw their testimony could be as effective as refuting Aldington's statement. He concocted a plausible basis for misunderstanding that would enable Amery, Lloyd, and Storrs to withdraw their statements without losing face, ending his letters to the three with an indication of the answer that he wanted: "When Lawrence told me of this proposal he conveyed that it was a sounding rather than a definite invitation. Moreover, I understood that it did not refer to the time when Allenby was actually removed, in 1925, but to the occasion in 1922 when Allenby offered his resignation and the Government (then L[loyd] G[eorge]'s) wanted to have someone ready to fill his place." Even before he heard from Amery, Lloyd, and Storrs, Liddell Hart took this line when the London correspondent for the *New York Times* asked for his reaction to Aldington's charge that there had been no "Egypt" offer. He answered that he had discussed this with Lloyd George during the 1930s: " 'Lloyd George was Prime Minister in 1922 at the time of the reported offer of the High Commissionership of Egypt to Lawrence. . . . He confirmed these facts which Lawrence told me." [7]

On 25 January, Liddell Hart wrote to Prime Minister Churchill, which was delicate since Liddell Hart had opposed Churchill's conduct of the war against Germany and since Major-General Sir Eric Dorman-Smith had enlisted Liddell Hart's cooperation in legal action against Churchill, who had made defamatory statements about the general's performance in the North African campaign. Liddell Hart began by mentioning that he had responded to a barrage of telephone calls from the press by recommending that those seeking a true assessment of TEL should read Churchill's *Great Contemporaries* (1937) and his tribute in *T. E. Lawrence by His Friends*. He reminded Churchill that he was already on record concerning "the positions [TEL] might have filled and your efforts in 1922 to persuade him to consider them—as you subsequently conveyed in your book."

Liddell Hart then indicated what he wanted Churchill to write:

It is evident that Aldington has jumped to the mistaken assumption that T.E. was speaking of 1925, and claiming that he had been offered the succession to Allenby then, before it was offered to [George] Lloyd. When T.E. mentioned it to me he conveyed that it was a suggestion rather than a definite invitation, and also that it happened in 1922.

Aldington, although he does not mention you by name, obviously implies that it was you who, in reply to his enquiry, said that T.E.'s "tale" was "wholly unfounded." That is the most damaging card he plays. I can hardly believe that you made such a reply—if the question was properly put to you.

It would be even better if you could make it publicly clear that what T.E. said was not "wholly unfounded."

Liddell Hart wrote to Collins on the same day, expressing his reluctance to see the publisher "associated with mud-slinging." He then reminded Collins of something that would have startled Aldington: "Over a year ago you told me you were worried about this book and asked me if I would 'vet' it as regards its accuracy, and I said I would certainly do so. You mentioned it again a bit later and said the book was being sent me. But it never came, though I sent messages to let you know I was still awaiting it." He regretted not having "the chance to safeguard you." He stated that Aldington had erroneously assumed that the "Egypt" offer came in 1925 rather than in 1922. Citing Amery, the present Lord Lloyd, and Storrs was "ludicrous" since none had direct knowledge, and there was "a particular reason why Amery should not have been told of it." He asked whether Collins's "extensive" checking had included "those who fought alongside Lawrence, and actually saw him in action with the Arab forces," providing a long list. Mistakenly thinking that Aldington's D. H. Lawrence biography was a "muck-rake," he opined that Aldington's penchant for debunking would reflect adversely on the firm and on Collins's personal reputation.

Collins marked his response of 29 January "CONFIDENTIAL." He informed Liddell Hart that "Aldington's book on Lawrence has been a problem to us for nearly two years now. When I originally spoke of sending it to you I had not read it all myself. After doing so there were so many points that worried me, including references to yourself, that I felt it would be useless to send you the manuscript in that state and that we must have a very careful check on all the references, and also try to persuade the author to do a good deal of re-writing." Collins indicated that, having "done all we can to check on the facts, we feel that in fairness to the author we must publish it." Then he explained that "Aldington deals with both occasions— 1922 and 1925—when Lawrence said he had been invited to succeed Allenby," and he argued that if Amery, Lloyd, and Storrs were not in a position to comment, they would not have given their written permission to print their statements. Collins confirmed that he would hold up the book if Liddell Hart disproved Aldington's position on "Egypt," but due to his "obligation to the author with whom one has made a contract," this required hard evidence.

Alerted by the *Evening Standard* announcement, other "Lawrence Bureau" members descended on Collins with telephone calls, letters, and personal visits, protesting the publication of a book that they had not read and challenging evidence that they had not examined. Colonel S. F. Newcombe, who had been responsible for the demolition of the Hejaz railway and had served with TEL during the Arab Revolt, offered to vet Aldington's proofs. For Aldington, who had nothing to lose by exposing TEL's shortcomings or those of his biographers, it was inconceivable that anyone knowing the "truth" about TEL could honestly defend him, and he felt that the "Lawrence Bureau" was acting from self-serving motives and consisted entirely of unprincipled liars. Opposition to Aldington's book sprang from a variety of motives, however, some more commendable than others. Many of TEL's partisans acted from their sincere conviction that TEL's heroism and genius outweighed any failings with which they were already familiar.

Before Collins had heard from Liddell Hart, Eric Kennington, who had met TEL in 1920 and who provided many of the illustrations for the 1926 subscriber's edition of *Seven Pillars of Wisdom*, wrote to demand that Collins withdraw Aldington's book. Collins responded on 29 January that Aldington's book had been a surprise to him but that a publisher should not "act as a censor of his author's views," that he was "genuinely sorry" to publish something that would offend and hurt others, but that "in the interests of history and scholarship it is right that Aldington should be free to put forward his views based as they are on very considerable research."[8] This soft answer did not turn away Kennington's wrath, and he replied on 31 January, "Your letter to me of the 29th reads as if from a simpleton or to a simpleton." He argued that the law required Collins to censor Aldington and concluded, "You cannot harm T.E., but you can weaken many by untruth, and you will kill his mother."

Kennington was fully aware of TEL's background, as he revealed to historian Arthur Bryant on 17 February, but he felt that Aldington had gone too far:

His mother *was* an adulteress, but why stone her publicly in page after page[?] T.E. *was* illegitimate and had characteristics which recur in bas-

tards. But I know his vast distance from sodomy, reject the claims that
he lied to everyone on all matters (almost on any) from birth to death,
that he was sadistic, cruel, vicious in almost every way, lived only for
self-aggrandisement, etc. etc.

As he wrote to Storrs on 18 April, Kennington also felt a personal obligation to honor TEL's request that the Kenningtons shield Sarah Lawrence
from revelations of her adultery.[9]

At first, Pat Knowles did not take Aldington's attack on TEL seriously.
The son of Sergeant Arthur Knowles, with whom TEL had served at Bovington, Knowles grew up across the road from TEL's Clouds Hill cottage.
Shortly after he had spoken with TEL on the morning of 13 May 1935, he
had the distressing experience of being summoned to identify TEL even
before he knew that the ultimately fatal motorcycle accident had occurred.
On 12 March 1954, he wrote to Liddell Hart, "It is walking on air to even
try to think what T.E. would have done. I fancy he would have held them
[critics of TEL] down with one hand, and with the other offered them the
means and privilege of doing something else, which they would have—
eventually—been proud of, instead of ashamed." By 9 April, however, it had
occurred to Knowles that Aldington's allegations concerning TEL's homosexuality might reflect on him. He wrote to Kennington, "The sodomy
business affects me—my brothers and my father, and would imply that CH
[Clouds Hill] was a place of evil retreat."[10] When Knowles wrote to Liddell
Hart on 17 April, he noted that Aldington's imputation of homosexual activity at Clouds Hill "would implicate me and the rest of my family."

TEL's biographers were also in a vulnerable position, largely because
they had concealed much of what they knew. Graves and Liddell Hart, beginning their long correspondence shortly after TEL's death, confided to
each other that TEL had greatly contributed to their books about him, had
given them contradictory accounts of his adventures, and had privately dis-
paraged each to the other. Graves wrote in June 1935 to Liddell Hart, "In
the papers that are on the way here [Mallorca] to me from England I have
a statement by him as to his purposeful lying about some points in the
campaign—especially the Damascus affair."[11] Graves, who had met TEL
at Oxford after the Great War, was grateful not only for TEL's help with
Lawrence and the Arabs, but also for TEL's friendship and financial assistance
when Graves had desperately needed both. He remained intensely loyal to
TEL.

Liddell Hart, who had met TEL in 1929, had a more complex mixture of personal and professional motives. TEL's friendship became immensely important to him. Adrian Liddell Hart has commented that his father "felt strongly about personal friendships and loyalties, transcending other loyalties, and this led him on occasions to disregard interests—and facts."[12] Liddell Hart wrote to Graves on 14 June 1935,

> . . . I did perhaps skip too lightly over his questionable aspects—first, because he had stood up so well to the severe cross-examination to which I had subjected him; second, because I had now found out what I believed to be the explanation of things in him which had caused me perplexity or doubt. I had come to feel that his faults and inconsistencies all lay on or near the surface, and that what lay below was marvellously solid. Having got through the surface strata myself, I was perhaps inclined to forget it might be worth enlarging upon it for others who might read the book.[13]

Brian Holden Reid has noted that Liddell Hart began "with a conviction of the essential truth of [TEL's] military ideas, tempered by doubts of his factual accuracy," and cross-examined TEL when he learned that TEL "was inclined to spin yarns and to claim too much."[14]

Liddell Hart's concern for his own reputation and place in history made his opposition to Aldington inevitable. Like Aldington, Liddell Hart lived in the shadow of the Great War, and his military theories and policy recommendations during the 1930s developed from his experiences at the Somme. TEL's military strategy—attacking matériel instead of personnel, weakening the enemy with few casualties to his own side, and winning "mainly by strategic means" instead of by throwing one large force directly against another—was an apt demonstration of Liddell Hart's "indirect approach," which won victories with brains rather than buy them with blood. It made no difference that the campaign itself was minor since " 'Quality of art, not quantity of force' was the important factor."[15] For Liddell Hart, "The opportunity of carrying the strategy of the Arab revolt to completion was not vouchsafed, for in September 1918—when it had reduced the Turkish forces on the Hejaz railway to a state of paralytic helplessness—the main Turkish forces in Palestine were overthrown by a single decisive stroke."[16]

Aldington's book challenged TEL's application of the "indirect approach" by treating the Arab Revolt as an unheroic series of meaningless hit-and-run skirmishes that provided loot and distraction for the Arabs without contributing to the Palestine campaign or to the "real war" in the trenches. For Aldington, who viewed TEL's reputation for military genius as sheer humbug, Turkey would have collapsed with or without TEL, with or without the "decisive stroke" in Palestine, after Germany lost the Great War in the trenches. If TEL's military achievements were fraudulent, so was Liddell Hart's alternative to a war of attrition.

As Adrian Liddell Hart has commented, " . . . Aldington's attack came out at a time when my father's reputation was recovering, after much struggle, from the buffeting it had received during—and to some extent on account of—the Second World War. And it was still being assailed (it still is) by a younger generation of writers. He could not afford to view this with equanimity, even if he were temperamentally inclined to do so."[17] During World War II, Liddell Hart's reputation had reached its nadir. He doubted that a policy of appeasement could prevent war with Hitler, but he opposed conscription, argued against sending British troops to the Continent, and maintained that France's Maginot Line could fend off German invasion. When the Blitzkrieg proved him wrong, he sent a memorandum to the War Office opposing Churchill's policy of unconditional surrender for Germany, urging a negotiated peace. Although some considered this "treasonous," Churchill "stopped further action against Liddell-Hart with the words: 'he seems more a candidate for a mental home than for more serious action.' "[18]

According to John J. Mearsheimer, Liddell Hart restored his reputation as a military strategist by manufacturing evidence that the Germans had learned Blitzkrieg tactics from his prewar writings.[19] Military historian Jay Luvaas comments that "Professor Mearsheimer correctly takes the Captain to task for putting words into the mouths of German Generals and manipulating history to demonstrate that 'the roots of the great German victory [in 1940] could be traced back to him.' " From firsthand knowledge, Luvaas describes Liddell Hart as "temperamentally incapable of letting ideas make their own way in the marketplace. He refought World War I every time a new book on the subject appeared, and on occasion he even tried to discourage publication of some offending book. . . . He was almost incapable of admitting error. . . . In conversation he might change his tone or opinions, but once in print—never!"[20]

Liddell Hart was by far the most formidable member of the "Lawrence Bureau," combining commitment, knowledge, and an ability to argue convincingly and authoritatively. Unfortunately for him, his most fervent allies, particularly Kennington and Knowles, were too strident to be effective. Others who might have provided valuable support were reluctant to involve themselves. Lionel Curtis, who was not particularly close to TEL, wrote to Liddell Hart on 28 January 1954 that "My advice to everyone is to ignore [Aldington]. . . . I'm afraid I can add nothing else." Lord Hankey, responding on 24 February to Liddell Hart's request for confirmation that TEL had "been offered Egypt," provided, after several rough drafts, only a very cautious statement: "I see no reason why Lawrence should not have been sounded out about the possibility of his succeeding Allenby." Lord Winterton responded to Liddell Hart's letter of 26 January to suggest "that just before the book comes out you and I and Ronald Storrs and possibly one or two others should meet in order to concert a counter-attack upon Aldington's credentials." Most exasperating for Liddell Hart was Prime Minister Churchill, who provided only evasive and noncommittal responses to repeated requests for testimony to refute Aldington. Unknown to Liddell Hart, Churchill had suffered a major stroke in 1953 (carefully kept secret by his family) that may have hindered his ability to respond effectively to Liddell Hart's appeals.

Some well-meant but ill-advised actions of other "Lawrence Bureau" members would have hurt the cause had they become public. Kennington wrote to Liddell Hart on 29 March to report a conversation with J. G. Wilson of Bumpus's bookshop in which Wilson seriously suggested that Churchill might bribe Collins with a knighthood. In a letter to Liddell Hart on 8 April, Newcombe suggested that Stirling change the pages in *Safety Last* (1953) that applied to TEL: "If Stirling would rewrite this part giving dates and places to fit in with Seven P., it would be very convincing? and supplement Seven P. as 1st witness evidence." On 17 March, R. G. Sims had written to ask Kennington whether Churchill might alter his introductory tribute to the *Home Letters*, to be published by Blackwell in June: "After Sir Winston told T.E. that 'governorships and great commands were at my disposal . . . ' could Sir Winston just allow to be added a slight extension of this as a footnote, to the effect that these governorships included that of Egypt, which he would have been glad for T.E. to accept, but T.E. refused[?]" [ellipsis in original].

Pat Knowles, who had become frantic, wrote to Kennington on 27 March to suggest that Churchill might use the occasion of his leaving office to solicit, as "his last request," the help of the Queen. On 10 April, Knowles sent Churchill a petition intended for Elizabeth II:

I plead that the good name of Lawrence of Arabia shall not be subject to slight or slander without incurring your displeasure. . . .

The chemistry of Life gave Lawrence his being as the natural and most worthy son of Sir Thomas Chapman.

A new biographer, of strange and lonely mind, has chosen to add this fact to lies and deceits of his own contriving, to achieve a narrow and debase purpose. . . .

We humbly beg that Your Majesty will debar this man his mean and evil objective, and that Captain Liddell Hart[,] the most competent historian amongst us, shall . . . record for Posterity, the true facts and life of Lawrence of Arabia. . . .

Knowles's comment to Churchill about the petition was, "if it fails, all England fails." Only Knowles, rather out of his depth, was surprised that nothing came of his effort.

Disproving Aldington's version of the "Egypt" offer was much more difficult than Liddell Hart had expected. Amery wrote on 25 January that he had no recollection of corresponding with Aldington and doubted "whether I would have been in a position to say that there was 'no truth whatever' in the suggestion about Lawrence." He added that TEL "may have read more into some casual reference that he would make an ideal High Commissioner than really implied any serious consideration on the part of the Cabinet." This suggested to Liddell Hart, as he replied to Amery on 26 January, that "It is obvious that Aldington's enquiry must have been made in a rather casual way" and that "it seemed to me very unlikely that you would have made such a definite statement about a matter that you were not in a position to know."

Churchill, in a letter to Liddell Hart dated 2 February and marked "*PRIVATE*," stated that he "was indignant with what I have read about the forthcoming Aldington book and am wondering what can be done about it," but that he had to "look up my papers of the time because 'old men forget,' and will communicate with you again." While Liddell Hart now had evidence that Churchill was "indignant," which might have weighed with Collins, a private letter that he could not show was worthless.

Liddell Hart tried Churchill again on 4 February 1954, identifying TEL's 30 September 1934 letter to George Lloyd in which TEL had mentioned his "Egypt" offer and adding that Lloyd George had confirmed what TEL "had said about his own part in the 1921–22 period." He then indicated what he needed:

You, of course, were better placed than anyone else to know about the matter. I can well understand the difficulty of recollecting a talk exactly at this very distant date. But it obviously seemed that you had such an appointment in mind when you wrote about how you had told T.E. that "the greatest employments" were open to him, and how "nothing availed" as an inducement. One took this as additional confirmation of what you had said earlier about your efforts to persuade him to accept further and bigger employment. So, naturally, did other friends of T.E. to whom he had mentioned the matter.

It is good of you to ask for suggestions as to what can be done. Your own testimony to T.E.'s great qualities is the best of all answers to Aldington's depreciation of him. But on this particular charge cited in the advance publicity about Aldington's book I think that by far the most effective counter would be a brief comment by you confirming that such an appointment was suggested—or at any rate that his story was *not* "wholly unfounded," as Aldington alleges.

He added, "I gather from Collins himself, who is evidently very worried, that he would hold up the book if he was convinced that any such suggestion was ever made to Lawrence." Despite Liddell Hart's care to spell out how the right sort of letter from the right person could stop Aldington's book, Churchill did not respond for a full month.

Lord David Lloyd's 5 February response to Liddell Hart's 23 January inquiry was even less helpful. After denying that he had ever said that there was "no truth" in TEL's "Egypt" claim, Lloyd quoted his actual statement: "My own guess would be that Lawrence was never asked either officially or unofficially to succeed Allenby in Egypt." After giving his reasons for standing by this statement, Lloyd added, "Indeed, I might almost ask you what proof you can produce that such an offer was ever made, beyond his own assertion." He emphasized that "the Evening Standard had no justification for saying that I had said that there was no truth in the story."

Lloyd did not mention that he had heard from Colin Mann, Aldington's intermediary, who enclosed a letter from Politzer. On 5 February, Lloyd wrote to Mann that "The quotation from my letter is fair enough," adding that Liddell Hart had "no proof and the weight of opinion is entirely against him. On the other hand, if Aldington is going to set up as an historian, then I think that he had better set out to tell the truth which is the very essence of history." In Lloyd's opinion, acknowledging that "none of the three witnesses in question can prove their point" would not seriously weaken Aldington's position since all three agreed in their rejection of TEL's

"Egypt" claim. He added, "For myself I do not greatly care whether in the introductory letter Mr. Aldington overstates his case and the evidence which I gave." He authorized Mann to show his letter to Politzer.[21]

Liddell Hart wrote to Lloyd again on 9 February, suggesting that it was "evident that you were misleadingly reported" and hoping that "you have taken steps to correct it." Aldington's "enquiry and mode of research were far too casual." Liddell Hart outlined his version of the 1922 "Egypt" offer, mentioning that Lloyd's father had not objected when TEL referred to "Egypt" in his 30 September 1934 letter. By then, the younger Lloyd had already received more guidance from Liddell Hart than he felt necessary. When he responded on 17 February, he rejected Liddell Hart's "deductions," Churchill's high opinion of TEL, and the claim in TEL's 1934 letter as evidence. His final words discouraged further discussion: "I hope that this will satisfy you. I am afraid that in any case it will have to."

Storrs presented another problem. Liddell Hart wrote to Lord Winterton on 5 February 1954 that "I am rather wondering about Ronald Storrs's attitude—for, unlike Amery, he has not replied to the letter I wrote him following the reference in the 'Evening Standard.' His attitude to T.E. often seemed somewhat ambiguous." Storrs's letter of 4 February, delayed or misdated, confirmed such suspicions. He had a "faint recollection of being appealed to by somebody, whom I now suppose to have been Aldington . . . [ellipsis in original]. I replied that in my opinion the suggestion was grotesque." Storrs added that since Amery and Lloyd shared his opinion, as well as " 'someone' who most certainly should know all there was to be known," he was confident in his view. Disturbed by Storrs's resolve to stand by his earlier statement, Liddell Hart wrote to him on 8 February that since Amery could not remember Aldington's query and Storrs had only a "faint recollection," therefore "It would seem that Aldington's enquiry and mode of research were far too casual, while it is evident that what you and Amery said has been misleadingly reported." After offering this rationale for Storrs to repudiate his support of Aldington, Liddell Hart outlined his version of the 1922 "Egypt" affair and awaited a reply.

Up to this point, Liddell Hart's knowledge of the contents of Aldington's book had depended on information from others. He wrote to Stirling on 29 January that "A letter just received from an American friend tells me that there has been much fuller advanced publicity in the American press, and that Aldington describes T.E. as a 'congenital liar.' It also says that Aldington's book delves into T.E.'s family background, and his illegitimacy, while also conveying that he was a notorious homosexual etc." Liddell Hart also had other sources. Therese Denny, who worked in Politzer's publicity department, had stayed at the Liddell Harts' home at Wolverton Park on the weekend of 30–31 January and had reported Collins's frustrations with Aldington's manuscript. Collins himself, in his letter of 29 January, had provided a wealth of information regarding Aldington's handling of the "Egypt" issue. Still, snippets of information about the book were no substitute for the text itself.

On 12 February 1954, Kennington wrote to Liddell Hart that Kennington would be able to read Aldington's proofs during the coming weekend and would copy "all questionable things" for Liddell Hart "in case *you* haven't got a copy." Collins had apparently provided a set of proofs to J. G. Wilson as a courtesy to a major bookseller, and Kennington had besieged Wilson for two days at Bumpus's before Wilson gave in and finally granted access. After Kennington returned the proofs to Wilson on the morning of Monday, 15 February, Liddell Hart and his wife, Kathleen, made a special trip to London. Lady Liddell Hart recalls that when they went to Bumpus's bookshop, they joked about the cloak-and-dagger nature of their after-hours entry, wondering whether there were Collins spies about. Since Wilson was not willing to let Liddell Hart take the proofs to Wolverton Park, he had to read them on the premises, a feat he accomplished in about five hours.[22]

Liddell Hart wrote to Churchill on 18 February that he had examined Aldington's book. "As an indictment, it is cleverly enough framed to look plausible. While the carping tone and interjected sneers may put off fair-minded readers, even these may be impressed by the crafty way the case against Lawrence is built up by half-truths, omissions, and twisted evidence. Even footnote references misleadingly suggest that the source referred to provides evidence supporting an allegation, when in fact it doesn't." He reported that Aldington had made the "Egypt" issue the "main plank" and remarked pointedly that "If that plank and its quoted supports were removed his case would manifestly be much feebler." Then he identified "Three of the worst aspects" of Aldington's "extremely nasty book": broadcasting TEL's illegitimacy while his mother was still alive, "portraying him as a sexual pervert," and making "the general insinuation that his reputation was merely a fiction created by British Government–inspired propaganda to promote our Imperial interests and gain American sympathy."

Aldington's proofs increased Liddell Hart's distrust of Storrs. Liddell Hart wrote to Stirling on 20 February that Aldington's book "pays frequent and fulsome tributes to Ronald Storrs, describing him as one of T.E.'s closest friends" and that "Storrs, too, has expressed himself more disparagingly about the H.C. of Egypt question than any of the others whom Aldington says he consulted." The proofs had convinced Kennington "that Storrs has had a hand in the book."

On 26 February, Liddell Hart met Mark Bonham-Carter at Collins's offices to present his case. Bonham-Carter listed Liddell Hart's objections: Aldington's book was "unpleasant," showed "basically bad taste" by exposing TEL's illegitimacy during his mother's lifetime, was replete with "minor and major inaccuracies," and would "be used to attack this country." Liddell Hart challenged Aldington's evidence on the "Egypt" question: the present Lord Lloyd had been nine and a half in 1922, his father had been in Bombay at the time of the offer, and Amery had thought that Aldington's question referred to 1925–26. Bonham-Carter added, "Liddell Hart is in touch with Mr. Churchill, and hopes to see him today about it." Bonham-Carter's notes of the meeting do not refer to Storrs. However, since Storrs had asked Kennington to sign a petition requesting postponement of publication, he seemed to be working on TEL's behalf. Liddell Hart wrote to AWL on 8 March that Storrs planned to tackle Collins regarding the quotation of Storrs's comment on "Egypt" as well as other points. On 10 March, Liddell Hart assured Stirling that "Storrs has recently been in touch with Kennington and seems to have disarmed his (K's) earlier suspicions. They may have been mistaken. At any rate Storrs now seems very anxious to help."

Storrs's visit to Collins did not work out as Liddell Hart had hoped. Politzer wrote to Aldington on 11 March, "Storrs has been in, having been told that he was being used in this book as chief witness against his former friend. We took him through every reference to himself and, apart from the few minor points detailed below, he was quite satisfied."[23] Politzer also telephoned Liddell Hart, who complained to Stirling on 12 March that Politzer had "rather gleefully told me that Storrs had been in to see them yesterday morning and had suggested only very trifling revisions. I rang up Storrs in the evening to see what he had to say. He seemed to have swung round to Collins's way of thinking, kept on saying what a nice man the latter was, and then admitted that he had agreed to let himself be quoted without modification as rejecting completely T.E.'s statement that he had been offered Egypt in 1922, and a Defence appointment in 1935."

On 12 March, Liddell Hart wrote to Storrs in very emphatic terms. Referring to "The way you are quoted by Aldington in denial of the fact that T.E. was sounded," he suggested that "both for your own sake and T.E.'s, you should ask Collins to alter the way you are quoted on these points, as dismissing both suggestions as 'grotesquely' improbable." With regard to the proposal that TEL should become deputy to Hankey on the Committee of Imperial Defence, Liddell Hart stated baldly that "To persist in a rejection of it would be tantamount to saying that I am a liar." Liddell Hart's reference to Storrs's "own sake" was not an idle threat. To undermine Storrs's reputation as TEL's close friend, Liddell Hart collected evidence that TEL had actually distrusted Storrs. TEL had discussed the "falseness of Storrs" in a letter to Stirling dated 15 October 1924. From the 1922 Oxford version of *Seven Pillars of Wisdom*, Kennington had unearthed an unflattering paragraph about Storrs that TEL had deleted from the 1926 subscriber's edition. Liddell Hart intended to make these comments public if it became necessary to discredit Storrs.

When Liddell Hart showed Storrs his evidence on 24 March, Storrs came around. Liddell Hart sent Collins a message the next day: "I saw Sir R. Storrs last evening and showed him the letters from Sir W. Churchill, and Mr. Amery. He asked me to convey to you that a withdrawal of the remarks quoted or ascribed to him in the book should also apply to him." Here Liddell Hart made a rare error in tactics. Since the message came from him and not directly from Churchill, Amery, and Storrs, the firm ignored it. Although Storrs seemed to have fallen back into line, Liddell Hart took precautions. On 27 March, he requested Stirling's permission to "utilise T.E.'s letter of 15.10.24" that referred to the "falseness of Storrs," adding his hope that such a step would not be necessary. Stirling sent his permission on 30 March. Liddell Hart's evidence against Storrs remained in his files.[24]

Churchill finally replied to Liddell Hart on 4 March that a search of his papers had revealed

> a brief letter of mine in 1951 in which I said that his claim to the offer of the successorship to Allenby was unfounded. This letter was written to Lord John Hope who had been asked by the Chairman of Heinemann's [Frere] (who it appears were then undertaking to publish Aldington's book) to approach me to help them by answering various questions about Lawrence. I would not however like this or any other informal opinions which may be attributed to me to be taken as modifying in any way my considered tributes to Lawrence contained in my published writings and speeches.

Liddell Hart responded on the same day, "your present letter will hardly have the desired effect, and might have the opposite effect—since it does not distinguish between 1922 and 1925, and can all too easily be read as confirmation of Aldington's prime assertion that Lawrence was lying when he said that he had been considered as a possibility 'for Egypt if Allenby came away' in 1922." Liddell Hart still needed a "clearer and more helpful answer to this question."

On 6 March, in a letter to Jane Portal, Churchill's secretary, Liddell Hart spelled out what Churchill should write: "the most effective answer to Aldington's charge would be if Sir Winston could say that Lawrence was then tentatively sounded (as the letter of 15 Feb. 1922 indicated) about whether he would be willing to go to Egypt in the event of Allenby persisting in his resignation and coming away." Failing that, "it might suffice if he were to say that Lawrence at that time (1922) was among the possible choices, in view of his influence with the Arabs and recent success in dealing with the crisis in Transjordan." She telephoned that Churchill would try again. After waiting six days for the revision, Liddell Hart complained to Kennington on 12 March that "This long continued delay is curious— and crippling to one's efforts. So long as he avoids the issue, on which he is the main witness still alive, Collins naturally are encouraged to maintain their stand."

Liddell Hart finally received Churchill's revision, dated 12 March:

> This letter [cited by Aldington] was written to Lord John Hope, who had been asked by the Chairman of Heinemann's (who it appears were then undertaking to publish Aldington's book) to approach me to help them by answering various questions about Lawrence. I had not then seen Lawrence's letter to his Mother of 15.2.22 which you were good enough to send me, but knowing Lawrence as I did, I have no reason to believe he was mistaken in saying there was a question of his having Egypt if Allenby came away.[25]

The revised statement was still cautiously evasive, but as Newcombe wrote to Liddell Hart on 15 March, "You can't expect Churchill to do more."

While Liddell Hart was tackling the "Egypt" question, AWL was instructing Kennedy, Ponsonby & Prideaux, the administrators of the Seven Pillars of Wisdom Trust, from afar. He was in West Africa when Burt announced Aldington's book and did not plan to reach England until late spring. AWL encouraged Liddell Hart to continue bringing pressure on Collins, but he did not discuss the intentions of the Seven Pillars Trust, confiding instead in Marshall Sisson and in Kennington, who kept Liddell Hart informed. AWL controlled the extent to which the Trust would fund legal action, and he did not want to attract unwelcome publicity to his mother. He had less at stake professionally than Liddell Hart since his stature as an archaeologist did not rest on his brother's reputation.

Liddell Hart and AWL had corresponded since mid–February, to little advantage for either. AWL tended to suggest actions long after Liddell Hart had implemented them. His advice that Liddell Hart should correspond with Lionel Curtis about "Egypt" arrived long after Liddell Hart had learned that Curtis could not help. AWL's letter of 23 February to Sisson, who passed it to Liddell Hart on 1 March, offered views on the "Egypt" question that, while sound, were too late to be useful: "Churchill will probably deny the offer of Egypt. It was not a creditable episode and so he is likely to have forgotten it, or if he remembers it, to prefer to suppress the facts. A Cabinet meeting may have discussed it; if so, the Minutes will say so but access will be very difficult—Lionel Curtis may contrive it (e.g. through Tom Jones if he is still alive) but even so might well fail to obtain leave to quote. I advise avoiding the Egypt issue." His assessment of some "Lawrence Bureau" members seemed painfully obvious to Liddell Hart by the time he saw it: "Storrs too is liable to rat. Kennington tends to take unwise action and so cause worse messes; Mrs. K[ennington] might pull strings in right directions."

Liddell Hart wrote to AWL on 8 March that he had seen Collins, "with his flanks buttressed by Smith (his chief editor) and Politzer (his publicity chief). Lack of privacy was somewhat of a handicap in the 1-to-3 argument—and lack of Churchill's expected letter a still bigger handicap. However, some of my points seemed to get home, and at the end of the two hours' discussion Collins asked if I would go through the page-proofs and say what corrections and cuts were required." Collins hoped that this would enable the firm to strengthen Aldington's book, but Liddell Hart intended to use the proofs to prepare a crushing refutation of Aldington's findings. He thoughtlessly revealed this when he wrote to Politzer on 17 March to thank him for the proofs, which he had "collected on my way through London" two days earlier, by disputing each point that Politzer had raised, contemptuously dismissing one with "there is nothing in this except to a hyper-sensitive mind." Collins realized that such "correction" would not help his firm, and on the evening of 17 March, Politzer telephoned to ask Liddell Hart to return the proofs.

Liddell Hart, however, did not return the page proofs for three more days, declaring in a letter to Politzer on 18 March that "the errors, distortions, and false assumptions are so numerous and so cumulative. To tackle this book is like wrestling with an all-pervasive 'smog.' " The criticism that he offered was too general to be of much use to Collins: "It seems evident that Aldington has gone to the printed sources to find support for his psychological thesis rather than in search of the truth. The book shows remarkable ingenuity, and an equally remarkable care to avoid going to witnesses who could have provided clarifying evidence on many of these points. But numerous comments are sheerly dishonest even on the printed evidence available. I'm afraid you have been led 'up the garden path.'" Although he had the proofs only briefly, Liddell Hart gained an important advantage. His earlier access at Bumpus's had enabled him to mail extracts in confidence to his "distribution list," but he could not openly quote Aldington's proofs as evidence without revealing that he had seen them surreptitiously. Now he could claim to have had Collins's permission to read the proofs.

Liddell Hart did not return the page proofs to Collins until 20 March, enclosing his "Note on a Few Sample Errors in Aldington's Book." Despite his earlier insistence that Aldington's comments were "sheerly dishonest," the errors were not very telling. One was that Aldington did not distinguish a "plan" from a "proposal." Another was that the expedition from Wejh did not travel "due north." Of the twelve "errors" that Liddell Hart identified, the publisher deleted only one—an erroneous statement about John Buchan's *Greenmantle* (1916) that Politzer, without Aldington's knowledge or approval, had added to the manuscript. On 24 March, a few days too late, AWL wrote to warn that "Any statement of yours as to errors in the proof is liable to be construed into acceptance of the rest of the text—which would be fatal, however violently you contradicted afterwards. I suggest that you restrict your report, if you do read the proof, to a statement that you consider the whole view A. takes to be madly unjustified while he includes a number of serious errors of fact."

Meanwhile, the Seven Pillars Trust administrators had received legal advice against attempting to injunct the book for libel or copyright infringement. The "Seven Pillars of Wisdom Trust Opinion," dated 3 February 1954, dismissed the prospect of suing for libel of TEL because "Defamation of the dead gives no cause of action to the living." Counsel recommended approaching a director of Collins informally to obtain prepublication proofs of Aldington's book. Since it had become evident that Aldington's book exposed TEL's illegitimacy, R. Henniker-Major, AWL and Sarah Lawrence's lawyer as well as an administrator of the Trust, investigated the feasibility of an action for libel on behalf of TEL's brothers and mother. His report to Sisson of 25 February was discouraging. He had considered "whether imputing adultery to Mrs. Lawrence is libellous and in my view clearly it is, by virtue of the Slander of Women Act 189, which says 'Words spoken and published after the passing of this act which impute unchastity or adultery to any woman or girl shall not require special damage to render them actionable.' " If the defendants could prove their charge, however, "they have a complete defence as 'the law will not permit a man to recover damages for injury to a character which he does not or ought not to possess.' This defence is known as justification." In that case, "all that would happen would be to incur costs and bring unpleasant publicity on Mrs. Lawrence." He suggested telling Collins that Mrs. Lawrence was still living so that the publisher "might then withdraw the passages dealing with her and save her and her family some pain."

The Trust also lacked grounds for claiming copyright infringement. In mid-February, Kennedy, Ponsonby & Prideaux had requested proofs from Collins, and Collins had communicated the request to Aldington, who mistakenly thought that this was merely another demand for the proofs in return for his access to *The Mint*. He wrote to Collins on 22 February that "I feel they are trying to construe a mere courtesy permission to see proofs into a right for them to censor. This last I emphatically deny." He suggested that the Trust lawyers not receive proofs until immediately before publication.[26] Collins then refused to send proofs to the Trustees. Since his lawyers had already spent months rendering the manuscript invulnerable to charges of infringement of *Seven Pillars of Wisdom*, the TEL/Charlotte Shaw letters, *The Mint*, and other writings by TEL, Collins was on solid ground, and he knew it.

On 18 February, Kennington wrote Liddell Hart to recommend a frivolous suit: "you have sure grounds for stopping publication, and if at the last he challenges them, you make it clear you have them, but don't say what. If he doesn't yield, you serve the injunction just before publication and he has to stop. . . . " John Holroyd-Reece had anticipated this strategy months before, in his 9 February 1953 "Confidential Memorandum" to Collins. He suggested having Jix investigate whether Collins could require anyone seeking an injunction to provide security for damages to the publisher should the basis for the injunction prove groundless. Holroyd-Reece felt that "the sum would probably be far larger than the family could produce."[27]

In a 15 February letter to Graves, Liddell Hart had expressed the hope that they might be able to prove copyright infringement of their works. "I understand that Aldington's book contains about 100 references to me, and

200 to you (and your book). Has Aldington ever got in touch with you, or got permission to quote from your book? I should like to hear your views as to any action we should take. I understand that the Trustees of the *Seven Pillars* have taken counsel's advice, and have written to Collins asking to see a copy of the book, as a first step, and are contemplating legal action." Graves responded on 19 February that "The only punitive action one can take, apart from action in defence of copyright, is to publicly strike Aldington and plead the book as provocation," a service that Graves declared himself ready to perform.

After arguing that TEL was essentially truthful, that "The suggestion that he was a homosexual is almost indecent," and that "The odd stories in Lowell Thomas's book were Arnie Lawrence's 'stuffing' of Thomas when he came calling for information at Polstead Road in 1923 (or whenever the date was)," Graves outlined his strategy:

> Well: I think that the first action to take against Aldington is to get him on copyright. The Lawrence Trustees, my agent (Bill Watt) and your agent should between them smother him with prohibitions—will you please ring up Bill (W.P.) Watt who also acted as T.E.'s agent before Savage cashed in on the racket and briefly explain the situation and ask him to protect my copyright in *Lawrence and the Arabs* and in *T.E. to his Biographer R.G.*[?] (He will be enraged against Aldington.) Then turn the heat on Collins.
>
> If Collins continues to handle the book in spite of all these démarches, we can think again about punitive action. But is Collins aware that Mrs. Lawrence is still very much alive and that any reflection on T.E.'s birth and that of his two brothers killed in World War I and of his missionary brother, and of Arnie who holds an important Museum position in W. Africa would be outrageous?
>
> It will be impossible to stop publication in U.S.A., I fear, but we could "lay on" reviews and démentis in good time.[28]

Liddell Hart also sought advice on his own account. He wrote to H. F. Rubinstein on 20 February, after he had examined the page proofs at Bumpus's, to ask whether Aldington had infringed his copyright.

> Aldington has about 100 references to my own biography of Lawrence, or to the twin volumes that Robert Graves and I produced in a limited edition "*T.E. Lawrence to his Biographers*," containing his letters and notes. The actual verbatim quotations are mostly short, but there is much paraphrasing. The numbered references are such as to convey an implication that the passages in my book support Aldington's interpretation. Ald-

ington in several places makes offensive remarks that seem to me to bor-
der on the libellous, while the general effect is to convey that I swallowed
many of T.E.'s tales without checking them from other sources.

Rubinstein responded on 23 February that Aldington had already approached him about issues of libel and copyright (when Aldington had
needed counsel to resist Joynson-Hicks's various demands), so Rubinstein
could not represent Liddell Hart due to conflict of interest.

On 22 March, W. P. Watt's legal counsel, K. Ewart of Field, Roscoe, sent
his opinion that Aldington was not vulnerable on grounds of copyright
infringement. The lawyer felt that, judging from the extracts provided by
Liddell Hart, "what has been taken cannot possibly be a substantial part of
Liddell Hart's work or of Graves' work" and that Aldington had two
defenses: either show that the portions he had quoted were not substantial,
which would end it, or demonstrate "that what he had done constituted a
fair dealing with the work for the purpose of research or criticism." Ewart's
view was that Aldington could easily do either. In terms of "defamation
of Graves or Liddell Hart," Ewart did "not think it is necessarily defamatory to say of a man writing a book about Lawrence that he has been
misled." He added, "I do not think the language which [Aldington] has
used is by any means so intemperate as that used in many other cases where
I have known a defence of fair comment to succeed." After stating his
opinion that Aldington would win any action brought for copyright infringement or libel of TEL's biographers, Ewart concluded that legal action
could not delay publication and he was therefore "averse to writing a threatening letter to people if I feel strongly, as I do here, that the threat is completely empty."

Despite the frantic activity behind the scenes, there had been surprisingly little comment in the English press after the initial *Evening Standard*
announcement. The *Evening Standard*'s "Londoner's Diary" of 4 February
carried a follow-up item pointing out that Aldington was not the first to
attack TEL since Sir Andrew Macphail's *Three Persons* had also questioned
aspects of the TEL legend, particularly "Why . . . was Lawrence, supposed
to be so modest and shy, so frequently photographed for Thomas's book?"
Macphail had offered a simple explanation for TEL's success: "it was British
gold that kept the revolt alive."[29] On 6 February, the *New Statesman and
Nation* reprinted excerpts from its 12 March 1927 review of TEL's *Revolt
in the Desert*. The reviewer had found the book "intensely irritating" for its
omissions and contradictions. The *New Statesman and Nation* concluded that

"On this showing, now apparently to be powerfully backed up by Mr. Aldington, Lawrence remains an undoubted writer of genius, producing a literary masterpiece, but not in any sense a reliable narrator of real events."[30]

The U.S. press was much more active and much more informative. An article entitled "Lawrence: Lies or Legends?" in the 15 February issue of *Newsweek* was the first major published comment on Aldington's book since the *Evening Standard*'s 19 January announcement. The *Newsweek* article clearly sympathized with Aldington, reporting his claim that "Lawrence was not a military genius, as the military expert Liddell Hart has claimed in volume after volume." *Newsweek* quoted, from "an interview at his retreat near Montpellier," Aldington's dismissal of TEL as a "phony Oxford esthete" and his statement that " 'Seven Pillars' [is] an incredibly boring book—filled with unimportant men shooting unimportant holes through unimportant water towers, and putting unimportant charges of dynamite under unimportant railroad ties." The article emphasized Aldington's view that TEL "was a creation of modern publicity. He was also its victim. Much of the publicity was American—either created by American admirers of Lawrence like Lowell Thomas or produced by Englishmen for export."

Newsweek ended with Thomas's reaction (solicited before the interview with Aldington). Thomas stressed that "in all [Thomas's] lectures and writings on Lawrence, no one came forward with a claim that Lawrence had not played a leading part in the Arab revolt" and that "most of those who could speak with authority about Lawrence—the men who really knew," particularly Allenby and Feisal, "are dead." His final comment was an emphatic declaration: "As for me, I'm not dead and will defend Lawrence until I am."[31] Liddell Hart sent typescripts of the article, along with copies of his "Notes" of refutation, to his "distribution list" without realizing that half the points he had countered were not Aldington's but insertions by *Newsweek* staffers.

A *New York Times* article, "T. E. Lawrence Issue Rallies His Friends," appeared on 15 February, reporting that "Friends of the late Col. T. E. Lawrence . . . are quietly organizing a campaign to refute a forthcoming book about him" and that "The possibility of a contribution from Prime Minister Churchill is not excluded, since he was Colonial Secretary after the war and had relied on Colonel Lawrence for help on Middle Eastern settlement."[32] On 19 February, the Bermuda *Royal Gazette* reprised the *New York Times* report, adding that "Lawrence's friends are privately greatly concerned at reports that Aldington is to go into intimate detail about Lawrence's family background and personal life in a search for a psychological explanation of Lawrence's admitted eccentricities."[33] Harvey Breit's column "In and Out of Books" in the *New York Times Book Review* of 28 February took up where *Newsweek* had left off, devoting about 90 percent of the article to the response of the "Lawrence Bureau" to *Newsweek*'s comments.[34] Peter D. Whitney's "Lawrence of Arabia Again Stirs a Storm" in the 28 February *New York Times* was more balanced, devoting about one-third of the column to Aldington's charges and his publisher's cross-checking, one-third to the appeal of the TEL story, and one-third to "Attack and Rebuttal." Whitney ended his article with the comment that despite "Strong pressures" on the publisher to withdraw the book, "So far the firm has held out against them."[35]

Thomas, TEL's first biographer, had not required encouragement from Liddell Hart to defend TEL from Aldington. Although Thomas realized that he had depended too greatly on "leg-pulling" anecdotes provided by TEL, members of the Egyptian Expeditionary Force, the young AWL, and others, he regarded any errors in *With Lawrence in Arabia* as his own fault even if others had misled him. He took to heart TEL's complaint that publicity from Thomas's film-shows had made TEL's life miserable. Thomas had written to Liddell Hart on 17 November 1952, "Some day I would like to chat with you about Lawrence, and the yarns that went around concerning my relations with him. Alas, I guess I was young, rather naive, and took him too literally. At any rate, the yarns that were told were far from true, although I did make several mistakes which have bothered me much down through the years."

On 4 March, Thomas discussed the controversy on his news broadcast. He recalled his role in making TEL known to the world and mentioned that he had not seen Aldington's book because it had not been published and possibly never would be. When Lord Beaverbrook had passed through New York, Thomas had solicited his opinion. " . . . Lord Beaverbrook, who has himself been in the middle of a hundred controversies, spoke warmly of the young Oxford archaeologist who became a hero in war and who then became a legend, and of whose greatness I myself feel just as sure as I did thirty-six years ago. Aldington was not there. I was. And this attack on Lawrence will probably just add to his fame. Lord Beaverbrook thinks so. He put it this way: 'No really great man ever escapes attack.' "[36]

When Thomas sent Liddell Hart the TEL portion of his broadcast on 9 March, he commented that TEL had not been without his detractors, such as Sir Arnold Wilson, and described his own rather strange relationship with TEL, including how he had lost almost all the money that the film-show "With Allenby in Palestine and Lawrence in Arabia" had brought him. Thomas declared, "Lawrence and I were friends, even if our relationship did end up in some confusion. All of which never dimmed my enthusiasm and admiration for him." The extent to which Thomas was informed must have surprised Liddell Hart. James McBey, who had been an official artist with Allenby in Palestine, wrote to Thomas on 9 March, and Thomas sent Liddell Hart a copy of the letter. McBey had told Thomas that he had seen Stirling in Tangier and had heard "hints regarding a certain knight who has always been jealous of L's reputation and may be the inspiration behind the forthcoming publication. This may be the same individual as you hint at in your letter." Thomas, in New York, had been as up to date on the "falseness of Storrs" as Liddell Hart.

On 8 March, Liddell Hart wrote to AWL, "A further question—which several friends of T.E. have raised—is whether, in view of all the advance publicity the book has by now received, its publication could be dropped without spreading suspicion that it had been suppressed to protect powerful interests rather than to preserve truth." Not realizing the extent to which Collins had already forced Aldington to change his manuscript, Liddell Hart added, "If on the other hand the publishers themselves are led to cut out some of the main planks in Aldington's indictment—those which have been publicized beforehand—reviewers and readers may realise that the book is untrustworthy. Moreover, without those planks the book would amount to no more than a series of niggling criticisms, unimpressive in content and tedious to read." AWL responded on 24 March that "after all this publicity we ought to prefer publication to suppression—which in any case could scarcely be managed in [the] U.S.A."

Liddell Hart had not convinced Collins that Aldington was wrong about "Egypt," and the "Lawrence Bureau" had found no legal basis for injunction, but the outlook still seemed to favor TEL's partisans. As Liddell Hart informed many on his "distribution list," his letter to Collins of 20 March had been very effective. He wrote to Basil Blackwell on 31 March that "It evidently made an impression, for I have heard from Politzer that, after conferences on the matter, Collins has gone off to America without taking a decision whether or not he would proceed with the publication of Aldington's book—leaving them all 'in the air.' Politzer kept on remarking, ruefully, 'what a mess we have got into with this book.' " Liddell Hart added, "I hope they will find some good way of getting out of the mess."

Newsweek's 5 April issue carried an article called "Lawrence's Defenders" in which Liddell Hart figured prominently as the leader of those "holding consultations to find means of fighting Aldington." The article tended to support Aldington's stance: "The problem of Lawrence's defenders is ironic. In volume after volume, praise has been heaped on Lawrence for heroic deeds that Aldington now says he could not have performed. The pro-Lawrence faction is now trying to prevent Aldington quoting from their works in praise of Lawrence. They are taking legal advice to see whether Aldington's publisher can be forced to omit such sections. Liddell Hart has sounded out the publisher about withholding the book entirely. The publisher said no."[37]

News to cheer the "Lawrence Bureau" and dismay Aldington soon followed. On 14 April 1954, the *New York Times* article "Publisher Delays Life of Lawrence" announced that Aldington's book "has been postponed following a number of protests, including a letter from Sir Winston Churchill." A "spokesman [Politzer] did not explain the delay, but from other sources" (Liddell Hart), the *New York Times* "learned that a considerable body of material protesting against and contradicting Mr. Aldington's 'debunking' of the hero of the Arab revolt in World War I had been submitted to Mr. Collins more than a fortnight ago." The article reported complaints that Aldington had "consulted very few of those who knew him well, preferring to draw heavily on previously published material," but Churchill had "reaffirmed his high opinion of Colonel Lawrence" by allowing a reprint of his 1936 Oxford Memorial tribute to TEL in the forthcoming *Home Letters*.[38] Less than three months after the *Evening Standard* announcement, the "Lawrence Bureau" seemed to be succeeding in its attempts to stop Aldington's book.

5

THE PUBLISHER IN SPITE
OF HIMSELF

By their mixture of hostility and stupidity they [Collins] have wrecked a most valuable property. Their trying to blame ME for their mistakes is ludicrous and impudent.

—Richard Aldington to Alister Kershaw, 5 April 1954

There is no shadow of doubt that Collins are on the side of Lawrence's friends, and are only publishing the book reluctantly. They are still trying to cut out true things which are damaging to TEL.

—Richard Aldington to William Dibben, 20 October 1954

I wish I could sue the bastards for heavy damages.

—Richard Aldington to Alister Kershaw, 10 December 1954

When Collins departed for the United States during the last week of March 1954, Aldington had only a vague notion of what the "Lawrence Bureau" had accomplished at Collins's during the previous ten weeks. His relationship with his publisher had deteriorated into mutual irritation bordering on hostility. When he wrote to press for a firm publication date, a formal publishing contract, an arrangement for U.S. publication, or cash advances, Collins left him dangling with either vague responses or no response at all. Aldington's literary earnings had dwindled because he had not published a book for nearly four years. His financial position was even more precarious due to the continuing demands of the Patmores and unforeseen expenses when his daughter's repeated failure of examinations mandated that she attend costly summer sessions. He also suffered from exhaustion, nervous prostration, and bronchitis. Since virtually all his meaningful contact with others occurred through the mail, his isolation and loneliness intensified his reaction to bad news. Even the slightest delay in responding to his frantic questions or concerns would send him into a rage.[1] Kershaw wrote to John Holroyd-Reece on 1 March 1954, "It has been a heartbreaking business over the Lawrence book and has reduced Richard to a state which is really alarming. It is a tragedy that what was intended to give him a much-needed breathing space has in fact upset him physically and mentally more than you can imagine."[2]

Tony Burt's announcement in the *Evening Standard* on 19 January 1954 had angered Aldington. He wrote to Kershaw on 23 January, "I am simply beyond any further disgust with Collins, whose imbecility is once more revealed by this Evening Standard leakage. It is damaging to have the news out too soon, giving full opportunity to the [Lawrence] Bureau to act. Fools, fools, fools. I'm certain Smith has sabotaged the book all along."[3] Actually, Burt's source had been Kershaw, who later recalled, "the 'Evening Standard' item was the work of a friend of mine who was anxious for a 'scoop.' I had explained that there should be no announcement of any kind until Collins was ready and he scrupulously respected this condition." After Ronald Politzer told Kershaw "that the time had come to release the news of the book's existence, I passed this on to my young friend[,] who thereupon published his snippet. Billy Collins promptly went out of his mind and [Politzer] hurriedly explained that I had authorised the item without referring the matter to him."[4] Politzer, writing to Kershaw on 25 January, tried to minimize the damage, arguing that the item was not "wholly deleterious." He added that since no other papers, to his knowledge, had carried the story, "it looks as if we have put a full stop to this for the moment."[5] When Politzer had confirmed the story for the *Evening Standard*, he had provided the singularly foolish claim that the book would "erase Lawrence from the pages of history," which Aldington resented as a distortion of his own views. Aldington wrote to Henry Williamson on 12 February that "Collins have misrepresented me by their sensational 'erasing from history' which I never said and don't believe."[6] Kershaw understandably kept silent about his role in alerting the "Lawrence Bureau" prematurely.

Aldington was more concerned with other matters. He was furious that nothing had been done to prepare the trust documents for a formal contract with Collins, and he was extremely upset by delays in arrangements for U.S. publication. He wrote to Kershaw on 23 March that "The absence of any news about the TEL is very ominous. I think that Collins have both sabotaged and mishandled the thing, and the Bureau have killed it before it is published if it ever is published." Collins had written to Kershaw on 4 May 1953 that "Knopf definitely offer 15,000 dollars advance,"[7] but after Knopf declined to publish the TEL book, Collins claimed that the contract had been "subject to legal advice which Blanche Knopf said she required."[8] In January 1954, despite Kershaw's urgent advice to the contrary, Aldington had resumed his attempts to market the U.S. rights. F. T. Smith wrote to Kershaw on 5 February that "Mr Collins was very alarmed to hear from Mr Aldington today that he thinks he will sell the American rights himself. This would lead to serious interference with rather delicate negotiations and I do hope you will impress on Mr Aldington that he must leave these negotiations to Mr Collins."[9]

After Collins's earlier equivocations, Kershaw could not persuade Aldington, whose own efforts quickly resulted in rejections from Doubleday, Random House, and Simon & Schuster. Still, Aldington had no reason to expect that Collins would do any better, informing Kershaw on 6 February, "I don't believe Collins has any offers. He doesn't want a US edition, so he can sell export there." The impropriety of having Aldington's English publisher act as Aldington's U.S. agent, and thus represent conflicting interests, had long troubled Holroyd-Reece, who had expressed his misgivings to Collins. On 26 February, Holroyd-Reece wrote to Kershaw that he had brought in a lawyer, Frank B. Cockburn of Horne & Birkett, because, as Holroyd-Reece put it, he had "never been forgiven for daring to differ on a matter of business 'morals' with the Chairman of Collins."[10]

Politzer wrote to Aldington on 24 March, asking him to clarify references that "are liable to hold back the book which is otherwise ready for press." [11] Aldington wrote to Kershaw on 6 April, "I still have not recovered from the last letter from Politzer—all the old nervous symptoms and insomnia back again." He had "gone over and over this damned Lawrence stuff until the mere mention of it makes me hysterical," and he told Kershaw to inform Collins by registered letter "That I am ill and cannot answer any more letters. It is particularly requested that no member of the firm writes to me again ever, and that they say what they have to say to you—and for God's sake keep it to yourself." On 9 April, Politzer wrote that "we will not bother you further on this score," but he addressed the letter to Aldington rather than to Kershaw and devoted five single-spaced pages, with lengthy enclosures, to more problems. He also revealed Collins's ethical unfitness to act as Aldington's agent for negotiating serial rights. Although Aldington desperately needed money, Collins had refused an offer from *Life* of $5,000 for a feature extract. (Pat Knowles reported to Liddell Hart that some *Life* photographers had been nosing around TEL's Clouds Hill cottage, but *Life*'s proposed extract never appeared.)

When newspaper reports indicated that Liddell Hart had seen Aldington's proofs, Aldington complained to Kershaw on 7 April, "What right Collins have to show an unpublished book of mine to Liddell Hart is hard to say; but it is obvious that Smith has been all along playing for the book's suppression." He scrawled a sarcastic note to Kershaw on the first page of Politzer's 9 April letter: "Since Messrs. C. are handing out my book to the Lawrence Bureau for pre-view, how about they send page proofs to Churchill?" On 20 April, after seeing newspaper reports that Collins had postponed his book indefinitely, he wrote to Kershaw, "As I have said so often, that book has been sabotaged in Collins's office from the start. We have no contract, therefore no means of enforcing publication. They have strangled American publication, and of course Amiot [Aldington's French publisher] is their accomplice! The Lawrence Bureau may agree to pay them to kill the book by constant delays, pretending to us they are 'going to' publish it some day."

Collins returned from New York, and Kershaw arranged to fly to London for a meeting on 30 April. On 28 April, Aldington advised Kershaw that "no agreement must be signed without a definite date for publication—failure to keep which will be penalised by total loss of the book by Collins without compensation." He felt that "If it is true as reported (and I think it is) that Smith showed Hart my book, you have a very valuable point in dealing with Collins. They showed to my enemy a book in which they have no property. Remember the book is still mine until the agreements are signed." Aldington warned Kershaw, "The American papers report that on pressure from Winston and Hart, Collins have withdrawn the book. Be very wary of them."

In the 11 April *Sunday Graphic*, Marshall Pugh had quoted Liddell Hart's statement that "The book should not be published in its present form" and the Seven Pillars Trust's solicitor's comment that "We find it intolerable that all sorts of intimate details of Lawrence and his family should be dragged in while Mrs. Lawrence is still alive."[12] Pugh also quoted Collins's statement that "Mr Aldington's book is a work of scholarship and research. Production is proceeding normally, as with any other book." Aldington later cited this as evidence of Collins's support when he wrote to William Dibben on 3 May,[13] but Collins saw Pugh's article as a harbinger of attacks on himself as Aldington's publisher. Also, Collins was angry that Aldington's chapter about Lowell Thomas's creation of the TEL legend had appeared in the 17 April issue of *Figaro* (Paris) in its unexpurgated pre-Jix form. Liddell Hart surmised to Eric Kennington on 27 April that "Presumably this serial use was arranged by Collins, though this way of 'beating the starter' [jumping the gun] is curious. I am wondering what the idea was."[14] So was Collins, and his meeting with Kershaw accomplished nothing.

Frank B. Cockburn of Horne & Birkett, acting as legal counsel for Aldington, did little better when he met Politzer and Smith at Collins's offices on 5 May. When he asked for a firm publication date in the trust documents that would comprise Aldington's contract with Collins, they replied that without a contract from Aldington, Collins could not negotiate with a U.S. publisher, who then would have to approve a date for simultaneous publication. They rejected Cockburn's suggestion that "Collins could continue to negotiate as Aldington's agent quite independently of any contract of their own," and when Cockburn, on instructions, insisted that Collins accept the offers from Putnam and *Life*, they maintained that they could accept Putnam's offer "only after the Agreement between Aldington and Collins had been completed." For Cockburn, the "real crux of disagreement" was the scheme to avoid taxes by drawing up the publishing contract between Collins and the Aldington trust. Collins was unwilling to "enter into any Contract which might involve Collins in any subsequent liability to account to the Revenue for Tax."[15] Referring to Pugh's *Sunday Graphic* article, Cockburn asked how Liddell Hart had seen Aldington's proofs. Politzer responded with a barefaced lie: "Clearly Liddell Hart had obtained a copy of the book, but how, Collins had no idea whatever."

Untimely intervention by Aldington had made matters worse for Cockburn. Politzer quoted a letter from Aldington dated Easter Sunday (18 April): "I thought Albatross was a subsidiary of yours. . . . Holroyd-Reece is not my representative; Kershaw is. . . . Indeed I fully believe that Holroyd-Reece is your representative. . . . I sometimes doubt if the legal documents will work . . . " [ellipses in original]. Since Aldington repudiated Holroyd-Reece as his representative and Holroyd-Reece had brought in Cockburn, Politzer disputed Cockburn's "authority to act for Aldington." He also insinuated that there was "some ulterior motive for the benefit of Holroyd-Reece and Kershaw, or one of them," and the meeting degenerated into smoke screening.

Holroyd-Reece's letter to Kershaw of 6 May (labeled "Confidential & how!") enclosed Cockburn's report. Kershaw, outraged by the implication that he was gaining anything besides insomnia and abuse from helping Aldington, wrote to Politzer on 7 May, "this whole wearisome business has been borne by me because of my desire to help Aldington and has cost me a great deal in effort, time and money. Any suggestion that I stand to benefit in any way from the proposed contracts is humourous but nonetheless unpleasant." He concluded, "I would like to say that if the Chairman has any doubts as to the correctness of my position throughout, I will have the greatest pleasure in asking Aldington to release me from my personal undertaking to help." Aldington wrote to Politzer on 12 May to express his complete confidence in Kershaw, even offering to give Kershaw "a Power of Attorney at any moment if that would expedite matters." He added, "It has been unfortunate that the Bureau has seemed to score this triumph, but it can be turned to a rout by the simple process of your announcing signature of the contracts and a publication date. I give you my word that I will sign the contracts as approved by Kershaw and 'my' solicitor, whose name I learn for the first time! I repeat I think it only fair that I should pay tax if the Inland Revenue so decide."

Aldington's letter simply made matters worse as far as Cockburn was concerned. As he wrote to Kershaw on 17 May, either Aldington, in his anxiety to publish, was ready to sign anything to end the present uncertainty and was thus willing to negate all the advantages of forming a trust ("This is what Collins want"), or Aldington "will be prepared to sign any document, or series of documents, that you are satisfied with as representing the best terms available to Mr. Aldington under the circumstances." Aldington's actions suggested the former to Cockburn, who was convinced that Aldington did not realize what was at stake. None of this surprised

The Publisher in Spite of Himself

Kershaw, who had been dealing with Aldington's exasperating and frequently bumbling interference for some time, but it bothered Cockburn, who insisted that Aldington understand what was going on.

Cockburn wrote to Kershaw on 25 May that Aldington's intervention continued to cause problems. Aldington's earlier refusal "to leave things entirely in [Kershaw's] hands" had made Aldington's signed approval necessary because "in his correspondence with Mr. Politzer he has from time to time shed such doubts on the abilities of his advisers, if not going to the lengths of disowning them, that Messrs. Collins and Messrs. Joynson-Hicks & Co. both feel that they cannot take things much further without some clear indication that the Scheme has met with Mr. Aldington's personal approval, that he does understand it, and that it is not merely being foist upon him, even if in his best interests, by his devoted admirers." Cockburn noted that Aldington had apparently written to Politzer on 24 May that he had "given instructions for Collins to be given all reasonable concessions, and in the event of any dispute would like Mr. [H. F.] Rubinstein to be the arbitrator." Rubinstein was a particularly unfortunate choice since he was not on good terms with Jix, so any involvement by him would be unacceptable to Collins and would thus obstruct the final negotiations. This was all the more frustrating because Cockburn was absolutely convinced, as he wrote to Holroyd-Reece on 31 May, that "Aldington is being taken for a ride."

Despite the complexity of the arrangements required for the contract, Cockburn and Jix managed to hammer out a provisional agreement. There were still a few unresolved issues raised in Jix's letter to Cockburn of 11 June. Collins, with Holroyd-Reece and Albatross in mind, insisted that there be no special Continental edition until one full year after English publication. While willing to "do their utmost" to meet a 4 October 1954 publishing deadline, Collins refused to "commit themselves to a binding undertaking to publish." Collins, however, excluded the French rights from the agreement, enabling Aldington to arrange publication by Amiot-Dumont, and ceded translation and film rights, provided that Collins had "a sole exclusive agency to deal in the rights." The Jix letter ended with a statement that if Aldington did not accept these terms, "further argument can only lead to delay in the publishing date." The lawyers, however, had agreed on the fundamental details of the Aldington trust, removing the last major obstacle to a contract.

Liddell Hart had continued his efforts to undermine Aldington's "Egypt" case. He wrote to Collins on 20 March that "It would be best from every point of view, before giving Churchill's and Amery's letters to the press, if one could say that you had corrected these mistaken imputations in the book, which have been reported in the press." Since Collins had departed for the United States without responding, Liddell Hart addressed subsequent letters to others at the firm. On 27 March, he wrote to Politzer to argue that Prime Minister Lloyd George's penchant for odd appointments made the "Egypt" offer more probable: "In the previous war he had made a railway expert a general and head of all the Army's transport, and later made him an admiral and Controller of the Navy. He also took a professor of anatomy into the Cabinet as Minister of National Service. To make Lawrence H.C. of Egypt would in fact have been much less startling than many of the appointments he actually made," and he sent Lord Rennell's confirmation that TEL had received a serious offer to become Secretary of the Bank of England. He also kept tabs on the status of Aldington's book. On 13 April, J. G. Wilson informed him that, as far as he knew, Aldington had no formal book contract and Collins had issued no printing orders.

In April 1954, Aldington published *Pinorman*, his reminiscences of Norman Douglas, Pino Orioli, and Charles Prentice. He had begun *Pinorman* a month after sending the TEL manuscript to Collins, mailing the completed *Pinorman* manuscript to A. S. Frere of Heinemann in January 1953. Frere had expected to release *Pinorman* in the wake of the TEL book, but after Collins had repeatedly postponed publication, Frere decided to wait no longer. On 1 March 1954, Aldington told Frere that Heinemann could "go ahead without corrections," and the book appeared on 15 April. *Pinorman* is an unpleasant book. The first half affectionately recalls various meetings and travels with Prentice, Orioli, and Douglas, but the second half attacks Douglas's pederasty, meanness, and hypocrisy, accusing Douglas of removing references to Aldington from Orioli's *Adventures of a Bookseller* (1938) and of misrepresenting, in "A Plea for Better Manners," D. H. Lawrence's role in the Maurice Magnus controversy. *Pinorman* hurt Aldington with his public by adding credibility to "Lawrence Bureau" charges that he was vindictive, venomous, and insensitive. Lady Kathleen Liddell Hart recalls "Nancy Cunard coming to see Basil at my mother's flat in London, when she was almost in tears about [Aldington's] savage book about her friend, Norman Douglas."[16]

Cunard reviewed *Pinorman* in *Time and Tide* on 17 April, calling the book "near to libel" and contrasting "Douglas, the erudite scholar, linguist, connoisseur and one of the best stylists of our time" with Aldington's "crazy creation." She wondered "What *can* have happened?" to explain how Aldington's friendship resulted in such a nasty book.[17] Perhaps she recalled her own perplexity two decades earlier when Aldington had fallen out with her for no discernible reason. Compton Mackenzie's *Spectator* review of 30 April objected to "hyenas nosing in the entrails of dead lions."[18] Constantine FitzGibbon commented in the 7 May *Times Literary Supplement* that although Aldington presented *Pinorman* as a supplemental text for Douglas's future biographers, "the pictures of Douglas and Orioli are so distorted that the biographer they could chiefly interest would be Mr. Aldington's own."[19] David M. Low's review in the *Listener* of 20 May declared that "Mr. Aldington's artistic principles are fortified by an unrelenting personal grudge. He thinks that Douglas deliberately ignored his merits and forced Orioli to suppress references to him in his two books. This is hazardous speculation, near to persecution mania."[20] The fuss over *Pinorman* helped the "Lawrence Bureau." Douglas's son Robin wrote to Liddell Hart on 18 May that *Pinorman* made him "hopping mad" and that "insofar as defending my Father and refuting Aldington [are] concerned, the biggest artillery I can muster will go into action." He added, "Please don't demolish him completely—leave a little for me!"

By September, Aldington had decided to have Forty-Five Press issue a pamphlet as a counterattack against those who had scathingly reviewed *Pinorman*, an idea that Roy Campbell had suggested in July. The title was to be "What Next? or Black Douglas and White Ladyship, Being a Herpetology of Literary London," a combination of allusions to Douglas's "On the Herpetology of The Grand Duchy of Baden" (1891–92) and Cunard's *Black Man and White Ladyship* (1931). He envisioned an introduction by Rob Lyle, five letters from Frieda Lawrence, an essay by Campbell, a postscript by himself, and "exhibits" of the reviews by Cunard, Mackenzie, and Low, among others. In November, however, the printers refused to set galleys, considering the pamphlet libelous. Aldington wanted to print the text outside England and distribute it in France, but by January 1955, he had abandoned the project.[21]

Meanwhile, Liddell Hart had been exploring other possibilities for taking legal action. Marshall Sisson had written to Eric Kennington on 8 April that "the book could not legally be stopped" for libel or infringement of copyright,[22] but there remained the prospect of a "Gladstone defense," probably suggested by "What Did Gladstone Do in 1881?" from the *Evening Standard* of 11 December 1953.[23] The article described the successful tactics of Prime Minister Gladstone's heirs against Peter Wright, whose biography of Gladstone had made several allegations. Liddell Hart informed his "distribution list" on 21 April, "I gather that A. W. Lawrence, and the Trustees, are now considering the possibility of dealing with Aldington's book in a similar way to that which Gladstone's family did in 1927 in the case of Captain Peter Wright's book attacking Gladstone's character. They counterattacked by a letter describing the book and author as foul, in such a way as to force him to sue for libel. When the case came into court he was unable to sustain his aspersions, and lost his case. That public exposure of his untruthfulness finished him."

Liddell Hart asked five questions: (1) whether "the denunciatory letter should come simply from the family, or be of a collective kind"; (2) whether the recipient would sign a collective letter; (3) whether the letter should attack only the author or also the publisher; (4) what the letter should emphasize; and (5) would the recipient, if unwilling to provoke a libel action, sign a collective letter to the press "of severe but not actionable criticism?" In a postscript amplifying the third question, he pointed out that while he had enjoyed "a very pleasant association with" Collins, he could "clearly see the force of the argument that the publishers of such a book as this are as blameworthy as the author." Eric Kennington, W. F. Stirling, and most of the others were willing to sign a libelous letter and desired to include the publisher, but Lord Winterton, as he wrote on 26 April, did not want to become involved in legal action and felt that the suit should be against the author only. Graves, responding on 25 April, suggested another course: "get Fleetstreet to agree to an unofficial censorship of the chapters relating to Mrs. Lawrence, as a mark of respect for T.E." Since the Paris *Match* for the week of 27 February–6 March had already referred to TEL's illegitimacy,[24] there was little likelihood that the English press would remain silent.

Nothing came of the "Gladstone defense." As Liddell Hart wrote to S. F. Newcombe on 5 June, AWL had argued that since Aldington lived abroad and belonged to no club where "such a denunciatory letter could be addressed" and since newspapers would not likely risk libel action by printing the defamatory letter, the tactic would not work. More significantly, AWL had decided not to make Trust funds available for legal expenses. Liddell Hart soon understood why AWL was unwilling to provoke a lawsuit. The Kenningtons told Liddell Hart that after TEL's death, AWL had learned from TEL's papers about the masochistic floggings that the *Sunday Times* later publicized in 1968. When Liddell Hart mentioned this to AWL on 15 June, he agreed that "it might be hazardous to embark on legal action along the 'Gladstone' line, in case A. has anything up his sleeve."

Aldington would certainly have included the floggings had he been aware of them, but the "Lawrence Bureau" did not realize this. In any case, since Aldington could document his allegations, a "Gladstone defense" would have generated only damaging publicity.

For Liddell Hart, the need to denigrate Aldington justified almost any means, including smear tactics. On 22 February, he had written to Lord Hankey that Sisson "had been informed on what seemed good authority that Aldington was far to the Left in his political views. Also, which is a matter of common knowledge, that Maclean's brother has been in Collins's firm since he left the F.O. following Donald Maclean's disappearance." Alan Maclean had joined the firm, as Mark Bonham-Carter recalled, after the Foreign Office had "*de facto* and monstrously sacked" him for being the brother of a traitor.[25] Liddell Hart found a willing ally in Celandine Kennington, who wrote on 5 May, "I believe that at the very bottom the A. book is communist inspired—maybe so deep down that A. himself is unaware of it." She added that such a charge would alienate people in the United States and "give friend Collins a nasty shake up en passant. It's probably difficult to *prove* factually, but it certainly could be made to smell very strong. We might be lucky to hit on a fact or two which would pin it down."

Such a fact would have been easier to fabricate than to find since there was no basis for the charge. To Eric Warman, Aldington had written on 18 September 1936, "The next time a Communist calls you 'liberal sentimentalist' call him 'brutal doctrinaire.' You might add that the liberal is one who tries to submit his passions to the discipline of Reason; whereas the Communist sacrifices Reason to hatred, envy and the prejudices of party."[26] He resented any trace of a party line in literature, as he wrote to Kershaw on 3 December 1954: "Golly [Gollancz] must be as much of a Commo as Frere always said he was. It is of course the party line, laid down also by Mr Auden of USA in his preface to the last vol of his anthology. Bastards. They might at least omit English poetry from their filthy propaganda." Aldington refused to go to the other extreme, however. He wrote to Alan Bird on 15 April 1960, "After all, the USSR and the USA are sisters under their skin, with nothing to offer the world but propaganda, machinery, and destruction."[27]

Published articles reflected growing support for Aldington's position on TEL. On 10 May 1954, Howard M. Sachar's article "The Declining World of T. E. Lawrence" appeared in the *New Republic*. After summarizing Aldington's charges and the response of the "Lawrence Bureau," Sachar argued that whatever the truth of Aldington's allegations, "the time clearly has arrived for an evaluation of the world T. E. Lawrence described." For Sachar, "it is unlikely today that military analysts would ascribe the influence to Arab railway skirmishes that Lawrence and Arab nationalists proclaimed at the Paris Peace Conference." Further, according to Sachar, the Arabs "were prodded, not led, by British officers" and "Arab forays recalled by [TEL's] talented pen are a chaos of cross-purposes and looting-parties." Sachar concluded, "It is likely that the luminous Arab world of the *Seven Pillars of Wisdom* existed only for Lawrence and others who wished that it were so. The legend of Thomas Edward Lawrence may survive the scrutiny of historians. But it is not likely that the stylized world he described will linger much longer to bewitch the Western imagination."[28]

More surprising to the "Lawrence Bureau" was the appearance of Henry Williamson's "Threnos for T. E. Lawrence," published in two parts in the *European's* May and June numbers. Williamson recounted that when he visited Aldington in France in 1949, Aldington had "retained . . . some of the despair, or bitterness of the 'twenties" although this "was not obviously apparent; for the perfect host never obtruded his views upon his guests." He did not refer to his part in Aldington's research, which had included lending books, providing copies of TEL's letters, acting as Aldington's intermediary with *Who's Who*, and reporting persistent rumors of TEL's illegitimacy. Instead, Williamson described how he came to regret Aldington's book:

> with every letter from Le Lavandou, and later from Montpellier, my perplexities grew with what I was told about the "T. E. Lawrence" biography. As more and more details of that perplexing life were found, checked, and cross-checked, it seemed that T.E. was—well, the book is to be published this Summer and so I will say no more now, except to add that I have read neither mss. nor proof: but I do know from what he wrote to me again, and again, that Aldington for a long time simply did not know how to treat the material. In the end, he declared, he would have to put down the facts, and the findings, and let them speak for themselves.
>
> But this I will declare now: Even if the much-publicised (by others) and mortifying (to "T.E.") Arabian Adventure turns out to be moonshine or mirage, it will make no difference to my feeling about "T.E." himself, as I knew him and perceived what he truly was, a wonderful man."[29]

In the first part of "Threnos," Williamson offered a rambling account of some of TEL's foibles. In the second part, he went further: "Liddell Hart's book on 'T. E. Lawrence' had just been published," and TEL had commented, "He makes it all fit in: afterwards: it didn't happen like that: but who will believe it now?" At the end of the second part of "Threnos," apostrophizing TEL, Williamson dropped several hints that both the "Lawrence Bureau" and Aldington would find disturbing:

> Were you conscious underneath your dither, despite the Arab robes, of that name of convenience, "Lawrence"? Is that the real reason why you refused all decorations? Were you afraid that one day one of those newspapers, making money by sensation, might risk an action for libel, and print a photograph of your birth certificate?
> . . . And you, I think, would be the last person to blame any biographer who accepted a contract job and then did his best to say what happened. (Though if it has been said this time in the way that it did happen that will be a wonderful thing.) Let the critic who has never slurred or twisted in his own life throw the first stone.[30]

Elie Kedourie, in the June 1954 *Cambridge Journal*, did not mention Aldington, but many of his assessments are startlingly close to Aldington's findings: "The consequences of his actions have touched numberless lives, and yet their motives were strictly personal, to be sought only in his intimate restlessness and private torment. . . . And the cruel irony of his fate is that, although he was intent chiefly on the salvation of the soul of T. E. Lawrence, a private person, it is as Colonel Lawrence, a public legend, engaged in a dubious adventure, that he may claim to survive in men's memories." He argued that TEL "objected to duplicity on the part of England, but not on that of the Sharif and his followers," noting one occasion when TEL tried to justify his disregard for facts: "When Liddell Hart asked him why then he portrayed Faisal in his reports as a heroic leader, Lawrence said that 'it was the only way to get the British to support the Arabs.' . . . " Kedourie concluded that *"The Seven Pillars* is a book which seeks to justify, and to prove right, not so much the Arab movement, as his own actions."[31] Aldington would have heartily agreed.

Although Collins had returned from the United States during the last week of April, he did not respond to Liddell Hart's letter of 20 March for some weeks. When Liddell Hart wrote on 24 May, Collins's secretary, Miss L. Reider, responded two days later that Collins would write when he had returned from Scotland. By 9 June, Liddell Hart still had heard nothing, so he wrote to Collins again: "I have not received the letter you said you were going to write me on your return from Scotland, the week before last. I would appreciate hearing from you." Collins had been reconsidering his position. He knew that if he declined to publish the manuscript, the firm would forfeit the £4,500 advance as well as additional payments to Aldington. Collins had concluded that, short of suppressing the book, he could expect no consideration from the "Lawrence Bureau." He also felt that Liddell Hart's evidence had failed to dislodge Aldington's. Since Jix and Cockburn had managed to agree on the important terms of a contract with the Aldington trust, Collins, after consulting his cousin in Glasgow, decided to proceed with the book.

Collins finally wrote to Liddell Hart on 15 June, after he had made up his mind.

> . . . I think the proper thing is for us to publish Aldington's book and to leave the critics and the public to be the arbiters. There will be plenty of opportunity following publication for you and others to criticise and refute Aldington's conclusions if you wish to do so.
>
> As regards the Egypt affair, I understand that there are two letters in which Lawrence said it was Churchill who offered him the post. If Churchill wishes to believe the letter of the 15th February, 1922 [from TEL to his mother], then he must also be prepared to believe Lawrence's other letters and that he himself made the offer to Lawrence. But you say it was Lloyd George, although you have not shown us any convincing evidence to support this. I must say I think it would be regrettable to embroil Churchill in this matter. His letter to you, if I may say so, is very noncommittal.
>
> Whatever the faults of the book, it presents a very decided point of view, and the author is entitled to his point of view whether one agrees with it or not.

Liddell Hart sent Collins's letter to Churchill on 19 June with a summary of the "Egypt" issue and suggested the line that he wanted Churchill to take: "It looks from Collins's letter as if he is still intending to retain you (and your 1951 statement) as witness for the prosecution against Lawrence. I hope you will feel moved to prevent that. For your 1951 statement is the main support of Aldington's case that Lawrence was a liar, and without that support Aldington's charge would carry little weight." He then pointed out, "As you will see, Collins virtually argues that your letter was self-contradictory, wishful and evasive." Liddell Hart quoted TEL's statements to George Lloyd in 1934 and to Charlotte Shaw in 1926 before ending with his plea: "Have you no recollection at all of having discussed such a possibility with Lawrence at that time [1922]?"

On 20 June, Liddell Hart responded angrily to Collins that Aldington's

The Publisher in Spite of Himself

book was "palpably destructive in aim and venomous in tone" and that publication would harm Collins's reputation, disputing Collins's claim to have seen no "convincing evidence" refuting Aldington's "Egypt" position. He accused Collins of putting "Churchill in the very awkward dilemma of admitting publicly that his 1951 answer was careless and misleading. . . ." He then quoted Lord Hankey's statement "that he would not be 'in the least surprised if Lawrence had been sounded on the subject.' " His conclusion was blunt: "It is a principle of British justice—to which all decent people subscribe, in public life as well as in law—that the onus of proof lies with the accuser. If you publish Aldington's accusations without proof of their truth, you will violate that principle."

To those on his "distribution list," Liddell Hart wrote on 22 June that "It rests with Churchill to convince Collins that T.E. was not lying," but no immediate help was coming from that quarter since Churchill had gone to the United States and would not see Liddell Hart's letter for nearly a month. Liddell Hart then wrote to Lord Trenchard on 23 June to ask about the "Egypt" offer, but on 28 June, Trenchard responded emphatically that he had "no intention of being drawn into any controversy about [TEL] and I have no comments to make on the correspondence you sent me." The "Egypt" question was essentially a dead issue as far as Collins was concerned, but it took Liddell Hart some time to realize this.

AWL arrived in mid-May and communicated directly with Collins on behalf of his family and the Seven Pillars Trust, displacing Liddell Hart as the center of opposition to Aldington's book. On 24 June, AWL visited Collins at the firm's offices, and as he reported to Celandine Kennington the next day, Collins had agreed "to show the stuff about my mother for its tone to be altered."[32] He was disposed to be reasonable about other aspects of the book, which relieved Collins considerably.

Collins wrote to Liddell Hart on 25 June that "We have now sent along a proof copy to Messrs. Kennedy, the understanding being that the proofs will not leave their office, but I suggested to Professor Lawrence that he might like to read them there. We have again said that we will do our very best to alter any specific points to which the family may object, or any facts that can be proved to be inaccurate." Collins summarized AWL's position:

> I understand from Professor Lawrence that at least three other books will be appearing that will refute the material in this one. He also seemed to feel that it is probably better for this book to come out now that it has

been so talked about, rather than that it should be suppressed. He did not fear it doing any permanent harm to his brother's reputation. But his main point was to avoid causing any distress to his mother, and that is what we want to avoid if we possibly can.

I realise how terribly difficult the position is for you but knowing us as you do I had hoped that you would have tried to see our point of view and would have helped us so far as you could.

This hardly mollified Liddell Hart, who wrote on 2 July to complain that Collins had ignored his earlier questions and had not specified what "corrections" Collins had made to Aldington's TEL book in response to Liddell Hart's evidence: "It is hard to conceive that anyone is obliged to publish false charges based on false facts after being given good evidence of their falsity that would satisfy any reasonable judge who was seeking the truth of the matter." Realizing that AWL's accord with Collins had reduced him to a cipher as far as the publisher was concerned, Liddell Hart complained to J. G. Wilson on 3 July that AWL had "seemed only too glad that others should be willing to bear the burden." By the end of July, however, Liddell Hart's standing as the official "Lawrence Bureau" liaison with Collins had all but ended. On 31 July, AWL wrote to Eric Kennington that Collins had "agreed to talk to [Sir Lewis] Namier" about what material Collins should cut. In AWL's view, "N will do his utmost & is a most formidable antagonist; the whole affair can safely be thought to be left to him. (Incidentally Collins was not aware of N's fervency on the matter.)"

Articles questioning the Lawrence legend continued to appear. A. J. Neame, in "T. E. Lawrence—Security Risk" in the July number of the *European*, claimed that "Lawrence was ideally equipped to play the hero of a national compensation neurosis." He described TEL's ambiguous position of ostentatiously shunning publicity while he was effectively and consistently attracting it, called Lowell Thomas's published denial that TEL had helped with Thomas's book "the master stroke," and poked fun at Liddell Hart's claim that "a cripple[d] child was sustained through nights of suffering by the possession of a copy [of Liddell Hart's TEL biography] autographed by Lawrence. No miraculous cures were reported." Neame pointed to TEL's apparent approval of homosexual lust in *Seven Pillars* and then commented, "About Lawrence the man, as opposed to Lawrence the myth and Lawrence the stylist, his friends have told us as much as they wish to tell, and we are thrown back for further information on what we can deduce from his writings." He argued that "The activities of Lawrence's manhood are the attempts to realise the fantasies of an arrested adolescence."

For Neame, "If Lawrence was bent on crusading, it would have been better for his integrity, to say nothing of the bodies of his neighbours, if he had decided *which* crusade he wanted to win."[33]

On 29 June, Basil Blackwell published *Home Letters* with Churchill's 1936 Oxford Memorial tribute to TEL as a preface and Churchill's comment that his views on TEL had not changed. As Eric Kennington informed Liddell Hart on 28 February, AWL had objected to M. R. "Bob" Lawrence's shoddy and "Mum"-serving editing. Sarah Lawrence had ordered M. R. Lawrence to change TEL's letters "as she decides, and to omit any passage which deviates from her education of T.E. A.W. was vitriolic over this." AWL, however, did recognize the potential propaganda value of the volume. After he learned that *Figaro* had published an excerpt from Aldington's book in April, he wrote to Liddell Hart on 21 June that he had "suggested to Blackwell that he might counter by sending *Figaro* extracts from my mother's [*sic*] book of *Home Letters*—which makes me squirm at every page but is opportune for that purpose as no reasonably edited book could be." On 4 July, David Garnett reviewed *Home Letters* for the *Observer*, quoting TEL's 15 February 1922 claim to his mother that "There was a question of me for Egypt, if Allenby came away: but that of course I wouldn't accept."[34] Graves reviewed *Home Letters* for the *New Statesman and Nation* on 24 July, emphasizing the "glowing introduction" by the Prime Minister.[35]

Reviews of *Home Letters* were generally favorable. The most surprising one appeared in the November issue of the *European*, where Henry Williamson recanted his earlier doubts about TEL's veracity:

> Recently I wrote about his *possible* fiction-life; his Irish blarney in embroidering his tale, inventing adventures, exaggerating his exploits from a sense of fun, self-scorn, or uneasiness. Since I wrote my *Threnos* in the May and June numbers of *The European*, I have been shown papers and letters which dispel all doubt. He was entirely truthful; and the records will eventually prove it. If there were occasional small discrepancies, when writing of details years later in letters, they were those of a man, sometimes savagely self-deprecatory, writing too many letters to too many people.[36]

Meanwhile, Aldington had signed the long-awaited trust documents, required for a formal publishing contract, on 25 June 1954. He expected Collins to sign the agreement immediately, announce 4 October as the publication date, and release the book. Collins, however, did not sign. On 24 July, still having heard nothing from Collins, Aldington wrote to Kershaw, "This delay, on top of all the others, plus the penury, is really driving me to a nervous breakdown. We must break the deadlock somehow." In a letter to Kershaw dated 5 and 6 August, after he had seen a Collins advertisement in the *Times Literary Supplement* that failed to mention the TEL book, Aldington became even more impatient. He was convinced that a showdown with his publisher was both desirable and necessary unless Collins announced a publication date and "a clearance of Aldington from the aspersions of [Liddell] Hart."

On 7 August, Aldington informed Kershaw that he had received a telegram: "Could you see Mark BonhamCarter our editor for urgent discussion certain problems about book he having authority to make final decision with you feel personal talk essential stop he would fly out on hearing from you Collins." Kershaw persuaded Aldington to let Kershaw represent him, pointing out on 7 August that Collins had "declined to sign the contracts, drawn up to their own specifications" and that Cockburn had assured Kershaw by telephone that Aldington was "in the strong position; Collins knows it; hence this effort to get you alone away from anyone who knows the full details and get you into a trap." Aldington agreed, and Kershaw met Collins, Smith, and Bonham-Carter at Collins's office on 12 and 13 August.

Collins had fresh demands, spelled out in Kershaw's "Notes": "He insisted that . . . the total absence of any effort to hint at remarkable qualities in Lawrence would cause the book to be attacked, not for its exposure of a legend, but for its lack of impartiality. He was convinced that in its present form, sales would be disappointing." Collins wanted a "less biased version which would still make substantially the same argument," and although Kershaw pointed out that this required a virtual rewriting of the entire book, Collins "repeated that he had only gradually come to see the need for revision and added that he did not think 'his conscience would permit him' to publish the book as it stood." He wanted Bonham-Carter to visit Aldington on 21 August to explain the necessary changes and agreed to pay travel expenses so that Kershaw could be present. Collins also offered additional payment to Aldington for rewriting.[37] Kershaw's "Notes" of 13 August summarized Cockburn's advice: "they can't force you to make changes; they can't reclaim advance; they can't stop book going elsewhere." Aldington replied on 15 August that he was so exhausted, ill, frustrated, and outraged that he could not bear the thought of revising.

On 21 August, Bonham-Carter and Kershaw met Aldington in Le Lavandou. Bonham-Carter urged that some passages be deleted as "unnecessary criticisms" and that "additional passages be inserted giving credit to Lawrence where Aldington could conscientiously agree." With one or two exceptions, Aldington accepted the proposed deletions. He also agreed to insertions if "the number involved was not unreasonable," following a procedure that would minimize his labor: Bonham-Carter would provide copy for the desired additions, Kershaw would recast these in Aldington's style, and Aldington would revise Kershaw's renditions "where he considers it necessary." Collins would advance £100, with an additional £300 to follow "on condition that [Aldington] has accepted a majority" of Bonham-Carter's insertions. Collins would immediately announce the book, specifying February 1955 as the publication date. After receiving the insertions from Aldington, Collins would provide a legal document guaranteeing the February publication date, with the provision that "should the book not have been published by 31 March, 1955, all rights in the book will revert to Aldington without his being liable to repay any of the sums so far advanced to him by Collins."[38]

After meeting Bonham-Carter, Aldington was willing to cooperate but not to compromise his book further. He wrote to Kershaw on 23 August,

> If you think it worth while point out to B.-C. (1) that there is no need to consult TEL's "friends" personally as all have recorded their recollections in the Friends book, which B.-C. has of course never heard of. (2) Challenge him to name any important "friend" of TEL not mentioned in the book. Specifically on the subject of the Arabia "war," my authorities are Antonius (includes Hussein and Feisal), Abdulla, Storrs, Brémond, Young, Bray, Buxton, Barrow, Allenby, Pisani, St[i]rling, Wavell, the Official history. If B.-C. has any other authorities up his sleeve, let him produce them!

Bonham-Carter recalled that Aldington "was very reasonable,"[39] and Aldington wrote to Kershaw on 27 August, "One thing I must say for Bonham-Carter—during 40 years of what is known as 'close association' with the publishing trade of England-America, I have never before met a gentleman. Now do not tell me about C.B.E. and knighthoods and peerages and sons at Eton and so forth. Like all Brits I am a snob and I know a gemmam when I sees one." Early in September, Bonham-Carter saw Aldington again. Ultimately, Aldington accepted twenty-six of Bonham-Carter's thirty-two suggested additions. He felt that he had gone far beyond the letter of the agreement since he might have obstinately accepted only seventeen insertions as the required majority. In his letter to Kershaw dated

10 September, Aldington emphasized that he would "make no more concessions, tell them, and am unyielding on the para[graph]s to which I have said 'No.' " He wanted Collins to announce publication "*at once*" and demanded that Collins "stand by the book and its author, or give the book WITHOUT MORE DELAY. I am sick of them and their treachery."

Aldington was soon ready to have done with Collins. Despite repeated promises, Collins had still not signed the agreement, announced the book, or sent the urgently needed £300. Aldington prepared three letters dated 30 September for Kershaw to mail if Collins failed to sign, announce, and pay by the end of the month. One to Bonham-Carter withdrew the book from Collins. Another to Cockburn explained the reasons for withdrawing the book and asked him to communicate the book's formal withdrawal to Collins's solicitors. The third, to Holroyd-Reece, indicated that Collins no longer had any interest in the book and asked that Holroyd-Reece consider the manuscript for an Albatross Continental edition: "We can supply a set of proofs as fully approved for publication on legal grounds by Joynson Hicks." The letter indicated that if Holroyd-Reece did not want the TEL book, Aldington would "take it to Frere" for publication by Heinemann.[40]

On 23 September, Aldington sent these letters to Kershaw with his comments: "I am determined to get away from these people, absolutely determined. This situation is intolerable and has gone on too long. It has beggared me and made me ill. Much better not have the book published. If John [Browning] and Frere won't have it, offer it to Golly [Gollancz]. But if Collins have not announced AND paid [£]300 AND signed agreements by the 30th Sept, mail the letter REGISTERED. Believe me, dear boy, it is the only way out. You are an honest Aussie, and you do not know what cits are English 'gentlemen.' " The *Evening Standard*, however, had announced on 20 September that Aldington's book would "appear early next year," quoting Aldington's earlier statement that "There were people who wanted to see the book suppressed" who "have not succeeded."[41] Collins met the other commitments, so Aldington's 30 September letters remained in Kershaw's files.

Meanwhile, impatiently awaiting a response from Churchill, Liddell Hart vented some of his exasperation by sending Graves TEL's comment on Churchill: "If Winston's interests are not concerned in a question, he wouldn't be interested." Churchill, who had returned from the United States, finally wrote to Liddell Hart on 17 July:

The Publisher in Spite of Himself

I am sure the post of High Commissioner in Egypt was never offered officially to Colonel Lawrence, but I think it very likely that I talked over the possibility of his being offered it and asked him how he felt about it. It is very likely also that his not welcoming the idea played its part in my not pressing it any further. However I cannot pretend to remember all these details and when Lord John Hope wrote to me on February 21, 1951, I replied only from what I remembered without refreshing my mind by studying all that was happening at the period, nor have I done so yet.

He then specified how Hope's letter might have misled him: "the word *officially* is underlined in typescript and I expect my words 'I think the first is certainly unfounded' applied to the *official* offering of the post and not to whether I ever mentioned it *unofficially* as a possibility in private conversation." Churchill added, "I cannot however undertake even now to embark upon a prolonged study and research as I have a lot of other things to think about."[42]

Liddell Hart did not receive Churchill's permission to show this letter to Collins until 22 August, the day after Aldington and Bonham-Carter had agreed to necessary revisions at Le Lavandou, and by then it was too late. Collins and Aldington paraphrased Churchill's 17 July letter for inclusion in a footnote to Aldington's original "Egypt" argument. Liddell Hart continued corresponding extensively with Lady Hardinge (whose son, George, worked in Collins's crime-fiction department), Celandine Kennington (who had visited TEL's two surviving Chapman half-sisters in Ireland in September), Namier (to whom AWL had handed over dealing with Collins), Bonham-Carter (who spent an October weekend at Wolverton Park), and many others, but he remained on the periphery. Information about the activities of the Seven Pillars Trust reached him only secondhand. As he wrote to Eric Kennington on 17 September, news of the forthcoming publication of *The Mint* had come as a "complete surprise."

That same day, Bonham-Carter dashed any remaining hope in a note marked "*CONFIDENTIAL*": "I thought I would drop you a line to say that Aldington's Lawrence will be published by us in February of 1955. It has been to a considerable extent altered since you saw it, though not possibly as much as you would like. In view of the course of the negotiations I do not think there was any alternative open to us but to publish." On 9 November, Bonham-Carter sent Liddell Hart excerpts from the recently issued *A Diary with Letters, 1931–1950* by Thomas Jones, former deputy secretary of the Cabinet, that mentioned TEL's illegitimacy.[43] Jones's book, published by Oxford University Press, took some wind from the sails of the argument against Aldington's "indecency." As Liddell Hart wrote to Lady Astor on 17 November, "In view of T.J.'s disclosures of T.E.'s illegitimacy etc., it becomes difficult to object to Aldington's—and Collins are evidently both pleased and relieved."

In October, there had appeared an abridged edition of *T. E. Lawrence by His Friends*, prepared especially to oppose Aldington. In March, writing to Eric Kennington about Aldington's TEL book, AWL had indicated that "For UK opinion an abridgement of T.E. by his friends is being published." The *Evening Standard* announced in its 24 September "Londoner's Diary" column, under the heading "Counter-attack," that AWL would "bring out a new abridged edition of T. E. Lawrence by His Friends, which was first published in 1937. Its reappearance has been hastened to counter Aldington's attack." In the *Evening Standard* account, AWL alluded to Aldington in words very close to those of his preface to the new edition: "I gather that a book is expected to appear in which a novelist has devoted his abilities to a steady denigration of my brother. Clearly no such attack can be restricted to the target of a single dead man; those who spoke well of him from their personal knowledge may well be made to appear fools, hypocrites or partners in a fraud."[44] Aldington wrote to William Dibben on 18 October that "They are republishing T. E. Lawrence by his Friends! But have you noticed that it is a *shorter* edition—i.e. they have cut out the parts I proved are lies!" The truncated edition was an effective "Lawrence Bureau" riposte.

In November, Amiot-Dumont published the French edition of the TEL book, including pre-Jix material cut from Collins's edition. Aldington had written to Dibben on 28 September that "The French version will be much franker and sharper than the English, and defy the English libel laws which don't hold in France." As he wrote to Kershaw on 6 November, he had not seen proofs, and the "infamous" translation distorted his statements and scrambled his references. It both amused and exasperated him that French reviewers quoted and praised obviously garbled passages. He wrote to Eric Warman on 3 December,

> the reviewers know nothing. One joke I think will please you much. A sapient chump says I rely very much on Freudian interpretations of TEL. In the first place I wouldn't dare do so, since I don't know enough about it—not a hundredth part of what you know; second, I specifically put aside the Freudian interpretation, as you will have noted; and third, the passages he quotes are in fact paraphrases of an unpublished letter of TEL

which the law and the Lawrence Bureau wouldn't allow me to quote verbatim. "Serious intellectual criticism" as she is wrote.

It irked Aldington that the title page of *Lawrence L'Imposteur* cited "T. E. Lawrence, The Legend and the Man" from the early galleys supplied to the French translator.

On 10 November, Liddell Hart wrote to Eric Kennington that David Garnett had brought an advance copy of the French edition to England. He informed his "distribution list" on 24 November that a special band around the French edition "tends to confirm the fears I expressed earlier that the book would be exploited for anti-British propaganda." Amiot-Dumont's offensive promotional statement was "L'étonnante vie truquée de celui qui fut le grand ennemi de la France en Orient, passée au crible par un célèbre écrivain anglais," which Liddell Hart translated as "The amazing life of fake of him who was the great enemy of France in the East, put through the sieve by a celebrated English writer." In London, the *Times* of 27 November printed a short notice, "French Criticisms of T. E. Lawrence." After erroneously claiming that Aldington's book had been published earlier in the United States, the article cited *Le Monde*'s criticisms that Aldington "did not question personally the survivors of Lawrence's Arab adventures" and that "a mediocre man would not have had the friends he did," omitting Aldington's revelations.[45] Lord Hankey, writing to Liddell Hart on 9 January 1955, reported that "I have also heard Aldington's book discussed in Paris, where most French people misjudge Lawrence. I have disillusioned some of those who were inclined to believe Aldington. I have not read the book myself."[46]

When Liddell Hart received his advance copy of Collins's edition of Aldington's book, he regarded the footnote paraphrasing Churchill's letter of 17 July 1954 as "dishonest." He resented the book's use of Amery's "Egypt" statement despite the request to withdraw it that Amery had sent to Liddell Hart on 18 February and that Liddell Hart had forwarded to Collins. As usual, Liddell Hart did not find Churchill very helpful. In response to Liddell Hart's 5 January 1955 letter describing the offensive footnote, Churchill merely commented on 11 January that "The footnote to which you refer certainly does not do justice to my letter of July 17." On 14 January, Liddell Hart expressed his "hope" that Churchill would "convey to Collins what you feel about the way that they have treated your statement," but nothing came of this. He also wrote to Bonham-Carter on 14 January, complaining that there was "little sign" of correction and calling

Collins's handling of the "Egypt" question "dishonesty," ending that he would "have to examine his quotations in a much more detailed way, and then consider what action to take."

Bonham-Carter did not mince words in his response of 18 January:

> If you think we are as dishonest as you appear to, there is clearly not very much I can do to convince you to the contrary; but I would like to point out that although you may find very little difference in Aldington's book [compared with the earlier proofs], from other quarters I have received several letters and telephone messages asking me why our edition is so different from the French edition. These people think, like you, that we are being dishonest, but in their case our dishonesty lies in the efforts which we have made to meet your, and other people's, objections.
>
> I can only say that we have been to very great trouble to make the book as inoffensive as we can, and that so far, neither you nor any of Lawrence's other friends who have seen it—and by now there have been several—were able or willing to point out an error in the argument which would justify us in breaking our agreement with the author.

On 14 January, Liddell Hart had urged Amery to send Collins a "letter of protest" objecting to the use of Amery's "Egypt" statement. Amery reluctantly complied on 19 January, writing that Aldington had approached him recently after working on the TEL book for some time and that therefore any attempt "to make my statement the beginnings of his doubts about Lawrence, looks highly disingenuous." To his surprise, he received a response directly from Aldington, dated 23 January, that demolished Amery's ground for complaint: "The 'application' to you for information on the topic of T. E. Lawrence was made to you on my behalf by Mr. Colin Mann, at that time Public Relations Officer of the Conservative Party, and his letter giving your reply and that of others is now with Messrs. Collins." After quoting the relevant passages of his book, Aldington stated that "You are quite inexact in stating that my reference to you was made 'not very long ago.' As the date of Mr. Mann's letter proves, it was made in 1951, at the outset of my investigation."[47] Amery sent Liddell Hart a copy of Aldington's letter on 26 January, commenting that "I am afraid he has rather the better of me if it is correct that Lawrence claimed to have been offered the Commissionership in 1925."

Liddell Hart received an unexpectedly supportive letter from Lord Lloyd, who wrote on 21 January that "Aldington has put into my mouth opinions which I never expressed and about the publication of which I was never consulted." He enclosed a copy of his 20 January letter to Politzer in which he made the same complaint, particularly objecting to a "false attribution" in Aldington's introduction. Almost a year earlier, however, on 5 February 1954, Lloyd had written to Mann that he had no particular objection to this attribution.[48] He had authorized Mann to show the letter to Politzer, who chose to treat Lloyd's letter as formal consent.

As the date of publication drew closer, Aldington became increasingly jittery about the prospect of treachery from Collins. He wrote to Dibben on 11 January that

> If those *blasted* Collins would only get the TEL out instead of weeing their old-school cricket pants and making Heath Robinson publicity plans, all would be well. They've only got to *publish* the bloody book, no matter how, because everyone wants to read it. Instead of which they fart about eternally like a pack of old bean-fed whores, and let the newspapers pinch the news to gratify the very natural curiosity of the public. I have to put on my desk a notice: DON'T WRITE TO COLLINS. Otherwise I should tick off the silly bastards to my own detriment. But they *are* fools, Bill. Everything in that book has been gone over and over by Jix and my own lawyer, so what are they funking? Of course they were sucking up for "Honours" and won't get them now—at any rate from Winston. But surely At[t]lee will soon be back?

On 12 January, he wrote to Dibben that "Collins gave me their word it should be January, and you see they made it the latest possible day. What friends." (Aldington forgot that Collins had agreed to publish in February.)

On 23 January, Aldington wrote to Kershaw with another accusation against his publisher:

> I have just discovered that Collins's printers have wrecked the whole recruiting passage by printing 5 ft 6 instead of 5 ft 8 [as the raised height requirement for military service during the 1914 deluge of volunteers]. Now they had it right in all earlier proofs, and it is one of the things given correctly in the French edition [translated from Collins's galleys]. This looks an additional indication that they actually distributed the type after the first blow-up, and then hastily re-set the book after we threatened withdrawal. You will remember I thought so as soon as I got the proofs.

The far-fetched notion that Collins had broken type and then reset reveals more about Aldington's frenzied state of mind than about his publisher's actions. On page 123, the incorrect height "5 feet 6 inches" does appear in the sixth line, but on the twenty-second line it appears correctly as "5 feet 8 inches."[49] When correcting proofs, no one had noticed the discrepancy.

Aldington caught the typographical error in the published text but missed the correct version sixteen lines later.

Aldington also worried about forthcoming reviews. Referring to James Mayo's "British Hero Debunked" in the 9 January *Sunday Chronicle*,[50] he wrote to Bird on 12 January, "the line indicating how to steal my news without paying me was evidently too much for the integrity of the Sunday Chronicle which is said to have published eight scurrilously virtuous columns with large headlines denouncing me."[51] He also wrote to Dibben on 12 January, "Do you see Storrs is to review for the BBC, in accordance with the well-known maxim of British law that a government-protected culprit should be tried by his accomplices?" On 23 January, he informed Kershaw,

> So far it looks as if the only papers on my side will be Sunday Chronicle (Hayter Preston), Punch (Muggeridge), Express and possibly N. Statesman. I think even the Telegraph will hedge, and that the rest of the "respectable" press will be against. You see what a fool B.-C. was to reject my plan of suddenly publishing in Dec without sending out press copies. He should have published about Dec 15, sending out review copies the same day. The book would then have had a chance to be judged on its merits, instead of in this atmosphere of lies and propaganda. Illustrated Features have that article and photos, and their man seemed very friendly.

Almost two years earlier, Aldington had feared concerted opposition in the reviews. He had written to Kershaw on 9 March 1953 to provide his "main list of bars": "Prof Lawrence, David Garnett, Liddell Hart, Robert Graves, Vyvyan Richards, Storrs, Henry [Williamson], [the] Sitwells, Raymond Mortimer. What I would like is a set of really impartial and competent reviewers, but where are they to be found?" Aldington's "main list of bars" was prophetic—almost everyone on the list either appeared in print to oppose the book before publication or defended TEL against Aldington in the storm of controversial reviews that broke even before the book officially appeared on 31 January 1955.

6

KILLING THE MESSENGER

[N]o honest reader (from whose ranks I carefully exclude most reviewers) can question my statements without verification.

— Richard Aldington to Henry Williamson, 6 February 1952

The level of reviewing in all the serious papers has been remarkably just and penetrating.

— B. H. Liddell Hart to Sir Linton Andrews, 28 February 1955

However it is small comfort to know that I shall be vindicated 20 years after I am dead!

— Richard Aldington to Alison Palmer, 13 November 1955

It now looks as though Mr. Aldington's biography of Lawrence of Arabia will not survive the malevolent and well-directed barrage of criticism which it provoked. The English literary establishment, having failed to kill the book before birth, has slaughtered it in early infancy. Nevertheless, it has largely achieved its purpose. Those of us who read it and were not already prejudiced in Lawrence's favour, now find it impossible to regard him with anything except contemptuous tolerance.

— Paul Johnson, *New Statesman and Nation*, 5 May 1956

REVIEW COPIES OF *Lawrence of Arabia: A Biographical Enquiry* went out on 31 December 1954, exactly a month before the official publication date. Aldington's biographer, Charles Doyle, notes that "By 3 March Aldington had collected nearly two hundred press cuttings concerning the biography. Three-quarters of these were hostile, and he began to feel many attacks were rooted in personal animus against him."[1] In the *Sunday Chronicle* of 30 January, Liddell Hart reiterated well-rehearsed points: Aldington's "venomous" and "monotonous" book consisted of "smears and sneers." It was "a catalogue of carping comment" that would help "anti-British propaganda everywhere." Exposing TEL's "family secret" was "an indecency," and Aldington's conclusions derived from false assumptions and misquotation.[2] Various reviewers wrote that Aldington's book was "dull," he was a cad to sensationalize Sarah Lawrence's adultery, his biased selection had "distorted" the evidence, he focused only on "trivialities," he had "no first-hand knowledge or evidence," and his "sustained sneer" was "resentful and vindictive."

Mervyn Jones reflected the response of many in the title of his 18 February review in the London *Tribune*: "Lawrence or Aldington? I Dislike Them BOTH."[3] In the *Sunday Times* of 30 January, Raymond Mortimer commented that "If Mr. Aldington had been personally slighted by Lawrence, he could hardly show himself more resentful and vindictive." Mortimer confessed to having "always had a prejudice against Lawrence, whom I never met, but this has been largely broken down by Mr. Aldington."[4] In the 30 January *Observer*, Harold Nicolson agreed that TEL's "habit of telling fibs was almost pathological," TEL "was himself a master of advertisement," and "it is difficult to-day for all those statesmen, admirals, field-marshals, air-marshals, historians, school-masters, and novelists to admit that their early enthusiasm was exaggerated or misplaced," but Aldington's attack had made him "think more highly of T. E. Lawrence than I ever thought before."[5]

In March, C. M. Woodhouse reviewed Aldington's book along with three "Lawrence Bureau" productions that had attempted to preempt it: *Home Letters*, the shortened *T. E. Lawrence by His Friends*, and *The Mint*. For Woodhouse,

> The consensus of opinion among reviewers has been that [Aldington's book] is bad but important. Its badness has been put in many different

ways: bad taste, faulty scholarship, slovenly writing, dullness, inaccuracy, irresponsibility and malice. On this form, it might well rank as the worst best-seller in the non-fiction class ever recorded; but most of the reviewers seem disinclined to put it in the non-fiction class. Its importance, on the other hand, has been not so much stated as implied: implied, for instance, in the speed and prominence and violence of the hostile reviews, as well as by the exhilarating race over the last year to bring rehabilitating material on to the market ahead of or alongside Mr Aldington's assault.

Woodhouse, who felt that "subjecting the book to a dispassionate detailed examination . . . would almost certainly leave it at least as badly mutilated as Mr Aldington believes himself to have left the Lawrence legend," noted that "the more important reviewers (especially those belonging to what Mr Aldington spitefully calls 'the Lawrence Bureau') have scarcely addressed themselves to factual criticism at all. . . . Beneath the overtones of emotion, controlled or uncontrolled, there are undertones of uneasiness in the reviews, as though it were not Lawrence that was on trial but the reviewers themselves and their generation. There has been a certain uniformity about them. . . ."[6]

Liddell Hart had accounted for part of the "certain uniformity" that bothered Woodhouse. While reading Aldington's proofs for Collins in March 1954, he prepared "Note on a Few Sample Errors in Aldington's Book" for his "distribution list." On 15 April, after receiving his copy, Graves wrote to ask Liddell Hart's "permission to mention you as having disproved some of the most specious lies, naming your sources, but not of course quoting the actual text—which would be unethical, since you will certainly be called on to review the book yourself, if it appears."[7] After Liddell Hart saw a set of emended proofs in mid-1954, he supplemented his "Note" with "Insertions added to page proof of Aldington's book."[8] In January 1955, he prepared "Aldington's 'Lawrence': His Charges—and Treatment of the Evidence," a seven-page single-spaced typescript (referred to as his "Analysis").[9] He and Eric Kennington duplicated it for mailing in batches of one hundred. After reading "Analysis," many reviewers brought up the same anti-Aldington arguments "independently."

In his review for the London *News Chronicle* on 31 January, Graves particularly resented Aldington's sarcastic treatment of TEL's rape by Turkish soldiers at Deraa. Graves quoted a comment by Aldington that "in better days would have earned him the horse-whip": "This catastrophe was a punishment for his . . . insolence and contempt for his enemies . . . whom he frequently called stupid [ellipses in original]. Who was stupid *this* time?"[10]

This statement was not in the book, however, for Collins had insisted on its deletion after Liddell Hart had seen the proofs. In an expanded version of Graves's review, published as "Lawrence Vindicated" on 21 March in the *New Republic*, Graves quoted the same passage and remarked indignantly, "Personally I cannot read this book without revulsion."[11] He apparently had not read it at all. He wrote to Liddell Hart on 10 February that the book had not arrived until the day that his *News Chronicle* review appeared in print, "but I had used the notes you sent me some months ago—which contained all the quotations I needed!" Graves added, "Now I am extremely grateful for your enclosure, because I have to write a 3000 word article on the book for *New Republic* and it gives me the necessary ammunition on points which I'd never checked myself."[12]

David Garnett may also have reviewed Aldington's book without reading it. His "Lawrence in the Dock," printed in the *New Statesman and Nation* on 5 February, relied extensively on Liddell Hart's extracts. After commenting that "There is a sneer on almost every page, sometimes in every paragraph; and the abundant documentation cannot conceal the silliness and malevolence of this estimate of Lawrence," Garnett focused on what he called "the crucial case of the bicycle," which would not strike most people as "crucial," quoting Aldington at length:

> Those who have come to realise Lawrence's irresistible propensity to dramatise his exploits and advertise himself will not be surprised to know that he circulated a very quotable little story about this bicycle which has been accepted by his friends. Vyvyan Richards says: "Lawrence had a light little racing bicycle which was built by Lord Nuffield when plain Mr. Morris at Oxford. The two of them put their heads together to perfect the design." Unfortunately for the truth of this story Lord Nuffield assured David Garnett that he gave up making bicycles before 1900.[13] It can and will be said that hitherto these exaggerations and untruths I am pinning on Lawrence are trifles, and so they are, though truth itself is not a trifle. But it so happens they can be convincingly shown to be untrue . . . [ellipsis in original]. And if he would deceive in trifles for the sake of a worthless astonishment and admiration, what guarantee is there that he did not do likewise in important matters?[14]

Garnett was not quoting the book that he had ostensibly read for review. The parallel passage that Collins published differs in phrasing, organization, and content, with "truth itself is not a trifle" embedded in the next paragraph's explanation for addressing admitted trivialities.[15]

When Liddell Hart mailed out post-review copies of "Analysis," his cover letter adopted one of two approaches. He congratulated those who had condemned Aldington without reservation for a perceptive review. To those who castigated Aldington but seemed to regard the book as having some basis in fact, he condoled that Aldington's misleading presentation of evidence had fooled many. Several received letters that included the substance of the following paragraph that Liddell Hart sent on 4 February to Donald McLachlan of the London *Daily Telegraph*: "While most of the reviews of Aldington's book that I have seen have reacted against his attitude, they have been apt to assume that it is at least careful and honest in its presentation of the evidence. That illusion ought to be dispelled." Liddell Hart did what he could to see that everyone received the message.

Dr. A. L. Rowse wrote his review for the London *Daily Mail*[16] before he corresponded with Liddell Hart, who first wrote to him on 1 February after reading Rowse's 31 January review. Rowse responded on 3 February, "I don't think Aldington's book will do any damage, except possibly to himself. By way of compensation he must be pleased at the amount of attention he is receiving—which will help to sell his book." He added, "He is a *mean* piece of work and I do detest professional denigrators of men more remarkable than themselves." The intervening years have not altered his view. He wrote on 24 August 1992, in his ninetieth year, "I don't think TEL would have cared. But Aldington should have been ashamed of himself." [17]

There was some support for Aldington. On 26 January, the BBC *Panorama* program had broadcast a debate between Malcolm Muggeridge of *Punch* and Sir Ronald Storrs. Muggeridge later commented that he had been "cautioned not to be too critical of Lawrence in my article of what he did before I interviewed Ronald Storrs."[18] *Panorama* focused on TEL, referring to a forthcoming "critical biography" without mentioning Aldington's name. Muggeridge asked Storrs how TEL, "so allegedly modest," willingly posed so often for photographs and paintings in Arab dress, whether he was truthful, and whether he was really a great man. Storrs conceded that TEL's character was inconsistent and that he had often "exaggerated."[19] On 28 January, the London *Daily Express* carried Sydney Smith's telephone interview with Aldington, who outlined his major points. Smith quoted the publisher's statement that "No one has been able to dispute the major facts" of Aldington's case.[20] Aldington's "Why I Decided to Debunk a HERO" appeared in the London *Evening News* on 31 January.[21] The *Daily Mail* paid Aldington for a rebuttal of Rowse on 1 February, which focused on the nature of his "biographical enquiry," his evidence that TEL was a liar, and the extent of his documentation (more than 1,300 references).[22] On 5 February, the London *Illustrated* published his "Why I Debunked the Lawrence Legend."[23]

The willingness of editors to accommodate Aldington ended early in February, but abusive reviews of his book continued to appear for some weeks. Collins did not help Aldington refute attacks on the book and refused to return important documentary evidence that Aldington needed, insisting that it remain at the firm's London office for "legal" reasons. The publisher also censored Aldington's defenders. On 25 February, Aldington complained to Kershaw that "Your Telegraph letter was criticised by B-Carter as 'inaccurate' on the subject of changes forced on me, so Mrs Colin [Aldington's London agent] thought we'd better not send it."[24] He warned Kershaw on 6 April, "Make any changes you wish, but don't insist on the *publisher* having cut or go beyond what I say in para I. According to Cockburn this is a sore point with Collins and they don't want their treachery and pusillanimity exposed." Aldington complained to his wife, Netta, on 29 April that "Collins wrote only one defensive letter—to the Booksellers' paper and that was simply to clear themselves on the possible libel."[25] Collins did not want to draw fire from the "Lawrence Bureau." AWL wrote to Liddell Hart on 26 February, "It appears to me that editors may be becoming chary of printing attacks on Aldington but would be glad to offer their public an attack on Collins for a change, and that would naturally be against A. too."

Lord Vansittart, in a review sympathetic to TEL, had unexpectedly corroborated some of Aldington's conclusions and even praised Aldington in the *Daily Telegraph* on 31 January. He stated that although he had expected more from Aldington's book, "it is well written and should be widely read," an endorsement that Collins later quoted in advertisements.[26] While agreeing that TEL courted attention, Vansittart took a stance that later reviewers quoted: "If he was a show-off he had something to show." He dismissed Aldington's "suggestion" of TEL's homosexuality since TEL "seemed sexless," but he concluded that "I do not think Mr. Aldington a hanging judge, though in this book he looks rather like one. I believe, on the contrary, that he has done good service in writing it. For it will provoke not only interest but anger, and in the clang a balance may be struck."[27] Liddell Hart sent Vansittart his reaction to this review on 7 February, enclosing a copy of "Analysis." Vansittart returned it on 9 February. He refused to alter his views, repeating that "no offer of the High Commissioner of Egypt was ever made to Lawrence in 1922."

Killing the Messenger

After publishing Vansittart's review, the *Daily Telegraph* opened its correspondence columns to some twenty-five letters about TEL. Most defended him, but on 4 February, Major R. M. S. Barton emphasized that TEL's "success" owed much to British gold, and on 10 February, General George de S. Barrow declared flatly that the Arabs had not been the first to enter Damascus. He criticized TEL's behavior in Arabia, particularly his refusal to stop "his Arabs" from "cutting the throats" of wounded Turks at Deraa.[28] On 5 February, Major General Lord Burnham attacked Liddell Hart and the "Lawrence Bureau": "If another Lawrence book had to be written, what was wanted was a reasoned assessment of the military value of his contribution to set against the absurd exaggeration of Capt. Liddell Hart in pursuance of the theory of the indirect approach." Burnham argued that "The whole Lawrence story has been clouded with prejudice and exaggeration. Richard Aldington's book is a good example of this, but it was the Lawrentians who started it." For Burnham, "Lawrence was a splendid and gallant adventurer who brought colour and inspiration into our lives at a time when we sadly needed both, and it is tragic that the adulation of his friends should have driven a costive penman into a paroxysm of debunking a rather vulnerable hero."[29]

On 12 February, Liddell Hart responded, declaring that Allenby had described TEL's work as "invaluable" and remarking caustically, "Before talking about 'the absurd exaggeration' of Lawrence's military contribution, and expressing conclusions contrary to both Commanders-in-Chief, Lord Burnham might have studied the facts." He also answered Barrow: "Lord Winterton, who was there at the time and closely acquainted with Allenby's inquiry into the matter, told me that Lawrence's account in 'The Seven Pillars' was 'completely accurate.' He authorises me to quote his testimony."[30] However, a letter from Marshal of the Royal Air Force Sir Arthur Harris, immediately following Liddell Hart's, diminished its impact. Harris wrote that "Anyone who has had the privilege of serving under Sir George, as I had on the North-West Frontier, and has experienced his invariable courtesy, kindliness and efficiency in dealing not only with his own command, but with the units of another Service at a time when overall relationships between the Services were at their lowest ebb, will accept without hesitation or reservation his opinions and his account of facts which he has at long last made public in the interests of historical accuracy."[31] Aldington's letter of 24 February disputed that Allenby had actually called TEL's military contribution "invaluable" and pointed to a minor discrepancy in Liddell Hart's quotation. On 26 February, Liddell Hart reciprocated in kind.[32]

The *Illustrated* asked Liddell Hart to respond to Aldington's "Why I Debunked the Lawrence Legend" but did not print his letter until 26 February and then sandwiched it between two pro-Aldington pieces. One, a long letter from Squadron Commander G. F. Breese, D.S.C. (Ret.), supported Aldington's view of TEL and offered comic glimpses of TEL's angling for special treatment when he was an R.A.F. recruit at Uxbridge. The other, from Major General R. Dening, declared, "Many of us soldiers in Palestine in 1918 had little doubt at the time that Lawrence was a charlatan and a self-advertiser." Liddell Hart's letter lost most of its effect when Breese and Dening countered it in the same issue.[33]

Publication of *The Mint*, TEL's account of his R.A.F. training, also helped Aldington. Breese wrote to Aldington on 10 February that "you warned me that [*The Mint*] was a scurrilous bit of Lawrence journalism but I was not prepared for such a complete tissue of lies and gross distortion of facts; I've only read two installments in [the] Sunday Times; but if it is all like that it's the worst book ever issued. However, it does one thing admirably and that is to confirm all YOU have written about L and his habits and twisted mind."[34] Major R. M. S. Barton's 29 February letter to Liddell Hart remarked that "Lawrence appears to have debunked himself in a stupid book called the Mint." Derek Marks, reviewing for the *Daily Express* on 14 February, declared that "Richard Aldington's nasty little biography published the other day did nothing to alter my opinion [that TEL was "one of the great heroes of the century"]. But now that I have read 'The Mint' I think that Lawrence merited a nasty little biography."[35] On 18 February, H. D. Ziman in the *Daily Telegraph* felt that *The Mint* "would have been turned down on at least three grounds—that the book was dull, that it was dirty, and that it was pretentious."[36] AWL wrote to Liddell Hart on 5 August, "I am surprised at the lukewarm reception of *The Mint*, which seems to me a far better book than *Seven Pillars* and likely to last. But no Arabs, no glamour, I suppose."

After the editors of *Merlin*, an English-language periodical published in Paris, asked for something on the TEL controversy, Aldington sent Kershaw material for an article.[37] Aldington preferred to let others defend his book, as he wrote to Kershaw on 6 April: "I don't want to get involved in a controversy with the Bureau. Rob Lyle is fighting the bastards in England. He squashed Kenning[ton] nicely,[38] and is tackling Hart in the Lon[don] Mag[azine]. It is much better for me to stand back and let others do the arguing, if I may count on a few helpers as I can on you." Lyle wanted *Merlin* to devote an entire issue to refuting the "Lawrence Bureau." As

Aldington wrote to Netta on 29 April, he liked the idea because "we can't be betrayed by the Lawrence Bureau bringing pressure on the editor" and because he could include "quotes of evidence I had but did not use, and evidence which came in to me spontaneously from others." *Merlin*, however, ended publication with its Spring/Summer 1955 issue.[39]

In Buenos Aires, the July/August *Sur* devoted a special issue to TEL that included Portuguese translations of Liddell Hart's *London Magazine* review, Churchill's 1937 *Great Contemporaries* tribute to TEL, Raymond Mortimer's 30 January 1955 *Sunday Times* review, and Storrs's review from the 3 February 1955 issue of the *Listener*, but this had little effect in England. Liddell Hart and others tried to prepare a pamphlet refuting Aldington, but the project collapsed when David Garnett declined to edit it, Jonathan Cape would not risk publishing it at a loss, and AWL would not release Seven Pillars Trust money to print it privately. Liddell Hart needed an editor who would provide space to refute Aldington at length and who would treat him with more consideration than had the editors of the *Daily Telegraph* and the *Illustrated*. John Lehmann, editor of the *London Magazine*, fulfilled both requirements. He had sent a telegram to Liddell Hart on 27 January 1955, a scant four days before the official publication date of Aldington's book: "If not retained for other journal will you please review Aldington[']s book together with the Mint for London Magazine." Although Lehmann wrote the next day that he was more interested in TEL the artist than in a refutation of Aldington, Liddell Hart sent a synopsis (probably "Analysis"), and Lehmann changed his mind, responding on 7 February, "I have not seen [Aldington's] nonsense answered more completely elsewhere."

When Liddell Hart's "T. E. Lawrence, Aldington and the Truth" appeared in the April 1955 *London Magazine*, Lehmann gave him every conceivable advantage. In the editor's introduction, Lehmann referred to Aldington's "reckless disregard of the revenge it will bring upon himself, in his pseudo-biographical attacks on Norman Douglas and T. E. Lawrence" and declared that "Captain Liddell Hart deals effectively with that part of Mr Aldington's new book on T. E. Lawrence which sets out to destroy the legend of Lawrence the hero of the Arab wars. Very little is left, one cannot help thinking, of the laboriously constructed case for the prosecution, after it has been riddled by Captain Liddell Hart's well-aimed bursts of machine-gun fire. . . ."[40]

After recapping his earlier *Sunday Chronicle* statements that Aldington had performed indecent "backstairs" detective work and that the entire book consisted of "smears and sneers," Liddell Hart laid out his case. Most of his points addressed Aldington's method. Aldington had "misleadingly framed" his letter of inquiry to Churchill to suggest that he had the "assistance of the executors and of the family." Aldington's letter had asked, "Was the post ever *officially* offered to Colonel Lawrence?" (with *officially* underscored), thus confusing Churchill. Amery, Lloyd, and Storrs "have all protested at the way their brief replies have been misleadingly exploited." The publisher's paraphrase of Churchill's "very likely" into "may" was deceptive. Aldington used misleading quotations. His selection of sources was slanted. He had misrepresented TEL's involvement in the surrender of Erzerum and the landing at Alexandretta. TEL had definitely received approaches regarding "Home Defence," Colonel S. F. Newcombe had firsthand evidence from Jemal Pasha that the Turks had offered a substantial reward for TEL's capture, and Allenby saw TEL's support as "invaluable." Liddell Hart's most convincing point was that Aldington misunderstood the importance of taking Akaba from the land. Although Akaba had fallen twice before, taken both times from the sea, on each occasion the Turks had driven out the Allies from the landward side. Liddell Hart made Aldington look both dishonest and careless.

Lyle, to whom Aldington had provided material, sent four and a half single-spaced pages of rebuttal to the *London Magazine*.[41] Lehmann wrote to Liddell Hart on 6 April that "A long letter has come in from a poet called Rob Lyle (I suspect the letter is really instigated and perhaps even written by Aldington), attempting to refute your article on Lawrence. The skill in it does not seem to me equal to the anger, and it seems to rely chiefly on long quotations from General Rankin. However, I shall have to publish it, though not necessarily in full, and I feel I ought to have your comments to add immediately at the end." Lyle had devoted more than a full single-spaced page to a sarcastic exposition of Liddell Hart's deficiencies as a biographer and an historian. Before sending the letter to Liddell Hart, Lehmann insisted that Lyle cut that page. On 14 April, Liddell Hart wrote that he was still awaiting Lyle's letter. By return post, without identifying the nature of the cuts, Lehmann wrote that Lyle "asked for his letter back to make some changes, and is also trying to object to me [*sic*] cutting various paragraphs out of it. I have told him that I must exercise my absolute editorial right to limit the space—far too much anyway, even with the cuts." After Lyle had made the required deletions, Lehmann sent the revised letter to Liddell Hart on 18 April, remarking that it could appear with a response in the June issue "if you're speedy!" Liddell Hart received Lyle's letter on

19 April, began his rebuttal that evening, finished it at 2:30 A.M. on 20 April, and sent it to Lehmann in that morning's post.

Refuting Liddell Hart's claim that he "had only a short time to check" Aldington's statements, Lyle pointed out that Liddell Hart "had access to the proofs in 1954. Were the book really such a tissue of falsehood, this would seem an adequate period in which to produce some real evidence to that effect. Instead we are treated to minor points, quibbles and, where necessary, downright falsifications." He remarked how odd it was that Churchill was unable to recall any "Egypt" offer until four years after he had repudiated it as "certainly unfounded" and dealt rapidly with other points before quoting an interview with General George Rankin from the 2 March Melbourne *Argus*, which had serialized Aldington's book. Rankin had commanded Australia's 4th Light Horse in Palestine and Sinai and had threatened to shoot TEL in Damascus unless he controlled "his" looting Arabs. Lyle quoted Rankin's report of a conversation: "I once asked Newcombe: 'Why do you stand this little tinpot fake swaggering around taking whatever kudos is going?' Newcombe replied: 'I am a regular Army officer, and it is not my job to attract attention to myself. Besides, it wouldn't help my work.' "

When Liddell Hart had seen Lyle's letter on 19 April, he had asked Newcombe, "Did you ever meet Rankin, and is there the slightest justification for his story?" Newcombe replied on 20 April that he "must have met" Rankin "sometime, somewhere if he says so" and that his comment to Rankin probably had been his way of saying tactfully, "Don't ask stupid questions." Liddell Hart nevertheless declared in print that General Rankin's "alleged talk" with Newcombe could not have occurred because Newcombe, who had been captured by the Turks, was not in Damascus when Rankin arrived, as if Rankin and Newcombe could have talked only in Damascus.[42] He suggested that Lyle, compared with Aldington, was merely "a novice in the art of distortion" and that Aldington had lied when his inquiry to Churchill had claimed "the assistance of the executors and the family." Lyle, outraged, wrote to the editor of the *London Magazine* on 23 May, the day he saw the June issue: "I must concede Captain Liddell Hart a point. Confronted by the example of such a master, I confess myself a novice in the art of distortion. Indeed, I have never aspired to any success in this field, let alone to the eminence which Captain Liddell Hart enjoys."[43] Lehmann did not publish Lyle's letter.

When Aldington saw the Lyle/Liddell Hart exchange, he wrote to Kershaw on 22 May for documentation that TEL's family and executor had supported his early inquiries: "It is too much to be called a liar for telling the truth!" Aldington immediately sent his rebuttal to Lehmann, who forwarded it to Liddell Hart. Kershaw then found Raymond Savage's 6 October 1950 letter proving that Aldington had not lied, and Aldington's 11 June letter to Lehmann quoted Savage: "I thought the best thing I could do was to wait until A. W. Lawrence got back to Cambridge before the beginning of Term and go up and talk to him about the whole thing for Aldington. Accordingly I went to Cambridge yesterday with a result which I am sure will please Aldington. A. W. has now become really co-operative and interested in Aldington's project."[44] When Liddell Hart sent his refutation of Aldington's earlier letter to *London Magazine* Assistant Editor David Hughes on 21 June, he wrote, "I presume you are not intending to publish Aldington's second letter (of the 11th June) in this issue, and have made an amendment to mine on that presumption." The editors did not print Aldington's 11 June letter, so Liddell Hart did not have to address its evidence.

Aldington's earlier letter appeared with Liddell Hart's rebuttal in August.[45] Aldington did not have a copy of Lord Hope's letter to Churchill and, relying on memory, he blundered by denying any claim of assistance from TEL's executors and family. Instead of retracting his earlier accusation that Aldington had lied, Liddell Hart simply pointed out that Hope's letter had mentioned such assistance, making clear in the process that Lehmann, who had "been shown the letter," could corroborate this. To Aldington's argument that Churchill had altered his original position on "Egypt," which had been unequivocal, Liddell Hart responded that Aldington's query had misled Churchill by asking "Was the post ever *officially* offered to Colonel Lawrence?" as if that were the entire question although Hope's letter (from Liddell Hart's file copy) had asked about unofficial offers as well: "(1). The statement has been made that Mr. Churchill 'tried to persuade' Colonel Lawrence to take over the post of High Commissioner of Egypt from Lord Allenby. Is this true? Was this post ever *officially* offered to Colonel Lawrence? Or, did Mr. Churchill ever mention it as a possibility, unofficially, in private conversation?"[46]

Aldington observed that Graves's statement about TEL's having read fifty thousand books in six years had been "read and passed" by TEL before it appeared in Graves's biography (despite the published denial that TEL had seen the book) and that Liddell Hart's qualification that TEL had claimed to read the books "which interested me" was not in print until

1938. Liddell Hart deflected attention from the fifty thousand figure by retorting that TEL had read only Graves's first draft and had not vetted the passage that Aldington quoted. The exaggeration, however, was TEL's. TEL himself had written on Graves's typescript, "You might perhaps help the outside public, by basing my knowledge on my really wide reading. I read every book which interested me in the library of the Oxford Union (best part of 50,000 vols. I expect) in 6 years."[47]

Aldington's book misquoted Lord Milner's comment as "although I am aware that I have almost every other Government authority, military and diplomatic, against me, I am totally opposed to the idea of trying to diddle the French out of Syria."[48] Lloyd George's *Truth About the Peace Treaties* had it as "My own opinion on the subject is very clear, although I am aware that I have almost every other Government authority military and diplomatic against me. I am totally opposed to the idea of trying to diddle the French out of Syria." Aldington argued that his unintended error of transcription had not changed Milner's meaning. Liddell Hart responded that Aldington had taken Milner's statement out of the context of the paragraphs preceding it. In his April *London Magazine* review, he had referred to Milner's clear endorsement of the British policy: "we had no desire to play the French out of Syria or to try to get Syria for ourselves." The quotation that Liddell Hart offers as official British policy, however, was not that at all, but what Milner had said to Clemenceau. Milner indicated his own doubt whether "we had no desire to play the French out of Syria or to try to get Syria for ourselves" was an accurate expression of official policy. He told Lloyd George, "I did not wish to go any deeper into it, until I was quite sure that I was pursuing a policy in accordance with your views."[49] Liddell Hart counted on the inability or unwillingness of his readers to consult Aldington's source, and he was undoubtedly correct in his assumption that they would not trouble to look up the passage to verify his statements.

Aldington also asked why, if TEL's version of his role in the "arranged surrender" of Erzerum was true, A. P. Wavell had described the Russian capture of Erzerum in the *Encyclopedia Britannica* as "one of the finest feats of arms of the whole War" and why Liddell Hart, who had commissioned Wavell to write the article, had failed to correct it. Liddell Hart retorted that Wavell had received the assignment before Liddell Hart became the *Encyclopedia Britannica*'s military editor and that Wavell had not been on the scene anyway. While implicitly disavowing Wavell's version, Liddell Hart had actually commended it on 14 January 1926: "I simply cannot refrain from a note of congratulation—it combines literary style with clearness and simplicity, perfectly easy to follow and yet of value to military as well as general readers. In fact it is, ideally, what I should like such articles in the E.B. to be—and if only a few more were like it I should feel happier over the general result of the military section."[50] (John Connell's biography of Wavell did not make this letter available until 1965, three years after Aldington's death.)

Liddell Hart ended his *London Magazine* response with the sentence, "It is a pity that Mr Aldington has not reserved his extraordinary imagination and inventive powers for the realm of fiction, to which he formerly devoted his efforts." Since this exchange was the only extended debate between Aldington and Liddell Hart, having the last word was important, and Liddell Hart was becoming weary of the struggle. He had complained to W. F. Stirling on 20 June, "That bloody man has wasted an appalling amount of my working time, and thus cost me a lot of money during the last eighteen months—while himself enjoying ill-gotten gains far exceeding what he could have gained by writing decent books." He wrote to Storrs on 21 June, "while Aldington's view of Lawrence has been generally rejected by reviewers, his accompanying view of the 'Lawrence Bureau' seems to have been swallowed by many who have forgotten or never studied the original books." When Liddell Hart had sent his rebuttal to Hughes on 21 June, he had commented, "I only hope that the Editor will now 'call it a day.' " The editor complied. Immediately after Liddell Hart's rebuttal came the announcement, "*This correspondence is now closed—Editor.*"

Coping with M. R. Lawrence's reaction to Aldington's exposure of the family secret had intensified Liddell Hart's resolve to end the matter once and for all. The birth certificate linking M. R. Lawrence with Montagu Robert Chapman, son of Thomas R. Chapman and Sarah Chapman, *née* Laurence, had convinced Jix that it was legally safe to reveal TEL's illegitimacy. TEL had not learned the full story of his origins from Sarah Lawrence until 1919, after his father's death.[51] His brothers Frank and Will, both killed in 1915, probably never knew. AWL told John E. Mack that he had learned the story from TEL in 1922 or 1923.[52] In his seventieth year, M. R. Lawrence still believed that his parents had married. Peter D. Whitney, the *New York Times* London correspondent, had reported on 6 February that "Incredible though it may seem, Lawrence's elder brother, Robert, a retired medical missionary in his sixties, did not know the truth until last year,"[53] but M. R. Lawrence still did not believe it. On 29 April 1954, Eric Kennington had written to Liddell Hart that at AWL's request, Celandine Kennington had informed TEL's elder brother that Aldington was about to reveal Sarah Lawrence's adultery and her children's illegitimacy, discussing the matter as if he knew the truth. She emphasized that AWL "wanted *him* to know so he could protect Mum." Even then, he refused to accept that his parents had not married.

On 23 February 1955, M. R. Lawrence wrote to Liddell Hart, "I do *not* believe this story of Ned being illegitimate. I know Father and Mother too well." He wanted documentation that would prove libel, but his mother had told him that his birth certificate had been destroyed when the Dublin law court had burned, "and I have wondered if the marriage certificate was destroyed at the same time." Lady Kathleen Liddell Hart recalls that her husband spent four hours in the garden one afternoon trying to convince him that the revelation about his parents was true.[54] Even this was not enough, but on 3 March, he wrote to Liddell Hart that "a *private* note" from AWL "alters matters considerably. Please take *no* action about the letter I sent you on 1st March written on 28 February, and do not allude to it in writing to us both." After accepting the truth, he tried to shield his mother from the news that Aldington had exposed the family secret.

Shortly after the *London Magazine* exchanges, Collins arranged for Henry Regnery to publish Aldington's book in the United States. Aldington learned of the October publication date not from Collins, but from Regnery's fall list. He wrote to Regnery on 25 August to describe the reviewing controversy in England and to report that the book had sold 31,709 copies as of 31 May 1955. When Regnery responded to Aldington on 15 September, he was encouraging: the advance sales figure of approximately 3,000 was promising, *Life* planned to feature "a major article," the *Atlantic* planned to publish an essay on the controversy, "and I am sure that Time will take up the issue."[55] Two years earlier, Aldington had accused Collins of deliberately delaying the U.S. edition so that he could export more copies, which would be profitable for him but not for Aldington since the reduced demand for a later U.S. edition would make it harder to find a publisher willing to pay more than a small advance. This is almost exactly what happened. Regnery paid an advance of only $3,000 and, on 29 September, reported that "Our sale, of course, will be somewhat reduced by the fact that the English edition was widely circulated in this country." *Time* had decided not to review the U.S. edition since there had been a major feature article in February in response to the English edition,[56] and *Life* had decided not to run the promised feature article.

Regnery wrote to Aldington on 16 November that "Most of the Reviews . . . have been rather unfavorable. We have sold only about 4,000 copies and will sell another two or three thousand, only with considerable difficulty." Vincent Sheean, a longtime friend of Lowell Thomas, called the book "a tirade of great venom" in the *New York Herald-Tribune Book Review* (25 September).[57] Carlos Baker in the *New York Times Book Review* (2 October) found it "tedious and pedantic."[58] In November, the *Atlantic* reprinted Liddell Hart's April *London Magazine* essay as "T. E. Lawrence: Man or Myth?"[59] Aldington wrote to the *New York Herald-Tribune* on 3 October to protest Sheean's review, offering his own evidence, but Irita van Doren responded that there was no space. When Aldington wrote to the *Atlantic* on 12 December that Liddell Hart's article was "the product of personal *animus*" and had "already been published in *The London Magazine* where its quibbles and mis-statements were exposed by Mr Robert Lyle and myself," the *Atlantic* declined to print his letter.[60] Two of his letters appeared in the *Montreal Gazette*,[61] but these had little impact elsewhere. Liddell Hart wrote to John Connell on 3 March 1956, "It may amuse you to hear that Aldington keeps on replying at great length to criticisms of his book in papers in remoter parts of the world, but seems to avoid the more central arenas where he could be refuted." Aldington, however, lacking access to "more central arenas," was defending his book wherever editors would provide space.

Lowell Thomas had stayed out of the Aldington controversy for the most part. He wrote to Liddell Hart on 31 March 1955, "The way in which T. E.'s countrymen came forth in rebuttal seemed to me to make it unnecessary to add my voice."[62] Nevertheless, he reviewed Aldington's book in *Middle East Journal* (Spring 1955),[63] and in a new edition of *With Lawrence in Arabia*, he added a preface that reiterated points from his March 1954 radio broadcast, addressed Aldington's comments about Thomas's role in creating the TEL legend, and quoted the letters that he had written to Aldington. As Thomas put it, "Now I know that I should have been more careful of what I said; that is, careful to make myself clear." He also added an appendix, "Notes in Defense of Lawrence," supporting his argument with quotations from hostile reviews of Aldington's book. Thomas's "Defense" thus became part of the record in a form more durable than ephemeral newspaper reviews. Those reading or rereading Thomas's TEL book would be more likely to reject Aldington's conclusions in the face of so much authoritative disapproval.[64]

Flora Armitage, Middle East Information Officer for the British Information Agency in New York, also provided a rebuttal of Aldington. She had been working on her TEL biography for almost a decade when she heard (presumably from the *New York Times* summary of the January 1954 *Evening Standard* announcement)[65] about Aldington's book. She wrote to Liddell Hart on 25 January 1954, "If, as Mr. Aldington says, the facts are completely falsified then, of course, the whole structure of my book collapses. For if the essential facts of Seven Pillars are a tissue of lies, then what Lawrence was before the war is irrelevant, and what he was afterwards loses all its force." Liddell Hart's response of 9 April was encouraging: "There is certainly no need to worry about the effect of his book on the one that you have been writing. Indeed, there may be all the more call for truthful books about Lawrence." After assuring her that Aldington had no firsthand information and that Liddell Hart had been sending evidence to Collins, he suggested that Aldington's book might not appear at all, adding that "no decent person would" reveal TEL's illegitimacy while his mother lived.

Armitage continued to correspond with Liddell Hart while she completed her research. After Aldington's book had appeared, she informed Liddell Hart on 10 April 1955 that "The letters to Mrs. Shaw in the British Museum were read for me and a precis sent me of the contents; and according to that precis Aldington has completely distorted Lawrence's confession to Mrs. Shaw." Although Liddell Hart had been unable to substantiate TEL's claim of a prewar enlistment in the Royal Artillery, Armitage believed TEL. She wrote to Liddell Hart on 21 April, "You will probably be interested to learn that, in view of Aldington's wild speculations, I tried to get to the bottom of the early enlistment by writing Arnold Lawrence. He replied that he knew nothing about it and that his elder brother (Dr. M. R. Lawrence) was of the opinion it never happened. Do you believe this? I don't. They are an odd family."

Henry Holt published Armitage's book in the United States on 29 August 1955. Her preface stated that Aldington's publication of TEL's illegitimacy had forced her to include the circumstances rather than to withhold them, that Thomas Jones had earlier revealed the facts "quietly and without ostentation," and that "the importance given the later revelation [by Aldington] is both exaggerated and misleading." She added that, "Shorn of its cumbersome detail, the main indictment of Aldington's *Biographical Enquiry* does not contain any strictures harder than those Lawrence imposed on himself and his actions."[66] As she wrote to Liddell Hart on 5 August, "My own disadvantage is that I have produced no new and startling revelations." The English edition, which did not appear until May 1956, included "Epilogue—The Imposter," a refutation of Aldington.[67] In one sense it boomeranged, for it called reviewers' attention to the contrast between Aldington's attempts to verify his statements and Armitage's glossing over the issues that he had made controversial. Aldington had written to William Dibben on 15 November, pointing out Armitage's connection to the British Information Agency, which he called "propaganda in N.Y.!": "I have suspected for some time that there was British official interference to stop the book and discredit me."[68]

In July 1957, Gordon Landsborough, managing director of Four Square Books, became interested in publishing a softcover edition. When Rosica Colin, Aldington's London agent, asked Collins the cost of paperback rights, he astonished her by demanding £1,000 (half that sum would have been high) and a share of the royalties. To her surprise, and perhaps to Collins's, Four Square paid, bringing out the paperback in November 1957. Aldington updated this edition, securing permission from General Rankin to quote the Melbourne *Argus* interview, from Squadron Commander Breese to quote his impressions of TEL as an R.A.F. recruit, and from Foreign Office official T. F. Breen to quote his account of the private audience during which TEL refused honors offered by George V. After the Four Square edition appeared, Aldington informed his brother, Tony, on 4 December 1957 that "The reprint of TEL is or seems to be faintly reviving the controversy with more people on my side. The views now are (1) that I am still a frightful cad and louse for libelling Our National Hero, (2) that he was on the way out anyway and my book had little to do with his downfall."[69] Landsborough wrote to Aldington on 20 February 1958 that "It may interest you to know that LAWRENCE OF ARABIA has virtually sold out its first printing of 30,000 copies."[70]

Aldington wrote to Lawrence Durrell on 6 November 1958,

> I couldn't get worked up to righteous indignation over Pasternak. It seems to me nearly as much a misuse of political power and attempt to stifle free speech that Winston Churchill, as P.M., signed two snivelling and quibbling letters on official Downing St paper, and sent his emissary, a journalist hack called Liddell Hart, (a) to try to bully Collins out of publishing my TEL, and when that failed (b) to bully editors and journalists into writing and publishing the stuff I showed you. The only difference is that the Russians have no Pecksniff stuff about it. I may add that Collins only published the book to get back their advance. As soon as that was done, they closed down, and said there was "no demand." Landsborough has since sold nearly another 40,000, but one gets nothing on those reprints.[71]

By 30 November 1961, as Aldington wrote to Eunice Black, his paperback TEL book had sold 42,848 copies and the original hardback some 30,000, "proving that the really desperate and unscrupulous efforts of the Lawrence Bureau to discredit and suppress the book have failed."[72]

A more long-range indicator of ultimate influence lay in recognition from serious scholars. Aldington received a letter dated 15 August 1957 from Anita Engle, then working on *The Nili Spies*, a history of the Israeli espionage group organized by Aaron and Sarah Aaronsohn that had provided valuable intelligence to Allenby. Engle's letter was heartening: "I've just read your 'Lawrence of Arabia.' From the review of Harold Nicolson, and that in the New Statesman [by David Garnett], I was under the impression that it was a venomous, distorted sort of book. I can't think why the reviewers have taken this attitude, as I find your book perfectly straightforward, unstrained and exceptionally fascinating. Do you think the objections come because of your revelations, not of Lawrence, but of others, rather more important than he?" Engle added, "Lawrence will take a small part in my book, for I have real deeds of real people to write about."[73]

Aldington promised Engle a copy of the forthcoming Four Square edition, complete with new material. Engle had sent him new information, but the Four Square edition was too far along in production for insertions. His descriptions of behind-the-scenes efforts to suppress him made Engle uneasy about the reception of her own book, but when *The Nili Spies* appeared in 1959, the reviews were favorable. Aldington was particularly pleased with some of her published comments: that "Lawrence claimed [the work of Nili] as part of his own achievements," that Lawrence and his Arabs confined most of their raids to areas well outside the danger zone, that "the whole story of the connection between Sarah [erroneously identified as the S. A. to whom TEL dedicated *Seven Pillars*] and Lawrence was started at least a year after Lawrence's death," and that various people spun tales to connect TEL with Nili because "no story about the Middle East during World War I would amount to a row of beans unless Lawrence could be dragged into it somehow." Engle's final chapter, "The Lawrence-Sarah Myth," disposed of the Sarah Aaronsohn/S. A. connection unequivocally, and Aldington appreciated Engle's quotation (translated from French) of Aaron Aaronsohn's assessment of TEL: "A little snot."[74]

Although many privately supported some of Aldington's findings, few corroborated him openly. Aldington had written gleefully to Eric Warman on 15 August 1956 that "an article in the N.Y. Nation by C. P. Snow says that although the 'Establishment' rallied against me to a man *publicly*, they now admit *in private* that I am at least 85% right."[75] (Snow had actually written "Yet in private, it is now tacitly assumed that in at least 80 per cent of his case, Aldington was right."[76] Aldington had the "80%" right in other letters.) In 1958, Lord Vansittart's memoirs, *The Mist Procession*, while sympathetic to TEL, dismissed the "Egypt" offer as fantasy:

> There is no truth in Lawrence's intimation that the job was offered to him. Even less substance is in his claim to have had the chance in 1922. The appointment lay with Curzon. If Winston had ever foolishly proposed Lawrence I should have heard, for Curzon would have laughed him out of court, and the laughter would not have been kind. Still more untruthful is the suggestion that anyone ever thought seriously of pushing out Maurice Hankey to let in Lawrence as Secretary of the Cabinet. Lawrence would have been fantastic in any high officialdom. Montagu Norman was mad enough to want the Prince of Mecca for Secretary of the Bank of England. Everyone was indeed potty about this flood-lit man, who deserved his Bath and Distinguished Service Order but nothing like apotheosis. What a gifted pair of *poseurs* Monty [Field Marshal Sir Bernard Montgomery] and T. E. would have made! . . .
> We could not risk fantasy in Egypt. . . . [77]

In *Middle East Diary* (1959), Richard Meinertzhagen purported to describe the basis of TEL's "Egypt" claims:

> Aldington explodes the myth that Lawrence was offered the High Commissionership of Egypt in succession to Allenby who threatened resignation. This must refer to an occasion in 1922 when, after a conference in Churchill's room at the Colonial Office, the question of Allenby's resignation was discussed. Churchill put his hand on Lawrence's shoulder saying "I think we shall have to send you out to Egypt." It was not intended seriously. We all smiled and thought it a harmless little joke. But I have little doubt that Lawrence let it be known to many friends that it was a serious offer.

Meinertzhagen supported many of Aldington's findings:

> Richard Aldington has just published a book exploding the Lawrence Myth. It is a venomous book but true. Lawrence was the victim of his own desire for publicity but I blame the so-called Lawrence Bureau for pushing him into such an impossible position—men like Lowell Thomas, Storrs, and his own family. There are also men like Lloyd George, Winston Churchill, Allenby and Wavell who helped erect the myth and made the most extravagant claims for Lawrence's military genius. Lawrence had

great charm, great ability and was in many ways a genius; he used all these virtues for deception. Not one single one of the men mentioned above had any first-hand knowledge of Lawrence's Arabian exploits, having gained their knowledge from Lawrence himself and from what he spread about, knowing it to be either false or exaggerated. Comparing him with Napoleon and Hannibal is just nonsense for Lawrence never commanded anything but a looting rabble of murderous Arab levies, he took part in no major military operation and his desert exploits had not the slightest bearing on Allenby's campaign. In his own words, his was a "side-show of a side-show."

He called *Seven Pillars* "a lie based on fact" and claimed that TEL "had no use for women, his sexual inclination being big strong men."[78]

Aldington wrote to Eunice Black on 10 September 1960 to thank her for alerting him to Meinertzhagen's *Middle East Diary*. "After much delay I managed to get the book, and the whole passage (by TEL's best friend) is simply devastating. I sent it to London and N.Y. Times, which both find excuses for not issuing it! And yet any silly pro-Lawrence lie is given full publicity. Of course, the Lawrence Myth is part of British government propaganda, and as long as they can block the truth, they'll do it. . . . The book seems to have been ignored in England."[79] Aldington did not realize that Meinertzhagen, embittered by history's neglect of his own deeds and veneration of TEL, had altered his diaries for publication. Meinertzhagen's so-called contemporary entries about TEL, written long after the fact, may actually have used Aldington's book as a source.[80]

Stanley Weintraub wrote to Aldington in October 1958 with questions about the relationship between TEL and Bernard Shaw. On 5 November, Aldington responded with information about the TEL/Charlotte Shaw letters and a warning not to use the sanitized 1954 version of *T. E. Lawrence by His Friends*, and he sent a copy of the Four Square edition with his handwritten corrections. His letter of 14 September offered "An astounding story which of course I cannot use" from Somerset Maugham "that the head of Scotland Yard (obviously Lord Trenchard) said TEL's death was no accident, but suicide. He had been using Clouds Hill as a rendezvous with private soldiers, and almost openly, relying on his quasi-immunity as the 'prince of Mecca.' Nothing was done while he was in the RAF, but within a few weeks after his discharge, the usual warrant was issued, and the usual inspector in plain clothes called to give the 24 hours warning to get out of England, or . . . [ellipsis in original]. TEL preferred suicide." He added, "I am sure Maugham would not have passed it to me if he had not had it from the head of Scotland Yard."[81] He warned Weintraub, as he had Engle, to expect opposition to a book unfavorable to TEL. On 28 September 1959, he wrote that Vansittart "admits that the claim to 'Egypt' was a falsehood— and Winston Churchill wrote two letters on Downing St notepaper trying to pretend it was true! Nize peepul. Watch out."

On the same day, Aldington sent a letter to support Weintraub's application for a Guggenheim fellowship. Aldington may have done more harm than good. He wrote to his brother on 22 October that when he had recommended Weintraub, "in my confidential report to the Guggs I spilled the beans, right down to Willy Maugham's tale that the Col committed suicide because there was a warrant out against him for buggering H.M.'s troops. Maugham swears he got that from Trenchard." After the Guggenheim Foundation turned Weintraub down, Aldington informed him on 14 September 1960 that " 'they' are afraid of any honest and impartial investigation." Aldington hoped to encourage Weintraub to prove what he himself could not. On 12 August 1961, he wrote, "It is a typical piece of 'Lawrence' impudence for AWL to persuade the Bodleian to withhold their TES [T. E. Shaw] material from honest researchers. Obviously there is a lot they are desperately trying to hide, just as they made every effort, dirty and otherwise, to prevent the publication of my Enquiry—which in the then state of knowledge could only be an Enquiry and not a definitive biography, which you ought to undertake some day."

On 10 September 1961, the *Sunday Times* ran the first of two extracts from a new TEL book by Anthony Nutting, then serving as "political advisor" for Sam Spiegel's *Lawrence of Arabia* film.[82] Nutting accused Aldington of dishonest scholarship: "Richard Aldington . . . claims that Lawrence did not in fact resist the Bey's homosexual advances and asserts that he admitted as much in a letter to Mrs. George Bernard Shaw. But the letter in which this alleged confession was made, and which Aldington states was in the British Museum when he wrote his biography, cannot today be traced." Weintraub wrote to Aldington on 30 September that he had sent "an indignant letter to the editor announcing that I had just re-read the letter. . . . But (as you may have seen) the *STimes* didn't print mine (so they wrote me) because another letter actually quoted the 'missing' letter." On 17 September, the *Sunday Times* had printed K. J. Fielding's letter, quoting TEL's 16 March 1924 statement that "I gave away the only possession we are born into the world with—our bodily integrity."[83] Weintraub commented, "The fact that the *Sunday Times* actually violated the Lawrence Trust copyrights . . . seems to have escaped them. But at least your state-

ment is now actually confirmed by the quotation, which has received the
Sunday Times's wide circulation."[84] Aldington wrote to Kershaw on 15 October, "Anyway, it is something that two people at least have seen the original, and cared enough to protest."

In the 17 September extract, Nutting referred to TEL's "silly pretensions that he had been offered the Secretaryship of the Cabinet, the High Commission in Egypt and other high-ranking positions." Liddell Hart wrote to Nutting the following day that he "was glad to see . . . you effectively contradicted the insinuations about Lawrence's homosexuality" but that he "was surprised and dismayed" that Nutting "spoke of his 'silly pretensions' about the high-ranking positions he had been offered." He referred Nutting to his *London Magazine* review of Aldington, adding, "I hope that a correction may still be possible before your book is printed." Nutting responded on 25 September that "I must of course accept what you say about the 'Secretaryship of the Cabinet,' but I would just say that other sources give me information contrary to your own on this score." After subsequent exchanges, Nutting emended the offensive sentence: "Hence his anxiety that it should be known that he had been offered the Secretaryship of the Committee of Imperial Defence and other high-ranking positions."[85]

In *Lawrence of Arabia: The Man and the Motive*, Nutting did not accuse Aldington of citing a non-existent letter, stating instead that Aldington "claims that Lawrence did not in fact resist the Bey's homosexual advances and asserts that he admitted as much in a letter to Mrs. George Bernard Shaw. But Aldington is as usual misleading his readers for this letter makes it perfectly clear that Lawrence had first resisted and only to save himself *further* torture eventually gave in."[86] Aldington had not misled his readers on this point. He had stated, "The truth was (he admits in this letter) that he had not been able to endure, and, to escape further torture of flogging, had yielded to the Bey's pederasty and so secured a respite and ultimate escape."[87] Whatever Nutting's source for Aldington's "misleading" statement, it was not Aldington's book.

Nutting took TEL from birth to the Arab Revolt in seven pages, and most of his text was essentially a paraphrase of *Seven Pillars*. TEL's "motive," featured in Nutting's title, appeared in a short concluding chapter that added nothing to the *Sunday Times* excerpt. Reviewers complained that Nutting might have written an essay instead of a book that merely followed the well-worn path of the established TEL legend, and they had little to report beyond Nutting's role as political advisor for the forthcoming TEL film and

140

Killing the Messenger

his connection with Anthony Eden's government. The reviewers missed the significance of Nutting's references to TEL's masochism and scourgings, but Liddell Hart had not. He wrote to Lord Winterton on 19 September 1961, "I am more anxious about Nutting's emphasis on T.E.'s masochism and 'habit of scourging himself' and wonder where Nutting obtained what he terms this 'known fact.' But it would be wiser not to press this point, or raise an argument about it in a public way."

The reviewer in the 20 October *Times Literary Supplement* angered Liddell Hart with the comment that "it was only the subsequent adulators, such as Mr. Robert Graves and Captain Liddell Hart, who provided Mr. Aldington with his opportunity by their ludicrous comparisons of Lawrence with Alexander the Great, Hannibal, Marlborough and Napoleon." The reviewer also disputed Nutting's statement that TEL "now knew that the best way to defeat the Turks was to avoid them" and remarked, "No one ever defeated an enemy by avoiding him: all that can be done by avoiding the enemy is to leave him to someone else to defeat. Otherwise he will never be defeated."[88] This double assault on his TEL biography and military theories was intolerable to Liddell Hart. He wrote a long letter on 25 October that the *Times Literary Supplement* printed on 3 November. To counter the comment that his comparisons of TEL with great leaders were "ludicrous," he specified the basis for his claims and cited supporting testimony from Churchill. To defend the notion that one could defeat an enemy by avoiding direct confrontations, he quoted Mao Tse-tung's dictum, "Avoid the solid, attack the hollow." He maintained that "Allenby could not have defeated the Turks without Lawrence" and that Allenby had said as much.

The *Times Literary Supplement* reviewer's response, printed at the end of Liddell Hart's letter, was blunt. He remarked that Liddell Hart "understandably wishes to adhere to the opinions which he formed in the 1920s, but other people must be allowed to revise earlier judgments in the light of later knowledge. In that process Mr. Aldington played an undeniable part, although it is common ground that he went much too far." He then stressed that TEL "materially helped Allenby's campaign, but he only *helped* it" and that Mao had not won by avoiding engagements with the enemy, as "his crushing victories in 1949" clearly demonstrated.[89] Liddell Hart wrote to Nutting on 7 November that "The reviewer's reply seemed to me very feeble, too feeble, in fact, to be worth answering." Aldington wrote to Eric Warman on 22 November that "Liddell Hart tried one of his bully-bluster letters to the TLS, and was quietly bashed down by the reviewer."

Weintraub reviewed the U.S. edition of Nutting's book in the 31 December 1961 issue of the *New York Times Book Review*. He commented that "no new study of Lawrence can escape the impact of Richard Aldington's controversial 'Lawrence of Arabia' (1955), which hacks away at the Lawrence image by disclosing Lawrence's suppressed shame resulting from his boyhood discovery of his illegitimacy, by evaluating acidly the contradictory statements by Lawrence about himself and his exploits, and by hypothesizing from some evidence and much inference that Lawrence had homosexual leanings."[90] Aldington appreciated both these comments and the statement that Nutting's accusation about the British Museum letter was demonstrably false. Weintraub had also been corresponding with Liddell Hart, to whom he wrote on 24 June 1962 that Nutting's "book had nothing new to contribute—which I indicated." Liddell Hart, no doubt relieved that Weintraub had not referred to Nutting's comments about TEL's masochism and scourgings, responded on 11 July, "It was refreshing to read such a discerning review."

Writing to Weintraub on 23 February 1962, Aldington summarized recent publications about TEL:

> The results of my original research are appropriated without acknowledgment; my name is coupled with abusive adjectives to arouse reader prejudice; I am accused of fabricating a document (Nutting) and of saying that L. joined the RAF for publicity when in fact I said it was mainly to escape his mother (Wheeler)[91] as L. himself wrote to Mrs. GBS; decisive evidence such as that of e.g. Meinertzhagen is ignored; other evidence is ignored or manipulated; and in the end we are left with a picture of a "complex" but maligned hero, but still a hero—who can make dollars for Rattigan [in his 1960 play *Ross*] and Spiegel [in the forthcoming film *Lawrence of Arabia*], and get Nutting back into Parliament.

Despite his grousing, Aldington was rather pleased with himself. The Nutting book increased sales of the Four Square edition. He was hopeful that Crowell-Collier would issue his TEL book in paperback in the United States, and he expected Weintraub's book to support his major conclusions about TEL.

Weintraub, however, had to consider the reaction of AWL, as he wrote to Norman T. Gates on 30 April 1991: "My problem in doing PRIVATE SHAW AND PUBLIC SHAW, which RA hoped might confirm some of the allegations he had picked up but couldn't prove, was that I had Arnold Lawrence sitting on me. Permission to quote was dependent entirely upon him and he had the last word on what I could or couldn't use."[92] As Weintraub later recalled, "For PRIVATE SHAW AND PUBLIC SHAW, AWL charged me 11% of my royalties to use TEL quotes, and retained a veto over what I used. . . . And he wanted to see the whole text—not just the quotes, so I couldn't be evasive through paraphrase. That meant, in those pre-Xerox days, sending him a large packet of onion-skin carbon copies. And I could use no publisher but TEL's own, Jonathan Cape, which gave their editors a lot of additional control."[93] When AWL responded on 15 April 1962 to Weintraub's request for permissions, he obliquely indicated this when he commented, "I can report to my co-Trustees that none of your individual quotations requires their attention."[94]

Weintraub's purpose was to illuminate the TEL/G.B.S. relationship, not to attack TEL or the "Lawrence Bureau." As Weintraub stated in his preface, it was of "no consequence" to his subject "whether [TEL's] reports of his military or diplomatic or personal activities then—or recounted later—were fact, hyperbole, or fantasy." Still, Aldington would have been pleased to see that Weintraub referred to TEL's lack of reliability, that he cited Aldington occasionally as an authority, that he sometimes contradicted Liddell Hart's view, and that he quoted Charlotte Shaw's comment that TEL was "such an INFERNAL liar." Weintraub made a number of points consistent with Aldington's book: that TEL aided and abetted his legend-makers, that TEL frequently "posed," and that TEL's "extravagant assistance" to Liddell Hart was "a response which often overwhelms the writer's critical faculties." [95] Aldington did not live to read Weintraub's book, but he recognized the truth in Kershaw's letter to him dated 3 November 1961: "you cannot deny that your Tribute to the Colonel has done its job. Ten years ago, nobody would have questioned anything about him: now nobody can refer to him without at least conceding that he was 50% phoney. And the rest will follow." [96]

It is unlikely that Aldington saw Christopher Sykes's 20 July 1962 review of AWL's edition of *Letters to T. E. Lawrence*, but he would have found evidence that "the rest will follow" in some of Sykes's comments. Sykes complained of the volume that "the correctives only affect relatively minor considerations; the great blot on Lawrence's reputation, his chronic untruthfulness, is not seriously touched on," and he presented Meinertzhagen's *Middle East Diary* as evidence that the charge of TEL's lying "cannot be dismissed as a prejudiced accusation."[97] Aldington wrote to Eunice Black on 1 January 1962 that "Still more and more writers have come over half-way [to Aldington's position] or even further, and when I'm dead, they'll say I was right but didn't go far enough."[98] Despite the attempts to suppress and discredit his book, by the time Aldington died on 27 July 1962, he had seen some effects of his pioneering work. He had put the "Lawrence Bureau" on the defensive.

7

HIS BROTHER'S KEEPER

The attitude of certain people to the evidence on T. E. baffles and depresses me. Why [are] the personal knowledge and research of yourself, the often-on-the-spot evidence like Young, Stirling, Joyce etc. and the opinions of Allenby, Wavell or, to have an Arab, Nuri, set aside in favour of the denigrators, whose information is often only second-hand?

     —A. W. Lawrence to B. H. Liddell Hart, 4 February 1967

Fundamentally kind behind his reserve and critical wit, Arnold has borne the burden of having to live two lives. For forty years he has conducted the job of being his famous brother's keeper with rare skill, fairness and, most of the time, patience while living simultaneously his own private life.

     —John E. Mack, *A Prince of Our Disorder*

[TEL] seems to answer some requirement. It's almost religious. In fact it *is* a religion. I had great difficulty in not allowing myself to be used as a Saint Paul of it!

     —A. W. Lawrence, in *Lawrence and Arabia* (BBC documentary)

Awl, BORN ON 2 May 1900, was TEL's literary executor from 1935 until his death in 1991. The extent to which he "knew" TEL is open to question, but the brothers shared many values, including a desire to keep their distance from their overbearing mother and their elder brother, M. Robert, who had never freed himself from his mother's apron strings. Their other brothers, Will and Frank, both died in the Great War in 1915. AWL married in 1925 despite apprehension of his mother's disapproval, and he had a distinguished career as a classical archaeologist, publishing several books and teaching at Cambridge and the University of Ghana. To the outside world, however, he was chiefly visible as TEL's brother. His duties as TEL's literary executor and trustee frequently interfered with his own work. Profits from TEL's writings, the Seven Pillars Trust, and the TEL Letters Trust supported various charities, chiefly the R.A.F. Benevolent Fund. Serving as guardian of TEL's words and their earnings was partly an obligation, partly a sideline, and partly a nuisance.

Slightly more than two weeks after his thirty-fifth birthday, he read TEL's diaries and private papers, making several discoveries that surprised him. TEL was still lingering between life and death after the 13 May 1935 motorcycle accident when John "Jock" Bruce, a young Scot who had served with TEL in the ranks, wrote to AWL on 17 May, making puzzling references to TEL's "uncle." AWL ultimately learned that TEL had gulled Bruce into flogging him. As John E. Mack noted, "Arnold Lawrence 'realized that my brother had invented a living uncle and that the "nephew," who was to be punished by beating and other trials, was T. E. himself.' "[1] AWL's brief meeting with Bruce at a railway station in July 1935 convinced AWL that Bruce still believed in the existence of TEL's fictional uncle. Bruce had promised to destroy TEL's letters to him, but he did not do so, writing to Mack on 8 February 1969 about his plan to publish the letters "someday."[2] The knowledge that Bruce might reveal TEL's flagellation episodes greatly influenced AWL's handling of TEL's literary legacy.

As TEL's literary executor and the major trustee of TEL's estate, AWL exercised considerable control over publications by and about TEL. He had used this power to oppose Aldington. In 1954, AWL had Cape reissue *T.E. Lawrence by His Friends*, abridged by half to remove material that Aldington had found revealing, and he authorized the 1955 publication of *The Mint* to compete with and deflect attention from Aldington's book. AWL had too much confidence in his brother's ultimate vindication and too much respect for history to destroy important material that might tarnish TEL's image, but he took great care to see that compromising papers remained under embargo. He encouraged some biographers and discouraged others, depending on his assessment of their attitude toward TEL and their willingness to heed his suggestions, and he limited the extent to which biographers and critics could quote. His primary concerns were loyalty to TEL and the need to shield his mother and missionary brother.

AWL worried about depictions of TEL on stage and screen that, in his view, were too much under Aldington's influence. His involvement in the early film projects had been minimal. Alexander Korda had secured rights to *Revolt in the Desert* in December 1934, during TEL's lifetime, and an agreement with the Seven Pillars Trust in August 1937 allowed Korda to use the title *Lawrence of Arabia*, empowering Colonel W. F. Stirling to approve any changes in the scenario.[3] After encountering financial difficulties and the politically motivated refusal of the British Board of Film Censors to license his film, Korda abandoned the project in 1939.[4] Anatole de Grunwald bypassed TEL's trustees by paying Liddell Hart £3,000 (under an agreement dated 18 March 1955) for film rights to *"T. E. Lawrence": In Arabia and After*, the basis of Terence Rattigan's screenplay. Grunwald planned to shoot his film in Jordan with Glubb Pasha's Arab Legion, but Glubb was ousted, and after Grunwald decided to film in and around Cairo, the 1956 Suez crisis erupted. He sold his project (including Rattigan's screenplay) to the J. Arthur Rank Organization on 8 February 1957. Aldington hoped that Rank's film would renew interest in his TEL book and wrote to Eric Warman on 23 February 1958, "it would sell me another 50,000 [copies of the book]."[5] Rank wanted to shoot the film in Iraq, but escalating costs and revolution (culminating in the 14 July 1958 assassination of Feisal II, grandson of Feisal of the Arab Revolt) ended his hopes. By March 1958, he had canceled the project.[6]

Rattigan converted the screenplay into a stage play, completing *Ross* in February 1959. G. Wren Howard of Cape sent a copy to AWL, who responded on 5 July that *Ross* presented TEL as "a weakling with a compensatory blood-thirst and other uncontrolled neurotic impulses."[7] When Sam Spiegel, who had discussed filming *Seven Pillars* with David Lean, learned about *Ross*, which he regarded as potential competition, he told AWL that if AWL protested, the Lord Chamberlain (Lord Scarbrough) would ban *Ross*. AWL duly complained, but the Lord Chamberlain approved *Ross* after Rattigan threatened to produce it for television, where the Lord Chamberlain's ban had no effect. Rattigan had asked Graves to vet *Ross*, and Graves mentioned AWL's objections to the play. On 14 October, Rattigan responded, "A. W. Lawrence's reactions seem to me perfectly understandable—although, as you'll appreciate—knowing so many parties concerned—it *is* a little hurting that Binkie B[eaumont, a powerful theatrical entrepreneur], Alec [Guinness], Glen Byam Shaw [director of *Ross*], the Lord Chamberlain's office (who approve the play) and myself should all be considered as being involved in some dark conspiracy to dishonour the memory of T.E.L.—five Aldingtons, in fact, for the price of one—when, of course, our purpose is the exact opposite." Rattigan added, "P.S. I didn't quite understand your phrase about 'the copyright laws preventing one from misrepresenting the dead.' Who or what prevented Aldington? I'm told his bloody book still sells. God, I hate him. Still that's beside the point." Then he added, "P.P.S. Or is it?"[8]

AWL wrote to Liddell Hart on 9 November, "On 23rd July I wrote [to the Lord Chamberlain] that I objected strongly and had been led to believe that my mother and elder brother would object quite as strongly," adding that Graves "had confirmed my own opinion of the play." The Lord Chamberlain, however, had issued a license for *Ross* because, according to AWL, "the play, if banned, could be produced in ways outside his control and would receive greater notoriety. He had therefore concluded that refusal of a license would not be in the best interest of the relatives. (I should have protested against this view if I had been given an opportunity to do so.)" He added that the Lord Chamberlain felt that Rattigan "would do his best to meet my objections to any particular passages" and that AWL "might appreciate a foreword on the programme," but AWL believed "that a foreword would be much worse than useless if it did not state clearly the conviction that the alleged portrait is a travesty." Liddell Hart suggested on 16 November that the best course was "to induce Rattigan to make the necessary changes in his script. It is a pity that Robert did not take him up on his offer" to correct errors if Graves would identify them. Neither AWL nor Liddell Hart realized that Graves had an interest in Spiegel's film. Spiegel bought film rights to Graves's TEL-related books, hiring Graves as an "advisor." AWL later wrote, "I was induced to accept Spiegel by recommendations of him by Robert Graves and Lairdner. Later, Graves told me he deeply regretted his action."[9]

Graves wanted to weaken or suppress *Ross* in favor of Spiegel's film. On 16 November, he suggested that AWL impose conditions that he felt the playwright would not accept: "insist on the removal of non-historical material where it misrepresents T. E. and the circumstances in which he found himself, and also exact a promise that in the acting version no 'business' is introduced that has the same effect." As an alternative, Graves recommended that AWL demand a disclaimer: "Playgoers are warned that his play is deliberately unhistorical, though the names included are historical. In particular, the character of 'Ross' and of the late Colonel Lawrence as he really was, are dissimilar." If Rattigan refused to alter his script and the Lord Chamberlain did not force compliance, Graves suggested that AWL write a letter to the *Times*: "If you can get your mother to sign the letter, it's in the bag!" In a postscript, Graves commented on the film project that was much more important to him than Rattigan's play: "I am very happy to hear that you are *allowing* Spiegel, David Lean and [screenwriter] Mike Wilson to make the T. E. film. It will be historical and heroic: the film of the year." Before passing Graves's letter to Liddell Hart in January 1960, AWL wrote in the margin that "I can't stop them and have an open mind whether to help much, little or not at all." He responded to Graves on 30 November that "If they make good in my eyes I'll help them actively."

In a 23 November letter, AWL explained to Liddell Hart that he wanted to be fair to Rattigan without seeming to approve his play: "I feel that R. will wreck his play if he makes even a small proportion of the changes we'd want, & I'd rather he did not make token changes just to demonstrate his amenability—or to claim cooperation in a manner which might suggest it was genuine cooperation. The more *obvious* mistakes the better, I'd say, in matters of fact." Liddell Hart reiterated on 25 November that "I ought at least to make an effort to point out to him where his portrayal of T. E. is misleading and wrong."[10] AWL outlined his strategy to Liddell Hart on 28 November: "Robert Graves' nuisance value is enormous in this business & I am anxious it should not be wasted prematurely. . . . I may be wrong, but my instinct at present is to await some move by the enemy before taking any action whatever." AWL then wrote to Graves on 30 November to suggest tactics: "restrict yourself to the *worst features attributed to T. E.*, and reserve as much as possible for a blasting article or speech timed to coincide with the first night. In any case Rattigan will claim dramatic license for factual errors." AWL did not tell Liddell Hart about his negotiations with Spiegel until January 1960.

When Liddell Hart had received a copy of Rattigan's script from Graves in October 1959, he had written almost immediately to his agent, David Higham. He had sold the screen rights to *"T. E. Lawrence": In Arabia and After,* but not the stage rights, and he felt that *Ross* included material that could have come only from his book. Rattigan, perhaps expecting such a reaction, had delayed sending the script. On 4 December, however, Liddell Hart reported to AWL that Rattigan had finally sent *Ross:* "He admitted that he had been 'stalling' about sending me a copy, apparently because he was nervous about my reaction to it in view of the way you and Robert had taken what he felt to be his counter-stroke against Aldington's attack on T. E.'s reputation." Rattigan had also sent a copy of an earlier encouraging letter from Graves, and Liddell Hart remarked, "It certainly differs markedly from Robert's wholesale condemnation of the script when he talked to me about it the following week. Rattigan naturally tends to connect this sweeping change of attitude with Robert's interest in the new film project." Liddell Hart, however, did not inform AWL of his own prospective financial interest in *Ross.*

Instead, Liddell Hart told AWL that he had reread the play "more carefully" and found that "Its jarring passages are not so numerous as they seemed at first sight, and I think that most of them could be quite easily corrected by relatively small cuts and changes of wording." Calling *Ross* "a brilliant piece of work" and attributing its "alteration of events" to requirements of the stage, he felt that any protest "might merely create a confusion favourable to the persistence of the Aldington view, and diminish the play's potential influence in countering this. For Rattigan's play could be a powerful antidote to Aldington, and all the more if its 'out of character' passages are corrected." AWL, still wanting to be fair to Rattigan, responded on 9 December that "Between ourselves, I should be more than satisfied if he cut out the passages in which 'Ross' exults in slaughter & atrocities, & the mythical desertion; I can scarcely expect him to eliminate the popinjay-pansy talk since that would oblige him to rewrite all through so many scenes." Liddell Hart suggested several changes to Rattigan, who jokingly called Liddell Hart his "collaborator" while incorporating virtually all Liddell Hart's emendations.

On 14 January 1960, AWL wrote to Liddell Hart that he had received "notes on how they would make a film out of *Seven Pillars.* It is a straightforward, perfectly decent & well-reasoned construction & I have informed them today that I shall have no objection, subject to a legal agreement. Of all the attempts at films & plays I have had to read, this is the only one that has kept to the facts, & the only one which has seemed to me likely to leave no bad taste in the mouth." He had seen a treatment by Michael Wilson, whose credits included rewriting the screenplay for *The Bridge on the River Kwai.* Wilson, who had been "blacklisted as a result of being an 'unfriendly witness' during the HUAC [House UnAmerican Activities Committee] hearings in 1951,"[11] had followed *Seven Pillars* closely and sympathetically, but after AWL had approved Wilson's version, Lean rejected it. Spiegel then brought in Robert Bolt, who began writing in December 1960. "When Bolt was subsequently given sole screenplay credit for the film, Wilson took the matter to a Screen Writers Guild arbitration. In late 1963, after examining all versions of the screenplay and related documents, the Guild determined that Wilson was entitled to equal credit for the screenplay."[12] Despite this decision, the 1989 "restoration" of the movie to its original 220 minutes did not credit Wilson.[13]

AWL realized that he might have blundered when the London *News Chronicle* of 18 February 1960 quoted Spiegel's remarks at the 17 February gala reception celebrating plans to film *Seven Pillars*. Spiegel, perhaps not realizing that the payment, like all other *Seven Pillars* income, was destined for charitable purposes rather than for private gain, stated that AWL had been paid "As much as he'll spend in a lifetime" and that "He gave us blanket approval to do 'Seven Pillars.' No further objections are expected from him, nor is he entitled to one."[14] On 19 February, AWL wrote to Liddell Hart that he was "annoyed at Spiegel's performances" but that "I still have some hold over Spiegel because he has undertaken not to call his film *SP of W* unless I approve the final (shooting) script. . . . The newspapers would make a fuss if in fact I were to say 'No,' which I'd do as publicly as I could." As AWL discovered later, there is no copyright in titles, so his "hold" on Spiegel had no force.

On 24 February, Rattigan sent his revision of *Ross* to Liddell Hart, reporting that he had made all but one of the changes that Liddell Hart had suggested. He had not altered "the phrase 'showing off' on Pages 1.2.25 and 2.6.58" because "Alec [Guinness] didn't like any of the alternatives (play acting etc) and pleaded eloquently for the exact expression which (since Aldington) will be in all audiences['] minds and for which any euphemism might seem cowardly and evasive." Rattigan then settled with Liddell Hart for stage rights to his book, paying £3,000 under an agreement dated 29 February 1960 that gave Liddell Hart "1 percent of the U.K., U.S., and Canadian box-office gross for all productions of *Ross*; 10 percent of Rattigan's rights for other country presentations of the play; and 10 percent of 'other rights' income. But the agreement specifically excluded film rights to *Ross*."[15] Since the receipts for *Ross* averaged between £4,500 and £5,000 each week, biweekly payments of £90 to £100 supplemented Liddell Hart's income during *Ross*'s extensive run, and more than thirty years later, Lady Kathleen Liddell Hart was still receiving small sums for *Ross* productions.[16] Rattigan, or his legal counsel, showed considerable foresight. Securing rights to Liddell Hart's book provided a defense against any claim that *Ross* infringed rights acquired by Spiegel.

Ross began a run of 762 performances at the Haymarket Theatre in London on 12 May 1960 and later ran for 159 performances at the Eugene O'Neill Theatre in New York, where it opened on 26 December 1961. AWL and Liddell Hart had expected *Ross* to offset Aldington's influence, but the homosexual undertones of the stage version and the contradictions implicit in TEL's character came through clearly, and several reviewers of *Ross* mentioned Aldington. J. C. Trewin in the *Illustrated London News* (28 May 1960) found Rattigan's motive for TEL's withdrawal into the ranks (TEL's torture at Deraa) more convincing than Aldington's (to escape both his mother and his responsibilities).[17] In *Action* (August/September 1960), Michael Harald took the opposite viewpoint: "If you want a sober factual examination of the *real* T. E. Lawrence, then you will have to go to Aldington's book, and from there to your own minds and hearts. Perhaps you *don't*; and I should be the last to blame you."[18] Constantine FitzGibbon in *Encounter* (November 1960), after dismissing Aldington and others who debunked the TEL legend, offered conclusions compatible with Aldington's: "The appeal [of the TEL legend] was immediate, enormous, and, as Lawrence knew, false. His war had been at least as disgusting as theirs, his victory more pointless and sterile, his lies even more profound and self-destructive."[19]

AWL was generally satisfied with Liddell Hart's improvements to Rattigan's earlier version and wrote on 21 May 1960 that "From a review in the 'Observer' I gather your work on Rattigan had all the effect one could have wished. My congratulations, & gratitude." Rattigan's high regard for TEL was apparent throughout *Ross*. Alec Guinness wrote nearly thirty years later, "Rattigan rather hero-worshipped T. E. so 'Ross' is a bit suspect. I don't think there is *any* doubt that T. E. was homosexual and Rattigan recognised this. In my opinion (and that of others) the whole humiliating and buggery incident at Deraa was total fiction. (Oddly he told G. B. Shaw and Mrs. Shaw absolutely contradictory accounts of it.)"[20] Aldington shared AWL's view that *Ross* bolstered the TEL legend. On 14 September 1960, he wrote to Stanley Weintraub, "You will of course have observed how cleverly and unscrupulously Rattigan and Guinness have put over their version of the myth, and an American movie is projected on the lines of the Bridge of Kwai—doubtless the theme song this time will not be the old British army march of 'Colonel Bogie' but a new 'Colonel Bogus.'"[21]

Rattigan purchased the film rights to his screenplay from Rank on 11

August 1960. Herbert Wilcox, who in 1926 had rejected an offer from TEL and Raymond Savage to film *Seven Pillars* after concluding that audiences would not be interested, now wanted to film *Ross*. Rattigan sold him the film rights (including those to Liddell Hart's book) on 8 September 1960 for an impressive £100,000. Spiegel had failed to keep *Ross* off stage, but he had more success keeping it off screen. When word spread that Spiegel's Horizon Pictures might sue Wilcox Holdings for infringement of Spiegel's acquired rights to *Seven Pillars*, Wilcox could not find the necessary financial backing. Before securing permission to film *Seven Pillars*, Spiegel had bought rights to several books about TEL, including those by Lowell Thomas, Robert Graves, David Garnett, and others, thus cornering the market. Knowing that he could not win, Wilcox sold his rights to Spiegel in March 1961 for a reported £140,000.

Graves decided that *Ross* had infringed the copyright of his TEL biography after he saw a performance on 7 October 1960. His solicitor, Maurice Bilmes, wrote to Rattigan on 11 October:

> I am instructed by my client that you, without his authority or consent, have included in your play dramatic scenes, events and direct quotations from my client's book entitled "Lawrence and the Arabs" which constitute a flagrant breach of my client's copyright. I understand that you are fully aware of these deliberate plagiarisms as my client, when he last spoke to you, specifically informed you that he did not wish you to include any part of his works in your play. Notwithstanding this request, you quite arbitrarily have deliberately chosen to infringe my client's copyright.

Bilmes sent a copy to Rattigan's agent, A.D. Peters, but Rattigan prepared his own response, a short but comprehensive cablegram: "I HAVE RECEIVED YOUR CABLE AND YOUR LETTER. MY SOLICITORS HAVE BEEN INSTRUCTED TO ANSWER YOUR INSULTING INACCURATE AND DEFAMATORY COMMUNICATION."[22] Rattigan had a willing ally in Liddell Hart, who wrote to Rattigan's solicitor, P. F. Carter-Ruck, on 17 December, "As regards the passages of which Robert Graves complains, I presume that the references you mention are to his book. In that case they are all well known points, covered in my book and elsewhere, and appear to be merely incidental in the script of the play."[23] Nothing came of Graves's threats of litigation.

By the end of 1961, AWL realized where he stood with Spiegel. In the 14 December London *Daily Mail*, he commented that "Film scripts start off all right, but they seem to get altered as they go along."[24] When he saw

Bolt's screenplay, he was extremely displeased and wrote a long letter to Spiegel on 1 August 1962 to complain that the film was not based on *Seven Pillars* and that it bore little resemblance to "the synopsis you originally gave me to read, on the evidence of which I sold you the rights in the book." Spiegel responded by inviting AWL to a showing of sequences of the film. After viewing about two-thirds of the movie on 5 September, AWL wrote to Spiegel the next day that what he had seen had intensified his negative impression of the script. He arranged to return to Spiegel the £5,000 that "would have been paid to me if I had allowed you to use the name or title 'Seven Pillars of Wisdom,' " and he enclosed a formal state-ment of his refusal. On 23 September, AWL wrote to Liddell Hart that "It is difficult to think of any way of attack which will not help to advertise the film."

The BBC, however, was preparing a TEL documentary, to be written by David Lytton and produced by Malcolm Brown and Philip Donnellan. AWL wanted the documentary to "redress the balance" and worried that Aldington's book might influence the program. Liddell Hart replied on 25 September that the BBC had already asked him to advise the project, that he had agreed in the "hope that it would be a way of keeping a check on the script," and that he "was favourably impressed by their attitude to the subject." He added, "I don't know who is still active in the Aldington school, but I do find many signs that his imputations have a continuing effect in many quarters, despite all efforts to expose the distortions in his book. . . . But it is essential in every sense to go on trying to correct them. . . ."

After an advertisement claimed that the Spiegel film would be based on *Seven Pillars*, AWL wrote to Liddell Hart on 8 October that Henniker-Major of Kennedy, Ponsonby & Prideaux "has asked for a recall of the advt. and thinks there is a case for injunction—which, if defended, would give us a splendid chance of attacking." Horizon withdrew the offending ad-vertisement, however, and offered to try to resolve AWL's objections to the film's treatment of TEL. On 9 October, AWL sent Henniker-Major a summary of his complaints to convey to Spiegel's representative, Cardew-Smith:

(1) When T.E.L. returns from Akaba he is made to tell Allenby that he has killed two men and enjoyed it. (2) His motive for entering Deraa is converted from reconnaissance to despairing bravado. (3) His instantane-ous rage at finding the massacred village (Tafas) is distorted to a slow

surrender to his alleged sadism, as is emphasized by Ali's repeated remonstrances. (4) As for the hospital scene, which a previous letter of Cardew-Smith said was being altered, the alterations should rectify the following misrepresentations[:] (a) T.E.L. is made to have "forgotten" a hospital of wounded Turks, some of them wounded by "his Arabs," whereas he did not know that the Turks had filled part of a barracks with sick; (b) his effective cleaning-up is distorted into futile gestures.

AWL informed Henniker-Major, "There are other passages of deliberately unpleasant misrepresentation, but I think the list of them should be withheld until we see how far Horizon Pictures are will[ing] to correct these four. I don't want to give them a chance to alter things of minor consequence and stick out on the more serious, but still be able to say they have made changes to suit my wishes. Also the delay will enable Liddell Hart to take a hand in drawing up the final list if one is called for."

On 10 November, however, AWL wrote to Liddell Hart, "Actually I doubt whether any serious alterations will be feasible at this eleventh hour, so we may escape having to prepare a list, and, instead, go straight to considering publicity—which we can't do much about till we know what alterations (if any) have been made." Since the scheduled royal premiere was only a month away, it was already too late for major alterations.

An article by Robert Bolt, "Clues to the Legend of Lawrence," had appeared in the *New York Times Magazine* months before, on 25 February 1962. Bolt seemed to accept Aldington's view of TEL's homoerotic inclinations and, to bolster this, noted that, "Of the forty contributors to the book 'Lawrence by His Friends,' only two are women and one of these his mother." (He had used the 1954 abridgement instead of the 1937 original edition, which had eight women among its eighty contributors.) His summary of TEL's character is close to Aldington's:

Take a man born a bastard, and unable to speak of it. Let him be clever, imaginative and vain, loving to play harsh jokes on others but chillingly resentful of a joke against himself. . . .

Now endow him with courage, physical toughness and above all a capacity for stoic suffering taken to extremes and exercised compulsively. Place him in the landscape and among the people where this minor virtue is so highly regarded that nothing else much matters. Give him gold to distribute.

For Bolt, "sadism was in [TEL's] nature," and after the war, TEL "had committed himself too deeply and had to remain a figure from an epic—

Lawrence of Arabia. I think that is why there are so many lies and so much misplaced poetry in the book."[25]

With AWL's approval, Liddell Hart wrote to Bolt on 21 November, disputing that homosexuality and sadism were part of TEL's makeup but conceding that "On the question of his truthfulness you are nearer the mark." Bolt's 22 November reply began, "Before I say anything else, I do hope that you don't place me in the Aldington category?" Bolt ultimately stood by his own interpretation of TEL's statement that, at Tafas, "By my order we took no prisoners, for the only time in our war," which, for Bolt, demonstrated sadistic complicity in a "war crime." In his final letter, on 29 November 1962, Bolt maintained that "it was my duty to take Lawrence as meaning what he says, not something else, in these pages as elsewhere. If I am to assume that he was lying wherever his statements are inconvenient to me, I have no right to take him as truthful when his account fits in with some theory of my own. The whole thing would become questionable, a quicksand of fantasy, which is the view of Aldington, not of myself."[26] Liddell Hart sent Bolt's letter to AWL on 30 November, and AWL responded on 3 December that "Bolt should be described in the 18th century manner as Mr. ***t. His last letter to you makes me feel slightly sick."

The BBC televised the documentary *T. E. Lawrence: 1888–1935* on 27 November 1962. In the *Radio Times*, Brown and Donnellan had stated that their purpose was not to present "a kind of television court-martial" of TEL or his debunkers, but "to tell the story of his life and death. By doing this with the richest and most authentic material available we hope that a real and credible Lawrence will emerge—someone a good deal more human and comprehensible than the figure the 1920s idolised, or the 1950s spurned."[27] The finished program included appearances by Lowell Thomas, Henry Williamson, AWL, and many others who had known TEL. At some points, the program contradicted the Spiegel film in advance (e.g., "No one could restrain" the Arabs at Tafas), but this was entirely coincidental. As Brown commented three decades later, "we did our TEL film without a clue as to what the Spiegel film would be like. We knew it was coming, but we knew nothing about it. Certainly I never talked to L-H about it while we were making ours."[28] The program's conclusion referred to those who had "proceeded to fashion the various versions of him that have puzzled the imagination since" into "the legend" that "still dogs him, growing, it would seem, more and more absurd." AWL then commented on film that TEL had "become a subject either for extreme adulation, or equally extreme denigration, the process having naturally gained strength as the witnesses to his actions have died off. In neither of these two figures, over-dramatised figures, the saint and the charlatan, can I really recognise more than a trace of the brother whom I knew and liked."[29]

The documentary could not offset the impact of Spiegel's film, which has survived as a modern cinematic classic. The film made its debut on 10 December 1962. On 14 December, the *Times* printed a letter by AWL identifying the film's historical inaccuracies pertaining to Allenby.[30] His article "The Fiction and the Fact" in the *Observer* on 16 December specified several discrepancies between the film and *Seven Pillars of Wisdom*, ending with the comment, "I need only say that I should not have recognised my brother."[31] He complained in the *New York Times* on 5 January 1963 that the film "completely misrepresents my brother" and referred to Bolt's well-known anti-war bias.[32]

In the *New York Times* on 26 January, Spiegel, more skillful with the press than AWL, shifted attention to aspects of TEL and his younger brother that were not always relevant to the film or to AWL's objections: "I quite understand what the movie must mean to someone who has lived in the shadow of a legend of an older brother for some 50 years. Professor Lawrence did not want family skeletons rattled. He wanted to preserve the Lawrence of Arabia legend in Victorian cleanliness." Spiegel then deliberately referred to skeletons that the film had barely implied, such as TEL's illegitimacy, or had omitted entirely, such as that TEL "was aware of homosexual tendencies but did not want to commit himself to homosexualism" and "became involved in all sorts of masochism as a result of his conflicts." He added that AWL "had never known his brother under these conditions" and doubted that AWL "realizes his brother was narcissistic enough to create a curtain of mystery as part of his sense of humor. If any man was capable of planting false footprints it was Lawrence of Arabia." Spiegel also indicated that TEL's partisans had been happy enough to profit by selling film rights, quoting one "biographer" (David Garnett): "I'm glad my hands are clean, but not empty."[33] AWL soon realized that he was fighting a losing battle. He wrote to Liddell Hart on 16 April 1963 that "Unless there is further provocation I do not feel that a concerted attack on the film just now will serve any useful purpose."

AWL was much more successful with publishers and scholars than he had been with film producers and screenwriters. As TEL's literary executor, he could exert considerable influence simply by extending or withholding permission to quote, as TEL scholars and their publishers well knew. Pat Knowles informed AWL of TEL books in progress since their authors almost invariably visited Clouds Hill cottage, which also provided a useful venue for distributing information. Knowles gave Clouds Hill visitors reprints of Liddell Hart's *London Magazine* refutation of Aldington at the rate of about one thousand each year. When AWL decided to update the Clouds Hill guidebook, he suggested to Liddell Hart on 17 February 1964 that "you might put some disguised propaganda v. Aldington & Co. into your Introduction." The National Trust *Clouds Hill* booklet still has this "disguised propaganda": "In his lifetime he made friends or enemies; few people, if any, could feel indifferent about him after meeting him. Since his death, he has continued to evoke no less intense reactions, and in the case of dislike these have led to rabid distortion of the evidence resting on nothing better than flagrant misquotation of many passages in the sources cited—as any reader can discover if he takes the trouble to check."[34]

Joyce Ludlow, who claimed to be writing a book about Aldington, wrote to Liddell Hart on 19 July, "Your comment in the Clouds Hill booklet about flagrant misquotation, which I realise is intended to refer to Richard Aldington, is so true. . . . I should give a lot to know exactly what it was that made Aldington hate him so, for hatred it definitely was. Perhaps with luck I shall one day find out."[35] After corresponding with Ludlow, AWL wrote to Liddell Hart on 26 August that she "struck me as almost certainly incapable of writing an interesting study of Aldington; indeed, I'd expect something too inept for publication. So I did not raise the subject; nor did she. I hope and almost trust that it is a mere way of feeding her apparent need for self-esteem, not a real project." Ludlow published nothing about Aldington or TEL, but she made one lasting contribution when she purchased Aldington's letters to his second wife, Netta, and ultimately bequeathed them to the British Library.[36]

While keeping tabs on prospective authors of TEL books and corresponding with them, AWL often defended his brother in print. In May 1965, the *Royal British Legion Journal* reported Colonel H. C. Joynson's claim "that the ignorance and incompetence of T. E. Lawrence in his early days of leadership often resulted in unnecessary heavy loss of life—and even succeeded in blowing up some of his own personnel." AWL responded in the September issue with a letter that challenged Joynson's credentials, questioned his claims of high casualties, and provided evidence that Joynson was not likely to have been on the scene that he described.[37] For the most part, however, he ignored books whose shoddy inaccuracies put them beneath notice and whose influence was inconsequential.

In 1966, Suleiman Mousa's *T. E. Lawrence: An Arab View*, translated from

Arabic, was too important for AWL to disregard. As Stephen E. Tabachnick comments, Mousa "expressed a point of view hitherto practically unheard in the West, namely that the Arab Revolt was far more important to Allenby than Aldington had claimed, and owed more to Arab needs, inspiration and execution than to Lawrence, who remained in the last analysis a 'British citizen with a great regard for his country's interest' and 'a real desire to see the Arabs win, simply because they were British allies.' . . . [H]e outstrips Aldington in claiming that Lawrence completely fabricated many incidents in order to call attention to himself in *Seven Pillars*." [38] (Mousa later wrote that he would have preferred "in order to call attention to himself in his secret reports and later in *Seven Pillars*.") [39] Addressing Mousa's most startling charges that TEL had "entirely fabricated . . . a northern journey behind Turkish lines in June 1917 and that he completely invented the Deraa incident," Tabachnick argues that "we must today accept the fact of this journey" but recognize that "With regard to the Deraa incident, the case is somewhat more ambiguous. . . . " He adds that because Mousa "was a Jordanian government employee when he wrote his book, he may have been committed to upholding the reputation of the Hussein family, who in his account can do no wrong." [40]

Mousa interviewed several Arab sources who had firsthand knowledge of TEL during his wartime activities in Arabia and investigated something that no one had previously bothered about. He identified the Turkish Bey at Deraa who had ostensibly lusted after TEL as Hajem Muhyi al-Din Bey, whose character was so divergent from TEL's description in *Seven Pillars* that even the Bey's enemies dismissed TEL's accusations. On 28 November 1953, writing to Kershaw, Aldington had rejected as preposterous the suggestion of New York attorney Morris Ernst that Aldington had libeled the Bey of Deraa, [41] but Mousa's evidence suggested that Ernst had been right. Mousa compared TEL's accounts in the *Arab Bulletin* with those in *Seven Pillars* (later, he gained access to the papers of Emir Zeid). Although Aldington and Mousa both question TEL's credibility, Mousa emphasized the significance of the Arab Revolt to Allenby's campaign while Aldington had contemptuously dismissed the Arabs as inconsequential looters. According to Mousa, "in the works of Lawrence's admirers and detractors alike one seeks in vain for a semblance of justice to the Arabs." [42]

As Mousa reported later, when John Bell, his editor at Oxford University Press, requested permission to quote *Seven Pillars*, AWL insisted on seeing Mousa's entire typescript, which he read at the Press's London office on 27 July 1965. Bell informed Mousa on 19 August that AWL and the

Seven Pillars Trustees would allow use of the quotations for a fee of £25. On 9 September, however, Bell wrote Mousa that "Professor Lawrence has suggested putting a note from the Trustees . . . at the beginning of the book in which they will give briefly their answer to what you have to say" [ellipsis in original]. Mousa might have refused to consider the notion, but Bell thought it "good diplomacy to let them say it politely in the book rather than to say it rudely in the Press after the book is published, and it will show that you and we are anxious to be fair." Mousa responded on 23 September that he did not object if he could vet AWL's comment, and Bell sent AWL's rough draft to Mousa on 18 January 1966. Mousa informed Bell on 30 January that he had found some of AWL's commentary "offensive and impolite" and suggested that AWL tone down his comments and limit them to two pages. He objected to putting AWL's criticism at the front of the book, where it could influence readers before they read Mousa's text, and stated that "If [AWL] does not agree, he may say whatever he likes in newspapers and I am ready to answer in detail."[43]

Oxford University Press included AWL's rebuttal as "Comment" at the end of Mousa's text, where it runs to eight printed pages. Bell wrote to Mousa on 9 March that his willingness to include the rebuttal "will reflect great credit on you and will serve to indicate that you have no doubt about the general fairness and balance of your own criticisms of Lawrence." AWL expressed a very different view to Liddell Hart on 11 April 1966: "After half a year of argument, back and forth to the Jordanian author, John Bell has now sent his book to be printed off complete with the destructive comments I wrote—though they were toned down & shortened a little at the author's demand. Still, a mild reply printed within the same cover is worth far more than any amount of unrestrained obloquy in the ephemeral press." Although Mousa did not regard AWL's comments as "destructive,"[44] their inclusion in Mousa's book gives them undue weight with later readers.

In 1967, intercession by AWL prevented publication of a TEL book by Edward H. T. Robinson. Gordon Grimley of Robert Maxwell, Publishers, had asked Liddell Hart on 16 August whether he would read a 360-page manuscript "by a civil servant who was clerk to Lawrence and through whose hands practically all the documents covering the campaign from Wejh to Damascus passed." However, on 4 September, Grimley wrote again, informing Liddell Hart that AWL had "cast such light on the T. E. Lawrence manuscript and the author that I am now returning the manuscript with a simple rejection slip. It would appear that the entire origin of the book is wholly questionable—a fact that you may wish to remember in the event that it should come to you for your opinion via any other publisher." [45] More than two decades earlier, in 1935, AWL had stated in an "Introductory Note" to Robinson's biography for juveniles, *Lawrence: The Story of His Life* (1935), that Robinson "was himself an eye-witness of many of the scenes described. I have read the proofs of the book, and find no errors of fact, while the general picture seems to me as accurate as could reasonably be expected in a book of its purpose." [46] Two years later, however, as the *New York Times* reported on 17 June 1937, Robinson received a three-month prison sentence after he sold manuscripts and photographs that AWL had lent him for research for an adult biography. [47] That book, *Lawrence the Rebel*, did not appear until 1946. Whatever manuscript Robinson was circulating in 1967 has yet to reach print.

Dr. John E. Mack had begun research for his biography of TEL in 1964. As he commented in his introduction to *A Prince of Our Disorder* (1976), Mack wrote from a sympathetic perspective: "Although I have attempted to give as thorough and objective an exposition of the historical evidence as possible in order to achieve a balanced view of the man, and to examine any personal reactions of my own which might lead to distortions of the data, I do not claim to be neutral to my subject. I unabashedly regard him as a great man and an important historical figure, and intend in the pages that follow to show how the evidence led to my opinion. But I have sought to suppress nothing that would lead to a contrary view." [48] Mack had the cooperation of AWL, M. R. Lawrence, David Garnett, Liddell Hart, Lowell Thomas, and several others during the twelve years from the inception of his project to its publication. AWL freely answered questions but did not volunteer highly sensitive information.

On 2 August 1967, Mack wrote to Liddell Hart about a startling discovery: "I was told that when [TEL] was in the Air Force he became involved with flagellation." Mack felt that "the matter, if true, should still not be published out of concern for the feelings of living family members," but he needed "the facts to help me in my understanding." [49] He later explained that he had learned from his Little, Brown editor at a luncheon in November 1966 that "William Sargant, an English psychiatrist and a friend of Robert Graves, had been told at one time by Graves that he was aware of certain facts concerning Lawrence's sexuality which were not generally known. Dr. Sargant put me in touch with Graves, whom I visited in Majorca during the summer of 1967. Graves told me that Lawrence had 'become a flagellant' in the ranks after the war, that he had become impotent as a result of the Der'a experience (not literally true)." [50] Liddell Hart passed Mack's letter to AWL, who wrote to Mack on 10 August 1967 that there was a "basis of fact" in the story, adding that "To write a statement not liable to be misunderstood would take more time than I can spare at present, whereas you would quickly get everything aright in conversation."[51] As Mack comments, "It is worth pointing out that this offer to discuss the matter occurred ten months before Arnold Lawrence had knowledge that Bruce had been successful in selling his story to a newspaper."[52]

Had it not been for the reappearance of John Bruce, Mack would surely have kept this knowledge to himself. AWL had not heard from Bruce since 1935 except for one (unanswered) letter in December 1962 and another in February 1963 enclosing a cutting from a Helensburgh, Scotland, newspaper announcing Bruce's plans to publish a book called *Lawrence after Arabia*, which failed to appear. In February 1967, Bruce accidentally (as he later told Mack) mailed AWL's solicitors a manuscript describing his relationship with TEL. On 1 January 1968, pleading ill health and financial woes, Bruce wrote to the solicitors that he would have to break his long silence and asked whether there were objections to his publishing the manuscript. The solicitors responded that there were indeed objections.

Early in March 1968, AWL learned that Bruce had sold the *Sunday Times* the typescript that would form the basis of articles on TEL's relationship with Bruce and "such other subjects as Lawrence's family background, alleged espionage activities, and relationship with Mrs. Shaw."[53] Colin Simpson would have primary authorship of the articles. AWL granted Simpson access to the material at the Bodleian Library on 28 March 1968, hoping that this might make the articles more accurate. Dreading that there would be "no background depicted, so that the story would seem just dirt," AWL wanted the *Sunday Times* to have Mack write "a companion article that would place the story of the beatings in an appropriate psychological and historical perspective," but this did not happen.[54] There apparently was no attempt to preempt the *Sunday Times* by publishing a sympathetic account of TEL's flagellation elsewhere.

The articles were sensational pieces, focusing on TEL's supposed rape at Deraa, his affectionate relationship at Carchemish with the Arab worker Dahoum, his flagellation episodes, and his relationship with Charlotte Shaw.[55] After these articles had interested publishers in a book version (McGraw-Hill offered $65,000 for U.S. rights), the *Sunday Times* put its extensive resources at the disposal of Simpson and his collaborator, Phillip Knightley, for further research. As Knightley later wrote, AWL, who had "been on the point of refusing collaboration of any kind" and was considering "denying use of any copyright material, . . . had reconsidered and was prepared to conclude a 'gentleman's agreement.' " Although "this gentleman's agreement eventually became a six-page legal contract" replete with obligations, one advantage of the arrangement for Knightley was that "Professor Lawrence had not only declined the editor's offer to vet the book but had incorporated in the contract an agreement that he would not be available for consultation and would not render any assistance."[56]

AWL agreed to allow quotation and continued access for Simpson to the Bodleian material until the book appeared in print. In turn,

> The authors expressly agreed to state that none of the material relating to Bruce was obtained from papers in the Bodleian Library or from Professor Lawrence; that Clouds Hill (Lawrence's cottage in Dorset) should not be associated with beating; that no indication be given that a British soldier was involved in a sodomy episode described in a cancelled chapter of the *Seven Pillars of Wisdom*; that no indication be given of where in the unpublished text this cancelled chapter could be found; that the authors would submit to Professor Lawrence for his approval all references in the book to himself; and that they would supply to Dr. John Mack (a psychiatrist from Harvard University, who was working on a book on Lawrence) copies of all the material they obtained from Jock Bruce.[57]

While Simpson worked at the Bodleian, Knightley coordinated the "T. E. Lawrence centre" at the *Sunday Times* offices. Mousa had written a letter to the *Sunday Times* on 19 June 1968 concerning "errors and mistakes regarding the Arab side," but instead of publishing the letter, the *Sunday Times* sought his help. He ultimately provided the bulk of new material from the Public Records Office. According to Mousa, he "succeeded in convincing Knightley (my connection was with him and not with his partner) of the real position of the Arab side, and I feel satisfied that his book contains much less error about the Arabs than most other books written about Lawrence. This is a consolation to me."[58]

The arrangement with AWL posed some logistical problems. As Knightley commented two decades later,

> A. W. Lawrence was always doing his best to make it difficult for anybody to write anything at all about T. E. All those trusts and everything that were being set up, administered by a firm of city solicitors—they just hinged them with so many restrictions that, while giving the appearance of being helpful and making material freely available, no censorship and all that sort of thing, the physical effort in what you had to do in order

to get copyright clearance and commissions and all that, and then in the
end the money you had to pay, were a very inhibiting factor in writing
anything about T. E. Lawrence.[59]

Knightley and Simpson had agreed to show AWL all references to himself
by 31 March 1969, and since failure to meet this deadline could delay publication for as much as a year, the *Sunday Times* team, working around the
clock, provided these by 8 April (which proved to be soon enough). Another
condition was that they could not publish TEL's letters without permission
from the recipients. (Garnett had to meet the same condition for his 1938
edition of TEL's letters and had received two refusals, one from Churchill
and the other from Charlotte Shaw.) On 18 July, Kennedy, Ponsonby &
Prideaux, the lawyers for the TEL trusts, reported that a typescript of the
book "had come onto the market," which was "a breach of the Agreement,"
but the bookseller agreed to withdraw it from sale.[60]

The Secret Lives of Lawrence of Arabia appeared on 29 September 1969
after a series of *Sunday Times* excerpts in late August and early September.
The book sold well, but Knightley felt that some reviewers were unethical
when they failed to identify their own interests in TEL projects. He particularly resented Mack's unfavorable review: "Nowhere in the review does
Dr. Mack mention that he himself is engaged in writing a biography of
Lawrence. . . . "[61] While *Secret Lives* offered a great deal of new material,
Tabachnick comments that "the use they make of their fresh material frequently raises doubts that invalidate their overall portrait of his life." Of
their argument "that Lawrence was a cold-blooded imperialist agent
who cared nothing for the Arabs and sought only to advance British interests," he writes that "the very documentation Knightley and Simpson
quote contradicts this one-sided view of Lawrence."[62] Tabachnick had expressed a similar objection to Aldington's approach, commenting that "Self-
contradiction infects much of Aldington's view" and noting Aldington's
tendency to form "negative judgements where positive ones were just as
plausible."[63]

Knightley, in 1988, commented that Aldington's book "coincides almost identically with my views on Lawrence. In fact, I think he went a
little bit further on some issues than I did, but I wouldn't add or take away
anything that he wrote." During his research, Knightley had learned about
the attempts of the "Lawrence Bureau" to suppress Aldington's book, and
he decided that a chapter on the efforts to censor Aldington would be an
appropriate epilogue for *Secret Lives*. The publisher, however, complained

that Knightley and Simpson had exceeded the agreed maximum number of words and insisted that they shorten the manuscript to the length specified in their contract. To avoid cutting material in the chapters devoted to TEL, Knightley had to jettison the Aldington epilogue. In 1973, he published the canceled chapter as an article, "Aldington's Enquiry Concerning T. E. Lawrence."[64]

AWL wrote a long letter, published in the *Times* on 22 November 1969, citing discrepancies between Knightley and Simpson's book and the June 1968 articles, emphasizing the inconsistencies in Bruce's various accounts. "I accept only one significant ingredient in Bruce's story, the basic fact that my brother, while in a condition of extreme physical and mental distress, invented the myth of an implacable uncle's demands, and induced Bruce to execute them. I believe that the rest of Bruce's narratives should be regarded with considerably greater caution than the authors of the recent book suggest.[65] Knightley and Simpson responded in a joint letter to the *Times* on 28 November that discrepancies between the 1968 and 1969 articles had resulted from what their intervening research had revealed and that their book had included a cautionary note about the reliability of Bruce forty-seven years after the fact. "Any sentence by sentence examination of Bruce's account so long after the events can only be a waste of time because surely the main point is that Bruce birched Lawrence at Lawrence's own request and this is not disputed even by Professor Lawrence himself." [66]

After Knightley and Simpson's June 1968 articles had made TEL's flagellation public knowledge, Mack published an article, "T. E. Lawrence: A Study of Heroism and Conflict," in the February issue of the *American Journal of Psychiatry* (a shorter version appeared as "The Inner Conflict of T. E. Lawrence" in the 8 February issue of the *Times Saturday Review*),[67] but his book did not appear until 1976. Mack's study, *A Prince of Our Disorder: The Life of T.E. Lawrence*, is the most convincing and plausible of the sympathetic portraits of TEL. Instead of categorically dismissing TEL's negative traits, Mack tries to explain them in the fuller context of TEL's personality. He wrote on 29 March 1991, "Above all, what Aldington's attack forced me to do was to explore the distinction between the psychology of an inner sense of fraudulence or falsehood, which T.E.L. felt, and the reality of it in narrower terms, i.e. whether in fact he lied, distorted his actions, misrepresented facts, etc. I did not find on the whole that the latter was true, but he has many of the elements of the psychology of the imposter in the feeling that he does not belong and that he is engaged in a false enterprise."[68]

In *A Prince of Our Disorder*, Mack describes the sources of TEL's confusion:

> The cloudiness of the family background; the uncertainty about his mother's origins; the discovery of his own illegitimacy and the related discrepancy between his parents' values and ideals and their violation of social codes; the deception of their silence on these matters; the perceived dominance of his father by his mother; his mother's deep need to find redemption for her sins through Lawrence and his brothers; perhaps the rejection experience in his only attempt as a young man to find a mate [in his alleged proposal to Janet Laurie]—all these adverse influences distorted, damaged, and interfered with Lawrence's development of his own self and left him vulnerable to the later problems which the traumata of the war years brought about.[69]

Mack emphasizes TEL's psychological gifts, ability to function as an "enabler," and remarkable traits, accounting for many of TEL's quirks and foibles without making them the occasion for judgment.

Rather than call TEL a charlatan or liar because of his conflicting accounts of various events, Mack refers to TEL's tendency to "embellish" in *Seven Pillars*, or to apply "exaggeration youthwards" in his recollections of his childhood, or to present a "less than completely accurate" description of his self-implied role in the surrender of Erzerum, or to "communicate selectively" to those whose relationships he kept in watertight compartments. Frequently, Mack acknowledges a major problem for any biographer of TEL—"How much of this romanticization is from Lawrence's yarn-telling and how much the embellishments of his admirers is beyond my capacity to determine"[70]—keeping in mind TEL's penchant for myth-making throughout. Since Mack puts specific events into a larger context than did Aldington, paying more attention to TEL's state of mind and to the psychological urgencies that he suffered than to various departures from literal truth, it is surprising on how many points Mack and Aldington seem to agree despite their diametrically opposed attitudes—what Mack calls "embellishment," Aldington called "lying."

Although Mack is usually careful to keep his focus on TEL's personality rather than argue about narrowly defined facts, occasionally, in both text and notes, he takes exception to specific remarks by Aldington, Mousa, and Knightley and Simpson. Mack's awareness of AWL's likely responses to his text may account for some of his references to minor points by others, but this is hard to determine since, as he later wrote, "I didn't want to offend

AWL. On the other hand I never had him in mind consciously when writing."[71] In one note, Mack comments, "In connection with Lawrence's challenge [in *Crusader Castles*] of Oman's views, Richard Aldington says of Lawrence, 'He tried to pretend that Oman was a relic of the past and not worth wasting time on, since he was a charlatan, an imbecile and a smatterer' (*Lawrence of Arabia*, p. 68). In the two references Aldington provides to support his assertion that Lawrence damned Oman in this way there is nothing of the sort to be found."[72] It is hard to recognize the original from Aldington's paraphrase, and Collins's lawyers had insisted that he drop several references, but on 15 March 1951 he had identified his source to Alan Bird: TEL wrote to Charlotte Shaw on 25 February 1928 that Oman was "a fool: a pompous pretence: a sciolist."[73]

In a few places, one senses cautious constraint on Mack's part. He cites AWL's conviction that had TEL "been allowed to remain in the RAF in 1923, he probably would not have succumbed to the residuum of the Der'a experience,"[74] which fails to address reports that during his 1922 R.A.F. induction physical, the doctors refused to pass TEL due to marks of recent flagellation. He quotes Sergeant Pugh's account of TEL's "stoically heroic conduct" when he broke his arm and reports that the medical officer ordered hospitalization, which TEL refused. "According to Sergeant Pugh this was the only time he ever saw a man refuse to go into the hospital with a broken arm."[75] That was certainly a remarkably stoical response to physical pain, but it seems odd that Mack, fully aware that TEL was involved in flagellation at that time, does not speculate whether TEL found enduring his pain preferable to having to disrobe, thus exposing his weals and facing the consequences of discovery.

Mack's book generated many favorable reviews and earned the Pulitzer Prize for biography in 1976, but not everyone was happy with it. Jeffrey Meyers, in the Autumn 1976 *Virginia Quarterly Review* (*VQR*), called the work "an improvement on the denigrating and destructive biography of Richard Aldington (1955) and the lively but unreliable biography of Knightley and Simpson (1969)," but he found it "far from satisfactory." He objected that Mack too readily accepted Janet Laurie's unsupported claim that TEL had proposed marriage to her and that Mack did not adequately examine the implications of TEL's homoerotic leanings, flagellation episodes, and "sexual pathology." The final page of the review addressed AWL's attempts to control information about TEL and his appointment of an "official biographer"[76] whom Meyers did not name. On 8 November 1976, Jeremy Wilson wrote to the editor of the *VQR* complaining that Meyers had defamed both AWL and himself (the "official biographer"). He demanded the immediate resignation of the editor and a written apology from the highest official of the University of Virginia confirming that the editor had resigned, with the condition that the *VQR* not refer to his demands in print. He further stated that he would have additional requirements if these demands were not met within four weeks and that meeting his demands would not prevent AWL from acting independently.[77]

Statements that Wilson found objectionable seem accurate enough. Meyers's claim that AWL had attempted "to suppress and conceal certain aspects of T. E.'s life" since 1935 is verifiable. So is his statement that those whom Aldington identified as the "Lawrence Bureau" tried to suppress his book. So is his statement that AWL had known about TEL's flagellation since 1935 and had been "able to keep it secret until 1968, when John Bruce, who administered the beatings, sold the story to the *Sunday Times*." Meyers also was accurate in his statement that AWL had authorized Knightley and Simpson access to the restricted Bodleian archives "but suppressed in their book some of the revelations first made in their newspaper serial." (According to Mrs. A. W. Lawrence, her husband had granted access to "two journalists,"[78] and in the agreement, AWL did insist that some material from the 1968 articles not be included, such as TEL's reference in a suppressed chapter of *Seven Pillars* to a British soldier caught in an act of sodomy with an Arab.) Meyers's statement that "Arnold Lawrence then encouraged Mack to balance Knightley and Simpson's interpretation" seems plausible, given AWL's failed attempt to have the *Sunday Times* publish "a companion article that would place the story of the beatings in an appropriate psychological and historical perspective."[79] Only Meyers's observation that AWL was "not very pleased with Mack's conclusions" eludes verification, resting on an unidentified "good authority."

The final paragraph of Meyers's review may explain the intensity of Wilson's reaction:

> When I was writing my literary study of *Seven Pillars of Wisdom*, I received permission from Arnold Lawrence to quote from the unpublished Oxford 1922 edition of that work, but the permission to quote from other manuscripts was withdrawn when I discussed Lawrence's homosexuality in my essay, "Nietzsche and T. E. Lawrence." Now Arnold Lawrence has appointed "an official biographer," less qualified than any of his predecessors, who, if he ever completes his book, will probably fail once again to satisfy the literary executor. The attempt to maintain secrecy has not

been effective, and there is still no first-rate biography of Lawrence. Since so many of the "closed" papers have already been published, it would best serve the interests of truth and scholarship if they were opened to qualified people. It would also be wise to initiate (after nearly 40 years) a new edition of Lawrence's letters, only a fraction of which have been published, before they are dispersed beyond recall.[80]

Staige D. Blackford, then (as now) editor of the *VQR*, responded to Wilson on 29 November 1976 that "under the appropriate American libel and defamation standards Dr. Meyers's comments on page 723 were within the allowable limits of fair comment and criticism of an academic subject." After receiving this letter, Wilson wrote directly on 9 December to the president of the university, Frank L. Hereford, Jr., summarizing his demands, enclosing a copy of Blackford's response, and threatening legal proceedings if his demands were not met. In an enclosed letter to Blackford, also dated 9 December, he argued that the review was indeed libelous and stated that AWL had withdrawn Meyers's permission to quote after Wilson had convinced him that Meyers had quoted improperly. Wilson repeated that the editor must resign, and he listed fifteen statements from Meyers's review that he found objectionable as false or malicious. After his signature, he listed an M.A. from Oxford and an M.Sc. from London University, and he identified himself as TEL's official biographer, the editor of *T. E. Lawrence Studies*, and the editor of *The Collected Letters of T. E. Lawrence* (still not in print).

Hereford wrote to Wilson on 5 January 1977 that the university was "prepared to counterclaim a tort action for abuse of process in the event you should name either the University or Mr. Blackford as a defendant in a legal proceeding." Wilson responded on 1 February that he intended to make available to the Bodleian some information about Meyers as well as copies of the correspondence pertaining to Meyers's review. He reiterated his case before requesting that the *VQR* publish a retraction, copy for which he enclosed. On 21 February, Hereford responded that he would not request Blackford's resignation or print any retraction, and he commented that depositing the papers at the Bodleian would enable subsequent researchers to draw their own conclusions. Writing to Meyers on 23 February, Wilson stated that *T. E. Lawrence Studies* would include a rebuttal of Meyers's *VQR* comments, and he wrote to Hereford on 25 February that support for Meyers would force him to include the *VQR* in any subsequent suit and in the forthcoming rebuttal. There the matter ended. Neither Meyers nor Hereford replied to Wilson, there was no suit, and the threatened issue of *T. E. Lawrence Studies* never appeared.

Meyers's reference to Wilson's meager qualifications must have rankled. According to his own account, Wilson had reached his position as official biographer gradually. In 1968, the Bodleian had requested that Wilson have access to the embargoed papers to catalogue them. As a result, AWL recommended Wilson "when Jonathan Cape [was] urgently looking for someone to replace Colin Simpson as editor of *Minorities. . . .* In 1971, when *Minorities* appeared, Cape suggested that I should write the official biography. I turned the project down, knowing that it would involve several years' very costly research. At the end of 1974, needing an occupation which would allow me to live in France, I changed my mind. Cape then secured A. W. Lawrence's agreement to the project."[81] At the time of Meyers's review, Wilson had published a thirty-four-page introduction to TEL's *Minorities* and had also edited the first (and only) issue of *T. E. Lawrence Studies*, much of which he had written himself. Even now, it is not easy to determine exactly what Wilson has published. During the early 1970s, both the *Encyclopedia Britannica* and the *Cambridge Bibliography of English Literature* listed Wilson's forthcoming descriptive bibliography of TEL, but that work has never appeared. In the authorized TEL biography, Wilson refers to four works with publication dates of 1990—TEL's *Military Report on the Sinai Peninsula* (with Wilson's introduction), *T. E. Lawrence, A Guide to Printed and Manuscript Materials*, *T. E. Lawrence, Bruce Rogers, and Homer's Odyssey*, and *T. E. Lawrence: Wartime Diaries and Letters* (edited by Wilson and J. Law).[82] These "1990" works are still not in print.

In 1977, Desmond Stewart's *T. E. Lawrence* claimed that TEL's postwar flagellation episodes derived not from his torture and rape at Deraa, which TEL had fabricated, but from his relationship with Sharif Ali ibn al-Hussein al-Harithi. Stewart also claimed that in 1922,

> Lawrence had unwisely attended flagellation parties in Chelsea conducted by an underworld figure known as Bluebeard [Jack Bilbo], and Bluebeard's impending divorce case threatened to release lubricious details concerning Lawrence and one of his aristocratic friends which had already been hinted at in a German scandal-sheet.
>
> Lawrence laid aside other ambitions to meet this challenge to his continued enjoyment of his all-male purgatory. Sacrificing caution, he wrote to the Home Secretary [Edward Shortt] asking for the expulsion of Bluebeard and a ban on the German magazine.[83]

His Brother's Keeper

On 12 June 1977, Simpson reviewed Stewart's book for the *Sunday Times*. After mentioning Stewart's rejection of TEL's account of the Deraa episode and Stewart's surmise that "Lawrence's death could have been political murder," Simpson commented that Stewart's views

> have upset the Lawrence Trust and Jeremy Wilson, who is writing an official biography of Lawrence for Oxford University Press.
>
> The Trust solicitors at first told Stewart's publishers, Hamish Hamilton, that unless certain changes were made in the book they would revoke copyright permission to quote from Lawrence's works. They later withdrew this condition but urged that the passages should be modified if not deleted. Hamish Hamilton refused.
>
> Wilson wrote that a story in the book that Lawrence had attended flagellation parties in Chelsea conducted by an underworld character called Bluebeard was an invention. "I shall challenge you to produce evidence for this myth," he wrote to Hamish Hamilton, "and also point out to the public that you published it in full knowledge that it could not be substantiated." [84]

On 19 June, the *Sunday Times* published Wilson's protest against some of Simpson's comments and Stewart's interpretation:

> I first saw Desmond Stewart's Lawrence biography in proof, and found a sensational story which for several reasons is most improbable. Mr Stewart ascribes it to an unnamed informant who has had access to the embargoed Lawrence archives at the Bodleian Library.
>
> I can definitely state that the story does not come from the Bodleian papers, which I catalogued. More important, it is recognisable as a sensationally garbled version of a real but insignificant incident.
>
> Trying to be helpful, I contacted Mr Stewart's publishers drawing attention to these facts and suggesting that they should get some evidence from their informant or drop the story. I now learn that the T. E. Lawrence Trustees complained about the same passages. Since Hamish Hamilton have retained the story, perhaps we shall be entitled to the evidence? [85]

The next *Sunday Times* issue, 26 June, carried Simpson's response. He identified himself as Stewart's "unknown informant." On 28 March 1968, AWL had granted him access to the holdings of the Bodleian but not to the "other and supplementary papers at the offices of Messrs Kennedy, Ponsonby and Prideaux." Simpson then described his discovery of a letter from TEL to the Home Secretary asking that Bluebeard be deported and that "something be done about the magazine" that had reportedly purchased

Bluebeard's confessions. AWL "and his legal advisers" had convinced him that TEL was innocent of Bluebeard's allegations, so Simpson did not refer to the episode in *Secret Lives*. He added that "Mr Wilson is correct in saying that the letter to which Mr Stewart refers is not there now. It was no longer there when I checked the proofs of my own book four months after I first saw it."[86]

Accompanying Simpson's letter was one from Stewart, who described his own negotiations with the guardians of TEL's papers. He had approached the Bodleian Library to no avail: the original agreement left access to "the discretion of the Librarian after 1970; but a new agreement had extended the closed season until 1999." AWL had refused access

> in view of the authorisation of an "official biographer"; in December 1975 Mrs Lawrence amplified her husband's letter: "Three exceptions to the embargo have been made—to two journalists [Knightley and Simpson] to allay their suspicions and to a psychologist [Mack] and neither he nor the Bodleian wish to make more"; she added that "the young man calendaring the papers" [Wilson] was to be the biographer.
>
> In this impasse Mr Colin Simpson kindly described the archive and his difficulties with the Lawrence Trust, persuading me that on balance I was fortunate to be working without Lawrentian "guidance."

After commenting that the Bluebeard letter "helped explain the origin of the weals which disposed the RAF doctors to reject Lawrence . . . in August 1922," Stewart offered a suggestion: "If Mr Wilson would release his own version of what he now calls a 'real but insignificant incident' (in his letter to my publisher he dismissed the whole story as an absurd fabrication deriving from Bruce) and if it convinces me, I should be only too happy to modify my lines about it in future editions."[87] Instead of making the evidence available, Wilson sent a brief note to the *Sunday Times*, which printed it on 3 July: "If Mr Desmond Stewart will write to me and ask for it, I will gladly provide him with the rather lengthy evidence which leads me as a trained research historian to take a different view of Mr Colin Simpson's Bluebeard story concerning T. E. Lawrence (Letters, last week)."[88] Whether Stewart ever saw Wilson's announcement or received anything from Wilson before Stewart's death some five years later is difficult to verify.

Almost all the books about TEL that appeared between Stewart's biography in 1977 and the centenary of TEL's birth in 1988 were favorable in their depictions of TEL. In 1982, however, H. V. F. Winstone's study *The*

Illicit Adventure followed Aldington in challenging the TEL legend, and in 1986, Charles D. Blackmore's *In the Footsteps of Lawrence of Arabia*, describing the 1985 attempt to retrace TEL's movements by using *Seven Pillars* as a guide, concluded that some of TEL's self-described accomplishments were flatly impossible. The 1986 BBC documentary *Lawrence and Arabia*, produced by Julia Cave and Malcolm Brown, interviewed TEL scholars (including Suleiman Mousa and Jeremy Wilson). It presented a more comprehensive view of TEL than had been possible in the earlier 1962 documentary and featured AWL, in the middle of his ninth decade, commenting on how sundry adulators and denigrators had shaped the TEL legend. During the centenary year, there appeared a volume of TEL's letters (edited by Malcolm Brown), *A Touch of Genius: The Life of T. E. Lawrence* by Malcolm Brown and Julia Cave, *T. E. Lawrence: A Bibliography* by Philip M. O'Brien, and *Images of Lawrence* by Stephen E. Tabachnick and Christopher Matheson, which made available a summary of TEL's public image as it had evolved through 1986, a photographic history of TEL, and an assessment of TEL's actual achievements.

After Sarah Lawrence's death in 1959 and M. R. Lawrence's death in 1971, it was no longer necessary for AWL to protect them. He remained concerned about TEL's reputation, but his direct participation in TEL projects declined. As Jeremy Wilson later remarked, "His advice to me [in 1974] was very simple: to do the work as best I could, and to publish whatever conclusion I reached. At the outset, he gave me carte-blanche to print any Lawrence copyright material I chose. My access to the Bodleian archive continued and, in addition, he wrote a note requesting help from others who might control access to relevant documents. That was the sum total of his assistance, and I asked for nothing more." After Meyers's comments in the 1976 *VQR*, Wilson and AWL "agreed" to have "minimal contacts." They did not meet again for ten years. Wilson indicated that "a deepening hostility to the biography project and perhaps to me personally . . . led to serious obstruction which forced me to take legal advice. . . . Following publication he at last wrote, praising the book very generously."[89]

AWL also gave a free hand to Malcolm Brown, who wrote to me on 14 January 1993,

> You asked if my excisions in the Lawrence *Selected Letters* were due to interventions by A. W. Lawrence. Not at all. His condition for my doing the book was that I shouldn't bother him about it—just get on with it. The cuts were my own or my editor's—many dictated by the fact that

the publisher demanded a major reduction when I submitted my first selection in order to get it down to approximately 600 pages; others by the fact that I wanted not to waste space on those inevitable passages in letters which are about uninteresting minutiae. The problem is you can't win: it looks as if you're excising to conceal, when you're really excising so as not to bore. Not all letters are worth reading from Dear So and So to Yours truly.[90]

In my own limited communication with AWL, I found him very helpful despite his knowledge of my appreciation of and sympathy for Aldington. He was extremely informative in a telephone interview, and he quickly provided formal written permission when I needed his consent to acquire copies of two BBC broadcast scripts.[91] Others received less cooperation. On 15 June 1987, AWL responded to Lawrence James's letter about TEL's political views that "I cannot help you, because I am already much involved in other biographical studies of my brother, and as far as I can see the subject you propose has already been well covered." On 21 June 1987, he refused James's request for access to the restricted Bodleian archives on the grounds that "there is nothing to your purpose in the posthumous transcripts of personal letters that compose the Bodleian collection, & the library has not completed sorting them."[92]

Now that AWL has died, access to the Bodleian papers and permission to quote TEL's words reside solely with the two TEL Trustees, M. V. Carey and the Hon. Henry Hankey. Carey reports that "It is unlikely that the embargo [on access to the Bodleian TEL archives] will be extended."[93] Sources at the Bodleian indicate that after the necessary "conservation and calendaring," researchers should be able to examine archival materials after 1999. A separate embargo on the copies of letters collected by E. M. Forster and David Garnett will expire in 2000. Since there are only about 400 letters in the restricted collections, many of which have appeared in print wholly or in part, the likelihood of significant discoveries does not seem great. That will not deter researchers from continuing to pursue the elusive and ever-controversial TEL in those documents.

8

ALDINGTON AND THE DOCUMENTS

The documents are liars. No man ever yet tried to write down the entire truth of any action in which he has been engaged. All narrative is parti pris. And to prefer an ancient written statement to the guiding of your instinct through the maze of related facts, is to encounter either banality or unreadableness. We know too much, and use too little knowledge.

—T. E. Lawrence to Lionel Curtis, 22 December 1927

Personally, I think my TEL book will be superseded in a few years['] time—younger writers will follow up my clues and will accuse me (as one of my "researchers" [Denison Deasey] did) of "pulling punches all the way."

—Richard Aldington to Henry Williamson, 22 February 1954

I do not pretend to have written the definitive biography of Lawrence, nor is this in any sense a final portrait of the man. Much of the evidence that is necessary for such a task is still not available.

—Richard Aldington, *Lawrence of Arabia*

ALDINGTON'S CONTRIBUTION TO our knowledge of TEL and the events in which he engaged has been considerable. Aldington provided a long-needed corrective to hagiography and pointed to questions that others might have raised years earlier had they bothered to investigate more diligently. He gave the lie to some romantic notions of the desert war. Most important, he defined the areas of controversy about TEL and made people face contradictions implicit in a myth that they had accepted without adequate investigation or reflection. Aldington's discoveries stand up surprisingly well despite the findings of TEL scholars during the past four decades. Much that shocked in 1955 is now standard knowledge—that TEL was illegitimate, that this profoundly troubled him, that he frequently resented his mother's dominance, that such reminiscences as *T. E. Lawrence by His Friends* are not reliable, that TEL's leg-pulling and other adolescent traits could be offensive, that TEL took liberties with the truth in his official reports and in *Seven Pillars*, that the significance of his exploits during the Arab Revolt was more political than military, that he contributed to his own myth, that when he vetted the books by Graves and Liddell Hart he let remain much that he knew was untrue, and that his feelings about publicity were ambiguous. Aldington's careful examination of the fragmentary evidence at his disposal enabled him to dispute many statements by TEL and by those who had exaggerated his achievements and suppressed his shortcomings.

In 1988, TEL's authorized biographer, Jeremy Wilson, dismissed Aldington's book as no longer relevant to TEL studies: "Today, its interest is mainly literary, since the documentary sources now available dispose of the contentious issues Aldington discussed."[1] AWL wrote on 17 June 1988 that "the Aldington episode is, to my mind, finished, and I am confident that you will be of the same opinion when you see J. M. Wilson's biography of T. E., due in the autumn."[2] Wilson's authorized TEL biography would draw from previously unpublished documents and the restricted archives of the Bodleian. If any book could dislodge Aldington by providing evidence that would refute the controversial questions that he had raised, Wilson's *Lawrence of Arabia: The Authorized Biography of T. E. Lawrence* would do it. Nevertheless, when Wilson's biography appeared in England in 1989 and in the United States in 1990, it left Aldington comparatively unscathed.

Wilson's biography has contributed to TEL scholarship by providing easier access to many of TEL's previously restricted papers. His thorough examination of the political background of the Arab Revolt offers the best context for understanding the nature of TEL's dilemma when he tried to serve conflicting British and Arab interests. Wilson has illuminated several aspects of TEL's personal life, including when and how he gradually acquired full understanding of his illegitimacy. As Stephen E. Tabachnick points out, however, Wilson simply provides fuller detail of what we have known for some time but does not resolve or even illuminate the more controversial issues.[3]

One reason that Wilson has failed to displace Aldington is his rejection of previously published research in favor of contemporary documents. Access to primary material is not enough. When TEL called the documents "liars," he meant that they lie because no writing can be entirely accurate or objective despite a person's desire to present the truth with complete candor and integrity. The selection of evidence, the evaluation of one fact as more significant than another, the writer's emotional or ethical or idiosyncratic response to an event, and the most dangerous assumption—that one has identified and subdued all one's own assumptions—combine to make purely objective recording beyond human reach. All documents are subjective since their contents are always under the conscious or unconscious influence of their human authors. Consulting others' views is necessary for testing not only the statements and evaluations in original documents, but also the interpretations and conclusions that one draws from such material, providing safeguards against uncritical acceptance of unreliable documents and against one's own biases.

Wilson rejects books and articles about TEL wholesale instead of trying to determine which specific arguments and evidence seem valid and which do not. As a result, he fails to profit from the evidence and analysis of earlier scholars. He passes over potentially useful sources without comment (as in the case of Lord Vansittart), or ignores them because at least one of the source's claims is demonstrably false (as in the case of John Bruce), or dismisses them for bias (as in the case of Aldington). In the process, he also rejects many insights and concerns that it is the business of an authorized biographer to address. Ironically, had he applied the same standards to *Seven Pillars*, he would not have been able to use it.

His statements about his predecessors are not always reliable. He claims that Aldington, finding inconsistencies in the biographies of Lowell Thomas, Robert Graves, and Liddell Hart, was "extremely naïve" to assume that TEL was responsible for these discrepancies,[4] but all three have identified TEL as the source of contradictory accounts, and one can verify several contradictions in TEL's own writing that Aldington cited. Wilson states that arguments by Suleiman Mousa, who drew from Arab witnesses and archives and later had access to the papers of Emir Zeid, "are adequately refuted by A. W. Lawrence in his 'Comment,' published as an appendix to Mousa's book (pp. 281–3)" (1070 n. 41), but a comparison of Mousa's text with AWL's "Comment" does not support this assertion. Wilson ignores other biographies on the ground that anything written before the 1968 release of British government documents is irrelevant, forgetting that major TEL biographies of the last thirty years have gone considerably beyond textual analysis. Knightley and Simpson drew from the government archives and also had access to the restricted Bodleian papers, but Wilson rejects them as sensationalists who relied overmuch on John Bruce. Mack drew from Bruce, the Bodleian, and the official archives, as well as from several interviews with those in a position to have had firsthand knowledge of TEL, but Wilson dismisses Mack as narrow in focus, commenting that his own "revisions and additions have considerably altered the biographical record given by Mack [in *A Prince of Our Disorder*], and have sometimes placed his argument in question; but in no sense did I set out to overturn his specialist analysis and judgments" (980 n. 4). Wilson has not put Mack's "argument in question" but has drawn much of his evidence and many of his conclusions from Mack.

Sometimes Wilson's justification for rejecting earlier TEL scholarship is weak. He dismisses the work of historian Elie Kedourie because "Although Kedourie's essay is sometimes described as 'definitive,' it was written before most of the Government papers became available" (1106 n. 56). After Janice J. Terry repeated this charge in a review, Kedourie answered it:

> Regarding the conquest of Damascus, your reviewer, copying the allegations of her author, declares that my study of this episode was written before all the documents were made available. This is not so. The episode was examined in a book published in 1956 and was reexamined in the light of the documents made available in 1968 in an essay included in a book published in 1970. The new evidence confirms and amplifies my account of 1956. In 1990, the "authorized biographer" finds nothing to add to the story, which is, briefly, that General Allenby forbade all his troops, with the exception of the so-called Northern Arab Army, to enter Damascus, and that this was followed by general disorder and looting.[5]

Another reason that Wilson has not dislodged Aldington is that his evidence depends too much on TEL. Aldington had complained that those writing authoritatively about TEL had been overly credulous in accepting TEL's version of events and inconsistent in their treatment of evidence. Refuting Aldington's charge that TEL was a charlatan who had fabricated his own legend requires independent corroboration of TEL's statements since one can hardly disprove a charge of lying by citing testimony from the purported liar. Wilson, however, treats as fact TEL's unsupported word for a number of events, including TEL's running away from home to join the Royal Artillery and subsequently having his father buy him out, TEL's being shot at during his 1909 Syrian walking tour (with no reference to TEL's contradictory accounts of the same event), TEL's meeting with Lord Kitchener in 1913, and many other claims that Aldington and others have disputed.

Instead of trying to determine the reliability of a statement by evaluating its plausibility and the integrity of its source, as Aldington did when he weighed TEL's description of the occupation of Damascus against that of General Barrow, Wilson tries to make chronology the sole criterion of accuracy. He argues that in his book "the essential points can be seen to rest everywhere on contemporary evidence rather than on some theory of my own" (14), but most of this evidence comes from TEL, and equating when TEL said something with whether it was true rather misses the point. Even so, Wilson depends primarily on accounts by TEL that are not really "contemporary." Wilson's evidence for TEL's involvement at Kut is chiefly *Seven Pillars* and *T. E. Lawrence to His Biographer Liddell Hart*. His authority that TEL explained the Sykes-Picot agreement to Feisal as early as February 1917 is a combination of the 1922 Oxford edition and the 1926 subscriber's edition of *Seven Pillars*. Too often a "contemporary" document turns out to be *Seven Pillars*, or his letters to Charlotte Shaw, or *T. E. Lawrence to His Biographer Liddell Hart*, written long after the fact.

Making chronology the test for reliability causes further problems when *Seven Pillars* (written and rewritten and ultimately published in 1926) disagrees with an earlier account. Chauvel, for example, frequently contradicted TEL's demonstrably false claim that the Arabs entered Damascus before the Australians. Since Chauvel's account "seems to date from 1923," Wilson tries to show that TEL's later account was actually the earlier: "Although Chauvel stated that his later accounts were 'copies' of notes he made at the time, these notes have apparently not been found. It is therefore misleading for [A. J. Hill in *Chauvel of the Light Horse*] to hold up 'Chauvel's unadorned contemporary recital of the events' as a corrective to *Seven Pillars* (p. 185). In reality, the 1922 text of *Seven Pillars* (*SP(O)*) was written earlier than the first of Chauvel's known accounts" (1109 n. 78). However, failure to locate Chauvel's notes in no way demonstrates that they did not exist or that Chauvel used them dishonestly. A 1923 account based on 1918 notes seems much more "contemporary" than *Seven Pillars*, which, according to Wilson, TEL rewrote at feverish pace, from memory, with only the fraction of his notes that had survived after the first version disappeared from Reading station in 1919. Also, since Hill is not talking about the 1922 *SP*(O) draft but the extensively reworked 1926 subscription edition, Wilson's comparison of the 1922 draft with Chauvel's 1923 version seems beside the point.

In order to put *Seven Pillars* as close as possible to the events that it describes, Wilson treats this drafted, redrafted, revised, and reworked narrative as a 1919 document. Trying to justify TEL's misrepresentation of the conditions under which he first went to the Hejaz, Wilson argues that "*Seven Pillars* was first drafted in 1919. At that period, when the future of the Middle East had yet to be settled, Lawrence may well have felt that it would be improper to reveal this kind of detail about wartime Intelligence work" (1031 n. 68). While it is true that TEL wrote and published material related to *Seven Pillars* in 1919, 1920, and 1921, Wilson's argument does not apply to the version that TEL had considerably enhanced and revised in 1926 after he had repeatedly claimed that the future of the Middle East had been settled in 1921.

When *Seven Pillars* conflicts with TEL's earlier report to Clayton, Wilson explains that "Lawrence simply confused two journeys," implying in this instance that TEL's contemporary account is confused but the later *Seven Pillars* is accurate (1072 n. 55). Elsewhere, when a letter that TEL "clearly dated '11.xii.22' " interferes with Wilson's preferred chronology, Wilson suggests that "the letter to Roberts is misdated, and was written on 11.1.1923 when Lawrence's continuation in the RAF hung in the balance" (1127 n. 51). Usually, however, misdatings in January have the year wrong and the month right, so in January 1923, TEL would have been more likely to write January 1922 than December 1922. It seems more probable that TEL expected to receive his walking papers earlier than Wilson believes.

Wilson treats TEL's letters to Charlotte Shaw as completely candid communications, for her eyes only, and regards TEL's 29 March 1927 letter to her as evidence that TEL thought "that his letters would be discarded" (11). However, TEL knew very well that she and others were preserving his letters (or selling them for £20 apiece). His letter to her of 29 March 1927 actually functions as a reminder to keep his papers for their future importance: "[O]f course somebody will want to write a life of me some day, and his only source will be such letters as chance has preserved. Had they been all kept, there would be a pretty complete history of events since 1910: volumes of stuff enough to discourage any historian: but chance will narrow his pile down" (Wilson, 11; Brown [TEL, *Selected Letters*, p. 321] has "winnow" instead of "narrow").

TEL was using Charlotte Shaw as an archivist for important documents, sending her a copy of his 15 July 1918 letter to Vyvyan Richards because he regarded it as historically significant and worth preserving. As Malcolm Brown notes, "When Richards showed Lawrence this letter seven years later (in much changed circumstances), Lawrence found it interesting enough to copy for himself. He subsequently sent his copy to Charlotte Shaw apparently believing it to be the only surviving letter of his 'Arab period.'"[6] TEL, as Wilson records, later expected her to pass material to Graves and Liddell Hart for their biographies and was surprised when she held back her letters and other TEL papers, but Wilson does not seem to realize the implications that the Charlotte Shaw "archive" has for the context in which TEL wrote to her. TEL did not intend his letters to her to remain private. He was writing for history as much as for her.

Sometimes Wilson's handling of accessible material casts doubt on his descriptions of documents that others cannot examine. He states that Bernard Shaw's response to *The Mint* reveals "a streak of prudishness in his character" (823), quoting Shaw's 12 April 1928 letter in excerpt, but Shaw's letter focused on TEL's purple prose and on a description that was gratuitously cruel, as Stanley Weintraub made clear three decades ago:

> As for his literary opinions, Shaw contented himself with suggesting two excisions, both from later parts of the manuscript. "Police Duty" (Part III, Chapter 12) was a retelling of a military policeman's story of a London adventure in which a tart concealed her dead infant in her bed while entertaining the corporal on a couch. Not condemning the tale as gratuitous bad taste, G.B.S. attacked it instead for its purple patchy descriptive passages, which read like a student effort. "Funeral" (Part III, Chapter 9), which G.B.S. also suggested scrapping, described a parade service Lawrence and his comrades were subjected to (including a long sermon on the Queen's reputation for beauty and virtue) on the day Queen Alexandra was buried. Hating what he considered to be folly and imposition even in good weather, let alone on a morning of chilly autumn fog (earlier, when the news had reached camp, they had to stand at attention while drums rolled and rolled, and the flag crept down agonizingly to half-mast), he recalled his last memory of the aged Queen, mummified-looking in her last, pitiful years. It was in bad taste, Shaw warned, and was unneces-

sarily cruel, savage and ignoble to so write of the infirmities of senil-
ity—which required instead man's most humane understanding.[7]

There is no evidence of Shavian prudery here.

Even those who have long awaited evidence disposing of Aldington
had to admit that Wilson's book has failed to provide it, partly because
Wilson glosses over or ignores those points that have formed the basis of
the post-Aldington TEL controversy and partly because Wilson relies too
much on TEL's testimony and too little on evidence from other sources.
This became even more clear in 1990 with the appearance of *The Golden
Warrior: The Life and Legend of Lawrence of Arabia* by Lawrence James, author
of a dozen books on British history. James did not see Wilson's biography
until after he had written his own book, but, ironically enough, this did
not matter because the authorized biography had ignored issues that had
been troublesome since Aldington raised them and that were the central
concern of James's investigation. As James comments in his preface to the
1993 U.S. edition, Wilson's book's "approach was radically different from
mine and having read it I felt no need to revise my conclusions."[8] One
surprise for those who have recognized the advantages of Wilson's privileged access to restricted material is that James's evidence frequently goes
beyond Wilson's, particularly on controversial matters. Wilson has enjoyed
exclusive access to the TEL papers at the Bodleian for a considerable period,
but James draws more meaningfully from government files, unearthing
many previously unknown official documents that bear directly on controversial aspects of TEL's activities and character. As a result, James's documentation provides a more useful reflection of current knowledge on Aldington's conclusions about TEL.

Wilson and James differ significantly in their evaluation and use of
evidence. Aldington had noted that TEL "was never married or engaged,
and, from the sexual point of view, there are no women recorded in his
life."[9] Wilson offers the disputable testimony of Janet Laurie, first provided
by Mack, that TEL once proposed marriage to her. Laurie, a very old lady
of questionable memory, may have fantasized herself into a stronger relationship with TEL than the facts warranted, perhaps for her self-esteem,
perhaps to secure a small niche in history. In his text, Wilson repeats her
unsubstantiated claim that TEL proposed to her, but in his notes he suggests
something else: "a number of people who knew [Janet Laurie] well have
suggested to me that her story of a proposal may be exaggerated" (990 n.
40). Despite this cautionary note, her supposedly close relationship with

TEL survives by inference later in Wilson's text, giving a misleading impression, particularly to those who habitually ignore notes. James dismisses Laurie's story for two reasons, her questionable credibility and TEL's character: "If this incident occurred, and there is only Miss Laurie's word for it, it appears more an instance of Lawrence's whimsicality than of his passion" (30).

Another problematic source that Wilson and James use differently is Meinertzhagen, a bitter and disappointed man who wrote sourly about those who achieved successes that he thought lacked merit while he languished in relative obscurity. Wilson emphatically rejects him because "Meinertzhagen's diaries are demonstrably incorrect on many points, and it seems to me that much of the content is pure fantasy" (1112 n. 3). Nevertheless, he cites Meinertzhagen to corroborate that TEL was working on *Seven Pillars* in Paris in 1919 because "None of [TEL's letters of early 1919] refer to *Seven Pillars*, and the only independent evidence of its existence is the fact that parts of the draft were read in Paris by another member of the British Delegation, Richard Meinertzhagen" (598). Thus he uses Meinertzhagen when his support is helpful but ignores him when his recollections are unwelcome.

Later, forgetting his earlier use of Meinertzhagen, Wilson declares that he has "not used Meinertzhagen's *Middle East Diary* . . . or his other works as source materials for this book. It is clear from the internal evidence that these diaries were very extensively 'written up' for publication, years after the events concerned. As the original diaries seem to have been destroyed, it would be a waste of time trying to guess which parts of the text we now have are contemporary" (1117 n. 6). The real problem with Meinertzhagen, however, is not the difficulty of figuring out which comments are "contemporary" but which ones are plausible. James, comparing *Middle East Diary* with other sources, has found corroboration for many of Meinertzhagen's statements, leading him to conclude sweepingly that "the substance of his anecdotes is beyond question" (310). At least some of Meinertzhagen's comments are potentially significant. James notes that after TEL related his alleged torture and rape at Deraa, Meinertzhagen had occasion to notice that TEL "was unscarred" (211). Determining the truth of this and other comments by Meinertzhagen poses a challenge, but simply dismissing such claims instead of addressing them is not sufficient.

The most damaging of Aldington's allegations was that TEL lied not only in personal letters and remarks, but also in *Seven Pillars* and in official documents. Wilson accepts TEL as a trustworthy source: "Now that the whole account in *Seven Pillars* can be compared with contemporary documents, it is clear that Lawrence was a reliable witness, and there is little reason to doubt his specific statements about Akaba" (1055 n. 13). Even so, he provides evidence to support the opposite conclusion, quoting TEL's comment to Graves that "I was on thin ice when I wrote the Damascus chapter . . . S.P. is full of half-truth, here" [ellipsis in original]. He calls TEL's remark "almost certainly a tactical error: on the basis of these omissions, detractors such as E. Kedourie have claimed that his whole account is discredited" (1107 n. 65), but he himself identifies many statements in *Seven Pillars* as inaccurate.[10]

Wilson also points out that TEL was not always reliable in official documents. TEL's 1918 memorandum to the Eastern Committee was "written from memory and not entirely accurate" (578). In his report for the *Arab Bulletin*, TEL "concealed the real reason" for the Arabs' late arrival at Wejh (1048 n. 58). Wilson comments that "Lawrence's reticence about Akaba in reports to Cairo cannot possibly have been unintentional" (1056 n. 15). In a letter to Sir Mark Sykes, TEL did not tell the truth because "It would not have been politic" (1081 n. 16). It is difficult to reconcile Wilson's confidence in TEL's reliability with the many instances of accidental and deliberate misstatements that Wilson has scrupulously listed.

Like Wilson, James is generally sympathetic to TEL, but he approaches TEL's unsupported statements with greater caution. At the same time, unlike Aldington, James does not reject something simply because TEL said it. For James, "Aldington exposed much of [TEL's] nonsense, but, I feel, went too far and assumed that Lawrence was a compulsive liar rather than an entertainer who fabricated tales."[11] Sometimes James exonerates TEL from unfounded charges, as when he draws from contemporary sources to demonstrate that despite the account of *Seven Pillars*, it is doubtful that TEL gave the "no prisoners!" order, citing evidence that TEL tried "to restrain the Arabs and stop the massacre of prisoners" (255). Wilson simply quotes TEL's "no prisoners!" version without comment.

At one point, James remarks, "As in earlier tales of hairbreadth escapes, it is impossible to distinguish invention from reality. Nor were there any bounds to [TEL's] capacity for expanding a tale" (59–60). In the 1922 Oxford *Seven Pillars*, TEL relates the discovery of an Arab and a British soldier in an act of sodomy. According to TEL, the Arab received a hundred lashes, the British soldier's fellow rankers gave him sixty lashes, and TEL covered up the matter. For James, "This stretches credulity to breaking point, for Lawrence would have had to have secured the collusion of Colonel Joyce and other officers who were unlikely to have shared his tolerance of homosexuality. Moreover, there might have been sturdy objections to compounding one offence with another: flogging had been illegal in the British army for over thirty years. No one else present has ever drawn attention to the incident and, fifty years later, Lawrence's surviving brother, Arnold, was anxious that it remain unknown" (216).

Aldington also claimed that TEL was a charlatan whose military accomplishments were highly overrated. Wilson usually follows TEL's line. James regards TEL's claim to have destroyed his "seventy-ninth" bridge as a deliberate lie: "An analysis from all available sources gives Lawrence's total of bridge demolitions as twenty-three, an honourable score. Battle fatigue may excuse the original slip, but not its translation from an official file to Lawrence's narrative. Quite simply, he lied twice, and he allowed Graves and Liddell Hart to repeat the falsehood" (296). There is another possibility, however. Suleiman Mousa calculated that TEL had been involved in the demolition of only seven bridges (including culverts) and that "when [TEL] claimed that he destroyed 79 bridges, . . . those were all the bridges destroyed by the forces of the Revolt."[12] Since it is customary for a field commander to claim the actions of those under his command as his own, it is conceivable that when TEL claimed seventy-nine bridges, he was simply following a long-standing military tradition in his reports.

Aldington doubted that the Turks had put a price on TEL's head, pointing out that neither General Liman von Sanders nor Jemal Pasha mentioned this in their memoirs and that the existence of this reward relied on TEL's unsupported word. Wilson often mentions the reward as a fact, but the information of his sources ultimately derives from TEL: Wingate mentioned a £5,000 price to the War Office (424), TEL claimed after the war that the price went up to £20,000 (460; 1084 n. 50), the Censorship and Press Committee and the War Office referred to it (552; 1102 n. 32), and TEL made the claim in a 1918 letter to G. Dawson of the London *Times* (594; 1112 n. 65). James comments that "In fact, the head money was a general reward first announced some months earlier by Fakhri Pasha for British officers taken dead or alive" (184). Wilson seems to corroborate this, not in his biography but in his 1993 edition of extracts from the War Office's 1918 *Summary of the Hejaz Revolt*, when he specifies that the reward for TEL was £5,000 (Turkish pounds, not British).[13] It seems likely that TEL's exaggeration of "his" price derived from the "general reward" for any British officer.

TEL's statements about the existence, nature, number, and seriousness of his wounds were contradictory. Wilson claims that TEL "was wounded several times" (414), and he quotes the highest estimate that TEL provided: "Like a tedious Pensioner I showed them my wounds (over sixty I have, each scar evidence of a pain incurred in Arab service) as proof I had worked sincerely on their side" (688–89). Wilson attempts to explain TEL's arithmetic in a note: "The apparent inconsistency in Lawrence's statements about the number of his scars is accounted for in a letter to John Buchan: 'The *Seven Pillars* doesn't perhaps bring out clearly enough that I was wounded in nine different scraps (sometimes two or three damages at once: I have about fifty scars tallied on me)' " (1127 n. 38). This still does not account for the discrepancies. Wilson quotes a letter in which TEL also says that "after seven bad air-crashes, after nine war-wounds, and many peace-ones," he is happy in the ranks (691). Wilson says nothing about those "seven bad air-crashes" although the records support TEL's involvement in only one.

Aldington found TEL's enumeration of wounds highly implausible. He wrote to Henry Williamson on 4 January 1951, "I have worked out seven of those nine wounds. Five were grazes and flesh cuts by bullets in one engagement (too slight to put him out of action); a sixth was a nick on the hip from the revolver of a Turkish officer in a train wreck; the seventh was cuts and bruises from a flying boiler plate. The other two I can't trace, but he doesn't seem to have been laid up. This would account for no traces being noticed by doctors at his RAF medical."[14] James also calculates more conservatively than had TEL, mentioning that in one skirmish "One shot grazed Lawrence's hip" (199) and that during the derailing of a train, "Lawrence was wounded in the arm by metal splinters from the exploding boiler. He had also suffered five or six grazes from bullets and a broken toe" (208).

Aldington chose to believe that TEL had suffered torture and rape at Deraa, but he questioned the need for the reconnaissance that was TEL's professed reason for being there. He noted that TEL's account in *Seven Pillars* differed from the version in his letters to Charlotte Shaw. Given earlier instances of TEL's physical endurance, Aldington thought it credible that TEL "was still able to ride after the outrage," but at the same time he worried about "one or two details left unexplained." According to TEL's account, "an Armenian dresser" bandaged the wounds, and Aldington wondered whether the dressing was "never changed." He also wanted to know how Halim, one of the Arabs accompanying TEL, "had gone into Deraa and, from the lack of rumour, knew that the truth of Lawrence's identity was undiscovered" without learning about TEL's flogging. Aldington concluded, "when you consider how all-powerful the motive of vanity was with Lawrence, it seems equally possible that at the time he concealed the flogging, even though in the end his romantic exhibitionism craved the partial and literary confession in *Seven Pillars*, completed afterwards by the letter to Mrs. Shaw" (RA, *Lawrence of Arabia*, 207). Because the R.A.F. examining-doctors initially rejected TEL (according to *The Mint*) when they saw evidence of flogging, and because it did not occur to Aldington that the weals or scars might have resulted from one or more different incidents, Aldington tended to accept TEL's story but left the matter open on the ground that "There is no evidence" (207).

Wilson has very little to say about Deraa in his book. He contradicts TEL's version by pointing out that TEL "must have been" recognized by his Turkish captors at Deraa (460), but he does not comment on the implications of this. He defends TEL's account in a note: "As there is no independent evidence, there can be no direct proof. However, there are strong indications that such an event took place in Lawrence's life at this time":

> a. Lawrence's post-war attitude towards all matters linked to sex appears typical of a male rape victim. . . . Lastly, the incident left scars on his body which were later seen and commented upon by men in the Tank Corps and RAF.
> b. As regards the timing of this incident: first, it is worth noting that as soon as he returned to Akaba he recruited a personal bodyguard. Secondly, those who doubt that the event took place at this time are accusing Lawrence of an elaborate and pointless lie. Such accusations were commonplace after the publication of R. Aldington's *Lawrence of Arabia: A Biographical Enquiry*. . . . However, I have found that Lawrence was not as Aldington claimed, a habitual liar, and that *Seven Pillars* is remarkably accurate on questions of fact. Those who wished in the 1950s to show that Lawrence was pathologically dishonest hoped that the contemporary documents would eventually demonstrate that they were right. In the event, the documents have done exactly the opposite. (1084 n. 49)

This is not very convincing. TEL's apparent post-war conformity to classic symptoms of male rape victims does not prove that his *Seven Pillars* account or his confessions to Stirling and Charlotte Shaw are accurate since he might have suffered physical abuse and indignities under very different circumstances. Those scars are also problematic. While Tank Corps and R.A.F. personnel claim to have seen scars, who can say when they were inflicted, or why? The timing of TEL's hiring a bodyguard is not evidence but an instance of the *post hoc ergo propter hoc* fallacy. The defense that those who doubt TEL's word "are accusing TEL of an elaborate and pointless lie" is merely a restatement of the charge. Whether "contemporary documents" actually sustain TEL or Aldington remains to be seen since Wilson does not present them, and the ones that he usually offers tend to be written by TEL long after the fact, making them neither sufficiently reliable nor sufficiently contemporary.

James disputes that the event occurred as TEL described it, citing official documents that convince him that TEL could not have been in Deraa on the night in question and referring to TEL's differing accounts to Stirling and Graves. He notes variations among TEL's 1922 Oxford *Seven Pillars* version, TEL's 1924 letter to Charlotte Shaw that provoked her to call TEL "such an INFERNAL liar!" (213), and TEL's 1926 *Seven Pillars* version. James points to other evidence contradicting TEL, including claims that Hajim Muhittin Bey (Hajem Muhyi al-Din Bey) was "a promiscuous womaniser" and that Hogarth, seeing TEL on 14 December, "reported that he was 'looking much fitter and better than when I saw him last' " (213–14). For James, "There is no direct corroborative evidence to support Lawrence" (210).

James tries to determine TEL's motive for providing his Deraa account: "Two explanations offer themselves. First, the tale was a fabrication created to illustrate a purely literary point; secondly, he was making a coded statement about his own sexuality. Something like this had occurred to him, but at another time and in different circumstances" (214). Some of the "literary point" also had a political dimension, for "the shocking business at Dera vindicated observations made by Lawrence at the beginning of *Seven Pillars*, where he outlined the rottenness of the Ottoman system manifested by the sodomy endemic among its officer caste. Dera proved the point. . . . Yet it was a major epidemic of pellagra rather than venereal diseases which really undermined the Turkish army, as Lawrence and the army's medical services knew well" (214).

In his investigation of TEL's credibility, Aldington found several of TEL's postwar stories extremely unreliable, including TEL's boast that he had made Lord Curzon burst into tears. TEL had provided his version in a "note on the draft of *Lawrence and the Arabs*, 1927" that later appeared in *T. E. Lawrence to His Biographer Robert Graves*. Ernest Barker in *T. E. Lawrence by His Friends* recalled hearing this account from TEL in 1920, and Graves's biography identified the source as a "late member of the F. O. staff" that turns out to be TEL. Wilson reports TEL's account as fact: When Curzon "began the proceedings with a eulogy of [TEL's] achievements in Arabia," TEL replied, "Let's get to business. You people don't understand yet the hole

Aldington and the Documents

you have put us all into." At this point, "Curzon burst promptly into tears, great drops running down his cheeks, to an accompaniment of slow sobs" (576). Aldington disputed this on the basis of the testimony of Viscount Cecil, who had been present when TEL appeared before the Eastern Committee of the War Cabinet on 29 October 1918. Cecil stated that this episode had never occurred and gave Curzon's daughter permission "to use this letter in any way you please" (RA, *Lawrence of Arabia*, 299–301). Cecil's willingness to let her cite him publicly suggests that his statement was more than an attempt to console her shortly after Curzon's death.

James accepts TEL's story but comments, "Although Lawrence later thought this was something to crow about, it had been a petty triumph, since the Marquess often wept publicly" (302). James has since indicated that he had this information from "Curzon's current biographer, David Gilmour, who told me that Curzon often burst into tears."[15] Still, only Aldington has presented corroborating evidence from someone who actually attended the meeting. Wilson provides evidence that casts doubt on the story when he quotes TEL's 4 August 1921 report to Curzon of talks with Hussein: "I gave him my candid opinion of his character and capacity. There was a scene remarkable to me in that not only the Foreign Secretary [Fuad] but the King also burst into tears" (657; brackets in original). It seems highly unlikely that TEL would have described this to Curzon in 1921 as "remarkable" if he had really inspired Curzon to tears in 1918.

Aldington commented scornfully on the discrepancy between TEL's various accounts of how he had refused decorations and his leaving them in the *Who's Who* entries that he vetted. Aldington added that in 1921, when Churchill sent TEL

> to negotiate a treaty with Hussein, the patent began thus:
>
> "Our most trusty and well-beloved Thomas Edward Lawrence Esquire, Lieutenant-Colonel in Our Army, Companion of Our Most Honourable Order of the Bath, Companion of Our Distinguished Service Order . . . " [ellipsis in original]
>
> If Lawrence had effectively resigned his honours, why were they cited in this patent? If he had not resigned them, why did he and his friends claim for him the *réclame* of having done so? (270)

If TEL refused the DSO medal from King George V but failed to disavow the citation in writing, and even let the honor remain in his *Who's Who* entry, then the renunciation was merely a piece of theater.

According to Wilson, TEL had decided not to accept any decorations "during the journey to Akaba in 1917." Wilson's evidence for this is TEL's letter home, and his contemporary source for TEL's claim to King George that "he did not know that he had been gazetted or what the etiquette was in such matters" is a letter to Liddell Hart written a decade after the fact, in 1928 (577). James comments that *Who's Who* listed the ostensibly rejected honors (as had Aldington), calls TEL's disavowal "a gesture which did nothing to promote the Arab cause," and adds that "Its insensitivity was surpassed when he used the ribbon of his Croix de Guerre as a collar for Hogarth's dog" (275). He also repeats a story suggesting that TEL sported his decorations long after their reputed rejection: "One airman remembered how Lawrence, then thirty-four, had been asked by an Uxbridge NCO why he wore no war-service medal ribbons. The next day Lawrence appeared on parade with his ribbons stitched to his tunic—including presumably the immediately recognisable DSO—which discountenanced the NCO. Whether or not such an incident occurred cannot be known for certain . . ." (354–55).

Aldington did not accept TEL's professed reasons for embarking on his ill-fated flight to Cairo in May 1919, and he discovered that TEL had been party to plans for a punitive expedition against Ibn Saud at least six weeks before his departure. As evidence, Aldington quoted the published records of the Commissioners Plenipotentiary of the United States describing a 20 March 1919 meeting: "(5) Memorandum No. 168 was read in which [U.S. Army] General [Marlborough] Churchill submitted a proposal that Captain William Yale accept an invitation tendered to him by Colonel Lawrence to accompany the British Forces on an expedition which they are planning for the month of May against the tribes of Nejd" (274). When TEL left for Cairo on 3 May and experienced his only documented airplane crash on 18 May, he seems to have been on his way to join Abdulla, whom Ibn Saud overran, as Aldington notes, on the night of 25–26 May.

Wilson accepts one of TEL's explanations, stating that he planned "to visit the Arab Bureau in Cairo in order to check his narrative against the messages and notes in its files" (611) rather than join in the long-planned punitive expedition against Ibn Saud. Wilson comments that "Lawrence himself would have become involved in the affair, had anyone been able to contact him earlier" and cites a cable from the Foreign Secretary to Allenby recommending that the British send TEL "to assist in Hussein's operations" (613). Wilson follows TEL's "cover story," but James provides new evidence corroborating Aldington's view that TEL was on his way to join the punitive expedition: "on 22 May, GHQ Cairo was instructed to allocate six

Mark VI tanks, their spares and a team of instructors for immediate service in Hejaz. A specific order, addressed to Lawrence, warned him to be careful how he deployed the tanks and not to use them too far from their operational base or a railway line" (312). By then, however, TEL's injuries had made it impossible for him to participate.

Aldington also did not believe TEL's story that he had lost the first draft of *Seven Pillars* at Reading station in 1919. TEL's letter to Charles Doughty of 25 November 1919 stated that the manuscript "was stolen from me in the train" as opposed to at the station, but a letter to Vyvyan Richards of 27 February 1920 reported that "It is on paper in the first draft to the middle of Book VI; and there are seven books in all." Aldington felt that "A first draft is a first draft" and questioned TEL's conflicting descriptions of the manuscript's progress after its supposed disappearance (315–16). Wilson reports that TEL lost his *Seven Pillars* manuscript at Reading station in November 1919 and that in January and February 1920, TEL "wrote out a new version of *Seven Pillars*. He later stated that he had recreated 95 per cent of the text in only thirty days, 'by doing many thousand words at a time, in long sittings' " (627–28). Wilson's sources for this are TEL's later account in *TEL to His Biographer Liddell Hart*, a 1942 memoir by Sir D. Brownrigg, and "contemporary press reports." James accepts TEL's version but reports conflicting views: "This version was completed by November, when the manuscript was stolen while Lawrence was changing trains at Reading station. Perhaps injudiciously, he carried the draft in a bank messenger's case, which tempted a thief. Some people, Robert Graves among them, cynically imagined that Lawrence, deeply dissatisfied with what he had written, had jettisoned the manuscript and concocted the theft story" (336). For Wilson, "There is no evidence whatsoever to support the theories advanced by some writers that Lawrence either did not lose the manuscript, or lost it deliberately" (1116 n. 17). Given the situation, there also is no evidence to the contrary.

Aldington and others have pointed out that the British rigged Feisal's "election" in Iraq in 1921 (even to the point of kidnapping Feisal's only serious opponent) and that Churchill and others presented the results as entirely democratic. Wilson glosses over the actual election in a transitional sentence: "By the end of 1921, Feisal was King in Iraq, where he reigned until his death in 1933 . . . " (663). Earlier, he surmises that at the beginning of 1918, "if the future of Syria were to be decided on the principle of self-determination, [the Syrian protestors'] complaints would at the very least confuse the issue, and might well obscure the extent of local support for Feisal" (472). Local support for Feisal, however, was already pretty obscure because the urban Syrians did not want to submit to Hashemite rule. James sees the matter differently from Wilson when he describes the agenda of the Cairo Conference: "The next problem was one of window-dressing, since it had to appear that Faisal had been chosen by the Iraqis rather than imposed on them by the British" (326), but he does not describe the election chicanery.

Although Aldington's conclusion that TEL was a vainglorious liar derived from TEL's claims that he received offers to become High Commissioner of Egypt in 1922 and 1925, he suspected, as he wrote to Kershaw on 10 February 1951, that TEL "may have believed it."[16] Wilson simply quotes as fact TEL's claim from his 15 February 1922 letter home without calling attention to the charges by Aldington, Lord Vansittart, and others that the offer existed only in TEL's imagination (672). James does not call the claim an outright lie since TEL seems to have believed in the offer: "It has been suggested that in 1922 and in 1925, when Allenby resigned as High Commissioner in Egypt, Churchill recommended Lawrence as his successor. Lawrence certainly imagined that he was a candidate and was both flattered and amused" (323). If TEL believed his claim, he was not deliberately lying.

One of Aldington's more contentious allegations concerned TEL's homoerotic sympathies. He devoted only slightly more than eight pages of his book to the issue because

> The opinions of those who without any concrete evidence assert that Lawrence was a homosexual cancel out the opinions of those who thought he wasn't. So far as I can discover, there is no legal or medical evidence whatsoever.
>
> The obvious course would be to leave it at that, but, though there is no evidence as to Lawrence's sexual actions, he has unconsciously left a record of his sexual sympathies. (333)

(It would have been more accurate to say that TEL "deliberately" recorded his sympathies.) Despite the admitted lack of evidence, Aldington did not "leave it at that" but cited passages from TEL's *Seven Pillars* (including the dedication to S. A.) and TEL's *Letters* to support his supposition. The revelations of John Bruce, presented in the *Sunday Times* in 1968 and in *The Secret Lives of Lawrence of Arabia* in 1969, conceded by AWL and examined further by Mack, indicate that TEL did indulge in flagellation and seems to have derived emotional satisfaction from the practice. Despite the rumors of more than half a century, however, there still is no evidence that TEL engaged in homosexual relations. Aldington's suspicions have had an effect disproportionate to their minor role in his book.

Wilson and James address the nature of TEL's sexual orientation and activities from almost opposite poles. For his part, Wilson focuses on TEL's relationship with R. A. M. Guy as if this were the only ground for raising the question, and his rebuttal (703–5) is not very convincing. He argues that TEL's referring to Guy as "Rabbit" or "Poppet" meant nothing because everyone addressed Guy by his "ordinary service nicknames," but Wilson does not speculate about how Guy had acquired them. According to Wilson, "the lack of privacy would make it far more difficult to conduct a homosexual affair in the ranks than in civilian life," as if this would deter someone of TEL's ingenuity, particularly since he had the Clouds Hill cottage. Wilson comments that TEL withheld the name of one of his female admirers from Guy, but TEL's remark of explanation ("Some of you youths are so impulsive") might have had a pointed irony. Although Wilson adds that Guy later married, this does not prove that there had been no homosexual activity or explain Guy's confident request (at least once) for £350, a substantial sum. Wilson contends that "One can discount such obviously leading remarks as Stewart's comment: 'Guy visited the cottage which became the focus of Lawrence's private life' " (1128 n. 81), but Clouds Hill was "the focus of Lawrence's private life," and Guy did visit.

The fragmentary evidence that James presents in support of TEL's alleged homosexuality is unreliable and secondhand: "To Robert Graves, Lawrence was more explicit. He confessed an urge to be whipped and, after his return to England in December 1921, admitted that he enjoyed being buggered [according to Martin Seymour-Smith's biography of Graves]" (216–17). James cites the story that Robin Maugham (like his uncle, Somerset, homosexual) had heard from an NCO at Bovington that "he had whipped Lawrence and then buggered him." He also mentions Somerset Maugham's 1958 letter to Aldington: according to Hugh Trenchard (Chief Commissioner of Police after his retirement from the R.A.F.), there was a warrant "for [TEL's] arrest to answer charges of indecent behaviour with servicemen at Cloud's Hill" shortly before TEL's fatal accident. The Home Secretary would have had to receive a formal complaint before anyone could issue such a warrant, but James has found no documentary evidence in the Home Office records to substantiate Maugham's allegation (219–20). James quotes the diary of Kathleen Scott, widow of Robert Falcon Scott, in which she records Colonel C. E. Vickery's statements that TEL was actively homosexual. When she confronted him with Vickery's allegations, TEL, according to her ambiguous diary entry, "Admitted his proclivities, but didn't affect his life" (369–70), which is susceptible to differing interpretations. Even if the widespread rumors justify investigation, they all derive from hearsay.

Wilson barely discusses TEL's involvement with flagellation. He argues that "Since Lawrence himself left no explanation, and there is no opportunity for detailed psychiatric questioning, further speculation as to the causes of this behaviour can lead to no conclusive result," and he dismisses TEL's flagellation disorder on the grounds that "private behaviour of this nature is usually totally independent of a person's everyday life" (751). Nevertheless, TEL arranged, enjoyed, and successfully concealed his flagellation episodes despite the lack of privacy in the military and the intense public interest in his activities. The flagellation episodes engaged his attention frequently and formed an important part of who he was. Proposing that this aspect of TEL's life was not important because it did not interfere with his other activities is a bit like arguing that Jack the Ripper's psychosis was irrelevant because it did not seem to hurt his work at the office.

According to James,

> Not long after [TEL's return to England in December 1921], if not before, Lawrence was willingly submitting himself to experiences akin to those he said he had had at Dera. The early stages of his addiction remain obscure; not surprisingly, since such behaviour broke the criminal law. At some time during 1922 he was present at flagellation parties held in Chelsea by a German, Jack Bilbo, who was also known as Bluebeard. This pander had offered his confessions to a German magazine and Lawrence, fearful of public exposure, even possibly prosecution, wrote in the autumn of 1922 to Edward Shortt, the Home Secretary, asking for Bluebeard's deportation and the suppression of the magazine. (217)

James cites Desmond Stewart's evidence, a letter from TEL to the Home Secretary, and summarizes the history of this elusive document:

> This letter was seen by Colin Simpson among the Lawrence papers held in the Bodleian Library, Oxford. In a letter to the *Sunday Times* (26.6.77) he claimed that it was removed shortly after and that he had been persuaded to exclude its contents from his biography, having heard from Arnold Lawrence and the Lawrence Trustees that Lawrence had been hounded unjustly by the German magazine. Publication by Stewart dismayed the Trustees [AWL, his wife, his daughter, and his friend Marshall

Sisson]. No copy of Lawrence's letter was kept in the Home Office files concerning deportations during 1922–3. No mention of this strange tale was made in Wilson's *Lawrence of Arabia*. (388 n. 24)

Contrary to TEL's belief, matters of deportation were outside the province of the Home Secretary. James records that

Bilbo was not prosecuted, nor did he attract police attention, since the Metropolitan Police possess no file on him. He seems to have left the country, for in October 1932 he was in Berlin where he was contemplating publishing his memoirs. Somehow aware of his intentions, Lawrence appealed directly to his distant cousin [actually his first cousin], Sir Robert Vansittart, at the Foreign Office. Backed by a departmental legal adviser, Vansittart agreed to contact the Berlin Embassy and secure the banning of the proposed book. Again it is unclear whether any action was taken, since no reference to Bilbo or what he had in mind to write appears in those Foreign Office files for the winter of 1932/3 which are publicly available. (217)

The 1922 letter from TEL to the Home Secretary has disappeared from view. In the Phillip Knightley/Colin Simpson T. E. Lawrence Research Papers at the Imperial War Museum, however, James found an intriguing note of a 30 September 1932 letter from TEL to the Hon. Edward G. Eliot, his solicitor and one of the original Seven Pillars Trustees: "I was lucky yesterday, in tumbling across one of the legal advisers of the Foreign Office. To him I told about Jack Bilbo's book. He opined that it concerned them— so we descended together on Vansittart, one of the big noises in the F.O. He said 'certainly' and his Ambassador in Berlin is to be written to, at once, so that steps may be taken about the book."[17]

One consequence of Aldington's TEL book is the conviction that any reticence about TEL signals an attempt on the part of his admirers to hide something. Such has been the case with reports that TEL attended flagellation parties at Jack Bilbo's Chelsea establishment in 1922. Jeremy Wilson stated in the 19 June 1977 *Sunday Times* that Desmond Stewart's TEL/Bilbo story was "recognisable as a sensationally garbled version of a real but insignificant incident,"[18] but he did not explain himself then, and whatever evidence he might have remains his private preserve two decades later. The natural result of his silence has been to increase curiosity about the incident and to encourage TEL biographers to speculate about what really happened.

Recent research by J. N. Lockman, however, suggests a plausible explanation for the "real but insignificant incident" that conforms to the existing evidence. According to Lockman,

> Jack Bilbo, born Hugo Baruch in Berlin in 1907, and therefore only fifteen years old in 1922, was, moreover, not even living in England at the time. . . . In 1932 he published a German pulp thriller called *Chicago-Schanghai* which featured Lawrence as infiltrating the Chinese underworld (undoubtedly inspired by headlines in the late 1920s falsely describing Lawrence as spying in Asia). Lawrence did not appreciate the criminal association, billed as nonfiction, and understandably tried to suppress the book.[19]

It would not have made much sense for TEL to approach Vansittart in 1932 to squelch a scandal concerning flagellation parties, but the Foreign Office would most certainly have wanted to stop rumors that England was using TEL as a master spy in China, particularly after the headaches that newspaper falsehoods about TEL's supposed spying in Afghanistan had caused the British government in 1928. This would account for TEL's 30 September 1932 letter to his solicitor, Edward G. Eliot. Since Bilbo was not in England in 1922, and since no one seems to be able to locate the letter, or any record of it, that TEL ostensibly sent to the Home Secretary in 1922, Lockman argues that "The mysterious '1922' letter, if it ever existed, was almost certainly just another harmless one written by Lawrence in 1932" (72–73).

Four decades after the publication of Aldington's TEL book, many of the mysteries remain. Because TEL's testimony is so frequently unreliable and since corroborating evidence simply does not exist for many of the events he has described, uncertainty about TEL is likely to continue. TEL once said that people would rattle his bones after his death, and he took the trouble to bury a good many misleading bones himself, inspiring one wit to refer to him as Piltdown of Arabia. We seem no closer now to determining emphatically one way or the other such matters as whether TEL actually enlisted in the Royal Artillery before the war, whether he actually lost his *Seven Pillars* manuscript in 1919, or to what extent he was really behind the activities of the Arabs during the revolt. Despite the claims that the documents would resolve the TEL mystery, in reality they have resolved surprisingly little except that Aldington, without access to official files, had asked the right questions.

Aldington's revelation of the complex and contradictory human being behind the TEL legend has not ended admiration for TEL's endeavors in the Arab Revolt, or for the flamboyance of his personality, or for his literary achievements, nor should it. The discoveries of Aldington and those who have continued to investigate the questions that he identified have made TEL more fascinating than the two-dimensional adventurous figure publicized by Lowell Thomas and certainly more sympathetic as a multi-dimensional human being. Now that we have a better sense of the challenging liaison role behind the TEL legend and can appreciate it in the context of its high personal cost to TEL, it is possible to respect him for what he was as much as for what he said he was. Perhaps the most ironical facet of Aldington's legacy is that although he knocked TEL from his pedestal, Aldington has made him an even more intriguing biographical subject.

9

CONCLUSION
ALDINGTON'S LEGACY

As a child in Scotland I received as a Sunday School Prize Lowell Thomas's "Boy's [*sic*] Life of Lawrence of Arabia." It has been a long wait for the "Adult's Life."

—Donald Malcolm to Richard Aldington, 17[?] July 1955

In the short term [Aldington's] book did harm to Lawrence's reputation; in the longer term it created a climate in which Lawrence's life and his legend could be examined more objectively.

—[A. J. Flavell], *T. E. Lawrence: The Legend and the Man*

Aldington made an enormous impact with his TEL book. No biographer after him could simply gloss over TEL's propensities for mythmaking and self-advertising. His painstaking care to document his findings introduced higher standards to TEL scholarship. Before Aldington, uncritical biographers depended excessively on TEL's unsupported and frequently unreliable word, but Aldington has forced TEL's admirers to face the inconsistencies in the legend, actions, and statements of their hero and to corroborate TEL's claims with independent evidence. The widespread demythologizing of TEL began with Aldington, and all the latter-day demystifiers ride on his shoulders. Whatever the disputable "facts," Aldington stands out everywhere as the one who derailed the burgeoning myth and whose book became the springboard for every unsaintly TEL biography since.

Exposing what Bernard Shaw once called the "maddening masquerade" of TEL's life, Aldington thus began one of the most persistent and fascinating biographical chases of all time. Far from inspiring people to dismiss TEL, he has added to TEL's interest. TEL has lost none of his power to fascinate posterity, and there is no reason to believe that he will. Now that TEL's authorized biography and the bulk of the significant letters are either in print or on the verge of publication, with the embargo on the restricted Bodleian papers due to expire by A.D. 2000, scholars can soon expect to proceed without fear of blockage. Part of Aldington's legacy is the enthusiasm with which future biographers will try to come to terms with the elusive TEL.

Paradoxically, Aldington's attempt to undermine TEL's significance has made TEL even more interesting, more compelling, more complex, and more worth exploring. Aldington revealed the inaccuracy of many claims by TEL and his admirers, and he successfully challenged inflated views of the military impact of TEL and the Arab Revolt in the context of the Great War, arguing that with or without TEL, the outcome would have been the same. It would have gratified him to know how much of his research has been accepted by subsequent TEL scholars despite their infrequent and begrudging acknowledgment of his contributions. It would also have baffled him to learn that despite his exposure of discrepancies between the legend and the man, TEL is now an infinitely more fascinating twentieth-century hero for the conflation of opposites in his personality and achievements than he was before Aldington began his demythologizing.

Part of the reason for this lies in what Aldington called TEL's "romantic exhibitionism," which compelled TEL to create in *Seven Pillars* a "literary confession" that remains the preeminent epic in prose of the twentieth century. Despite TEL's own claims and those of his defenders, he was not writing scholarly history, and he and his defenders were wrong to claim historical status for his work. He wrote a self-consciously literary epic that he conceived as being along the lines of *Moby-Dick* and *Thus Spake Zarathustra*. We cannot read *Seven Pillars* solely for factual accuracy any more than we can read Homer for real facts despite his catalogues of names, ships, and battles.

As Stanley and Rodelle Weintraub have pointed out,

> One of the problems raised by consideration of *Seven Pillars* as a major twentieth-century work of literature is that despite its confessed inexactitude and subjectivity it *is* a work of history—a work which has the poetry of history. G.B.S. seems to have hoped as he saw it in progress that it would become history on the Thucydidean model, where the events were brought to vivid life, however great the cost was in the loss of exactitude; but Lawrence's book of the Arabian revolt is only history as is the *Iliad* history. As *literature* it does not approach so great a work as the *Iliad* but rather has the inaccuracies, extravagances, diffuseness, artificiality—and sustained genius for language—of an epic in the Miltonic manner but misplaced in time: misplaced because in its frank subjectivity and its naturalism we see its peculiarly twentieth-century aspects.[1]

TEL was also a literary character in the sense that he wrote himself. The major question for his biographers is the credibility of TEL's invented persona as reinforced in his letters, in his confidences to his friends, and in material that he provided directly to Thomas, Graves, and Liddell Hart. Frequently, he was carried away with his own myth, and, like other mythologizers, he was often inconsistent. While TEL created an epic from his own experience, it was like other epics in being deliberately inventive and literary as well as essentially historical. Contention arises when partisans of Aldington and of TEL continue to argue on the assumption that TEL's validity depends entirely on whether *Seven Pillars* is factually accurate in its recording of events and in its evaluation of the significance of the Arab Revolt.

Parties on both sides of the TEL controversy err alike when they use literalness to obscure metaphorical truth. TEL's own obsession with secrecy and role-playing, as well as the posthumous cover-ups by the "Lawrence Bureau," have only tempted demythologizers the more. TEL knew early on that every letter he wrote would be saved, possibly sold, eventually archived, and he knew that he was always on the stage of history. On occasion he forgot his sense of role and let the mask slip, contradicting himself enough to enable Aldington to ask the right questions and to provide support for his rejection of TEL as England's emblematic national hero. One consequence has been a tendency on both sides to separate facts from their contexts when biographers try to present a positive or negative portrait of TEL.

Those who have come after Aldington have often used allegation and supposition too eagerly, stretching the implications of their evidence in an attempt to deify or dismiss TEL. Nevertheless, a point-by-point refutation will not determine the ultimate validity of TEL's contribution to history or literature any more than will uncritical acceptance of every statement by TEL. Nor should one expect that the eventual availability of previously restricted material will enable a future biographer to resolve the contradictory facts about TEL to everyone's satisfaction. Myths, like truth, remain beyond facts.

Whether Aldington was right or wrong, or too harsh in his judgments, he paid a heavy price for trying to tell the truth as he saw it. The TEL project was financially ruinous for him. Delays in the book's appearance required him to meet almost five years' living expenses and the costs of his daughter's schooling with less than £3,000 (the advance from Collins less the money that he had to return to Evans Brothers and to Duell, Sloan & Pearce when those firms released him from his TEL contracts). The book was a best-seller, but Collins withdrew it as soon as it had sold enough copies to recoup the firm's expenses (including Aldington's advance), claiming that there was no demand. Although Four Square issued the book in paperback in 1957 and sold nearly 40,000 copies, Aldington received little from this edition. Collins did reissue the book in 1969 as a result of the renewed interest generated by Phillip Knightley and Colin Simpson's *Secret Lives of Lawrence of Arabia*, but by then Aldington had been dead for seven years.

Aldington's courage and feistiness in bucking the various people with a stake in TEL's spotlessness, Boy Scout behavior, military prowess, and literary genius also deprived him of his future earnings by alienating many of his readers. He had already lost part of his audience by his attack on Norman Douglas in *Pinorman*. In 1954, Graham Greene wrote a review so libelous that *London Magazine* refused to publish it without Aldington's permission (which was not forthcoming).[2] Greene remained angry enough to publish his *Pinorman* review belatedly in 1966, four years after Aldington's death.[3]

Conclusion: Aldington's Legacy

The storm of abuse that followed the release of the TEL book made publishers reluctant to associate themselves with Aldington. Between 1955, when the TEL book appeared, and 1962, the year of his death, he published only three books, all under pre-TEL agreements with friends of long standing. In 1956, A. S. Frere of Heinemann published *Introduction to Mistral*, for which Aldington won the *Prix de Gratitude Mistralienne* in 1959, and in 1957, Frere issued *Frauds*, a collection of narratives about various charlatans, pointing the moral that "The English dearly love a fraud." Aldington did not include TEL in his summaries of the careers of those who had imposed on British gullibility, but to his exasperation, Frere censored references connecting Churchill to Maundy Gregory, who had been involved in the selling of titles. In 1957, L. J. Browning of Evans Brothers published *Portrait of a Rebel: The Life and Work of Robert Louis Stevenson*. None of these books sold well. Later, when Eric Warman arranged for him to work on four travel books (*Italy*, *Austria*, *France*, and *Switzerland*) in return for £25 each, his eagerness to accept this time-consuming but unremunerative commission was pathetic.

The TEL controversy also deprived him of earnings from his many earlier volumes of poetry, fiction, criticism, and biography. Booksellers, frequently in response to complaints by TEL's partisans, withdrew Aldington's books from their shelves, so his income from earlier books disappeared virtually overnight. Except during his military service in the trenches, Aldington had supported himself solely by his writing since 1912. Although he had complained as early as the 1920s that it was becoming impossible for a writer to succeed without independent means, he had been able to earn enough to live as he chose, but the TEL storm ended Aldington's ability to support himself by his pen. In 1957, Kershaw bought a small cottage in Maison Sallé and made it available to Aldington, rent free. Bryher (Winifred Ellerman), the wealthy friend of Aldington's first wife, H.D., generously provided an annual stipend of £500 and also assumed Catherine's educational expenses. Without this help, Aldington could not have made ends meet during the last five years of his life.

Ironically, while other countries ignored him, he remained a popular and respected figure in the Soviet Union where, as he had frequently complained, thousands of copies of his works circulated while he received no royalties. In 1957, Aldington had declined an invitation to visit Moscow, but he agreed in 1962 to be the guest of the Soviet Writers' Union on the occasion of his seventieth birthday. The genuine admiration of thousands of people moved him deeply and restored his confidence in himself and in his work. Generous as always, he spent the little free time he had shopping for presents for his friends, including the children of his neighbors. Some three weeks after his return, he died in Maison Sallé on 27 July 1962 with renewed faith in the importance of his life's work, the validity of his passion for truth, and his conviction that posterity would vindicate his conclusions about TEL and those to whom he referred as the "Lawrence Bureau."

The various forms of resistance to Aldington's TEL book have symbolic significance for truth in biography. A myriad of external pressures can legally prevent publication of what the biographer believes to be the truth about the biographical subject. Aldington had to confront them all.

The most demanding censor of biography is the publisher, chiefly for financial reasons. Collins had every reason to worry about Aldington's obvious hostility toward TEL, particularly when Aldington refused to indemnify the firm against damages for libel. In addition to the legal concerns, Collins had to protect his firm's reputation, which would suffer from publishing a book that violated standards of taste. He had to consider the reaction not only of TEL's influential partisans, but also of the booksellers who provided his market. Publishing this particular book was a serious risk.

Collins was therefore in a predicament. The profit motive had made him welcome the prospect of a sensational book by a noted author, but the legal constraints under which all publishers must operate made him apprehensive. Publishers can rake in huge profits from scandal but are timid when the truth can invite injunctions that will consume those profits. As a result, Collins had to invest both time and money in efforts to make the book less vulnerable to suit. When publication resulted in critical and popular outrage, Collins kept the firm's involvement in public argument to a minimum, withdrew the book as soon as he had recouped his initial investment, and did not revive the book until fourteen years after its initial English publication.

Like all biographers, Aldington was caught in the middle. He could not reveal his findings without a publisher, yet he frequently found that his own publisher was the most demanding of his censors. After extensive "editorial" emendations and the further demands of Collins's legal advisors, Joynson-Hicks, so many externally imposed alterations mutilated the original manuscript that Aldington barely recognized his own book. The publisher, for his own protection, had insisted on "editing" beyond the literal requirements of vaguely worded law to avoid providing grounds for suit. Threats to delay publication were a form of extortion that forced Aldington to alter his book against his will.

The broader implication for authorship and publication in general is that money controls the truth in publishing in many ways. When the author's livelihood depends solely on literary earnings, the pressure becomes even more intense to exact a share of translation and reprint rights, urge the publisher to promote sales and keep books in print, and cope with a business relationship that frequently becomes adversarial when the interests of author and publisher are in conflict.

Even before his publisher saw the manuscript, Aldington had to consider the opposition that his book would arouse from TEL's estate, executors, and relatives. As soon as he realized that his portrait of TEL would be negative, he knew that he would have to contend with adversaries armed with two powerful legal weapons, the laws of copyright and the laws of libel. The nature of Aldington's TEL book precluded cooperation from AWL and the Seven Pillars and Letters Trusts, so Aldington had to be extremely wary of what he quoted or paraphrased. In some cases, the paraphrase was so distant from the original that it is difficult to identify the source, as when Aldington paraphrased TEL's "a fool: a pompous pretence: a sciolist" as "a charlatan, an imbecile and a smatterer." Paradoxically, even biographical subjects who dislike the biographer's use of their words have good reason to prefer the original version to the paraphrase.

Much of the legal oversight of biographers is legitimate protection of assets and reputations that would certainly suffer from dishonest manipulation of quotations, particularly when the biographers are clearly hostile to their subjects. The copyright laws provide legitimate protection for the owners of literary property from theft or misappropriation, and the libel laws offer legitimate protection for individuals from defamation and allegations that, once public, can damage a reputation even after the allegations have proven to be entirely false. Although copyright and libel laws both serve worthy ends, threat of suit for copyright infringement or libel can suppress or warp the truth.

Faced with the expensive prospect of defending in court, and recognizing that an injunction, even if ultimately overturned, can kill a book, a publisher will compromise by deleting passages offensive to those who can offer or withhold permissions. This occurs even when those passages are vital to an author's conception of a biographical work and reflect matters that the public ought to know.

Truth is frequently held hostage to the cost of permissions to quote or even to examine evidence. The Sinclair Lewis Estate demanded 50 percent of the profits to permit Mark Schorer to include copyright letters in his biography of Lewis. The TEL Estate demanded that Stanley Weintraub submit the entire manuscript of *Private Shaw and Public Shaw* in advance, pay 11 percent of the profits, and publish the book with Cape as conditions of quotation and access. In some instances, withholding permission to quote can suppress a biography when the permission would not be necessary for other types of studies. When James E. Miller, Jr., applied an approach to the early years of T. S. Eliot that Mrs. Valerie Eliot found unpalatable, he had to rewrite his book as a critical study. Only by changing genre to something other than biography was he able to publish *T. S. Eliot's Personal Waste Land: Exorcism of the Demons* (1977) without the imprimatur of Eliot's literary heirs.[4]

Others have been less fortunate. Violation of copyright can suppress a book even without formal legal action. B.C. Rosset's *Shaw of Dublin* (1964), the best treatment of Bernard Shaw's formative years, remains generally unavailable three decades after its physical production because Rosset failed to acquire formal permission to quote.[5] When the Shaw Estate offered to waive penalties and forgo legal action if the publisher would immediately stop selling the book, Penn State Press halted distribution. Copies remain in storage that will not be legally available until the twenty-first century, when Shaw's published works will go out of copyright.

The reviewing system is another weapon for those who wish to suppress or discredit a book. Editors routinely ask acknowledged experts to review new books in their field, but this frequently means that the reviewer has both a personal and a professional interest in the work under scrutiny—sometimes even in its failure. Earlier biographers, and subjects in their biographies, want to protect their own reputations in the context of subsequent revelations. In Aldington's case, they did this by smearing his reputation in advance, some without troubling to read his book. The savage reviews did not hurt sales since, in the process of attacking Aldington's approach, they suggested by the intensity of their hostility that the book was important, but negative reviews can easily submerge a worthy book that offers less sensational revelations.

Those who lied, invented, overpraised, covered up, or otherwise deliberately misrepresented TEL's character and accomplishments had a vested interest in concealing their distortions and in sustaining the image of TEL that they exploited. To complicate matters, many had been the dupes or victims of their subject. TEL, like Bernard Shaw, attempted to preempt biographers by providing so much information that they saw little need to verify his statements or to investigate matters further. Overwhelmed and flattered, they failed to realize that TEL was cleverly feeding them only the information that he wanted them, and posterity, to have. TEL was not new or original in this practice, but he was a genius at it. As a result, the earlier TEL biographies now seem hagiographies.

Biographers must contend with restrictions on their access to the evidence long after the death of the biographical subject. AWL, for generally commendable motives, spent years exerting his powers as literary executor to control access to information about TEL, partly to spare the sensibilities of his mother and his eldest brother. One of his powers was to determine who could read such restricted material as *The Mint*, which Aldington saw before AWL, or Aldington, knew the direction that his research would take. AWL could confine access to a privileged few.

After Aldington publicized TEL's illegitimacy, AWL continued to be extremely protective as the guardian of his brother's posthumous reputation. He became less stringent, however, after Knightley and Simpson revealed TEL's flagellation episodes, which suggests that this was the last major revelation that he had been dreading since he had assumed the role of TEL's literary executor in 1935. He imposed no restrictions on the content of Jeremy Wilson's authorized biography or on Malcolm Brown's edition of TEL's letters. AWL cooperated with others to varying degrees, granting access to the Bodleian papers for Knightley and Simpson's *Secret Lives* and John E. Mack's *Prince of Our Disorder* but withholding that advantage from Desmond Stewart and from Lawrence James.

Until the authorized life and letters of a subject appear in print, biographers face a censorship of exclusivity granted to those working on the official projects. During the years that Leon Edel produced his five-volume biography of Henry James and his edition of James's letters, the availability of James's papers to others was restricted. Valerie Eliot has imposed similar impediments pending completion of her edition of T. S. Eliot's letters, and since only the first volume has appeared, the embargo is likely to continue for some time. One consequence of this practice is that others have no opportunity to examine important evidence or to investigate a subject until the authorized or official version has appeared, thus delaying the emergence of information that the subject's partisans prefer to conceal or gloss over. Frequently, the biographies appearing in the wake of the official publications contest and overturn the sanitized version produced by their privileged predecessor. Many unofficial biographers tend to prevail over the favored few, but only if they live long enough.

Aldington's most striking achievement was to challenge the TEL legend despite encountering practically every obstacle that a biographer might face. With a minimum of resources and in virtual isolation, he overcame organized and dedicated opposition from powerful and influential friends of TEL, an uncooperative literary estate, a reluctant publisher, limitations on access to significant material, and severe restrictions from libel and copyright laws, all of which hampered his ability to tell the truth as he saw it. That he succeeded was the result of incredible courage, intellectual rigor, and determination even as he coped with crises of confidence, domestic troubles, financial woes, and failing health. His passion for truth gave him little choice. Had he foreseen the high personal cost of his TEL book, he would have written it anyway.

Notes

Bibliography

Index

NOTES

Abbreviations

AK	Alister Kershaw
ALS	autograph letter signed
AWL	A. W. Lawrence
BHLH	B. H. Liddell Hart
FDC	Fred D. Crawford
HWLE	Henry Williamson Literary Estate
IWM	Phillip Knightley/Colin Simpson T. E. Lawrence Research Papers, Department of Documents, Imperial War Museum, London
LHCMA	Liddell Hart Centre for Military Archives, King's College London
LTCCA	Lowell Thomas Communications Center Archives, Marist College
RA	Richard Aldington
SIU	Special Collections, Morris Library, Southern Illinois University at Carbondale
SIU 67	Selected Richard Aldington Correspondence (1906–1910, 1930, 1945–1963)
SIU 68	Richard Aldington Papers (1910–1962)
SIU 69	Alister Kershaw Collection of Richard Aldington Papers (1947–1962)
SIU 70	Eric Warman Collection of Richard Aldington Papers (1932–1962)
TEL	T. E. Lawrence
TLS	typed letter signed

1. The Unlikely Biographer

Epigraphs: RA to Eric Warman, 27 July 1950, SIU 70; RA to Alan Bird, 15 August 1952, *A Passionate Prodigality: Letters to Alan Bird from Richard Aldington 1949–1962,* ed. Miriam J. Benkovitz (New York: Readex Books, 1975), p. 52; and AK to FDC, 18 March 1983.

1. RA, *Lawrence of Arabia: A Biographical Enquiry* (London: Collins, 1955), p. 12. Subsequent references to RA, *Lawrence of Arabia* appear in the text.

2. *T. E. Lawrence: The Selected Letters,* ed. Malcolm Brown (New York: Norton, 1989), p. 181. This letter appeared in TEL, "Two Unpublished Letters to Ezra Pound," *Nine* 2 (Summer 1950): 180–82.

3. *Lawrence of Arabia, Strange Man of Letters: The Literary Criticism and Correspondence of T. E. Lawrence,* ed. Harold Orlans (Rutherford, N.J.: Fairleigh Dickinson University Press, 1993), p. 174.

4. AK, *The Pleasure of Their Company* (St. Lucia: University of Queensland Press, 1986), p. 93.

5. *Richard Aldington: An Autobiography in Letters*, ed. Norman T. Gates (University Park: Penn State University Press, 1992), p. 214.

6. AK, *Pleasure of Their Company*, p. 109.

7. For information about RA's life and work, see particularly RA, *Life for Life's Sake: A Book of Reminiscences* (New York: Viking, 1941); AK and F.-J. Temple, eds., *Richard Aldington: An Intimate Portrait* (Carbondale: Southern Illinois University Press, 1965); Selwyn Burnett Kittredge, "The Literary Career of Richard Aldington" (Ph.D. dissertation, New York University, 1976); and Charles Doyle, *Richard Aldington: A Biography* (Carbondale: Southern Illinois University Press, 1989). There are five published volumes of RA's letters: *A Passionate Prodigality: Letters to Alan Bird from Richard Aldington 1949–1962*, ed. Miriam J. Benkovitz (New York: Readex Books, 1975); *Literary Lifelines: The Richard Aldington—Lawrence Durrell Correspondence*, ed. Ian S. MacNiven and Harry T. Moore (London: Faber & Faber, 1981); *Richard Aldington: An Autobiography in Letters*, ed. Norman T. Gates (University Park: Penn State University Press, 1992); *Richard Aldington and H.D.: The Early Years in Letters*, ed. Caroline Zilboorg (Bloomington: Indiana University Press, 1992); and *Richard Aldington and H.D.: The Later Years in Letters*, ed. Caroline Zilboorg (Manchester: Manchester University Press, 1995).

8. RA, *Life for Life's Sake*, p. 215.

9. RA, *Autobiography in Letters*, p. 294.

10. Letters from RA to AK are in SIU 69.

11. RA quotes TEL, *Seven Pillars of Wisdom: A Triumph* (Garden City, N.Y.: Doubleday, Doran, 1935), p. 661.

12. RA, *Autobiography in Letters*, p. 30.

13. Margery Lyon-Gilbert, interview with David J. Wilkinson, 30 January 1982, private collection of David J. Wilkinson.

14. RA, *Passionate*, p. 81.

15. RA, *Literary Lifelines*, p. 150.

16. HWLE (quoted in Anne Williamson, TLS to FDC, 20 March 1992).

17. HWLE.

2. From "Biography" to "Biographical Enquiry"

Epigraphs: RA to Henry Williamson, 4 January 1951, HWLE; RA to AK, 5 August 1952, SIU 69; and RA, *Lawrence of Arabia*, p. 14.

1. RA, *Lawrence of Arabia*, p. 58.

2. Letters from AK to RA are in SIU 68.

3. Letters from RA to AK are in SIU 69.

4. RA, *Autobiography in Letters*, p. 241.

5. SIU 69.

6. SIU 68.

7. SIU 69.

8. SIU 68.

9. RA, *Lawrence of Arabia*, pp. 25–26, 33.

10. HWLE.

11. HWLE.

12. AWL, ed., *T. E. Lawrence by His Friends* (London: Cape, 1937), p. 198.

13. LH 9/13/44, LHCMA.

14. LH 1/171, LHCMA. The quotation of Churchill had appeared in *The Letters of T. E. Lawrence* [1938], ed. David Garnett (New York: Doubleday, Doran, 1939), p. 845.

15. LH 1/171, LHCMA.

16. HWLE.

17. LH 9/13/44, LHCMA.

18. LH 9/13/44, LHCMA.

19. LTCCA.

20. SIU 67.

21. LTCCA.

22. SIU 67.

23. LTCCA.

24. LTCCA. For RA's April 1940 visit to the Dutch Treat Club as the guest of Colonel Theodore Roosevelt, Jr., see Doyle, *Richard Aldington*, pp. 202–3.

25. LTCCA.

26. HWLE.

27. *T. E. Lawrence to His Biographer Robert Graves* (London: Faber & Faber, 1938), p. 59; Robert Graves, *Lawrence and the Arabs* (London: Cape, 1927), p. 5.

28. HWLE.

29. Ronald Storrs, "Lawrence, Thomas Edward (1888–1935)," *Dictionary of National Biography, 1931–1940* (London: Geoffrey Cumberlege, 1949), p. 528.

30. John E. Mack, *A Prince of Our Disorder: The Life of T. E. Lawrence* (Boston: Little, Brown, 1976), p. 473 n. 38.

31. Léon Boussard, *Le Secret du Colonel Lawrence* (Clermont-Ferrand: Mont-Louis, 1941), p. 31.

32. National Library of Australia, Canberra, NLA MS 3957.

33. RA, *Passionate*, p. 15.

34. HWLE.

35. National Library of Australia, Canberra, NLA MS 3957.

36. David Roseler, *Lawrence, Prince of Mecca* (Sydney: Cornstalk, 1927).

37. RA, *Lawrence of Arabia*, p. 195; see General Sir George de S. Barrow, *The Fire of Life* (London: Hutchinson, 1942), p. 215.

38. RA, *Lawrence of Arabia*, p. 238; see Barrow, *Fire of Life*, p. 211.

39. RA, *Lawrence of Arabia*, p. 201.

40. RA, *Passionate*, p. 29; see Général Ed[ouard]. Brémond, *Le Hedjaz dans la Guerre Mondiale* (Paris: Payot, 1931), p. 72 n. 3.

41. TEL, *Letters*, p. 277.

42. RA, *Lawrence of Arabia*, pp. 274–75; RA cited *Papers Relative to the Foreign Relations of the United States*, 11:123.

43. HWLE.

3. Dangerous Liaisons

Epigraphs: RA to AK, 15 April 1952, SIU 69; RA to Alan Bird, 22 November 1952, *Passionate*, pp. 70–71; and RA to Alan Bird, 23 October 1953, *Passionate*, p. 96.

1. The memorandum is in SIU 69.

2. Letters from RA to AK are in SIU 69.

3. AK, interview with FDC, Maison Sallé, 14 May 1988; AK, TLS to FDC, 8 July 1988.

4. Correspondence between W. A. R. Collins and AK is in SIU 69.

5. RA to W. A. R. Collins, 8 September 1952, and "Notes of Memorandum from Collins' Reader/From Richard Aldington," are in SIU 68. Correspondence between RA and Collins is in SIU 68 unless otherwise specified.

6. Lord Mark Bonham-Carter, interview with FDC, London, 1 June 1988.

7. Correspondence between John Holroyd-Reece and AK is in SIU 69. This letter, misdated on the first page as dictated on 29 August 1951 and typed on 2 September 1951, was dictated in London on 29 August 1952 and typed in Florence on 2 September 1952.

8. Correspondence between AK and F. T. Smith is in SIU 69.

9. RA, *Passionate*, pp. 59, 80.

10. SIU 69, accompanying Smith's letter of 16 October 1952 to AK; Storrs, "Lawrence, Thomas Edward," pp. 528–31.

11. RA, *Passionate*, p. 67.

12. Correspondence between RA and Holroyd-Reece is in SIU 69.

13. SIU 69.

14. RA, "Notes on Messrs Joynson-Hicks Memorandum/Chapman-Lawrence Problem," SIU 68.

15. Holroyd-Reece's typed copy of Cass Canfield's letter, mailed to AK on 24 December 1952, is in SIU 69.

16. SIU VFM 1079.

17. RA, *Autobiography in Letters*, p. 258. A slightly different version appears in RA, *Passionate*, p. 79.

18. SIU VFM 1079.

19. SIU 68.

20. RA, *Passionate*, p. 89.

21. HWLE.

22. SIU 69.

23. RA, *Lawrence of Arabia*, pp. 44, 68.

24. RA, *Passionate*, p. 103.

25. SIU 68.

4. The "Lawrence Bureau" Mobilizes

Epigraphs: BHLH, "Notes on the Article in 15 Feb. issue of Newsweek (U.S.) 'Lawrence: Lies or Legends'," LH 9/13/44; W. A. R. Collins to S. F. Newcombe, 20 March 1954, LH 9/13/44; and Eric Kennington to BHLH, 24 July 1954, LH 9/13/44.

1. Letters from RA to AK are in SIU 69.

2. AK, interview with FDC, Maison Sallé, 14 May 1988.

3. "Londoner's Diary," London *Evening Standard*, (19 January 1954), p. 4.

4. Jay Luvaas, TLS to FDC, 1 September 1988.

5. Correspondence and documents in this chapter, unless otherwise specified, are from BHLH's file copies, LH 9/13/44, LHCMA.

6. SIU 69.

7. "Lying Attributed to T. E. Lawrence: Biographer Aldington Says He Will 'Erase from History' Author of 'Seven Pillars'," *New York Times* (25 January 1954), p. 13.

8. IWM 69/48/3.

9. IWM 69/48/3.

10. IWM 69/48/3.

11. Robert Graves, *In Broken Images: Selected Correspondence* [1982], ed. Paul O'Prey (Mt. Kisco, N.Y.: Moyer Bell, 1988), p. 251.

12. Adrian Liddell Hart, TLS to FDC, 18 August 1988.

13. Graves, *In Broken Images*, p. 252.

14. Brian Holden Reid, "T. E. Lawrence and Liddell Hart," *History* 70:229 (June 1985): 221, 221 n.

15. Reid, "T. E. Lawrence and Liddell Hart," p. 225.

16. BHLH, *Strategy: The Indirect Approach* [1954] (New York: Frederick A. Praeger, 1967), p. 198.

17. Adrian Liddell Hart, TLS to FDC, 18 August 1988.

18. Martin Gilbert, *Winston S. Churchill, Volume VI: Finest Hour, 1939–41* (Boston: Houghton Mifflin, 1983), p. 934.

19. John J. Mearsheimer, *Liddell Hart and the Weight of History* (Ithaca, N.Y.: Cornell University Press, 1988). See particularly chapter 7, "The Resurrection of a Lost Reputation," pp. 178–217.

20. Jay Luvaas, "Liddell Hart and the Mearsheimer Critique: A 'Pupil's' Retrospective," *Parameters* 20:1 (March 1990): 12, 17.

21. SIU 69.

22. Lady Kathleen Liddell Hart, interview with FDC, Medmenham, 17 June 1988.

23. Letters from AK to RA are in SIU 68.

24. LH 9/13/64, LHCMA.

25. IWM 69/48/3.

26. SIU 68.

27. SIU VFM 1079.

28. Robert Graves, *Between Moon and Moon: Selected Correspondence* [1984], ed. Paul O'Prey (Mt. Kisco, N.Y.: Moyer Bell, 1990), pp. 123–24.

29. "Londoner's Diary: The Lawrence Myth," London *Evening Standard*, (4 February 1954), p. 4.

30. "London Diary," *New Statesman and Nation* 47 (6 February 1954): 150.

31. "Lawrence: Lies or Legends?" *Newsweek* 43 (15 February 1954): 100–2.

32. "T. E. Lawrence Issue Rallies His Friends," *New York Times* (15 February 1954), p. 21.

33. "Not a 'Phoney': Friends Prepare Answer to Attack on Lawrence of Arabia," Bermuda *Royal Gazette* (19 February 1954), p. 9.

34. Harvey Breit, "In and Out of Books—The Dispute," *New York Times Book Review* (28 February 1954), p. 8.

35. Peter D. Whitney, "Lawrence of Arabia Again Stirs a Storm: Mystery of the Desert Hero Is One That Touches Noted Personages," *New York Times* (28 February 1954), section E, p. 10.

36. LTCCA.

37. "Lawrence's Defenders," *Newsweek* 43 (5 April 1954): 97–98.

38. "Publisher Delays Life of Lawrence," *New York Times* (14 April 1954), p. 9.

5. The Publisher in Spite of Himself

Epigraphs: RA to AK, 5 April 1954, SIU 69; RA to William Dibben, 20 October 1954, Richard Aldington Letters to William Dibben (1947–1956), SIU Acc 946; and RA to AK, 10 December 1954, SIU 69.

1. AK, interview with FDC, Maison Sallé, 14 May 1988.

2. Correspondence between AK and John Holroyd-Reece is in SIU 69.

3. Letters from RA to AK are in SIU 69; letters from AK to RA are in SIU 68.

4. AK, TLS to FDC, 24 May 1992.

5. Letters from Ronald Politzer to AK are in SIU 69; letters from AK to Politzer are in SIU 68.

6. HWLE (quoted in Anne Williamson, ALS to FDC, 25 March 1993).

7. Letters from W. A. R. Collins to AK are in SIU 69.

8. Holroyd-Reece, "Private Notes," SIU 68.

9. Letters from F. T. Smith to AK are in SIU 69.

10. Holroyd-Reece, "Private Notes," SIU 68.

11. Correspondence between Ronald Politzer and RA is in SIU 68.

12. Marshall Pugh, "What Is the Truth about Lawrence of Arabia? At 92, She Defends Her Hero Son," London *Sunday Graphic* (11 April 1954), from BHLH's typescript for his files, LH 9/13/44, LHCMA.

13. Letters from RA to Dibben are in SIU Acc 946.

14. Letters from or to BHLH are in LH 9/13/44, LHCMA.

15. Frank B. Cockburn's letters to AK and to Holroyd-Reece and Joynson-Hicks's letters to Cockburn are in SIU 69.

16. Lady Kathleen Liddell Hart, TLS to FDC, 20 November 1990.

17. Nancy Cunard, " 'Bonbons' of Gall," *Time and Tide* 35 (17 April 1954): 517.

18. Compton Mackenzie, "Sidelight," *Spectator* 192 (30 April 1954): 518.

19. [Constantine FitzGibbon], "Group Portrait," *Times Literary Supplement* (7 May 1954), p. 300.

20. David M. Low, "East Wind," *Listener* 51 (20 May 1954): 892.

21. RA, *Passionate*, pp. 121–22 n. 12.

22. IWM 69/48/3.

23. Joseph Dean, "What Did Gladstone Do in 1881? Action for Libel," London *Evening Standard* (11 December 1953), p. 13.

24. "Un Écossais démasque Lawrence d'Arabie," Paris *Match* (27 February–6 March 1954), p. 79: "Archives secrètes à l'appui, Aldington affirme: 'Mégalomane pour se venger de sa condition d'enfant naturel, Lawrence a fabriqué de toutes pièces son mythe' " ("A Scot Unmasks Lawrence of Arabia": With secret archives to back him up, Aldington states: "A megalomaniac seeking to avenge himself for his illegitimate condition, Lawrence has fabricated his own myth"). The identification of RA as a Scot is an error.

25. Lord Mark Bonham-Carter, interview with FDC, London, 1 June 1988.

26. Letters from RA to Warman are in SIU 70.

27. RA, *Passionate*, p. 278.

28. Howard M. Sachar, "The Declining World of T. E. Lawrence," *New Republic* 130 (10 May 1954): 18–19.

29. Henry Williamson, "Threnos for T. E. Lawrence: I," *European*, no. 15 (May 1954): 46–47, 48.

30. Henry Williamson, "Threnos for T. E. Lawrence: II," *European*, no. 16 (June 1954): 52, 60.

31. Elie Kedourie, "Colonel Lawrence," *Cambridge Journal* 7 (June 1954): 515, 525, 527, 530.

32. Letters from AWL to Celandine and to Eric Kennington are in IWM 69/48/3.

33. A. J. Neame, "T. E. Lawrence—Security Risk," *European*, no. 17 (July 1954): 45, 47, 48, 54, 55, 59.

34. David Garnett, "The Eagles' Nest," London *Observer* (4 July 1954), p. 11.

35. Robert Graves, "No. 2 Polstead Road," *New Statesman and Nation* 48 (24 July 1954): 106.

36. Henry Williamson, "New Books" (review of *Home Letters of T. E. Lawrence and His Brothers*), *European*, no. 21 (November 1954): 50–51.

37. SIU VFM 1079.

38. SIU VFM 1079.

39. Lord Mark Bonham-Carter, interview with FDC, London, 1 June 1988.

40. SIU 68.

41. "Londoner's Diary: Lawrence Attacked," London *Evening Standard* (20 September 1954), p. 4.

42. SIU 67.

43. Thomas Jones, *A Diary with Letters, 1931–1950* (London: Oxford University Press, 1954), pp. 149, 173–74.

44. "Londoner's Diary: Counter-attack," London *Evening Standard* (24 September 1954), p. 4.

45. "French Criticisms of T. E. Lawrence: Old Memories Stirred by New Book," London *Times* (27 November 1954), p. 5.

46. LH 1/352/179–80, 181, LHCMA.

47. Leo Amery's letter to Collins and RA's letter to Amery are in LH 9/13/44, LHCMA.

48. SIU 69.

49. RA, *Lawrence of Arabia*, p. 123.

50. James Mayo, "British Hero Debunked. *Lawrence L'Imposteur*: New Book Creates World Sensation," London *Sunday Chronicle* (9 January 1955), pp. 1, 3.

51. RA, *Passionate*, p. 150.

6. Killing the Messenger

Epigraphs: RA to Henry Williamson, 6 February 1952, HWLE; BHLH to Sir Linton Andrews, 28 February 1955, LH 9/13/44; RA to Alison Palmer, 13 November 1955, RA, *Autobiography in Letters*, p. 280; and Paul Johnson, "Fallen Pillars," *New Statesman and Nation* (5 May 1956), p. 490.

1. Doyle, *Richard Aldington*, p. 271.

2. BHLH, "What Authority Has Aldington for Writing This Niggling, Disparaging Book? Lawrence: His Friend, a Great Historian, Answers the Smears and Sneers," London *Sunday Chronicle* (30 January 1955).

3. Mervyn Jones, "Lawrence or Aldington? I Dislike Them BOTH," London *Tribune* (18 February 1955).

4. Raymond Mortimer, "T. E. Lawrence: Mr. Aldington's Charges," London *Sunday Times* (30 January 1955), p. 5.

5. Harold Nicolson, "The Lawrence Legend," London *Observer* (30 January 1955), p. 6.

6. C. M. Woodhouse, "T. E. Lawrence: New Legends for Old," *Twentieth Century* 157 (March 1955): 228, 231.

7. Robert Graves, *Between Moon and Moon*, p. 134.

8. LH 9/13/44, LHCMA.

9. BHLH, "Aldington's 'Lawrence': His Charges—and Treatment of the Evidence," private collection of Philip M. O'Brien.

10. Robert Graves, "The Lawrence I Knew," London *News Chronicle* (31 January 1955), p. 4.

11. Robert Graves, "Lawrence Vindicated," *New Republic* 132 (21 March 1955): 20, 16.

12. Letters to and from BHLH, unless otherwise specified, are in LH 9/13/44, LHCMA.

13. See TEL, *Letters*, p. 44 n. Despite Nuffield's statement to Garnett, he was making bicycles as late as 1908. See J. N. Lockman, *Scattered Tracks on the Lawrence Trail* (Whitmore Lake, Mich.: Falcon Books, 1996), p. 28.

14. David Garnett, "Lawrence in the Dock," *New Statesman and Nation* 49 (5 February 1955): 182.

15. See RA, *Lawrence of Arabia*, p. 59.

16. A. L. Rowse, "Legend or Only a Lie?" London *Daily Mail* (31 January 1955), p. 4.

17. A. L. Rowse, ALS to FDC, 24 August 1992.

18. Malcolm Muggeridge, TLS to Lawrence James, 1 November 1988, private collection of Lawrence James.

19. *Panorama*, 26 January 1955, BBC Written Archives Centre.

20. Sydney Smith, "Why I Decided to Debunk a Hero: Richard Aldington Talks to Sydney Smith about His Life of Lawrence of Arabia, Which Started a Row on TV's 'Panorama'," London *Daily Express* (28 January 1955).

21. "I Stand By My Book on Lawrence, Says Author," London *Evening News* (31 January 1955), late extra, p. 1.

22. RA, "The Battle over 'Lawrence of Arabia': Richard Aldington Defends His Book," London *Daily Mail* (1 February 1955), p. 4.

23. RA, "Why I Debunked the Lawrence Legend," London *Illustrated* (5 February 1955), pp. 32–33.

24. Letters from RA to AK are in SIU 69.

25. Letters from RA to his wife are in the collection of Richard Aldington Letters to Netta Aldington (1951–1962), Add. Mss. 54211, British Library.

26. See, for example, London *Sunday Times* (9 February 1955), p. 10.

27. [Lord Robert] Vansittart, "The Lawrence Legend," London *Daily Telegraph* (31 January 1955), p. 6.

28. R. M. S. Barton, "Lawrence of Arabia" [letter], London *Daily Telegraph* (4 February 1955), p. 6; George de S. Barrow, "Desert Encounters with Lawrence: 'Acts of Discourtesy' " [letter], London *Daily Telegraph* (10 February 1955), p. 6.

29. [Lord] Burnham, "Lawrence the Soldier: Case for Reasoned Reassessment" [letter], London *Daily Telegraph* (5 February 1955), p. 6.

30. BHLH, "Lawrence and His Arabs: Help to Allenby 'Invaluable' " [letter], London *Daily Telegraph* (12 February 1955), p. 6.

31. Arthur T. Harris, "Lawrence and His Arabs" [letter], London *Daily Telegraph* (12 February 1955), p. 6.

32. RA, "Lawrence's Friends" [letter], London *Daily Telegraph* (24 February 1955), p. 6; BHLH, "Lawrence's Arabs" [letter], London *Daily Telegraph* (26 February 1955), p. 6.

33. G. F. Breese, "The Storm over Lawrence: Lawrence as a Recruit" [letter], London *Illustrated* (26 February 1955), p. 6; BHLH, "The Storm over Lawrence: Quoting Churchill" [letter], London *Illustrated* (26 February 1955), pp. 6, 9; R. Dening, "The Storm over Lawrence: Arabs Liked His Bravery" [letter], London *Illustrated* (26 February 1955), p. 9.

34. Letters from AK to RA are in SIU 68.

35. Derek Marks, "Lawrence of the Cookhouse," London *Daily Express* (14 February 1955), p. 4.

36. H. D. Ziman, "Damaging Self-Portrait of T. E. Lawrence," London *Daily Telegraph* (18 February 1955), p. 6.

37. AK, "Aldington's Notes," *Merlin* 2:4 (Spring/Summer 1955): 298–301.

38. After Eric Kennington's review of RA appeared in *Truth* on 4 February 1955, Rob Lyle refuted it in a letter to the editor that appeared on 25 February. Kennington answered on 4 March but did not respond to Lyle's subsequent letters that *Truth* printed on 11 March and 18 March.

39. I am indebted to Christopher Logue for providing his recollections of *Merlin*, ALS to FDC, 17 November 1992.

40. John Lehmann, "Foreword," *London Magazine* 2 (April 1955): 13, 15; BHLH, "T. E. Lawrence, Aldington and the Truth," *London Magazine* 2 (April 1955): 67–75.

41. Rob Lyle's original letter is in SIU 67.

42. Rob Lyle's letter appears as "Correspondence," *London Magazine* 2:6 (June 1955): 75–79; BHLH's response immediately follows on pages 79–81.

43. LH 9/13/44, LHCMA.

44. LH 9/13/44, LHCMA.

45. RA's letter appears as "Correspondence," *London Magazine* 2:8 (August 1955): 66–69; BHLH's response immediately follows on pages 69–71.

46. LH 9/13/44, LHCMA.

47. *T. E. Lawrence to His Biographers Robert Graves and Liddell Hart* [1938] (Garden City, NY: Doubleday, 1963), 1:64. This reissue of the Faber & Faber limited edition of 1938 presents the two volumes in one binding, retaining the original pagination of each.

48. RA, *Lawrence of Arabia*, p. 273.

49. David Lloyd George, *The Truth about the Peace Treaties* [1939] (New York: Fertig, 1972), 2: 678–79.

50. John Connell, *Wavell: Scholar and Soldier* (New York: Harcourt, Brace & World, 1965), p. 153.

51. Jeremy Wilson, *Lawrence of Arabia: The Authorized Biography of T. E. Lawrence* [1989] (New York: Atheneum, 1990), pp. 621–22.

52. Mack, *Prince*, p. 477 n. 1 (chapter 3).

53. Peter D. Whitney, "Lawrence-of-Arabia Book Creates Literary Storm: British Critics Deal Roughly with Author Who Questions Soldier's Exploits," *New York Times* (6 February 1955), section 4, p. 3.

54. Lady Kathleen Liddell Hart, interview with FDC, Medmenham, 17 June 1988.

55. Correspondence from Regnery to RA is in the Henry Regnery Collection, box 2, folder 6, Hoover Institution on War, Revolution and Peace.

56. "Autopsy of a Hero," *Time* 65 (14 February 1955), p. 29.

57. Vincent Sheean, "T. E. Lawrence Seen in a Harsh Picture Designed to Blight His Name: Richard Aldington Looks with a Dark Eye on Every Aspect of That Controversial Figure," *New York Herald-Tribune Book Review* (25 September 1955), p. 5.

58. Carlos Baker, "A Hero Challenged," *New York Times Book Review* (2 October 1955), pp. 24–25.

59. BHLH, "T. E. Lawrence: Man or Myth?" *Atlantic* 196 (November 1955): 70–71, 74, 76.

60. SIU 68.

61. RA, "An Author Replies" [letter], *Montreal Gazette* (26 December 1955), p. 6; RA, "An Author Replies to Criticism" [letter], *Montreal Gazette* (26 January 1956), p. 8.

62. *T. E. Lawrence* Collection (Miscellaneous), Harry Ransom Humanities Research Center, University of Texas at Austin.

63. Lowell Thomas, "Lawrence of Arabia: A Biographical Inquiry," *Middle East Journal* 9:2 (Spring 1955): 197–98.

64. Lowell Thomas, *With Lawrence in Arabia* [1924] (New York: Grosset & Dunlap, 1955). "Preface" consists of four unnumbered pages. The refutation, "Notes in Defense of Lawrence," appears on pp. 304–16.

65. "Lying Attributed to T. E. Lawrence: Biographer Aldington Says He Will 'Erase from History' Author of 'Seven Pillars'," *New York Times* (25 January 1954), p. 13.

66. Flora Armitage, *The Desert and the Stars: A Biography of Lawrence of Arabia* (New York: Holt, 1955), p. vii.

67. Flora Armitage, "Epilogue—The Imposter," in *The Desert and the Stars: A Portrait of T. E. Lawrence* (London: Faber & Faber, 1956), pp. 302–23.

68. Letters from RA to Dibben are in SIU Acc 946.

69. Letters from RA to his brother, "Tony" Aldington, are in the P. A. G. Aldington Letters from Richard Aldington (1945–1962), SIU 66.

70. SIU 68.

71. RA, *Literary Lifelines*, pp. 62–63.

72. Private collection of David J. Wilkinson.

73. SIU 68.

74. Anita Engle, *The Nili Spies* (London: Hogarth, 1959), pp. 102, 134, 233, 238, 230.

75. Letters from RA to Warman are in SIU 70.

76. C. P. Snow, "The Irregular Right: Britain Without Rebels," *Nation* 182 (24 March 1956): 239.

77. Robert Vansittart, *The Mist Procession: The Autobiography of Lord Vansittart* (London: Hutchinson, 1958), p. 327.

78. Richard Meinertzhagen, *Middle East Diary, 1917–1956* (London: Cresset Press, 1959), pp. 41–43.

79. Private collection of David J. Wilkinson.

80. See J. N. Lockman, *Meinertzhagen's Diary Ruse: False Entries on T. E. Lawrence* (Grand Rapids: Cornerstone, 1995).

81. Letters from RA to Weintraub are in the private collection of Stanley Weintraub.

82. Anthony Nutting, "Lawrence of Arabia: The Secret of a Tormented Spirit," London *Sunday Times* (10 September 1961), magazine section, p. 21; Anthony Nutting, "Lawrence of Arabia: The Mirror of Degradation," London *Sunday Times* (17 September 1961), magazine section, p. 27.

83. K. J. Fielding, "Lawrence's Confession," London *Sunday Times* (17 September 1961), magazine section, p. 42.

84. SIU 68.

85. Anthony Nutting, *Lawrence of Arabia: The Man and the Motive* [1961] (New York: Signet, 1962), p. 239.

86. Nutting, *Lawrence of Arabia*, p. 110.

87. RA, *Lawrence of Arabia*, p. 206.

88. "Man of Destiny," *Times Literary Supplement* (20 October 1961), p. 751.

89. BHLH, "Lawrence of Arabia" [letter], *Times Literary Supplement* (3 November 1961), p. 789; the reviewer's response immediately follows BHLH's letter.

90. Stanley Weintraub, "Political Motivations Wrapped in a Personal Enigma," *New York Times Book Review* (31 December 1961), p. 4.

91. RA refers to Keith Wheeler, "The Romantic Riddle of Lawrence of Arabia," *Life* 52 (12 January 1962): 94–102, 104, 106, 108. This was devoted to the forthcoming Spiegel film, *Lawrence of Arabia*.

92. Private collection of Norman T. Gates.

93. Stanley Weintraub, TLS to FDC, 19 March 1992.

94. Private collection of Stanley Weintraub.

95. Stanley Weintraub, *Private Shaw and Public Shaw: A Dual Portrait of Lawrence of Arabia and G.B.S.* (New York: George Braziller, 1963), pp. xiv, 269, 179. Jonathan Cape published the English edition in the same year.

96. SIU 68.

97. Christopher Sykes, "Mystery Motorist," *Spectator* 209 (20 July 1962): 89.

98. Private collection of David J. Wilkinson.

7. His Brother's Keeper

Epigraphs: AWL to BHLH, 4 February 1967, LH 9/13/58; Mack, *Prince*, p. 17; and AWL, in *Lawrence and Arabia*, produced by Julia Cave and Malcolm Brown, BBC *Omnibus*, 18 April 1986.

1. AWL, "My Knowledge of Bruce" (1970), quoted in Mack, *Prince*, p. 428.

2. Mack, *Prince*, p. 429.

3. Ron Paquet, "Early Scripts of *Lawrence of Arabia*," *T.E. Notes* 5:7 (September 1994): 1–2. Paquet quotes revealing excerpts from John Monk Saunders's 1935 screenplay for Alexander Korda's film.

4. For an account of Korda's problems with his TEL film project, see Jeffrey Richards and Jeffrey Hulbert, "Censorship in Action: The Case of *Lawrence of Arabia*," *Journal of Contemporary History* 19:1 (January 1984): 153–70; and Andrew Kelly, James Pepper, and Jeffrey Richards, eds., *Filming T. E. Lawrence: Korda's Lost Epics* (London: I. B. Tauris, 1997), pp. 1–21.

5. Letters from RA to Warman are in SIU 70.

6. For a detailed narrative of attempts to film TEL's adventures, including previously unpublished correspondence, see L. Robert Morris and Lawrence Raskin, *Lawrence of Arabia: The 30th Anniversary Pictorial History* (New York: Doubleday, 1992).

7. Letters from AWL and letters from BHLH and Robert Graves to AWL are in LH 9/13/58, LHCMA, unless otherwise specified.

8. Letters from Terence Rattigan are in LH 9/13/50, LHCMA.

9. AWL, ALS to FDC, 9 October 1988.

10. LH 9/13/50, LHCMA.

11. Gary Crowdus, "Lawrence of Arabia: The Cinematic (Re)Writing of History," *Cineaste* 17:2 (1989): 17.

12. Crowdus, "Lawrence of Arabia," p. 17.

13. For Michael Wilson's extensive but unacknowledged contributions to the *Lawrence of Arabia* screenplay, see Joel Hodson, "Who Wrote *Lawrence of Arabia*?: Sam Spiegel and David Lean's Denial of Credit to a Blacklisted Screenwriter," *Cineaste* 20:4 (Fall 1994): 12–18.

14. Leslie Mallery, "Marlon Brando to Play Lawrence of Arabia," London *News Chronicle* (18 February 1960), p. 1.

15. Morris and Raskin, *Lawrence of Arabia*, p. 35.

16. Lady Kathleen Liddell Hart, interview with FDC, Medmenham, 17 June 1988.

17. J. C. Trewin, "The World of the Theatre: Arabia and Illyria," *Illustrated London News* (28 May 1960), p. 944.

18. Michael Harald, "Call Me Ishmael: 'Ross' by Terence Rattigan," *Action* (August/September 1960), p. 8.

19. Constantine FitzGibbon, "The Lawrence Legend," *Encounter* 15 (November 1960): 55–56.

20. Sir Alec Guinness, ALS to FDC, 16 August 1988.

21. Private collection of Stanley Weintraub.

22. LH 9/13/50, LHCMA.

23. LH 9/13/51, LHCMA.

24. Paul Tanfield, "Dear Mr Lawrence . . . ," London *Daily Mail* (14 December 1961), p. 4.

25. Robert Bolt, "Clues to the Legend of Lawrence," *New York Times Magazine* (25 February 1962), pp. 16, 48, 50.

26. LH 9/13/52, LHCMA. Morris and Raskin, *Lawrence of Arabia*, pp. 149–53, includes the BHLH/Bolt correspondence almost in its entirety but omits the reference

to RA in Bolt's letter of 22 November 1962 as well as BHLH's response of 23 November.

27. "The Life and Death of T. E. Lawrence," *Radio Times* (22 November 1962).

28. Malcolm Brown, TLS to FDC, 16 March 1993.

29. Malcolm Brown and Philip Donnellan, producers, *T. E. Lawrence: 1888–1935*, BBC documentary, 27 November 1962.

30. AWL, "Lawrence of Arabia: Changes Made for Film Version" [letter], London *Times* (14 December 1962), p. 13.

31. AWL, "The Fiction and the Fact," London *Observer* (16 December 1962), p. 25.

32. "Brother Rejects Lawrence Film: Professor Says Movie Gives False View of the Man," *New York Times* (5 January 1963), western edition, p. 7.

33. Murray Schumach, " 'Lawrence of Arabia' Producer Defends Film Story of Hero: Spiegel Charges Professor Wanted to Hide Facts about His Brother," *New York Times* (26 January 1963), p. 5.

34. *Clouds Hill, Dorset* (London: National Trust, 1986), p. 22.

35. LH 9/13/69, LHCMA.

36. Add. Mss. 54211, British Library.

37. "Critic of Lawrence of Arabia," *Royal British Legion Journal* 45:5 (May 1965): 19; AWL, "Lawrence—And Col. Joynson" [letter], *Royal British Legion Journal* 45:9 (September 1965): 8.

38. Stephen E. Tabachnick and Christopher Matheson, *Images of Lawrence* (London: Cape, 1988), p. 67.

39. Suleiman Mousa, TLS to FDC, 7 March 1993.

40. Tabachnick and Matheson, *Images*, pp. 67–68.

41. Letters from RA to AK are in SIU 69.

42. Suleiman Mousa, *T. E. Lawrence: An Arab View* [1962], trans. Albert Butros (London: Oxford University Press, 1966), p. vii.

43. Suleiman Mousa, TLS to FDC, 20 August 1989. Mousa, drawing from his files of correspondence with Oxford University Press, quotes the letters between him and Bell.

44. Suleiman Mousa, TLS to FDC, 7 March 1993.

45. LH 9/13/69, LHCMA.

46. AWL, "Introductory Note" to Edward Robinson, *Lawrence: The Story of His Life* (London: Oxford University Press, 1935), p. 5.

47. "Writer on Lawrence Sentenced in Fraud: Edward H. T. Robinson, 39, Sold Manuscripts Borrowed for Biography on the War Leader," *New York Times* (17 June 1937), p. 25.

48. Mack, *Prince*, p. 20.

49. LH 9/13/60, LHCMA.

50. Mack, *Prince*, pp. 523–24 n. 51.

51. LH 9/13/58, LHCMA.

52. Mack, *Prince*, p. 524 n. 51.

53. Mack, *Prince*, pp. 429–30.

54. Mack, *Prince*, p. 430.

55. Colin Simpson and Phillip Knightley, "The Secret Life of Lawrence of Arabia.

1: The Night of the Turks," London *Sunday Times* (9 June 1968), pp. 49–50; "The Sheik Who Made Lawrence Love Arabia," London *Sunday Times* (16 June 1968), pp. 49–50; "How Lawrence of Arabia Cracked Up," London *Sunday Times* (23 June 1968), pp. 45–46; and "How T. E. Lawrence Found Another Mother," London *Sunday Times* (30 June 1968), pp. 45–46.

56. Phillip Knightley, "T. E. Lawrence," in *The Craft of Literary Biography* [1984], ed. Jeffrey Meyers (New York: Schocken Books, 1985), p. 158.

57. Knightley, "T. E. Lawrence," pp. 158–59.

58. Suleiman Mousa, TLS to FDC, 6 October 1989.

59. Phillip Knightley, interview with FDC, London, 24 May 1988.

60. Knightley, "T. E. Lawrence," pp. 169–70.

61. Knightley, "T. E. Lawrence," p. 172.

62. Tabachnick and Matheson, *Images*, p. 73.

63. Tabachnick and Matheson, *Images*, p. 55.

64. Phillip Knightley, interview with FDC, London, 24 May 1988; see Phillip Knightley, "Aldington's Enquiry Concerning T. E. Lawrence," *Texas Quarterly* 16 (Winter 1973): 98–105.

65. AWL, "T E Lawrence: A Brother Gives His Testimony" [letter], London *Times* (22 November 1969), p. 7.

66. Phillip Knightley and Colin Simpson, "Lawrence of Arabia" [letter], London *Times* (28 November 1969), p. 11.

67. John E. Mack, "T. E. Lawrence: A Study of Heroism and Conflict," *American Journal of Psychiatry* 125:8 (February 1969): 1083–92; John E. Mack, "The Inner Conflict of T. E. Lawrence," London *Times Saturday Review* (8 February 1969), p. 17.

68. John E. Mack, TLS to FDC, 29 March 1991.

69. Mack, *Prince*, p. 444.

70. Mack, *Prince*, p. 73.

71. John E. Mack, ALS to FDC, 5 March 1993.

72. Mack, *Prince*, p. 479 n. 24.

73. RA, *Passionate*, p. 20.

74. Mack, *Prince*, p. 524 n. 59.

75. Mack, *Prince*, p. 515 n. 27.

76. Jeffrey Meyers, "A Wanderer after Sensations," *Virginia Quarterly Review* 52:4 (Autumn 1976): 717–23.

77. The correspondence generated by Meyers's review is at the Alderman Library, University of Virginia, in two collections: *Virginia Quarterly Review* Records, RG–24/3/1.801, boxes 13 and 15, University Archives; and President's Papers (Frank L. Hereford), RG–2/1/2.791, box 27, University Archives.

78. Mrs. A. W. Lawrence to Desmond Stewart, quoted in Desmond Stewart, "Lawrence: The Lost Letter" [letter], London *Sunday Times* (26 June 1977), p. 13.

79. Mack, *Prince*, p. 430.

80. Meyers, "Wanderer," p. 723.

81. Jeremy Wilson, in "The Crawford-Wilson Letters," *T. E. Notes* 4:5 (May 1993): 4.

82. Jeremy Wilson, *Lawrence of Arabia*, pp. 966, 968, 975.

83. Desmond Stewart, *T. E. Lawrence* [1977] (London: Paladin, 1979), p. 275.

84. Colin Simpson, "Lawrence Made Up Rape Story, Says Author," London *Sunday Times* (12 June 1977), p. 2.

85. Jeremy Wilson, "T. E. Lawrence: A New Myth" [letter], London *Sunday Times* (19 June 1977), p. 12.

86. Colin Simpson, "Lawrence: The Lost Letter" [letter], London *Sunday Times* (26 June 1977), p. 13.

87. Stewart, "Lawrence: Lost Letter," p. 13.

88. Jeremy Wilson, "Lawrence Evidence" [letter], London *Sunday Times* (3 July 1977), p. 12.

89. Jeremy Wilson, "Crawford-Wilson," pp. 4–5.

90. Malcolm Brown, TLS to FDC, 14 January 1993.

91. AWL, ALS (dictated) to FDC, 17 June 1988; AWL, ALS to FDC, 9 October 1988.

92. Private collection of Lawrence James.

93. M. V. Carey, TLS to FDC, 18 January 1993.

8. Aldington and the Documents

Epigraphs: TEL to Lionel Curtis, 22 December 1927, TEL, *Letters*, p. 559; RA to Henry Williamson, 22 February 1954, HWLE; and RA, *Lawrence of Arabia*, p. 14.

1. Jeremy Wilson, *T. E. Lawrence: Lawrence of Arabia* (London: National Portrait Gallery, 1988), p. 241.

2. AWL, ALS (dictated) to FDC, 17 June 1988.

3. Stephen E. Tabachnick, "T. E. Lawrence Authorized Biography," *English Literature in Transition* 35:1 (1992): 89–93.

4. Jeremy Wilson, *Lawrence of Arabia*, p. 8. Subsequent citations appear parenthetically in the text.

5. Elie Kedourie, "Communications" [letter], *American Historical Review* 97 (June 1992): 1006.

6. TEL, *Selected Letters*, p. 149 n. 2.

7. Weintraub, *Private Shaw*, p. 149.

8. Lawrence James, *The Golden Warrior: The Life and Legend of Lawrence of Arabia* [1990] (New York: Paragon House, 1993), p. xiii. Subsequent citations appear parenthetically in the text.

9. RA, *Lawrence of Arabia*, p. 331. Subsequent citations appear parenthetically in the text.

10. Wilson points out many discrepancies in *Seven Pillars*: TEL omitted material (486); *Seven Pillars* reflects "bitterness towards Hussein" that TEL felt in 1921 (661); his account of a battle was "somewhat inaccurate" (1030 n. 61); TEL "concealed the fact that his journey to the Hejaz was really an Intelligence mission for Clayton" in a version that Wilson calls "much less than the truth" (1031 n. 68); TEL puts a conversation between Storrs and al Masri into the wrong journey, and Wilson comments that "this trivial error is only worth noting because *Seven Pillars* contains few such lapses" (1033 n. 11); TEL deliberately "presented Newcombe's failure with the Arabs in the most favourable light possible" (1073 n. 4); TEL made "no allusion to the ibn Saud problem, and implies that Hussein's refusal to send troops north was merely capricious," but TEL

reported a different version in the *Arab Bulletin* (1097 n. 8); TEL misdated an attack, and Wilson comments that "the last book of *SP* has several small errors of this kind" (1101 n. 17); and "Lawrence's figure of four thousand [Arabs entering Damascus] in *SP* . . . may be exaggerated" (1107 n. 66). Wilson cites several further instances: 1029 n. 47; 1034 n. 12; 1035 n. 21; 1035–36 n. 24; 1046 n. 43; 1047 n. 47; 1058 n. 42; 1060 n. 2; 1064 n. 31; 1067 n. 18; 1070 n. 46; 1071 n. 54; 1082 n. 24; 1083 n. 49; 1089 n. 40; 1093 n. 39; 1102 n. 36; and 1107 n. 65.

11. Lawrence James, TLS to FDC, 1 May 1991.

12. Suleiman Mousa, TLS to FDC, 7 March 1993.

13. Jeremy Wilson, "Extracts from *Summary of the Hejaz Revolt*, War Office, London, 1918," *Journal of the T. E. Lawrence Society* 3:1 (Spring 1993): 37 n. 2.

14. HWLE.

15. Lawrence James, TLS to FDC, 13 February 1993.

16. Letters from RA to AK are in SIU 69.

17. IWM 69/48/4, quoted in Lawrence James, TLS to FDC, 21 January 1993. James did not quote this letter in his book, but it appears in Lockman, *Scattered Tracks*, p. 69.

18. Jeremy Wilson, "T E. Lawrence: New Myth," p. 12.

19. Lockman, *Scattered Tracks*, pp. 68–69. Subsequent citations appear parenthetically in the text.

9. Conclusion: Aldington's Legacy

Epigraphs: Donald Malcolm to RA, 17[?] July 1955, SIU 68; and [A. J. Flavell], *T. E. Lawrence: The Legend and the Man* (Oxford: Bodleian Library, 1988), p. 87.

1. Stanley Weintraub and Rodelle Weintraub, *Lawrence of Arabia: The Literary Impulse* (Baton Rouge: Louisiana State University Press, 1975), p. 62.

2. Doyle, *Richard Aldington*, p. 256.

3. Graham Greene, "Poison Pen," *London Magazine* 5 [n.s.] (March 1966): 70–73.

4. James E. Miller, Jr., *T. S. Eliot's Personal Waste Land: Exorcism of the Demons* (University Park: Penn State University Press, 1977).

5. B.C. Rosset, *Shaw of Dublin: The Formative Years* (University Park: Penn State University Press, 1964).

BIBLIOGRAPHY

A date in brackets immediately after a title indicates the year of first publication when this differs from the edition used in this book. A bracketed citation at the end of an entry is a cross-reference to *T. E. Lawrence: A Bibliography* (Boston: G. K. Hall, 1988) by Philip M. O'Brien, whose revised and expanded edition (Winchester: St. Paul's Bibliographies, 1997) includes more than five thousand new entries.

Archives and Private Collections

Alderman Library, University of Virginia
BBC Written Archives Centre, Caversham Park, Reading
British Library, London
Harry Ransom Humanities Research Center, University of Texas
Henry Williamson Literary Estate Archives, Chichester, West Sussex
Hoover Institution on War, Revolution, and Peace, Stanford, California
Imperial War Museum, London
Liddell Hart Centre for Military Archives, King's College London
Lowell Thomas Communications Center Archives, Marist College
Morris Library, Southern Illinois University at Carbondale
National Library of Australia, Canberra
Private Collections of Norman T. Gates, Lawrence James, Alister Kershaw, John E. Mack, Suleiman Mousa, Philip M. O'Brien, Stanley Weintraub, and David J. Wilkinson

Books and Articles

"The Air We Breathe: Art of Detraction." *Times Educational Supplement* (4 February 1955), p. 104.
Aldington, Catherine. "Le Gout Amer de la Vache Enragée." *L'Evénement du Jeudi*, no. 132 (14 May 1987).
Aldington, Richard. "An Author Replies" [letter]. *Montreal Gazette* (26 December 1955), p. 6.
———. "An Author Replies to Criticism" [letter]. *Montreal Gazette* (26 January 1956), p. 8.
———. "The Battle over 'Lawrence of Arabia': Richard Aldington Defends His Book." London *Daily Mail* (1 February 1955), p. 4. [H0464]

———. "Correspondence" [letter]. *London Magazine* 2:8 (August 1955): 66–69. [G0813]

———. *D. H. Lawrence: Portrait of a Genius, But . . .* New York: Duell, Sloan & Pearce, 1950.

———. *The Duke, Being an Account of the Life and Achievements of Arthur Wellesley, 1st Duke of Wellington.* New York: Viking, 1943.

———. *Frauds.* London: Heinemann, 1957.

———. "The Gullibility of the British." *Saturday Review* 41 (18 January 1958): 11–12, 61–62.

———. *Introduction to Mistral.* London: Heinemann, 1956.

———. *Lawrence L'Imposteur.* Trans. Gilberte Marchegay, Jacques Rambaud, and Jean Rosenthal. Paris: Amiot-Dumont, 1954. [E190]

———. *Lawrence of Arabia.* London: Four Square, 1957. [E195]

———. *Lawrence of Arabia: A Biographical Enquiry.* London: Collins, 1955. [E192]

———. *Lawrence of Arabia: A Biographical Enquiry.* Chicago: Regnery, 1955. [E198]

———. *Lawrence of Arabia: A Biographical Inquiry.* Intro. Christopher Sykes. Harmondsworth, Middlesex: Penguin, 1971. [E197]

———. "Lawrence's Friends" [letter]. London *Daily Telegraph* (24 February 1955), p. 6.

———. "La Légende du colonel Lawrence" [letter]. Paris *Le Monde* (9 July 1955), p. 7. [H0529]

———. *Life for Life's Sake: A Book of Reminiscences.* New York: Viking, 1941. [F0011]

———. *A Passionate Prodigality: Letters to Alan Bird from Richard Aldington 1949–1962.* Ed. Miriam J. Benkovitz. New York: Readex Books, 1975. [F0013]

———. *Pinorman: Personal Recollections of Norman Douglas, Pino Orioli and Charles Prentice.* London: Heinemann, 1954.

———. *Portrait of a Rebel: The Life and Work of Robert Louis Stevenson.* London: Evans Brothers, 1957.

———. *Richard Aldington: An Autobiography in Letters.* Ed. Norman T. Gates. University Park: Penn State University Press, 1992.

———. *Richard Aldington and H.D.: The Early Years in Letters.* Ed. Caroline Zilboorg. Bloomington: Indiana University Press, 1992.

———. *Richard Aldington and H.D.: The Later Years in Letters.* Ed. Caroline Zilboorg. Manchester: Manchester University Press, 1995.

———. "Richard Aldington's Letters to Herbert Read." Ed. David S. Thatcher. *Malahat Review* 15 (July 1970): 5–44.

———. *The Strange Life of Charles Waterton, 1782–1865.* New York: Duell, Sloan & Pearce, 1949.

———. "A Translation" [letter]. London *Daily Telegraph* (21 February 1955), p. 6.

———. "Translator's Note." In Pierre Custot, *Sturly.* Boston: Houghton Mifflin, 1923, pp. 7–8. [D0008]

———. *Voltaire.* London: George Routledge & Sons, 1925; New York: E. P. Dutton, 1925.

———. "Why I Debunked the Lawrence Legend." London *Illustrated* (5 February 1955), pp. 32–33. [G0711]

Aldington, Richard, and Lawrence Durrell. *Literary Lifelines: The Richard Aldington–Lawrence Durrell Correspondence.* Ed. Ian S. MacNiven and Harry T. Moore. London: Faber & Faber, 1981. [F0012]

Alexander, S. W. "Lawrence of Arabia and the Man Serge Rubinstein." London *City Press* (4 February 1955), p. 2.

Allen, Trevor. "Arabia's Hero under Fire." *Everybody's* (5 February 1955), p. 6.

———. "Lawrence's 'Iron Book'." *Everybody's* (19 February 1955), p. 6.

"Allenby Praises Lawrence's Work." *New York Times* (20 May 1935), p. 10.

Alpert, Hollis. "A Great One." *Saturday Review* 45 (29 December 1962): 29–30. [G1046]

Alvarez, A. "Arabia Deserta." *New Statesman* 59 (21 May 1960): 749–50. [G0933]

———. "Testimonials." *New Statesman* 64 (3 August 1962): 150–51.

Anderegg, Michael A. "Lawrence of Arabia: The Man, the Myth, the Movie." *Michigan Quarterly Review* 21:2 (Spring 1982): 281–300. [G1643]

"Another Reader's View of Deraa." *T. E. Notes* 2:7 (September 1991): 4–5.

" 'Arab' Lawrence Accused of Lying: Biographer Aldington Says He Will 'Erase from History' Author of 'Seven Pillars'." *New York Times* (25 January 1954).

Armitage, Flora. *The Desert and the Stars: A Biography of Lawrence of Arabia.* New York: Holt, 1955. [E212]

———. "Epilogue—The Imposter." In Flora Armitage, *The Desert and the Stars: A Portrait of T. E. Lawrence.* London: Faber & Faber, 1956; pp. 302–23. [E213]

Astor, [Lord]. "Courageous Story of Mrs. Lawrence." London *Observer* (22 November 1959), p. 12. [H1282]

Atkins, John. "He Merged Life with Fantasy: T. E. Lawrence and the Desert of Truth." *Books and Bookmen* (November 1957), p. 11.

"Autopsy of a Hero." *Time* 65 (14 February 1955), p. 29. [G0718]

Baker, Carlos. "A Hero Challenged." *New York Times Book Review* (2 October 1955), pp. 24–25. [G0834]

Barrow, George de S. "Desert Encounters with Lawrence: 'Acts of Discourtesy' " [letter]. London *Daily Telegraph* (10 February 1955), p. 6. [H0480]

———. *The Fire of Life.* London: Hutchinson, 1942. [F0062]

Barton, R. M. S. "Lawrence of Arabia" [letter]. London *Daily Telegraph* (4 February 1955), p. 6.

Bastable, Gilbert. "Lawrence of Arabia" [letter]. London *Sunday Times* (13 February 1955).

Bates, H. E. " 'The Mint' Is Bound to Shock." London *News Chronicle* (14 February 1955). [H0474]

Béraud-Villars, Jean. "L'Affaire T. E. Lawrence." *La Table Ronde* 83 (26 November 1954): 105–9. [G0683]

———. *T. E. Lawrence, or the Search for the Absolute* [1955]. Trans. Peter Dawnay. New York: Duell, Sloan & Pearce, 1959. [E206]

Berton, Joseph A. *See* Crawford, Fred D., and Joseph A. Berton

Beum, Robert. *See* Doyle, Charles, and Robert Beum

Bidwell, R. L. "Queries for Biographers of T. E. Lawrence." *Arabian Studies* 3 (1976): 13–27. [G1518]

Bidwell, Shelford. "A Military View of T. E. Lawrence." *Army Quarterly and Defence Journal* 100 (1970): 71–73. [G1397]

Bissell, Andy. "Has This Man Found the Real Lawrence of Arabia?" Bournemouth *Evening Echo* (4 March 1989).

Blackmore, Charles D. "Following Lawrence of Arabia." *British Army Review* 82 (April 1986): 11–14. [G1671]

———. *In the Footsteps of Lawrence of Arabia.* London: Harrap, 1986. [E406]

Bolt, Robert. "Clues to the Legend of Lawrence." *New York Times Magazine* (25 February 1962), pp. 16, 45, 48, 50. [G0994]

———. "Lawrence Meets Feisal: An Episode from Robert Bolt's Distinguished Scenario." *Show: The Magazine of the Arts* 2 (December 1962): 68–69, 132.

———. "The Playwright in Films." *Saturday Review* 45 (29 December 1962): 15–16. [G1047]

Boussard, Léon. *Le Secret du Colonel Lawrence.* Clermont-Ferrand: Mont-Louis, 1941. [E143]

Bowden, Ann. "The T. E. Lawrence Collection at the University of Texas." *Texas Quarterly* 5 (Autumn 1962): 54–64. [G1021]

Bray, N. N. E. *Shifting Sands.* London: Unicorn Press, 1934. [F0139]

Breese, G. F. "The Storm over Lawrence: Lawrence as a Recruit" [letter]. London *Illustrated* (26 February 1955), p. 6. [G0729]

Breit, Harvey. "In and Out of Books—Cross-Section." *New York Times Book Review* (20 February 1955), p. 8. [G0726]

———. "In and Out of Books—The Dispute." *New York Times Book Review* (28 February 1954), p. 8. [G0658]

Brémond, Général Ed[ouard]. *Le Hedjaz dans la Guerre Mondiale.* Paris: Payot, 1931. [F0140]

Brent, Peter [Peter Kilner]. *T. E. Lawrence.* Intro. Elizabeth Longford. New York: G. P. Putnam's Sons, 1975. [E357]

"Brother Rejects Lawrence Film: Professor Says Movie Gives False View of the Man." *New York Times* (5 January 1963), western edition, p. 7. [H0661]

Brown, Malcolm. "An Introduction to the BBC 1962 Documentary *T. E. Lawrence: 1888–1935.*" *Journal of the T. E. Lawrence Society* 1:1 (Spring 1991): 79–84.

———. "Reflections on *A Dangerous Man.*" *T. E. Notes* 4:9 (November 1993): 1–3.

Brown, Malcolm, and Julia Cave. *A Touch of Genius: The Life of T. E. Lawrence* [1988]. New York: Paragon House, 1989.

Bruce, John. "I Knew Lawrence." *Scottish Field* (August 1938), pp. 20–21. [G0474]

Bibliography

Buchan, James. "Romancers Entwined: How T. E. Lawrence and John Buchan Invented One Another." *Times Literary Supplement* (29 May 1992), pp. 13–14.

Bunting, Harold. "Hearsay Is Not Good Enough: Was Lawrence a Liar?" *Sheffield Telegraph* (31 January 1955), p. 5.

Burnham, [Lord]. "Lawrence the Soldier: Case for Reasoned Reassessment" [letter]. London *Daily Telegraph* (5 February 1955), p. 6.

Caldwell, Peter. "Another Side of Richard Meinertzhagen." *T. E. Notes* 5:7 (September 1994): 11.

Cantwell, Robert. "In Grave Adversity." *New York Times Book Review* (20 March 1955), pp. 3, 22–23. [H0489]

Carchidi, Victoria. Review of *Lawrence of Arabia: The Authorised Biography of T. E. Lawrence* by Jeremy Wilson. *Biography* 17:3 (Summer 1994): 301–3.

Carpenter, Humphrey. "Too Good for This World." London *Sunday Times* (26 November 1989), p. G14.

Carrington, C. E. "Lawrence." *Time and Tide* 36 (5 February 1955): 172, 174. [G0713]

———. "T. E. Lawrence." *Contemporary Review* 215 (December 1969): 281–87.

———. *See also* Edmonds, Charles

Cave, Julia. *See* Brown, Malcom, and Julia Cave.

Chainey, Graham. "Lawrence Biographer." *T. E. Notes* 5:4 (April 1994): 3.

Chambers, Jock. "Lawrence of Arabia" [letter]. London *Sunday Times* (6 February 1955), p. 6. [H0470]

Champness, H. M. "Prince of Mecca." *Spectator* 194 (4 February 1955): 131–32. [G0710]

Cherryman, A. E. "Lawrence of Arabia" [letter]. *Truth* (11 March 1955), pp. 288–89.

Churchill, Randolph. "Randolph Churchill Finds Lawrence a Liar in Little Things, But . . . The Big Lie Is Not Proved." London *Evening Standard* (31 January 1955), p. 6.

Churchill, Winston. *Great Contemporaries* [1937]. London: The Reprint Society, 1941; pp. 129–41. [F0211]

———. *See also* Sur

Clements, Frank. *T. E. Lawrence: A Reader's Guide.* Newton Abbot, Devon: David & Charles, 1972. [E331]

Clouds Hill, Dorset. London: National Trust, 1986.

Clouston, Erlend. "T E and the Sands of Time." Manchester *Guardian Weekly* (10 February 1991), p. 21.

Cohen, Gustave. "L'affaire Aldington *contre* Lawrence d'Arabie." *Hommes et Mondes* 29 (March 1956): 487–96. [G0857]

"Collapse of an Idol?" *Washington Post* (26 January 1954), p. 14.

Connell, John. "The Man Who Loathes Lawrence: A Protest." London *Evening News* (31 January 1955), p. 4.

———. "T. E. Lawrence—the Man and the Myth." Manchester *Evening News* (20 August 1955), p. 4.

———. *Wavell: Scholar and Soldier.* New York: Harcourt, Brace & World, 1965. [Fo226]

Conrad, Peter. "Laundering of an Antedeluvian [*sic*] Hero." London *Observer* (3 December 1989), p. 46.

Corbett, Capt. H. A. "A Critic in Action." *Journal of the Royal United Services Institute* 108 (November 1963): 366–70. [G1141]

"Correspondence: Lawrence of Arabia" [letter, signed "Desert Sands"]. London *Daily Telegraph* (27 January 1954).

"Counterfeit or True?" *Times Literary Supplement* (18 February 1955), p. 199. [Go720]

Craig, Alec. *The Banned Books of England and Other Countries: A Study of the Conception of Literary Obscenity.* London: Allen & Unwin, 1962.

Crawford, Fred D. "The Campaign Against Aldington's *Lawrence of Arabia*." *London Magazine* 33:3–4 (June/July 1993): 48–59.

———. "Fred Crawford Responds to Harold Orlans." *T. E. Notes* 4:2 (February 1993): 9–10.

———. "Fred Crawford Responds to Jim Ramage." *T. E. Notes* 4:2 (February 1993): 11–12.

———. "Henry Williamson, Richard Aldington, and the 'Lawrence Bureau'." *T.E. Notes* 5:10 (December 1994): 9–11.

———. "How Aldington Came to Write about T. E." *T. E. Notes* 4:2 (February 1993): 5–7.

———. "New Biography: Lawrence of Arabia." *English Literature in Transition* 36:4 (1993): 495–98.

———. "Reader Notes on *Richard Aldington: An Autobiography in Letters*." *T. E. Notes* 4:2 (February 1993): 12–13.

———. "Richard Aldington." In *Research Guide to Biography and Criticism: Literature.* Washington, D.C.: Research Publishing; 1985; pp. 16–19.

———. "Richard Aldington, Lowell Thomas, and the Ethics of Biography." *T.E. Notes* 3:9 (November 1992): 1–6. Reprinted in *Richard Aldington: Essays in Honour of the Centenary of His Birth.* Ed. Alain Blayac and Caroline Zilboorg. Montpellier: Université Paul Valéry, 1994; pp. 187–201.

———. "Richard Aldington's Biography of Lawrence of Arabia." In *Richard Aldington: Reappraisals.* Ed. Charles Doyle. Victoria, B.C.: University of Victoria Press, 1990; pp. 60–80.

———. "The 'Weather-Vane Soul' of Henry Williamson." *Henry Williamson Society Journal*, no. 30 (September 1994): 5–21.

Crawford, Fred D., and Joseph A. Berton. "How Well Did Lowell Thomas Know Lawrence of Arabia?" *English Literature in Transition* 39:4 (1996): 298–318.

Crawford, Fred D., and Jeremy Wilson. "The Crawford-Wilson Letters." *T. E. Notes* 4:5 (May 1993): 1–6.

"Critic of Lawrence of Arabia." *Royal British Legion Journal* 45:5 (May 1965): 19. [G1209]

Crowdus, Gary. "Lawrence of Arabia: The Cinematic (Re)Writing of History." *Cineaste* 17:2 (1989): 14–21.

Crowdus, Gary, and Alan Farrand. "Restoring Lawrence: An Interview with Robert Harris." *Cineaste* 17:2 (1989): 22–23.

Cruikshank, Ian. "Lawrence of England: Home from Arabia, the Dashing Desert Raider Created Another, Little-Told Legend." *MD* 32:8 (August 1988): 98–102, 105.

Cummings, A. J. "Where Does Monty Go from Here?" London *News Chronicle* (4 February 1955), p. 4.

Cunard, Nancy. " 'Bonbons' of Gall." *Time and Tide* 35 (17 April 1954), p. 517.

Curran, Charles. "Hero or Fake? Why Lawrence Hated the Secret of His Life." London *Daily Mirror* (27 January 1955), p. 7.

Dangerfield, George. "The Parody of a Hero." *Nation* 181 (22 October 1955): 345. [G0835]

"Dans son modeste appartement de la villa 'Les Rosiers' le grand écrivain Richard Aldington a écrit son 'Lawrence l'imposteur' avec lequel il va froisser ses compatriotes en détruisant le mythe du héros de l'Arabie." *Midi Libre* (20 January 1955), p. 4.

Daumas, Philippe. "Richard Aldington, *Lawrence of Arabia: A Biographical Enquiry* (1955): An Historian's Point of View." *T. E. Notes* 4:2 (February 1993): 1–5.

Dawson, Graham. "The Public and Private Lives of T. E. Lawrence: Modernism, Masculinity and Imperial Adventure." *New Formations: A Journal of Culture, Theory, and Politics* 16 (1992): 103–18.

Dean, Joseph. "What Did Gladstone Do in 1881? Action for Libel." London *Evening Standard* (11 December 1953), p. 13.

Deasey, Denison. "Death of a Hero." *Australian Book Review* (February 1970), pp. 84–86.

———. "Lunch at the Villa." *Sydney Bulletin Literary Supplement* (23, 30 December 1980), pp. 177–80.

"Death of a Hero." London *Private Eye* (1 August 1969), p. 18. [G1355]

Dening, R. "The Storm over Lawrence: Arabs Liked His Bravery" [letter]. London *Illustrated* (26 February 1955), p. 9.

Dennis, Nigel. Reply to "Snuggling With Lawrence" by Desmond Stewart [letter]. *New York Review of Books* 24 (9 February 1978): 46.

Dorrell, Karen. "Lawrence of Arabia Still Relevant Today." Norman, Okla., *Transcript* (4 October 1990), pp. 1–2.

Doyle, Charles. *Richard Aldington: A Biography*. Carbondale: Southern Illinois University Press, 1989.

Doyle, Charles, and Robert Beum. "Richard Aldington (8 July 1892–27 July 1962)." *Dictionary of Literary Biography, Volume 100: Modern British Essayists, Second Series.* Detroit: Gale Research, 1990; pp. 3–15.

Duff, Douglas V. "The Mysterious S. A." [letter]. *New Statesman and Nation* 53 (January 1957).

Dunbar, Janet. *Mrs. G.B.S.: A Portrait.* New York: Harper & Row, 1963. [F0291]

"Un Écossais démasque Lawrence d'Arabie." Paris *Match* (27 February–6 March 1954), p. 79.

Edmonds, Charles [C. E. Carrington]. *T. E. Lawrence (of Arabia).* New York: D. Appleton-Century, 1936. [E081]

Edwards, Oliver [Sir William Haley]. "Richard Yea and Nay." London *Times* (3 January 1957).

Ellis, Harry B. "From the Bookshelf: A Biographical Inquiry." *Christian Science Monitor* (17 October 1955), p. 9.

Engle, Anita. "Imperial Warrior" [letter]. *Times Literary Supplement* (30 April 1993), p. 15.

———. "The Mysterious S. A." *New Statesman and Nation* 52 (22 December 1956): 812–13. [G0874]

———. *The Nili Spies.* London: Hogarth, 1959. [F0310]

Engle, Paul. "Desert Tale Challenged by Aldington." *Chicago Sunday Tribune Magazine of Books* (16 October 1955), p. 4.

Étiemble. "Aldington L'Imposteur." *Les Lettres Nouvelles* 3:28 (June 1955): 873–91. [G0782]

———. " 'La Matrice' ou la Réponse d'un Imposteur." *Évidences* 7:53 (December 1955): 29–35. [G0849]

Fetherstonhaugh Frampton, R. H. C. " 'Fantasy' Phase in the Life of Lawrence of Arabia" [letter]. London *Sunday Times* (18 August 1968), p. 8.

Fielding, K. J. "Lawrence's Confession." London *Sunday Times* (17 September 1961), magazine section, p. 42. [H0623]

Fisher, P. F. "Turning New Leaves." *Canadian Forum* 35 (June 1955): 67–68.

FitzGibbon, Constantine [unsigned]. "Group Portrait." *Times Literary Supplement* (7 May 1954), p. 300.

———. "The Lawrence Legend." *Encounter* 15 (November 1960): 55–56. [G0944]

Fitzsimons, M. A. "Agonizing Reappraisal of T. E. Lawrence." *Commonweal* 63 (25 November 1955): 202, 204. [G0848]

Flavell, A. J. "T. E. Lawrence and the Bodleian." *Journal of the T. E. Lawrence Society* 1:1 (Spring 1991): 30–42.

———. "T. E. Lawrence, *Seven Pillars of Wisdom* and the Bodleian." *Bodleian Library Record* 13:4 (April 1990): 300–13.

———. [unsigned]. *T. E. Lawrence: The Legend and the Man.* Oxford: Bodleian Library, 1988.

Forster, E. M. *See Sur*

Frédérix, Pierre. "Lawrence l'imposteur précéde d'une réponse de R. Aldington à de Fallois." *La Revue de Paris* (June 1955), pp. 55–78. [Go786]

"French Criticisms of T. E. Lawrence: Old Memories Stirred by New Book." London *Times* (27 November 1954), p. 5.

Friedman, L. "Politics of A/c Shaw" [letter]. London *Times* (10 May 1968), p. 11.

Gardner, Brian. *Allenby of Arabia: Lawrence's General* [1965]. Intro. Lowell Thomas. New York: Coward-McCann, 1966. [Fo386]

Garnett, David. "The Eagles' Nest." London *Observer* (4 July 1954), p. 11.

———. "The Enigma of Lawrence." London *Sunday Times* (22 October 1961), p. 32.

———. "Lawrence in the Dock." *New Statesman and Nation* 49 (5 February 1955): 182–84. [Go712]

———. *See also* Lawrence, T. E., *The Essential T. E. Lawrence*; Lawrence, T. E., *The Letters of T. E. Lawrence*; Ocampo, Victoria, *338171 T. E.*; Williamson, Henry, Extracts from ALS to David Garnett

Garteiser, André. "A Propos du Colonel Lawrence." *Hommes et Mondes* 30 (May 1956): 310, 312. [Go864]

Gates, Norman T. *A Checklist of the Letters of Richard Aldington*. Carbondale: Southern Illinois University Press, 1977. [Fo393]

———. "The Richard Aldington Collection at Morris Library." *ICarbS* 3:1 (Summer/Fall 1976): 60–68.

———. "Richard Aldington in Russia." *Texas Quarterly* 21 (Summer 1978): 35–57.

George, William. "Lawrence of Arabia" [letter]. *Truth* (25 February 1955), p. 229.

Gilbert, Martin. *"Never Despair": Winston S. Churchill, 1945–1965*. London: Heinemann, 1988.

———. *Winston S. Churchill, Volume VI: Finest Hour, 1939–41*. Boston: Houghton Mifflin, 1983.

Gillett, Eric. "Sleuths at Work." *National and English Review* (February 1955), pp. 101–4, 106.

Glubb, John Bagot. *Britain and the Arabs: A Study of Fifty Years, 1908 to 1958*. London: Hodder & Stoughton, 1959. [Fo402]

Goodspeed, D. J. "The End of a Legend." *Canadian Army Journal* 10:2 (April 1956): 107–9.

Graham-Little, Helen. "Lawrence of Arabia" [letter]. *Truth* (18 February 1955), p. 201.

Graves, Richard Perceval. *Robert Graves and the White Goddess 1940–85*. London: Weidenfeld and Nicolson, 1995.

Graves, Robert. *Between Moon and Moon: Selected Correspondence* [1984]. Ed. Paul O'Prey. Mt. Kisco, N.Y.: Moyer Bell, 1990.

———. *Goodbye to All That* [1929]. New York: Penguin, 1986.

———. *In Broken Images: Selected Correspondence* [1982]. Ed. Paul O'Prey. Mt. Kisco, N.Y.: Moyer Bell, 1988.

——. *Lawrence and the Arabs*. London: Cape, 1927. [E030]

——. "The Lawrence I Knew." London *News Chronicle* (31 January 1955), p. 4. [H0461]

——. "Lawrence of Arabia" [letter]. *New Republic* 132 (16 May 1955): 46. [G0779]

——. "Lawrence Vindicated." *New Republic* 132 (21 March 1955): 16–20. [G0745]

——. "No. 2 Polstead Road." *New Statesman and Nation* 48 (24 July 1954): 105–6. [G0670]

——. "The Riddle of 'SA' of the Seven Pillars" [letter]. London *Times* (23 June 1968), p. 15. [H0854]

——. "T. E. Lawrence and the Riddle of 'S. A.'" *Saturday Review* 46 (15 June 1963): 16–17. [G1116]

——. *See also* Lawrence, T. E., *T. E. Lawrence to His Biographer Robert Graves*

Greene, Graham. "Poison Pen." *London Magazine* 5 [n.s.] (March 1966): 70–73.

Guinness, Sir Alec. *Blessings in Disguise.* New York: Knopf, 1986.

Guthrie, James. "Call Me Ishmael." *Literary Guide* (30 January 1955), pp. 27–29. [G0705]

Haley, Sir William. *See* Edwards, Oliver

Harald, Michael. "Call Me Ishmael: 'Ross' by Terence Rattigan." *Action* (August/September 1960), p. 8.

Harris, Arthur T. "Lawrence and His Arabs" [letter]. London *Daily Telegraph* (12 February 1955), p. 6.

Hartley, L. P. "A Failed Masterpiece." *Listener* 53 (14 April 1955): 658–59. [G0764]

Hawkins, G. R. "Lawrence of Arabia: Legendary Figure or Fraud?" *Bristol Evening Post* (14 February 1955), p. 2.

Hennessy, Peter. "Lawrence's Secret Arabian 'Slush Fund'." London *Times* (11 February 1980), p. 12. [H1237]

Herrington, J. M. "A New View of Lawrence of Arabia: His Admirers Are Now Asked to Believe He Was 'Half a Fraud'." *Field* (10 February 1955), p. 233.

Higgs, A. S. "T. E. Lawrence: A Remoulding of the Legend." *Army Quarterly and Defence Journal* 107 (January 1977): 71–74. [G1567]

Hodson, Joel C. *Lawrence of Arabia and American Culture: The Making of a Transatlantic Legend*. Westport, Conn.: Greenwood Press, 1995.

——. "Who Wrote *Lawrence of Arabia*?: Sam Spiegel and David Lean's Denial of Credit to a Blacklisted Screenwriter." *Cineaste* 20:4 (Fall 1994): 12–18.

Hopkirk, Peter. "The Postcard Poll Puts Lawrence First." London *Times* (8 August 1967), p. 8.

Hough, Graham. "Disgruntlements." *Times Literary Supplement* (6 November 1981), p. 1290.

Howarth, David. *The Desert King: A Life of Ibn Saud.* New York: McGraw-Hill, 1964. [F0536]

Hughes, Colin. "Britons Relive Desert Legend of Lawrence." London *Times* (19 March 1985), p. 36.

Hulbert, Jeffrey. *See* Richards, Jeffrey, and Jeffrey Hulbert

Humphreys, Humphrey. "Lawrence of Arabia: An 'Enquiry'." *Birmingham Post* (31 January 1955).

Hunt, Bob. *The Life and Times of Joyce E. Knowles.* Weymouth, Dorset: E. V. G. Hunt, 1994.

———. *See also* Knowles, Pat, Joyce Knowles, and Bob Hunt

Hyde, H. Montgomery. *Solitary in the Ranks: Lawrence of Arabia as Airman and Private Soldier.* London: Constable, 1977. [E373]

Irwin, Robert. "The Riddle of the Sands." *Listener* 122 (21–28 December 1989): 62–63.

"I Stand By My Book on Lawrence, Says Author." London *Evening News* (31 January 1955), late extra, p. 1.

James, Lawrence. "Deraa Revisited: Lawrence James Refutes Jeremy Wilson." *T.E. Notes* 2:7 (September 1991): 3–4.

———. *The Golden Warrior: The Life and Legend of Lawrence of Arabia* [1990]. New York: Paragon House, 1993.

———. *Imperial Warrior: The Life and Times of Field-Marshal Viscount Allenby 1861–1936.* London: Weidenfeld & Nicolson, 1993.

———. "Lawrence of Fantasia." *Scotland on Sunday* (10 December 1989).

———. "The Subtle Art of Being a Hero." *Scotland on Sunday* (19 August 1990).

Johns, W. E. "How Lawrence Joined the R.A.F." London *Sunday Times* (8 April 1951), p. 5. [H0425]

Johnson, F. W. "The Quiet Man" [letter]. London *Evening Standard* (10 September 1954), p. 5.

Johnson, Paul. "Fallen Pillars." *New Statesman and Nation* 51 (5 May 1956): 490–91. [G0865]

Johnston, Monroe. "Lloyd George, Allenby Had Faith in Lawrence[,] Lowell Thomas States." *Toronto Daily Star* (11 May 1954), p. 10.

Jones, Mervyn. "Lawrence or Aldington? I Dislike Them BOTH." London *Tribune* (18 February 1955).

Jones, Thomas. *A Diary with Letters, 1931–1950.* London: Oxford University Press, 1954. [F0574]

Joost, Horst K. "Lawrence of Arabia. A Biographical Enquiry. By Richard Aldington." *Military Review* 36:3 (June 1956): 108.

Kaplan, Carola M. "Conquest as Literature, Literature as Conquest: T. E. Lawrence's Artistic Campaign in *Seven Pillars of Wisdom*." *Texas Studies in Literature and Language* 37:1 (Spring 1995): 72–97.

Kedourie, Elie. *The Chatham House Version and Other Middle-Eastern Studies* [1970]. Hanover, N.H.: Brandeis University Press, 1984.

———. "Colonel Lawrence." *Cambridge Journal* 7 (June 1954): 515–30. [G0664]

———. "Communications" [letter]. *American Historical Review* 97 (June 1992): 1006.

———. "The Lives of Lawrence." *New Republic* 201 (21 August 1989): 37.

———. "The Real T. E. Lawrence." *Commentary* 64:1 (July 1977): 49–56. [G1579]

Kelly, Andrew, James Pepper, and Jeffrey Richards, eds. *Filming T. E. Lawrence: Korda's Lost Epics.* London: I. B. Tauris, 1997.

Kelly, Lionel, ed. *Richard Aldington: Papers from the Reading Symposium.* Reading, England: University of Reading, 1987.

Kennedy, Ponsonby & Prideaux. "Lawrence of Arabia" [letter]. London *Times* (2 January 1963), p. 9.

Kennington, Celandine. "Lawrence" [letter]. London *Observer* (13 February 1955).

———. "T. E. Lawrence: Was He a Woman-Hater?" *Housewife* (July 1955), pp. 55, 125–26. [G0730]

Kennington, Eric. "Lawrence of Arabia" [letter]. *Truth* (4 March 1955), p. 260. [G0735]

———. "On Books and People." *Truth* (4 February 1955), p. 141. [G0708]

Kershaw, Alister. "Aldington's Notes." *Merlin* 2:4 (Spring/Summer 1955): 298–301.

———. "Lawrence and History" [letter]. London *Times* (18 September 1967), p. 9.

———. "Pen Pals." *Sydney Bulletin Literary Supplement* (22–29 December 1981), pp. 210–16.

———. *The Pleasure of Their Company.* St. Lucia: University of Queensland Press, 1986.

Kershaw, Alister, and F.-J. Temple, eds. *Richard Aldington: An Intimate Portrait.* Carbondale: Southern Illinois University Press, 1965.

Kervin, Roy. "The Legend May Still Survive." *Montreal Gazette* (19 February 1955), p. 23.

Kilner, Peter. *See* Brent, Peter

Kimche, Jon. "Lawrence and the Arabs" [letter]. London *Times* (31 July 1969), p. 9. [H0873]

King, Daniel P. Review of *Lawrence of Arabia: The Authorized Biography of T. E. Lawrence* by Jeremy Wilson. *World Literature Today* 65:2 (Spring 1991): 310–11.

Kinross, Lord. "Still Another Theory of T. E. Lawrence." London *Daily Telegraph* (20 October 1961), p. 18.

Kirkbride, Sir Alec. *An Awakening: The Arab Campaign, 1917–18.* Tavistock: English University Press of Arabia, 1971. [F0597]

———. *A Crackle of Thorns: Experiences in the Middle East.* London: John Murray, 1956. [F0598]

———. "T. E. Lawrence: A Memory of the Hedjaz, 1918." *Manchester Guardian* (20 August 1956), pp. 4, 6. [H0551]

Kittredge, Selwyn Burnett. "The Literary Career of Richard Aldington." Ph.D. dissertation, New York University, 1976.

Knightley, Phillip. "Aldington's Enquiry Concerning T. E. Lawrence." *Texas Quarterly* 16 (Winter 1973): 98–105. [G1483]

————. "Another Twist in the Lawrence Tale." London *Sunday Times* (26 April 1981), p. 13. [H1243]

————. "Blame It on Lawrence of Arabia." Portland *Sunday Oregonian* (23 December 1990), p. C5.

————. "The Girl Who Snubbed Lawrence of Arabia." London *Sunday Times* (9 May 1976). [H1192]

————. "The Sandcastle." *New Statesman* 94 (8 July 1977): 56. [G1582]

————. "Stripped." *New Statesman* 91 (21 May 1976): 684. [G1543]

————. "T. E. Lawrence." In *The Craft of Literary Biography* [1984]. Ed. Jeffrey Meyers. New York: Schocken Books, 1985; pp. 154–72.

————. "Was There Really a Rape in Dera?" London *Independent on Sunday* (19 August 1990), Home section, p. 6.

Knightley, Phillip, and Colin Simpson. "Lawrence: A Desperate Man." London *Sunday Times Weekly Review* (7 September 1969), pp. 45–46. [H0853]

————. "Lawrence and the Arabs" [letter]. London *Times* (4 August 1969), p. 9. [H0877]

————. "Lawrence of Arabia" [letter]. London *Times* (28 November 1969), p. 11.

————. "Lawrence: The End of a Legend." London *Sunday Times Weekly Review* (31 August 1969), pp. 21–22. [H0853]

————. "Lawrence: The Secret Life of Aircraftman Shaw." London *Sunday Times Weekly Review* (14 September 1969), pp. 49–50. [H0853]

————. *The Secret Lives of Lawrence of Arabia* [1969]. London: Nelson, 1969; New York: McGraw-Hill, 1970. [E302, E309]

————. *See also* Simpson, Colin, and Phillip Knightley

Knowles, Pat, Joyce Knowles, and Bob Hunt. *Cloud's Hill—Dorset: "An Handful with Quietness"*. Weymouth, Dorset: E. V. G. Hunt, 1992.

LaBadie, Donald W. "The Reel Lawrence." *Show: The Magazine of the Arts* 3 (March 1963): 31. [G1082]

Laird, J. T. "T. E. Lawrence: The Problem of Interpretation." *Australian Quarterly* 32 (March 1960): 93–99. [G0930]

Lalou, René. "Essais: Lawrence l'imposteur *par* Richard Aldington." *Les Nouvelles Littéraires* (9 December 1954), p. 3. [G0684]

Larès, Maurice. "De Lawrence à Learoyd." *Revue de Littérature Comparée* 1 (January–March 1984): 51–86. [G1658]

————. "T. E. Lawrence and France: Friends or Foes?" In *The T. E. Lawrence Puzzle*. Ed. Stephen E. Tabachnick. Athens: University of Georgia Press, 1984; pp. 220–24. [E396]

Lawrence, A. W. "The Fiction and the Fact." London *Observer* (16 December 1962), p. 25. [G1040]

————. "Introductory Note." In Edward Robinson, *Lawrence: The Story of His Life*. London: Oxford University Press, 1935; p. 5. [E083]

——. "Lawrence—And Col. Joynson" [letter]. *Royal British Legion Journal* 45:9 (September 1965): 8. [G1224]

——. "Lawrence Letters" [letter]. London *Times* (24 May 1935), p. 17.

——. "Lawrence of Arabia: Changes Made for Film Version" [letter]. London *Times* (14 December 1962), p. 13.

——. "Lawrence of Arabia in the R.A.F.: The Making of 'The Mint'." London *Sunday Times* (23 January 1955), p. 6. [H0454]

——. "T E Lawrence: A Brother Gives His Testimony" [letter]. London *Times* (22 November 1969), p. 7. [H0910]

——, ed. *T. E. Lawrence by His Friends.* London: Cape, 1937. [E107]

——, ed. *T. E. Lawrence by His Friends* [1937]. Rev. ed. London: Cape, 1954. [E108]

——. *See also* Ocampo, Victoria, *338171 T.E.*

Lawrence, Frieda. *Frieda Lawrence and Her Circle: Letters from, to, and about Frieda Lawrence.* Ed. Harry T. Moore and Dale B. Montague. Hamden, Conn.: Archon Books, 1981.

——. *Frieda Lawrence: The Memoirs and Correspondence.* Ed. E. W. Tedlock. London: Heinemann, 1961.

——. *See also* Ravagli, Frieda Lawrence

Lawrence, M. R. *See* Lawrence, T. E., *The Home Letters of T. E. Lawrence and His Brothers*

Lawrence, T. E. *The Essential T. E. Lawrence* [1951]. Ed. David Garnett. Harmondsworth, Middlesex: Penguin, 1956. [A239]

——. *Evolution of a Revolt: Early Postwar Writings of T. E. Lawrence.* Ed. Stanley and Rodelle Weintraub. University Park: Penn State University Press, 1968. [A255]

——. "A Hitherto Unpublished TE Letter." Trans. Suleiman Mousa. *T. E. Notes* 2:4 (April 1991): 7.

——. *The Home Letters of T. E. Lawrence and His Brothers.* Ed. M. R. Lawrence. New York: Macmillan, 1954. [A247]

——. *Lawrence of Arabia, Strange Man of Letters: The Literary Criticism and Correspondence of T. E. Lawrence.* Ed. Harold Orlans. Rutherford, N.J.: Fairleigh Dickinson University Press, 1993.

——. "Lawrence's Own Epitaph: In a Letter to Robert Graves He Made an Estimate of His Life Accomplishments." *New York Times* (26 May 1935), section 4, p. 5. [H0292]

——. *The Letters of T. E. Lawrence* [1938]. Ed. David Garnett. New York: Doubleday, Doran, 1939. [A204]

——. *Revolt in the Desert* [1927]. Garden City, N.Y.: Garden City Publishing, n.d. [A109]

——. *Secret Despatches from Arabia and Other Writings.* Ed. Malcolm Brown. London: Bellew, 1991.

——. *Seven Pillars of Wisdom: A Triumph.* Garden City, N.Y.: Doubleday, Doran, 1935. [A054]

———. *T. E. Lawrence: The Selected Letters.* Ed. Malcolm Brown. New York: Norton, 1989.

———. *T. E. Lawrence to His Biographer Liddell Hart.* Ed. B. H. Liddell Hart. London: Faber & Faber, 1938. [A211]

———. *T. E. Lawrence to His Biographer Robert Graves.* Ed. Robert Graves. London: Faber & Faber, 1938. [A210]

———. *T. E. Lawrence to His Biographers Robert Graves and Liddell Hart* [1938]. Ed. Robert Graves and B. H. Liddell Hart. Garden City, N.Y.: Doubleday, 1963. [A217]

———. "Two Unpublished Letters to Ezra Pound." *Nine* 2 (Summer 1950): 180–82. [B0046]

———. "An Unpublished Letter of Lawrence of Arabia." *National Review* (10 September 1963), pp. 203–5. [B0051]

"Lawrence Accused of Faking Heroism." *New York Times* (31 January 1955), p. 17.

"Lawrence and His Legend: Mr. Aldington's 'Enquiry'." London *Times* (2 February 1955), p. 10. [H0465]

"Lawrence: Herunter von den Säulen." *Spiegel* 8:33 (11 August 1954): 27–31. [G0673]

"Lawrence: Lies or Legends?" *Newsweek* 43 (15 February 1954): 100–2. [G0657]

"Lawrence of Arabia: A Biographical Enquiry by Richard Aldington: A Bookseller's Opinion." *Publisher's Circular* (5 February 1955), p. 115.

"Lawrence of Arabia a Fake, New British Book Charges." *Baltimore Sun* (20 January 1954).

"Lawrence of Arabia's Rejected Post: Secretaryship of Bank of England." London *Times* (6 December 1950), p. 6.

"Lawrence of Arabia: Venture in Debunking." *Newsweek* 43 (8 February 1954), p. 88. [G0656]

"Lawrence Reminted." London *Times* (19 April 1956), p. 13.

"Lawrence's Defenders." *Newsweek* 43 (5 April 1954): 97–98. [G0661]

Leach, Hugh. "Further Comments on the Robinson Obituary." *T. E. Notes* 5:4 (April 1994): 3–4.

Lean, David. "Out of the Wilderness." *Films and Filming* 9:4 (January 1963): 12–15. [G1054]

"A Legend Shaken." *Economist* 264 (2 July 1977): 112. [G1581]

Legg, Rodney. *Lawrence of Arabia in Dorset.* Sherborne, Dorset: Dorset Publishing, 1988. [E407]

Lehmann, John. "Foreword." *London Magazine* 2 (April 1955): 13, 15.

Lengyel, Emil. "Behind the Hero." *Saturday Review* 38 (12 November 1955): 16, 44. [G0846]

———. "Enigma of the Sands." *Saturday Review* 38 (3 September 1955): 13. [G0822]

———. *World Without End: The Middle East.* New York: John Day, 1953. [F0633]

Lewis, Peter. "Uncrowned King of Arabia." London *Sunday Times* (19 November 1989), p. G9.

Lewis, Wyndham. "Perspectives on Lawrence." *Hudson Review* 8 (Winter 1956): 596–608. [G0872]

Liddell Hart, Adrian. "Plus ça change . . . " [letter]. *History Today* 41 (March 1991): 56.

Liddell Hart, B. H. *Colonel Lawrence: The Man Behind the Legend* [1934]. Rev. ed. New York: Halcyon House, 1937. [E062]

———. "Correspondence" [response to Aldington]. *London Magazine* 2 (August 1955): 69–71. [G0813]

———. "Correspondence" [response to Rob Lyle]. *London Magazine* 2 (June 1955): 79–81. [G0787]

———. "Lawrence and His Arabs: Help to Allenby 'Invaluable' " [letter]. London *Daily Telegraph* (12 February 1955), p. 6.

———. "Lawrence and History" [letter]. London *Times* (21 September 1967), p. 11.

———. "Lawrence of Arabia" [letter]. London *Times* (19 December 1962), p. 9. [H0655]

———. "Lawrence of Arabia" [letter]. *Times Literary Supplement* (3 November 1961), p. 789. [H0625]

———. "Lawrence of Arabia: A Genius of War and Letters: The Desert Revolt." London *Times* (20 May 1935), pp. 15–16. [H0240]

———. "Lawrence's Arabs" [letter]. London *Daily Telegraph* (26 February 1955), p. 6.

———. *The Liddell Hart Memoirs.* New York: G. P. Putnam's Sons, 1965. [F0647]

———. *The Liddell Hart Memoirs: The Later Years.* New York: G. P. Putnam's Sons, 1966. [F0647]

———. "Propagandist" [letter]. London *Sunday Times* (5 February 1967). [H0828]

———. *The Real War 1914–1918* [1930]. Boston: Little, Brown, 1964. [F0649]

———. "The Storm over Lawrence: Quoting Churchill" [letter]. London *Illustrated* (26 February 1955), pp. 6, 9. [G0729]

———. *Strategy: The Indirect Approach* [1954]. New York: Frederick A. Praeger, 1967. [F0651]

———. "T. E. Lawrence, Aldington and the Truth." *London Magazine* 2 (April 1955): 67–75. [G0760]

———. "T. E. Lawrence: Man or Myth?" *Atlantic* 196 (November 1955): 70–71, 74, 76. [G0839]

———. "What Authority Has Aldington for Writing This Niggling, Disparaging Book? Lawrence: His Friend, a Great Historian, Answers the Smears and Sneers." London *Sunday Chronicle* (30 January 1955). [H0460]

———. *See also* Lawrence, T. E., *T. E. Lawrence to His Biographer Liddell Hart; Sur* "The Life and Death of T. E. Lawrence." *Radio Times* (22 November 1962).

Lipton, Dean. "The 'Lawrence of Arabia Myth'." *Nexus* 1 (August 1963): 1–11. [G1125]

Bibliography

Lloyd George, David. *The Truth about the Peace Treaties* [1939]. 2 vols. New York: Fertig, 1972. [F0666]

Lockman, J. N. *Meinertzhagen's Diary Ruse: False Entries on T. E. Lawrence.* Grand Rapids, Mich.: Cornerstone, 1995.

———. *Scattered Tracks on the Lawrence Trail.* Whitmore Lake, Mich.: Falcon Books, 1996.

"London Diary." *New Statesman and Nation* 47 (6 February 1954): 150.

"Londoner's Diary." London *Evening Standard* (19 January 1954), p. 4. [H0432]

"Londoner's Diary: Counter-attack." London *Evening Standard* (24 September 1954), p. 4.

"Londoner's Diary: Lawrence Attacked." London *Evening Standard* (20 September 1954), p. 4.

"Londoner's Diary: Lawrence in Fiction." London *Evening Standard* (22 February 1954), p. 4.

"Londoner's Diary—The Lawrence Myth." London *Evening Standard* (4 February 1954), p. 4.

"Lost Lawrence." London *Times* (20 November 1971), p. 12. [H1164]

Lovelock, R. C. O. "The Mint—and the Metal: T. E. Lawrence's Life in the R.A.F." *Flight* 67 (18 March 1955): 356. [G0740]

Low, David M. "East Wind." *Listener* 51 (20 May 1954): 891–92.

Lunt, J. D. "An Unsolicited Tribute." *Blackwood's Magazine* 277 (April 1955): 289–96. [G0755]

Luvaas, Jay. "Liddell Hart and the Mearsheimer Critique: A 'Pupil's' Retrospective." *Parameters* 20:1 (March 1990): 9–19.

"Lying Attributed to T. E. Lawrence: Biographer Aldington Says He Will 'Erase from History' Author of 'Seven Pillars'." *New York Times* (25 January 1954), p. 13.

Lyle, Rob. "Correspondence" [response to B. H. Liddell Hart]. *London Magazine* 2 (June 1955): 75–79. [G0787]

———. "Lawrence, Aldington and Some Critics." *Nine* 11 (April 1956): 39–42. [G0862]

———. "Lawrence and His Detractor" [letter]. London *Daily Telegraph* (7 February 1955), p. 6.

———. "Lawrence of Arabia" [letter]. *Truth* (25 February 1955), p. 229. [G0727]

———. "Lawrence of Arabia" [letter]. *Truth* (11 March 1955), p. 288. [G0727]

———. "Lawrence of Arabia" [letter]. *Truth* (18 March 1955), p. 322. [G0727]

Mack, John E. "The Inner Conflict of T. E. Lawrence." London *Times Saturday Review* (8 February 1969), p. 17. [G1343]

———. *A Prince of Our Disorder: The Life of T. E. Lawrence.* Boston: Little, Brown, 1976. [E353]

———. "Psychoanalysis and Historical Biography." *Journal of the American Psychoanalytic Association* 19:1 (January 1971): 143–79. [G1436]

———. "T. E. Lawrence: A Study of Heroism and Conflict." *American Journal of Psychiatry* 125:8 (February 1969): 1083–92. [G1345]

———. "T. E. Lawrence: Charlatan or Tragic Hero?" [letter]. *American Journal of Psychiatry* 125:11 (May 1969): 1604–7.

Mackenzie, Compton. "Sidelight." *Spectator* 192 (30 April 1954): 518.

MacLean, James N. M. "Book Review: *Lawrence of Arabia* [by] Richard Aldington." *Scottish Regimental Gazette* 64 (December 1959): 218–21. [G0926]

Macphail, Sir Andrew. *Three Persons.* New York: Louis Carrier, 1929. [E048]

Majdalany, Fred. "The Last Word on and by Lawrence: He Had His Bed of Nails." London *Daily Mail* (14 February 1955).

Mallery, Leslie. "Marlon Brando to Play Lawrence of Arabia." London *News Chronicle* (18 February 1960), p. 1.

Malraux, André. "Lawrence and the Demon of the Absolute." *Hudson Review* 8 (1955): 519–32. [G0873]

"Man of Destiny." *Times Literary Supplement* (20 October 1961), p. 751.

Marks, Derek. "Lawrence of the Cookhouse." London *Daily Express* (14 February 1955), p. 4.

Marwil, Jonathan. *Frederic Manning: An Unfinished Life.* Durham, N.C.: Duke University Press, 1988.

Matheson, Christopher. *See* Tabachnick, Stephen E., and Christopher Matheson

Maugham, Robin. *Escape from the Shadows: An Autobiography.* New York: McGraw-Hill, 1973.

Maxwell, Elsa. [Untitled column]. *New York Journal-American* (20 February 1954), p. 20.

Mayo, James. "British Hero Debunked. *Lawrence L'Imposteur*: New Book Creates World Sensation." London *Sunday Chronicle* (9 January 1955), pp. 1, 3.

McAree, J. V. "Lawrence Restored." Toronto *Globe and Mail* (5 December 1955), p. 6.

McDonnell, Mary E. "Arnold Lawrence." *T. E. Notes* 2:6 (June 1991): 8.

———. "E. H. T. Robinson, 1897–1994." *T. E. Notes* 5:4 (April 1994): 3.

McFee, William. "A Hot Time in Arabia" [letter]. *New Republic* 132 (23 May 1955): 23.

———. "Lawrence of Arabia" [letter]. *New Republic* 132 (18 April 1955): 23.

McHandy, Rev. Archibald. "Lawrence of Arabia" [letter]. London *Sunday Times* (6 February 1955), p. 6. [H0470]

Mearsheimer, John J. *Liddell Hart and the Weight of History.* Ithaca, N.Y.: Cornell University Press, 1988.

Meinertzhagen, Richard. *Army Diary, 1899–1926.* Edinburgh: Oliver & Boyd, 1960. [F0720]

———. *Middle East Diary, 1917–1956.* London: Cresset Press, 1959. [F0721]

Mengay, Donald H. "Arabian Rites: T. E. Lawrence's *Seven Pillars of Wisdom* and the Erotics of Empire." *Genre* 27:4 (Winter 1994): 395–416.

Meyers, Jeffrey. "Imaginative Portraits of T. E. Lawrence." *Bulletin of Bibliography* 45:1 (March 1988): 15–16.

———. "Lawrence Unveiled." *Virginia Quarterly Review* 66:4 (Autumn 1990): 752–59.

———. "O'Brien, Philip M. *T. E. Lawrence: A Bibliography.*" *Bulletin of Bibliography* 46:1 (March 1989): 54–56.

———. " 'The Secret Lives of Lawrence of Arabia'." *Boston Globe* (7 May 1970), p. 39. [H1106]

———. "The Secret Lives of Lawrence of Arabia." *Commonweal* 93 (23 October 1970): 100–4. [G1424]

———. "T. E. Lawrence: A Bibliography." *Bulletin of Bibliography* 29 (January–March 1972): 25–36. [G1454]

———. *T. E. Lawrence: A Bibliography.* New York: Garland, 1974. [E338]

———. "A Wanderer after Sensations." *Virginia Quarterly Review* 52:4 (Autumn 1976): 717–23. [G1560]

———. *The Wounded Spirit: T. E. Lawrence's "Seven Pillars of Wisdom".* New York: St. Martin's Press, 1989. [E336]

———, ed. *The Craft of Literary Biography* [1984]. New York: Schocken Books, 1985.

———, ed. *T. E. Lawrence: Soldier, Writer, Legend.* New York: St. Martin's Press, 1989.

Miller, James E., Jr. *T. S. Eliot's Personal Waste Land: Exorcism of the Demons.* University Park: Penn State University Press, 1977.

" 'The Mint' and Mr. Aldington." *Bookseller* (15 January 1955).

Mitchison, Naomi. "Lawrence the Imp: Teasing on a Large Scale—and Quiet Intensity." *Manchester Guardian* (1 February 1955), p. 5.

Monroe, Elizabeth. *Britain's Moment in the Middle East, 1914–1916.* London: Methuen, 1965. [F0750]

———. *Philby of Arabia.* London: Faber & Faber, 1973. [F0751]

———. "The Round Table and the Middle East Peace Settlement, 1917–1922: 'Principles of Architecture' in the Middle East." *Round Table* 60 (November 1970): 479–90. [G1425]

Moore, Harry T. "Richard Aldington in His Last Years." *Texas Quarterly* 6 (Autumn 1963): 63, 66–68. [G1133]

Morris, John. "The Lawrence Enigma." *Encounter* 4 (April 1955): 78–80. [G1699]

Morris, John A. "Aldington, Edward Godfree 'Richard'." *Dictionary of National Biography, 1961–1970.* Ed. E. J. Williams and C. S. Nicholls. New York: Oxford University Press, 1981; pp. 12–15.

Morris, L. Robert, and Lawrence Raskin. *Lawrence of Arabia: The 30th Anniversary Pictorial History.* New York: Doubleday, 1992.

Mortimer, Raymond. "T. E. Lawrence: Mr. Aldington's Charges." London *Sunday Times* (30 January 1955), p. 5. [H0458]

———. *See also Sur*

Mousa, Suleiman. "Arab Sources on Lawrence of Arabia: New Evidence." *Army Quarterly and Defence Journal* 116:2 (April 1986): 158–71. [G1670]

——. "A Matter of Principle: King Hussein of the Hijaz and the Arabs of Palestine." *International Journal of Middle East Studies* 9 (1978): 183–94.

——. "The Role of Syrians and Iraqis in the Arab Revolt." *Middle East Forum* 43:1 (1967): 5–17. [G1285]

——. *T. E. Lawrence: An Arab View* [1962]. Trans. Albert Butros. London: Oxford University Press, 1966. [E256]

——. "T. E. Lawrence and His Arab Contemporaries." *Arabian Studies* 7 (1985): 7–21. [F0951a]

——. "Whose Debt? A Reply to Sidney Sugerman's Article on T. E. Lawrence." *International History Magazine*, no. 12 (December 1973): 78–80.

——. *See also* Lawrence, T. E., "A Hitherto Unpublished TE Letter"

"Mud on the White Robe." *Times Educational Supplement* (4 February 1955), p. 102. [G0709]

Muggeridge, Malcolm. "A Legend That Dies Hard." London *Observer* (28 September 1969), p. 29. [G1357]

——. "London Diary." *New Statesman* 64 (3 August 1962): 139.

——. "Poor Lawrence." *New Statesman* 62 (27 October 1961): 604, 606. [G0971]

——. "Richard the Lion-Heart." London *Observer* (28 March 1971), p. 33.

Munson, James. "The Lawrence Legend Lives On." *Contemporary Review* 253 (September 1988): 166–67.

——. "Lawrence of Arabia: A Biography to End Biographies." *Contemporary Review* 256 (April 1990): 222–23.

——. "T. E. Lawrence Revisited." *Contemporary Review* 258 (January 1991): 53–54.

Nathan, David. "Brando to Play Lawrence of Arabia." London *Daily Herald* (18 February 1960), p. 1.

Neame, A. J. "T. E. Lawrence—Security Risk." *European*, no. 17 (July 1954): 44–59.

Neame, Alan. Review of *Lawrence of Arabia: A Biographical Enquiry* by Richard Aldington. *Shenandoah* 6:2 (Spring 1955): 69–72.

"New British Book Calls Lawrence a Phony Hero." *Christian Science Monitor* (20 January 1954).

Nicolson, Harold. "The Lawrence Legend." London *Observer* (30 January 1955), p. 6. [G0704]

Nicolson, Nigel. " 'Never Forget That You Have Seen Him'." *New York Times Book Review* (10 June 1990), p. 42.

"Not a 'Phoney': Friends Prepare Answer to Attack on Lawrence of Arabia." Bermuda *Royal Gazette* (19 February 1954), p. 9.

Nutting, Anthony. *Lawrence of Arabia: The Man and the Motive* [1961]. New York: Signet, 1962. [E238]

——. "Lawrence of Arabia: The Mirror of Degradation." London *Sunday Times* (17 September 1961), magazine section, p. 27. [H0624]

——. "Lawrence of Arabia: The Secret of a Tormented Spirit." London *Sunday Times* (10 September 1961), magazine section, p. 21. [H0622]

——. "A Masochist?" [letter]. London *Sunday Times* (7 July 1968), p. 16.

O'Brien, Philip M. *T. E. Lawrence: A Bibliography*. Boston: G. K. Hall, 1988.

——. "*T. E. Lawrence: A Bibliography*. Status Report on Revisions and the Supplement." *T. E. Notes* 4:1 (January 1993): 10–11.

——. "T. E. Lawrence: The Man." *T. E. Notes* 2:10 (December 1991): 1–3.

——. "T. E. Lawrence: The Printed Word." *T. E. Notes* 3:1 (January 1992): 1–3.

O'Brien, R. Barry. "Life of Lawrence Costs Author £200,000." London *Daily Telegraph* (20 February 1989), p. 3.

Ocampo, Victoria. *338171 T.E. (Lawrence of Arabia)* [1942]. Trans. David Garnett. Intro. A. W. Lawrence. New York: Dutton, 1963. [E154]

——. *See also Sur*

O'Connor, John J. "Confused, Complex Lawrence of Arabia." *New York Times* (6 May 1992), pp. C17, C22.

——. "Lawrence of Arabia by Richard Aldington." *America* 94 (20 October 1955): 134. [G0837]

O'Donnell, Thomas J. *The Confessions of T. E. Lawrence: The Romantic Hero's Presentation of Self*. Athens: Ohio University Press, 1979. [E383]

O'Hearn, Walter. "Lawrence, the Man or Myth—Mr. Aldington's 'Enquiry'." *Montreal Star* (19 February 1955).

Orlans, Harold. "Jeremy Wilson Rebuts Lawrence James' Charge." *T. E. Notes* 2:1 (January 1991): 4.

——. "The Many Lives of T. E. Lawrence: A Symposium." *Biography* 16:3 (Summer 1993): 224–48.

——. "Obstacles to the Scholarly Biography of Contemporaries." *T. E. Notes* 6:8–9 (October/November 1995): 15–17.

——. "On Biographical Ethics and Truth." *T. E. Notes* 4:2 (February 1993): 7–9.

——. "On Lady Chatterley." *T. E. Notes* 2:10 (December 1991): 6.

——. *See also* Lawrence, T. E., *Lawrence of Arabia, Strange Man of Letters*

Ottaway, Robert. "He's Still a Hero to Churchill." London *Sunday Graphic* (30 January 1955), p. 6.

Palmer, Alison McK. "Aldington's 'Biography of Enquiry' on Lawrence" [letter]. *Montreal Gazette* (8 December 1955), p. 8.

Paquet, Ron. "Early Scripts of *Lawrence of Arabia*." *T. E. Notes* 5:7 (September 1994): 1–6.

Patch, Blanche. *Thirty Years with G.B.S.* London: Gollancz, 1951. [F0825]

Patrick, David H. "The T. E. Lawrence Collection: Its Historical Uses for the Biographer." *Library Chronicle* 20:3 (1990): 16–47.

Payne, Robert. *Lawrence of Arabia: A Triumph*. New York: Pyramid, 1962. [E260]

——. *Lawrence of Arabia: A Triumph* [1962]. Rev. ed. London: Robert Hale, 1966. [E261]

Pearce, Bryan. "Lawrence and the Arabs" [letter]. *New Statesman and Nation* 49 (12 February 1955).

Pearl, Cyril. "Aldington Recalled." *Sydney Morning Herald* (17 August 1968), p. 18.

Pepper, James. *See* Kelly, Andrew, James Pepper, and Jeffrey Richards

Peterborough. "A Blurb—For Mr. Aldington." London *Daily Telegraph* (10 February 1955), p. 6.

——. "Debunking: 1890–1955." London *Daily Telegraph* (16 March 1955), p. 6.

——. "An Eye on Lawrence." London *Daily Telegraph* (1 June 1963), p. 6. [H0702]

——. "Lawrence: Not Quite the Lady's Man." London *Daily Telegraph* (20 August 1992), p. 6.

——. " 'Master of Arabic'?" London *Daily Telegraph* (31 January 1955), p. 6.

Pfaff, William. "A Critic at Large: The Fallen Hero." *New Yorker* (8 May 1989): 105–15.

Philby, Harry St. John. *Forty Years in the Wilderness*. London: Robert Hale, 1957. [F0846]

Phillips, Hugh. "Yes, Lawrence Did Tell Lies." *Daily Worker* (3 February 1955), p. 19.

Pomeroy, Laurence. "Lawrence's Bicycle" [letter]. *New Statesman and Nation* 49 (19 February 1955): 249.

Pound, Ezra. *The Cantos of Ezra Pound*. New York: New Directions, 1972. [F0862]

Powell, Anthony. "Songs of Araby." *Punch* 228 (2 February 1955): 184. [G0706]

Powell, Jeremy, and Anne Powell. *Richard Aldington 8 July 1892–27 July 1962* [catalogue 16]. Cann, Dorset: Palladour Books, 1992.

"Publisher Delays Life of Lawrence." *New York Times* (14 April 1954), p. 9.

Pugh, Marshall. "What Is the Truth about Lawrence of Arabia? At 92, She Defends Her Hero Son." London *Sunday Graphic* (11 April 1954).

Ramage, Jim. "Reader Notes on 'Richard Aldington, Lowell Thomas, and the Ethics of Biography'." *T. E. Notes* 4:2 (February 1993): 10–11.

Ravagli, Frieda Lawrence. "Pinorman" [letter]. *Time and Tide* 35 (29 May 1954): 724.

——. *See also* Lawrence, Frieda

Read, Herbert. *A Coat of Many Colors*. London: Routledge & Kegan Paul, 1956. [F0888]

——. "The Listener's Book Chronicle: Letters to T. E. Lawrence." *Listener* 68 (26 July 1962): 145. [G1008]

——. "The Seven Pillars of Wisdom." In *Bibliophiles' Almanack for 1928*. London: Fleuron, 1928; pp. 35–41. [F0093]

"The Real Lawrence." London *Sphere* (12 February 1955), p. 246.

"Rebirth of a Hero," *Economist* 174 (5 February 1955): 449.

Reid, Brian Holden. "Lawrence and the Arab Revolt." *History Today* 35 (May 1985): 41–45. [G1663]

——. "T. E. Lawrence and His Biographers." In *The First World War and British Military History*. Ed. Brian Bond. Oxford: Clarendon Press, 1991; pp. 227–59.

——. "T. E. Lawrence and Liddell Hart." *History* 70:229 (June 1985): 218–31. [G1664]

"Restored Portrait." *Times Literary Supplement* (27 June 1956).

Rice, John. "Lawrence Isn't a Hero in Arabia." *San Francisco Chronicle* (9 September 1986), p. 16. [H1269]

Richards, Jeffrey. "The Untold Legends of Lawrence of Arabia." London *Weekend Telegraph* (13 August 1988), p. 10.

———. *See also* Kelly, Andrew, James Pepper, and Jeffrey Richards

Richards, Jeffrey, and Jeffrey Hulbert. "Censorship in Action: The Case of *Lawrence of Arabia*." *Journal of Contemporary History* 19:1 (January 1984): 153–70. [G1655]

Richards, Vyvyan. *Portrait of T. E. Lawrence* [1939]. New York: Scholastic Book Services, 1964. [E126]

Richford, Frank. "Fate of a Joker" [letter]. London *Illustrated* (26 February 1955), p. 9.

Riesman, Janet. "Life-Long Friendships: HW on TEL and RA." *T.E. Notes* 5:10 (December 1994): 6–9.

Robinson, Edward. *Lawrence the Rebel*. London: Lincolns-Prager, 1946. [E164]

———. *Lawrence: The Story of His Life*. London: Oxford University Press, 1935. [E083]

Rodman, Selden. "To Glory and Back." *New York Times Book Review* (4 September 1955), pp. 7, 11. [G0823]

Rogers, Newell. "America Column: Literary Row." London *Daily Express* (11 February 1954), p. 2.

Rolo, Charles J. "Book with a Past." *Atlantic Monthly* 195 (May 1955): 80, 82–83. [G0772]

"Romantic Riddle." *MD* 4:4 (April 1960): 221–27. [G0931]

Rosebery, Lord. "Kept the Arabs 'Sweet': A Balanced View of Lawrence" [letter]. London *Daily Telegraph* (15 February 1955), p. 6.

Rosenthal, Michael. "England's Desert Warrior Retains His Elusiveness." *Boston Globe* (17 June 1990), pp. B43, B45.

Rosselli, John. "The Devil's Advocate: Mr Aldington's Lawrence." *Manchester Guardian* (31 January 1955), p. 6. [H0463]

———. "Was T. E. Lawrence a Fake?" *Reporter* 12 (21 April 1955): 49–52. [G0767]

Rosset, B.C. *Shaw of Dublin: The Formative Years*. University Park: Penn State University Press, 1964.

Rota, Bertram. "Lawrence of Arabia and *Seven Pillars of Wisdom*." *Texas Quarterly* 5 (Autumn 1962): 46–53. [G1022]

Rothenstein, John. *Summer's Lease: Autobiography, 1901–1938*. London: Hamish Hamilton, 1965. [F0908]

Rowse, A. L. "Legend or Only a Lie?" London *Daily Mail* (31 January 1955), p. 4.

Ruthven, Malise. "A Hero and His Discontents." *Times Literary Supplement* (15–21 June 1990), pp. 635–36.

Sachar, Howard M. "The Declining World of T. E. Lawrence." *New Republic* 130 (10 May 1954): 18–19. [G0663]

——. *The Emergence of the Middle East, 1914–1924*. New York: Knopf, 1969. [F0930]

Scawen, William. "Lawrence of Arabia: A Biographical Inquiry by Richard Aldington." *Adelphi* (May 1955), pp. 292, 294.

Schumach, Murray. " 'Lawrence of Arabia' Producer Defends Film Story of Hero: Spiegel Charges Professor Wanted to Hide Facts about His Brother." *New York Times* (26 January 1963), p. 5.

Seligo, Hans. "Lawrence—Held oder Hockstapler? Ein Mythos soll zerstört werden." *Tagesspiegel* (9 January 1955), p. 6. [H0452]

Seymour-Smith, Martin. "Lawrence of Arabia" [letter]. *Truth* (18 March 1955), pp. 322–23.

Sheean, Vincent. "T. E. Lawrence Seen in a Harsh Picture Designed to Blight His Name: Richard Aldington Looks with a Dark Eye on Every Aspect of That Controversial Figure." *New York Herald-Tribune Book Review* (25 September 1955), p. 5.

"Shortage of Lawrences: British Intelligence Criticised." *Manchester Guardian* (1 February 1955), p. 7.

Simpson, Colin. "Lawrence Made Up Rape Story, Says Author." London *Sunday Times* (12 June 1977), p. 2. [H1213]

——. "Lawrence: The Lost Letter" [letter]. London *Sunday Times* (26 June 1977), p. 13.

Simpson, Colin, and Phillip Knightley. "How Lawrence of Arabia Cracked Up." London *Sunday Times* (23 June 1968), pp. 45–46. [H0853]

——. "How T E Lawrence Found Another Mother." London *Sunday Times* (30 June 1968), pp. 45–46. [H0853]

——. "The Secret Life of Lawrence of Arabia. 1: The Night of the Turks." London *Sunday Times* (9 June 1968), pp. 49–50. [H0853]

——. "The Sheik Who Made Lawrence Love Arabia." London *Sunday Times* (16 June 1968), pp. 49–50. [H0853]

——. *See also* Knightley, Phillip, and Colin Simpson

Sims, George. "Richard Aldington at Home." *Antiquarian Book Monthly Review* (December 1982), pp. 460–67.

——. "Richard Aldington at Home: Part 2." *Antiquarian Book Monthly Review* (January 1983), pp. 4–11.

Smith, Clare Sydney. "This Sordid Tale Changes Nothing." *Sheffield Telegraph* (31 January 1955), p. 5.

Smith, Richard Eugene. *Richard Aldington*. Boston: G. K. Hall, 1977.

Smith, Sydney. "Why I Decided to Debunk a Hero: Richard Aldington Talks to Sydney Smith about His Life of Lawrence of Arabia, Which Started a Row on TV's 'Panorama'." London *Daily Express* (28 January 1955), p. 4.

Snodgrass, W. D. "Nobodies of Prominence." *Western Review* 20 (Spring 1956): 234–39. [G0859]

Bibliography

Snow, C. P. "The Irregular Right: Britain Without Rebels." *Nation* 182 (24 March 1956): 238–39.

"Solitary in the Ranks." London *Times* (17 February 1955). [H0476]

Sperber, Manès. "False Situations: T. E. Lawrence and His Two Legends." In *The Achilles Heel*. Trans. Constantine FitzGibbon. London: André Deutsch, 1959; pp. 175–204. [F0984]

Spiegel, Sam, et al. "Lawrence of Arabia." *Journal of the Society of Film and Television Arts* 10 (Winter 1962–63): 1–24. [G1032]

Spring, Howard. "Lawrence Myth Exploded?" *Country Life* (10 February 1955).

Squire, Sir John. "The Case for the Prosecution." *Illustrated London News* (12 February 1955), p. 264. [G0716]

Stadelmayer, Peter. "*Kritik*: Die Aufzeichnungen von 352087 A/c Ross und die Enthüllungen des Richard Aldington." *Frankfurter Hefte* 10:5 (1955): 371–73. [G0687]

Stanford, Derek. "Lawrence of Arabia." *Contemporary Review* 186 (May 1955): 351–52.

Stephens, Robert. "Lawrence and the Arabs." London *Observer* (10 July 1966). [G1689]

Stewart, Desmond. "Lawrence: The Lost Letter" [letter]. London *Sunday Times* (26 June 1977), p. 13.

———. "Snuggling with Lawrence" [letter]. *New York Review of Books* 24 (9 February 1978): 46. [G1599]

———. *T. E. Lawrence* [1977]. London: Paladin, 1979. [E369]

———. "T. E. Lawrence" [letter]. *Times Literary Supplement* (17 February 1978), p. 202.

———. "T. E. Lawrence and the Arabs." *European*, no. 30 (August 1955): 50–60.

Stewart, Gordon. "General Rankin Speaks Out: I Threatened Lawrence." Melbourne *Argus* (2 March 1955).

Stirling, W. F. "Friends of Lawrence" [letter]. London *Daily Telegraph* (19 February 1955), p. 6.

Stookey, Mark. "Reader Comments." *T. E. Notes* 4:2 (February 1993): 13–14.

Storrs, Ronald. "Lawrence of Arabia." *Listener* 53 (3 February 1955): 187–89. [G0707]

———. *Lawrence of Arabia, Zionism, and Palestine*. Harmondsworth, Middlesex: Penguin, 1940. [E141]

———. "Lawrence's Way." London *Sunday Times* (20 February 1955), p. 5. [H0479]

———. "Lawrence, Thomas Edward (1888–1935)." *Dictionary of National Biography, 1931–1940*. London: Geoffrey Cumberlege, 1949; pp. 528–31. [F0266]

———. *See also Sur*

Sugerman, Sidney. "Available Evidence" [letter]. London *Times* (2 August 1969), p. 9.

———. "Finally, after Half a Century of Legend: The Truth about T. E. Lawrence and the Arab Revolt." *Jewish Observer and Middle East Review* (12 September 1969), pp. 17–20. [G1356]

——. *A Garland of Legends: "Lawrence of Arabia" and "The Arab Revolt"*. Hanley Swan, Worcestershire: SPA, 1992.

——. "Lawrence and the Arabs" [letter]. London *Times* (6 August 1969), p. 9.

——. "No Longer Lawrence of Arabia: End of an Old Legend—Or the Beginning of a New One?" *Jewish Observer and Middle East Review* (8 July 1966), pp. 14–15.

Sur (Buenos Aires), no. 235 (July–August 1955): 1–72. Includes "T. E. Lawrence" by Winston Churchill (2–11), "T. E. Lawrence, Aldington y la Verdad" by B. H. Liddell Hart (11–21), "T. E. Lawrence y el Libro de Aldington" by Sir Ronald Storrs (22–30), " 'El Troquel' de T. E. Lawrence" by E. M. Forster (31–38), "Las Accusaciones de Richard Aldington" by Raymond Mortimer (39–42), and "Felix Culpa" by Victoria Ocampo (42–72). [G0800–0805]

Sykes, Christopher. "Introduction." In Richard Aldington, *Lawrence of Arabia: A Biographical Enquiry*. London: Collins, 1969; pp. 2–10. [E193]

——. "Introduction." In Richard Aldington, *Lawrence of Arabia: A Biographical Inquiry*. Harmondsworth, Middlesex: Penguin, 1971; pp. 13–23. [E197]

——. "The Lawrence Legend: An Inspector Calls." *Tablet* (5 February 1955), p. 131.

——. "Lawrence of What?" London *Observer* (23 May 1976). [H1208]

——. "Mystery Motorist." *Spectator* 209 (20 July 1962): 89. [G1010]

Symons, Julian. "T. E. Lawrence." London *Sunday Times* (29 January 1967), magazine section, p. 23. [H0827]

"T. E. Lawrence: Another Point of View." *Spectator* 195 (8 July 1955): 42. [G0807]

"T. E. Lawrence Issue Rallies His Friends." *New York Times* (15 February 1954), p. 21.

"T E Lawrence's Arabic." London *Times* (30 June 1967), p. 10. [H0836]

Tabachnick, Stephen E. "Lawrence after Arabia." *Forward* (1 May 1992), pp. 9–10.

——. Review of *The Golden Warrior: The Life and Legend of Lawrence of Arabia* by Lawrence James. *World Literature Today* 68:1 (Winter 1994): 137–38.

——. "T. E. Lawrence Authorized Biography." *English Literature in Transition* 35:1 (1992): 89–93.

——. "The T. E. Lawrence Revival in English Studies." *Research Studies* 44:3 (September 1976): 190–98. [G1559]

——. "Two 'Arabian Romantics,' Charles Doughty and T. E. Lawrence." *English Literature in Transition* 16:1 (1973): 11–25. [G1461]

——, ed. *The T. E. Lawrence Puzzle*. Athens: University of Georgia Press, 1984. [E396]

Tabachnick, Stephen E., and Christopher Matheson. *Images of Lawrence*. London: Cape, 1988.

Taggart, Joseph. "A Honeymoon Gamble." London *Star* (3 February 1955), p. 11.

Taliaferro, Frances. "Nonfiction in Brief: *Literary Lifelines*." *New York Times Book Review* (11 October 1981), p. 18.

Tanfield, Paul. "Dear Mr Lawrence . . . " London *Daily Mail* (14 December 1961), p. 4.

Taylor, Martin. "T. E. Lawrence" [letter]. *Times Literary Supplement* (28 January 1994), p. 15.

Temple, F.-J. "Lawrence L'imposteur." *L'Evénement du Jeudi*, no. 132 (14 May 1987).

———. "Richard Aldington." *Sud* 11 (1973): 102–5.

———. *See also* Kershaw, Alister, and F.-J. Temple

Terrell, Carroll F. *A Companion to the Cantos of Ezra Pound*. 2 vols. Berkeley: University of California Press, 1980, 1984.

Terry, Janice J. "Jeremy Wilson. *Lawrence of Arabia: The Authorized Biography of T. E. Lawrence*." *American Historical Review* 96:5 (December 1991): 1587–88.

Thesiger, Wilfred. "In Defense of Lawrence." London *Observer* (6 June 1976), p. 18. [H1207]

Thomas, Lowell. *The Boys' Life of Colonel Lawrence*. New York: Century, 1927. [E023]

———. *Good Evening Everybody: From Cripple Creek to Samarkand*. New York: William Morrow, 1976. [F1042]

———. "I Remember Lawrence of Arabia." *TV Guide* 21 (27 January 1973): 19–21. [G1463]

———. "Lawrence of Arabia: A Biographical Inquiry." *Middle East Journal* 9:2 (Spring 1955): 197–98. [G0733]

———. "Letter to the Editor." *Michigan Quarterly Review* 21:2 (Spring 1982): 301–2.

———. "The Real Lawrence of Arabia." *Reader's Digest* 84 (June 1964): 252–56, 258, 260–62, 264–65, 271–72, 274. [G1170]

———. "Scorn for Honors Marked Romantic Career of Lawrence, Hero of Arabia: Lowell Thomas Describes Meeting with British 'Blue-Eyed Bedouin'." *New York Times* (19 May 1935), p. 34. [H0205]

———. *So Long until Tomorrow: From Quaker Hill to Kathmandu*. New York: William Morrow, 1977.

———. "With Lawrence and Feisal in Arabia." *Asia* 19 (October 1919): 998–1016. [G0012]

———. *With Lawrence in Arabia*. New York: Century, 1924. [E006]

———. *With Lawrence in Arabia* [1924]. Rev. ed. New York: Grosset & Dunlap, 1955; pp. [ix–xii], 304–16. [E009]

———. *With Lawrence in Arabia* [1924]. Rev. ed. Garden City, N.Y.: Doubleday, 1967; pp. vii–xix, 283–320. [E011]

Thomson, George Malcolm. "Whom *Did* Lawrence Love?" London *Evening Standard* (12 October 1954), p. 16.

Thomson, Lloyd V. "T. E. Lawrence Defended" [letter]. *New York Times* (9 March 1954), p. 26.

"The Times Diary: The Politics of A/c Shaw." London *Times* (7 May 1968), p. 10.

Toynbee, Philip. "Lawrence into Ross." London *Observer* (13 February 1955), p. 9. [G0717]

Trevor-Roper, Hugh. "A Humbug Exalted." *New York Times Book Review* (6 November 1977), pp. 1, 34, 36, 38. [G1594]

Trewin, J. C. "The World of the Theatre: Arabia and Illyria." *Illustrated London News* (28 May 1960), p. 944. [G0936]

Urnov, Mikhail V. "Richard Aldington and His Books." *News: A Soviet Review of World Events* (April 1956), pp. 29–30.

Vansittart, Lord Robert. "The Lawrence Legend." London *Daily Telegraph* (31 January 1955), p. 6. [H0459]

———. *The Mist Procession: The Autobiography of Lord Vansittart.* London: Hutchinson, 1958. [F1083]

Vogler, Sidney. "Lawrence" [letter]. London *News Chronicle* (7 February 1955), p. 4.

Walsh, Pat. "Lawrence Defended Against Attacks" [letter]. *Montreal Gazette* (5 January 1956), p. 8.

———. "New Facts about Lawrence of Arabia" [letter]. *Montreal Gazette* (29 November 1955), p. 6.

Warde, Robert. *T. E. Lawrence: A Critical Study.* New York: Garland, 1987.

Watson, Mark S. "Selected New Books in Review: Biography and Novel." *Baltimore Evening Sun* (25 October 1955), p. 24.

Waugh, Alec. "The Soldier Poets." In *My Brother Evelyn and Other Portraits.* New York: Farrar, Straus & Giroux, 1967; pp. 52–72. [F1099]

Weintraub, Rodelle. *See* Weintraub, Stanley, and Rodelle Weintraub

Weintraub, Stanley. "The Gift of Anonymity." *Times Literary Supplement* (13 January 1978), p. 29. [G1598]

———. "How History Gets Rewritten: Lawrence of Arabia in the Theatre." *Drama Survey* 2 (Winter 1963): 269–75. [G1148]

———. "Humanities Research Center: A Consumer's Report." *Texas Humanist* 5:5 (May/June 1983): 7.

———. "Lawrence of Arabia." *Film Quarterly* 17 (Spring 1964): 51–54. [G1159]

———. "Low-Key Lawrence." *Washington Post,* (9–15 July 1990), national weekly edition, pp. 35–36.

———. "Political Motivations Wrapped in a Personal Enigma." *New York Times Book Review* (31 December 1961), p. 4. [G0981]

———. *Private Shaw and Public Shaw: A Dual Portrait of Lawrence of Arabia and G.B.S.* New York: George Braziller, 1963; London: Cape, 1963. [E275, E277]

———. "The Riddle of the Sands." *Book World* (1 July 1990), p. 4.

———. "The Secret Lives of Lawrence of Arabia." *New York Times Book Review* (22 March 1970), pp. 8, 27. [G1394]

———. " 'The Seven Pillars of Wisdom' " [letter]. *Times Literary Supplement* (20–26 July 1990), p. 775.

Bibliography

———. *Shaw's People: Victoria to Churchill*. University Park: Penn State University Press, 1996.

Weintraub, Stanley, and Rodelle Weintraub. *Lawrence of Arabia: The Literary Impulse*. Baton Rouge: Louisiana State University Press, 1975. [E346]

———. *See also* Lawrence, T. E., *Evolution of a Revolt*

West, Anthony. "The Fascinator." *New Yorker* 31 (10 December 1955): 215–16, 218, 220. [G0851]

"What Do *You* Think about the Storm over Lawrence?" *Picture Post* (February[?] 1955).

Wheeler, Keith. "The Romantic Riddle of Lawrence of Arabia." *Life* 52 (12 January 1962): 94–102, 104, 106, 108. [G0988]

Whitney, Peter D. "Lawrence of Arabia Again Stirs a Storm: Mystery of the Desert Hero Is One That Touches Noted Personages." *New York Times* (28 February 1954), section E, p. 10.

———. "Lawrence of Arabia Assailed as Charlatan." *New York Times* (27 January 1954).

———. "Lawrence-of-Arabia Book Creates Literary Storm: British Critics Deal Roughly with Author Who Questions Soldier's Exploits." *New York Times* (6 February 1955), section 4, p. 3.

Williams, Kenneth. "The Lawrence Family." *Britain To-Day*, no. 218 (June 1954): 43.

———. "T. E. Lawrence: Fact and Legend." *Fortnightly Review* 138 (September 1935): 373–74. [G0320]

Williamson, Anne. "The Genius of Friendship—Part 1: T. E. Lawrence." *Henry Williamson Society Journal*, no. 27 (March 1993): 18–35.

———. "The Genius of Friendship—Part 2: Richard Aldington." *Henry Williamson Society Journal*, no. 28 (September 1993): 7–21.

———. "Ten Biographical Panels." *T. E. Notes* 5:10 (December 1994): 1–6.

Williamson, Henry. Extracts from ALS to David Garnett (5 February 1955). In *A Modern Miscellany: 19th and 20th Century Literature* [catalogue 1139]. London: Maggs Bros. Ltd., 1992; item 296.

———. *Genius of Friendship: "T. E. Lawrence"*. London: Faber & Faber, 1941. [E146]

———. "Henry Williamson on T.E." *T. E. Notes* 5:10 (December 1994): 13–15.

———. Review of *The Home Letters of T. E. Lawrence and His Brothers*. *European*, no. 21 (November 1954): 50–51.

———. "Threnos for T. E. Lawrence: I." *European*, no. 15 (May 1954): 44–61. [G0662]

———. "Threnos for T. E. Lawrence: II." *European*, no. 16 (June 1954): 43–60. [G0662]

Wilson, Arnold T. *Loyalties: Mesopotamia, 1914–1917. A Personal and Historical Record* [1930]. New York: Greenwood Press, 1969. [F1138]

———. Review of *Revolt in the Desert* and *With Lawrence in Arabia*. *Journal of the Central Asian Society* 14:3 (1927): 282–85. [G0088]

Wilson, Colin. *The Outsider*. London: Gollancz, 1956. [F1142]

Wilson, Jeremy. "An Appeal from Damascus: The Mohammed Abdulla Bassam Affair." *Journal of the T. E. Lawrence Society* 1:1 (Spring 1991): 60–67.

———. "A. W. Lawrence, 1900–1991." *Journal of the T. E. Lawrence Society* 1:1 (Spring 1991): 7.

———. "Catalogue Raisonné of Works by, about, and Relating to T. E. Lawrence." *T. E. Lawrence Studies* 1:1 (Spring 1976): 44–53. [E363]

———. "Documentary Proof or Wishful Thinking? Lawrence James on the Deraa Episode." *Journal of the T. E. Lawrence Society* 1:1 (Spring 1991): 85–88.

———. "English Editions of Works by T. E. Lawrence in Print." *T. E. Lawrence Studies* 1:1 (Spring 1976): 58–60. [E363]

———. "Extracts from *Summary of the Hejaz Revolt*, War Office, London, 1918." *Journal of the T. E. Lawrence Society* 3:1 (Spring 1993): 20–44.

———. "Introduction." In T. E. Lawrence, compiler, *Minorities: Good Poems by Small Poets and Small Poems by Good Poets*. Ed. J. M. Wilson. Garden City, N.Y.: Doubleday, 1972; pp. 17–50. [A260]

———. "Jeremy Wilson Refutes Lawrence James' Deraa Claims." *T. E. Notes* 2:4 (April 1991): 2–3.

———. "Jeremy Wilson Responds [to Lawrence James]." *T. E. Notes* 2:7 (September 1991): 4.

———. "Lawrence Evidence" [letter]. London *Sunday Times* (3 July 1977), p. 12.

———. *Lawrence of Arabia: The Authorized Biography of T. E. Lawrence* [1989]. New York: Atheneum, 1990.

———. "Legend of the Desert King." London *Independent* (16 August 1988).

———. "Register of Current Research." *T. E. Lawrence Studies* 1:1 (Spring 1976): 60–63. [E363]

———. "Sense and Nonsense in the Biography of T. E. Lawrence." *T. E. Lawrence Studies* 1:1 (Spring 1976): 3–10. [E363]

———. "*Seven Pillars of Wisdom* by T. E. Lawrence [The Complete 1922 Text]." *T. E. Notes* 7:1 (Spring 1996): 1–3.

———. "T. E. Lawrence and the Printing of *Seven Pillars of Wisdom*." *Matrix* 5 (Winter 1985): 55–69. [G1666]

———. T. E. Lawrence: A New Myth" [letter]. London *Sunday Times* (19 June 1977), p. 12.

———. "T. E. Lawrence at Clouds Hill." *Journal of the T. E. Lawrence Society* 3:1 (Spring 1993): 45–65.

———. *T. E. Lawrence: Lawrence of Arabia*. London: National Portrait Gallery, 1988.

———. "T. E. Lawrence: Notes for Collectors, Part I." *Antiquarian Book Monthly Review*, no. 3 (April 1974): 1–4. [G1489]

———. "T. E. Lawrence: Notes for Collectors, Part II." *Antiquarian Book Monthly Review*, no. 4 (May 1974): 3–6. [G1489]

———. "Works Received and Forthcoming 1975–1976." *T. E. Lawrence Studies* 1:1 (Spring 1976): 54–58. [E363]

———. *See also* Crawford, Fred D., and Jeremy Wilson

Winstone, H. V. F. *The Illicit Adventure: The Story of Political and Military Intelligence in the Middle East from 1898 to 1926.* London: Cape, 1982. [F1156]

———. "Lawrence, and the Legend That Misfired." London *Times* (6 November 1982), p. 8. [H1249]

———. "Was Lawrence a Red Herring?" [letter]. London *Sunday Times* (10 May 1991), p. 19. [H1244]

Winterton, Deryck. "Lawrence of Arabia: The Controversy. Now a Book Debunks Him. Prince of Bluffers?" London *Daily Herald* (28 January 1955).

Winterton, Lord Edward. *Fifty Tumultuous Years.* London: Hutchinson, 1955. [F1158]

———. "Lawrence and His Detractor: An Old Friend's Rebuke" [letter]. London *Daily Telegraph* (7 February 1955), p. 6. [H0478]

Woodhouse, C. M. "T. E. Lawrence: New Legends for Old." *Twentieth Century* 157 (March 1955): 228–36. [G0734]

"Writer on Lawrence Sentenced in Fraud: Edward H. T. Robinson, 39, Sold Manuscripts Borrowed for Biography on the War Leader." *New York Times* (17 June 1937), p. 25. [H0384]

Yale, William. "*The Desert and the Stars*, by Flora Armitage." *Middle East Journal* 10 (Winter 1956): 89–90.

———. "The Greatness of T. E. Lawrence." *Yale Review* 28 (Summer 1939): 819–22. [G0521]

———. "Richard Aldington. *Lawrence of Arabia: A Biographical Enquiry.*" *American Academy of Political and Social Science Annals* 307 (September 1956): 167–68. [G0869]

Yardley, Michael. *T. E. Lawrence: A Biography* [1985]. New York: Stein & Day, 1987. [E398a]

Young, B. A. *The Rattigan Version: Sir Terence Rattigan and the Theatre of Character.* London: Hamish Hamilton, 1986.

Young, Hugo. "Explaining Lawrence." *Yorkshire Post* (23 November 1961), p. 6.

Ziman, H. D. "Damaging Self-Portrait of T. E. Lawrence." London *Daily Telegraph* (18 February 1955), p. 6. [H0477]

Zinsser, William K. "In Search of Lawrence of Arabia." *Esquire* 55 (June 1961): 101–4. [G0959]

Zweig, Paul. "*A Prince of Our Disorder.*" *New York Times Book Review* (21 March 1976), pp. 1–2. [G1530]

INDEX

Aaronsohn, Aaron, 135
Aaronsohn, Sarah, 135
Abdulla ibn Hussein, 34–36, 109, 188
Aldington, Catherine (RA's dau.), 5, 17, 33, 92, 200–201
Aldington, Netta (RA's 2nd wife), 5–6, 17, 122, 125, 156
Aldington, P. A. G. "Tony" (RA's bro.), 6, 17, 134, 138
Aldington, Richard (RA): biographical method of, 11, 14, 16, 18–25, 27–28, 32–39, 102–3, 114, 122; and Churchill, 22–23, 66, 80, 126–28, 134; and Cockburn, 93, 95–97, 104, 108, 110, 122; and Collins, 42–46, 50–51, 61–64, 66, 92–94, 107–10, 115, 122, 134; as debunker, 2, 7–12, 21, 28, 112, 176–77; finances of, 6, 11, 17, 92, 108, 200–201; and Garnett, 19, 32–33, 36; on Graves, 28, 34, 50, 52, 56, 58, 60, 71, 116, 128–29; impartiality attempted by, 12, 19, 32, 37–39, 48; and Jix, 48–54, 57–58, 62–63, 86, 97; and A. W. Lawrence, 15–16, 18–19, 21, 28–29, 31–33, 36–37, 50, 53, 116, 128, 144; and D. H. Lawrence, 2–3, 5–6, 10–11, 17, 19, 45, 48, 69, 98; and TEL, 3–4, 7–12, 19; and TEL, later works on, 133–42, 145–50, 152–57, 162–65, 171, 174–77, 180–91, 194–95, 198; on TEL as fraud, 2, 7–8, 11–12, 21–23, 36–37, 77, 177, 181, 183; on TEL's illegitimacy, 2, 21, 28–30, 45, 57, 130–31; and TEL's *Mint*, 15–16, 18–20, 84, 87, 185, 205; on TEL's *Seven Pillars*, 9–10, 37, 66, 87, 189–90; and "Lawrence Bureau," 19, 35, 66, 70, 101, 118–19, 124–25, 130, 135, 142, 202; on Liddell Hart, 28, 34, 45, 56, 58, 108, 123, 128–30, 132, 134, 140; literary career of, 2–9, 11, 16–17, 29, 63, 200–202, 206; and *London Magazine*, 124, 127–32, 156, 200; mental state of, 5, 17, 44, 47, 59–60, 63, 66, 92, 94, 108, 115; *Pinorman*, 98–99, 125, 200; and Politzer, 60–61, 63, 76, 79, 83, 94, 96–97; and Thomas, 24–25, 27, 37, 45–46, 52, 56, 58, 211 n. 24; and Williamson, 12, 14, 18,

23–24, 28–29, 32, 63, 102–3, 116, 184; and World War I, 7–9, 19, 198, 201. *See also* Holroyd-Reece, John; Kershaw, Alister; *Lawrence of Arabia: A Biographical Enquiry*
Aldington Trust, 42, 51, 61, 64, 93–97, 104, 107–8
Alexandra, 179
Allenby, Gen. Sir Edmund, 21–22, 87, 89, 109, 135, 152, 155, 176, 188; and Churchill's "Egypt" offer, 68–69, 74, 76, 80–81, 107, 128, 136, 190; on TEL, 34, 37, 123, 126, 136, 140; TEL's value to, 2, 7, 34, 36, 123, 126, 137, 140, 157
Amery, Leo[pold] S., 22, 77–80, 97–98, 113–14, 126; value of "Egypt" testimony of, 66–70, 75, 77
Amiot-Dumont, 94, 97, 112–13
Antonius, George, 36, 109
Arab Bulletin, 157, 182, 224 n. 10
Arab Bureau, 42, 188
Armitage, Flora, 132–33
Astor, Lady Nancy, 46, 112
Attlee, Clement, 115
Auda abu Tayi, 36
Auden, W. H., 101

Baker, Carlos, 132
Barker, Ernest, 186
Barrow, Gen. Sir George de Symons, 34, 109, 123, 177
Barton, Maj. R. M. S., 123–24
BBC, 4, 116, 121, 152, 154, 171–72
Beaumont, Binkie, 146
Beaverbrook, Lord William, 88
Beeson, C. F. C. ["Scroggs"], 19
Bell, John, 157–58
Bernard Shaw Estate, 204
Bey of Deraa (Hajem Muhyi al-Din Bey), 119–20, 138–39, 157, 186
Bilbo, Jack, 168–70, 192–94
Bilmes, Maurice, 151
Bird, Alan, 14, 20, 31, 48, 56–58, 115, 165
Black, A. & C., 23–24, 63

Fred D. Crawford is an associate professor of English at Central Michigan University and the editor of *SHAW: The Annual of Bernard Shaw Studies*. He has written several books and articles on modern literature and history. Currently he is completing a biography of Lowell Thomas and editing a volume of Thomas's selected letters.